English Satire

and the

Satiric Tradition

Edited by

CLAUDE RAWSON

Assisted by

JENNY MEZCIEMS

Basil Blackwell

© Modern Humanities Research Association 1984

First published 1984
Basil Blackwell Publisher Limited
108 Cowley Road, Oxford OX4 1JF, England

Basil Blackwell Inc.
432 Park Avenue South, Suite 1505
New York, NY 10016, USA

The essays in this book were first published in The Yearbook of English Studies
Volume 14, 1984

British Library Cataloguing in Publication Data
English satire and the satiric tradition
1. Satire, English — History and criticism
I. Rawson, Claude
827'.009   PR931

ISBN 0–631–13668–1
ISBN 0–631–13667–3 Pbk

Typesetting by W. S. Maney and Son Ltd, Leeds,
Printed in Great Britain by T J Press Ltd, Padstow,

Contents

FOR BOB ELLIOTT
1914–1981

Introduction

CLAUDE RAWSON
University of Warwick

Satire, as we have long been accustomed to think, is a learned art: elaborately allusive, cunning in secret stings and subtle indirections. It is also, and this is less often remembered, an instrument of aggression. In ancient Greece and Ireland, in pre-Islamic Arabia, and in various primitive cultures, a poet's curses had power to kill (or were believed to, which often came to the same thing). The fact was known to Renaissance and later poets, who self-consciously proclaimed it, often in works more conspicuous for their ironic obliquity, their studiously literary procedures, and their high moral claims, than for unadorned punitive fury. The late Robert C. Elliott's *The Power of Satire: Magic, Ritual, Art* (1960) reminded us forcefully of satire's aggressive origins without losing sight of its artful transformations. Elliott reaffirmed the primacy of the hurtful and the punitive core. Proclamations of moral purpose and disclaimers of personal malice were seen by him as having often a secondary, self-justifying and *ex post facto* quality, necessary though they might be to the satiric enterprise. It was precisely because the essential purpose was aggressive that the poet needed to convince himself and others that he was not personally vindictive or anti-social. Apologies for satire quickly became commonplace in satire.

Stephen Halliwell's discussion of Aristophanes takes us behind the dramatist's own assertions of public-spirited motivation to those traditions of licensed insult and festal play from which Old Comedy derives. A standard ingredient of the *kōmos* was 'the abuse of bystanders, or a general mockery of those outside . . . the celebrating group'. Its licensed freedoms provided an enabling context for verbal aggressions that were more concerned to insult than to reform. The custom (Halliwell stresses that he is not, like some students of Old Comedy, speaking of ritual) has one feature which distinguishes it from those primary satiric aggressions in which damage to the victim was the singleminded objective. The context of sanctioned 'play' offered free scope for real abuse, but at one remove from the normal social consequences of such abuse. This is not merely a case of controlling the aggression by confining it within prescribed occasions, as legislation (from ancient tribal interdictions to our modern libel laws) controlled it by defining the limits of acceptability. The custom seems to have generated a pleasure in the exercise of insult which was relatively independent of practical purpose or the fear of reaction and which might be described as *aesthetic*.

The pleasures of invective are well-understood by poets. Two who are cited in this book are Keats ('Though a quarrel in the streets is a thing to be hated, the energies displayed in it are fine') and Auden, whose remarks on flyting are quoted by Douglas Gray:

Flyting seems to have vanished as a studied literary art and only to survive in the impromptu exchanges of truckdrivers and cabdrivers. The comic effect arises from the contradiction between the insulting nature of what is said which appears to indicate a passionate relation of hostility and aggression, and the calculated skill of verbal invention which indicates that the protagonists are not thinking about each other but about language and their pleasure in employing it inventively.

Both Keats and Auden are speaking as artists largely about the activities of non-artists, men quarrelling in the street, and are viewing the situation from a specialized angle of vision. As Auden says, flyting was once a 'studied literary art' (Douglas Gray's essay deals with examples of this art), though now largely confined to the stylized spontaneities of the street. Halliwell's Greek festivals, like other festal gatherings, doubtless preceded the invective contests of poets. They seem to have been group-manifestations, with popular crowd appeal, and they perhaps lacked some of the self-conscious feeling for individual performance and craftsmanship of Auden's truckdrivers and cabdrivers. The examples suggest no simple chronology of development: but they show 'art' and custom (and no doubt personal instinct too) collaborating to make satire 'artificial', deflecting or pretending to deflect it from its nakedly hostile intentions.

But they do not succeed in deflecting it, and were never meant to. Gray cautions us against Auden's view that 'playfulness' is invariably dominant in flytings. The play factor, moreover, whether in popular festivals or in the stylizations of artists, is simultaneously a restraining and an enabling force. The very things which divert, attenuate or disguise the aggression are those which make possible its expression in the first place. Satire moved from 'magic' to the domains of 'play' and of 'art' not only because people realized that it did not really kill or were embarrassed to pretend that it did, but because they felt shy of seeming to want it to. The death-dealing utterances of Jonson, or Swift, or Roy Campbell, or Céline, are hedged by a protective irony, often exuberantly hyperbolic, which signals both that the author is 'playing' with invective in the sense described by Auden, and that he knows he is being outrageous and excessive. The satirist thus escapes the disapproval of the reader, who cannot pin him down to a murderous intention seriously contemplated and does not know how to define the aggressive residue. When Jonson boasts Archilochan powers or the bardic gift of rhyming 'to death, as they doe *Irish* rats / In drumming tunes', or when Swift says he would gladly exterminate this or that person or group, we know that an element of self-mockery plays over the calculated extremism of the utterance. Without it, the thing could not be said, and if said, would not be taken seriously. As I have argued elsewhere, the satirist cannot in such places be said to mean literally that he can kill, or would if he could: but he does not *not mean* it either.

It is in Swift more than any other important satirist that the death-dealing curse, often with the personalized intensity which bards directed at particular offenders, is extended to whole classes of men (beggars, bankers, the nation's representers) and indeed to the human race itself. 'Drown the World', he said half jokingly, evoking the biblical Flood in a letter written as he was finishing *Gulliver's Travels* , in a correspondence with Pope about his 'misanthropy' in that work. In *Gulliver's Travels* itself, the Houyhnhnms debate 'Whether the *Yahoos* should be exterminated from the Face of the Earth' in language which expressly recalls God's words immediately before the deluge in Genesis 6.7: 'I will destroy man whom I have created from the face of the earth.' The parallel is not cited as often as it might be, and seldom by critics who believe the satire to be critical of the Houyhnhnms and of Gulliver's veneration of them. William Anderson's interesting exploration of biblical resonances in *Gulliver's Travels* is an exception, whose argument, however, seems flawed by an insufficient recognition that such collective aggressions, whether or not they are hedged by humorous undercutting or by angry hyperbole, are common in Swift's writing. He was in particular quite capable of entertaining such sentiments, and indeed such language, in his own name (e.g. on country beggars 'fitter to be rooted out off the Face of the Earth, than suffered to levy a vast annual Tax upon the City'). The close verbal resemblance of the Houyhnhnms' proposal about the Yahoos to God's decision to destroy the human race suggests not (of course) that Swift would enact the killing if he could, but that the Yahoos, like mankind in Genesis, deserve the punishment. Satire's killing impulse has been diverted from a single enemy to all men, and it is worth noting that although the retribution is in both cases based on moral outrage at the world's depravity, it is punitive rather than reformative.

John Traugott's reading does recognize this. He sees the Utopian invention of Houyhnhnmland as a form of game, an idealist game whose other face is a punitive disappointment with things as they are: 'When one longs to make men good and wise, free and reasonable (runs an adage), one is inevitably led to want to kill them all. Rage is the other face of idealism.' His essay explores the 'tension' between the killing urge and 'play'. The latter element is no longer a matter of popular or primitive ludic custom, but a sophisticated evocation of childhood freedoms. That the fantasy which generated Lilliputian dolls and made of *Gulliver's Travels* a children's classic should coexist with famous intensities of anger need not surprise us if we remember that one of the strongest surviving relics of satirical cursing is to be found in the lore and language of schoolchildren.

Murderous imprecations are not the only feature of satire. In so far as 'play', or the invention of satiric fictions and of surrogate speakers whose voice is formally dissociated from the satirist's own, are strategies of circumvention, they are analogous to the sophisticated indirections of irony, of parody and literary allusion (notably mock-heroic, which blends parody and allusion), as these are found in those urbane or soft-spoken satirists whose high classical model was Horace and whose greatest English exemplar is Pope. Medieval invectives find their urbane counterpart in Chaucer (here considered, in his mock-heroic aspect, by J. A. Burrow), as Swift has his counterpart in Pope. Simple demarcations between the two types do not bear scrutiny: Jonson has been considered an upholder of classical restraint and Horatian values, as well as an Archilochan scourge; Swift, alleged to be Juvenalian in his indignations, preferred and mimicked the more low-pitched manner of Horace, while Pope, the Imitator of Horace, was notoriously given to Juvenalian majesties (in this book some Horatian connections are explored in both Swift and Pope).

Emphases were changing in the seventeenth century. Ian Donaldson finely distinguishes Jonson's angers from the 'new gentlemanliness' which emerges in Dryden ('there's a sweetness in good Verse, which Tickles even while it Hurts': compare this with Pope's comment on *The Rape of the Lock* as 'a sort of writing very like tickling'). The Augustanizing refinement that this implies finds its major expression in Pope's and in Swift's Horatian poems, although both Pope and Swift insisted against Dryden on satire's right to certain kinds of aggressive forthrightness and especially on its right to be personal and to name names. Before them come Rochester and Oldham (discussed in these pages by Ken Robinson and by Raman Selden), strong, 'rough' voices in whom the 'fragile relationship . . . between violence or cruelty on one side and rational and artistic restraint on the other' is evident in an active and richly unresolved state.

This represents a late stage (perhaps the beginning of a terminal phase) in the history of satire and its progress from hurtful magic to object of aesthetic admiration, from weapon to artefact. By the time of Addison and Chesterfield, as Donaldson notes, the emphasis is on suppressing, not displaying anger. In the second half of the eighteenth century, satire came strongly under fire from the 'men of feeling'. A paradoxical feature of satire is that while it is in one sense subversive of order, it tends to be deeply traditional. The most outspoken and most alienated satirists, Juvenal or Swift, have spoken not for a new order but for the restoration of older values, under threat in a bad new world. Satire is a conservative art and the example of Augustan England suggests that it flourishes most in an order-minded culture, perhaps at moments when order is felt to be slipping: hence the peculiar desperation of Swift and at times of Pope, even as they assert values confidently believed in. The opposition to it in the eighteenth century came from 'liberalizing' or 'progressive' sources, and the great art of revolutionary aspiration at the end of the century is not in the main satiric.

Satire did not, of course, simply stop. The most one could say is that few writings of the highest imaginative stature since the age of Swift and Pope have been predominantly satiric in character. Satire went on being written, both in the more or less generic sense in which Horace or Pope wrote verse satires and Lucian or Swift wrote prose satires, and in the wider sense which includes the satiric elements in writings not formally described as satires: especially in novels, those of Fielding and Smollett for example, where the characteristic features of Augustan irony and of Jonsonian caricature are still strongly visible, and more diffusely and variously in later fiction. Of the last five essays in the volume, which cover the period from the Romantics to the present, four are devoted to novels and short stories, and the single exception deals with a poem strongly charged with the idiom and atmosphere of some stories of the 1920s. The energies which once went into the great satiric genres have largely been absorbed into the mode of prose fiction. Formal verse satire is dead: the progressive decline from Pope to Churchill to Gifford to Roy Campbell is inescapable. The best satire in verse, from *Beppo* and *Don Juan* onwards, is itself saturated with elements from prose fiction. Eliot's 'Prufrock' and 'Portrait of a Lady', as Barbara Everett notes, have a notable relationship with Henry James, and her analysis of *Sweeney Agonistes* reveals some vivid and surprising links with the work of Ring Lardner and Anita Loos.

Perhaps the decisive switch from satire to prose fiction occurred with Sterne. Fielding or Smollett have many satirical scenes and characters, as well as a style reminiscent of the Augustan ironists. They can be said to have made the novel-form hospitable to the satiric spirit, but they did not effect any radical transformation or synthesis. *Tristram Shandy*, on the other hand, is both a genuinely new work and one whose essential character derives profoundly from the great prose satires of Rabelais and Swift, and in particular from *A Tale of a Tub*, whose self-consciously digressive and open-ended or endlessly 'unfinished' form it assimilates in depth. It is full of mockery and self-mockery, but where the *Tale* mimicked a modern self-assertion in derisive rejection, Sterne indulged the mockery, refashioning it into a primary mode of self-assertion in itself. It is the *Tale* turned inside out, cheekily outfacing the parody, so that in one sense the *Tale* comes to seem a parody of Sterne *avant la lettre*.

The satiric dimension in *Tristram Shandy* remains pervasive and radical, not (as in so many novels before or since) sporadic and incidental. But it has been transvalued and internalized, cherished in itself as a mode of self-expression and self-scrutiny. The book brings to a peculiar and unexpected culmination a tendency inherent in many earlier satires, in which the satirist variously allows himself to be included in the satire (laughing at his own excess, or at his foolish expectation that the world can be mended; or registering, as Swift often does, that the follies universally ascribed to mankind must implicate the satirist too). Such self-implicating extensions of the scope of satire belong to the theme which Elliott has conveniently described as that of 'the satirist satirized'. The extraordinary and seminal further extension of this theme in Sterne, where the satire is simultaneously a critique and an expression of self-consciousness, did not greatly interest Elliott. Nor is it overtly treated in the present book, though some aspects of it were touched on by another contributor, Ronald Paulson, in a book much influenced by Elliott, *Satire and the Novel in Eighteenth-Century England*, (1967). But Marilyn Butler's discussion of Romantic satire, as manifested notably in Hazlitt's autobiographical fiction, the *Liber Amoris* (not usually regarded as a satire), describes what is surely an extension of the Shandean satiric perspective. Her argument, applicable also to a number of Romantic poems, including narrative poems of a quasi-autobiographical kind, is that the satiric impulse, like so much else in the Romantic period, became internalized and self-conscious, and was specifically exploited as a critique of self-sufficiency and self-preoccupation. It is to some extent *self-punitive*, and there is a curious aptness in the fact that Hazlitt's raw exposure of his amorous vulnerabilities, however ironically intended, should have brought upon himself some of the public ridicule that an older satirist might have hoped to inflict on other persons.

Martin Price's study of Conrad takes us from autobiographical fictions to the novel in its full state of development, with all the sense of authorial disengagement which this especially implies in a novelist schooled in the craftsmanship of Flaubert, James and Ford. Price's interest is in Conrad's ironic exposure of selves which are cut off from the reassurances of civilized life. Martin Decoud in *Nostromo* is a character who is himself an ironist, and who is placed in the kind of testing isolation which Conrad normally reserves for characters untouched by the ironic spirit, whether they are unimaginative (like the pair of gross and stupid Belgians in 'An Outpost of Progress', or the solid and decent Captain MacWhirr of 'Typhoon') or overimaginative (Lord Jim or the self-deceived Kurtz). The 'easy cynicism . . . Conrad attacks in Martin Decoud' is surely implicated in that tradition of the 'satirist satirized' to which Price also refers at the beginning of his essay. As Price says, the fact that Conrad 'attacks' Decoud's cynicism in *Nostromo* 'does not, of course, acquit him of participation in it elsewhere (or even there)'. We may recognize here too the raw materials of that self-referential satire which Marilyn Butler identified in the Romantics. The internal disorientations have been depersonalized and transformed in the novelistic medium, externalized into fictional characters with lives and personalities not confined to a merely autobiographical, any more than to a merely satiric, dimension.

Price only refers to *Nostromo* in passing here, having discussed it at length in his recent book, *Forms of Life*. But his essay explores the necessarily uneasy relation between a novelistic genre committed to a large sympathetic imagination of others and the specialized and non-sympathetic aggressiveness of satire. He brings out finely Conrad's satirical portraitures in 'An

Outpost of Progress' and *The Secret Agent* (the Professor in the latter, who 'has replaced radical Protestantism with a "frenzied Puritanism of ambition"', is surely a Swiftian fanatic, with his appalling sincerity and his interest in large-scale extermination.) Such things 'raise the question of how one can relate the satiric brilliance to the fictional adequacy': a question explored throughout this probing essay, and which Conrad is felt to have only intermittently resolved. The issue of overlapping and uncertainly compatible aims is posed in rather different terms in an essay of 1955 by John Lawlor, on 'Radical Satire and the Realistic Novel'. Lawlor's argument is that Swift, having registered mankind's incurability, left satire with nothing further to do, thus opening the way for the 'realistic novel', in the guise of Flaubert's misanthropic but unmoralized notation of human folly.

'The "realist" school of prose-fiction is apt to deal with people who do little credit to the highest aspirations of our human-nature, just like Satire', Wyndham Lewis said in an essay in *Men Without Art*. He identified Flaubert as a 'realist' in this sense, and saw him as 'a great civilizing influence' with a 'very healthy appetite for destruction'. Lewis asserted satire's kinship with fiction (with some qualifications, saying notably that satire *magnifies*, working 'not as "realism" works, but in an heroical manner of its own'). He insisted especially that satire 'often is nothing else but *the truth* . . . objective, non-emotional truth of the scientific intelligence . . . bent not so much upon pleasing as upon being true'. A chapter in *Men Without Art* is entitled 'The Greatest Satire is Non-Moral' ('The artistic impulse is a more primitive one than the ethical'), and it opens with some paragraphs of admiring discussion of Flaubert's hatred of the bourgeois. Lewis's comments on satire closely resemble Flaubert's on truth in art, down to the claim of *scientific* truthfulness; and Lewis sometimes liked to claim that art and satire were the same thing. Flaubert might not have seen it that way, but Lewis is often close to Flaubert's view that a truthful gaze on humanity, stripped of personal emotion, prejudice or programmatic design, would by its very exactitude expose evil and arouse the indignation or repugnance appropriate to the case. Both men saw a deep equation between 'objective truth' and an angry contempt for large sections of the human species.

Lewis's satiric enterprise was conducted largely through novels very unlike Flaubert's. They may be seen as aiming in places to reintroduce the simplified aggressions of the primitive satirist. Hugh Kenner's essay proposes a contradiction. Satire in Kenner's account is a *written* art (studied, dependent on 'textual storage' and the technologies of print), variously external and externalizing. Lewis insisted on the importance of externality in art 'in a world that is literally inundated with . . . the "dark" gushings . . . of *The Great Within*'. In fiction, he hated 'the *tellers-from-the-inside*' : Joyce, Woolf, Stein, Proust, Lawrence. Kenner sees Lewis as a neo-primitive, a *fauve* (and even, in his twin capacity as blaster and bombardier, a 'professional killer'), paradoxically aiming in an advanced literate medium to project the energies of a barbarian imagination: 'the true barbarian is an ear-man, illiterate. Lewis's barbaric pose . . . was that of a literate and sophisticated eye-man, seeking homeopathic remedy for distortions introduced by the eye'.

Borges, the last subject of this book, shows a different alliance of fiction and satire. Like Lewis and many other satirists, he has a temperament which is reactionary and classicist: but this finds expression not in Archilochan, or Juvenalian, or Lewisian angers, but in a fastidiousness and sceptical wit closer, as John Sturrock says, 'to Peacock than to *Private Eye*', but closer still to Conrad than to Peacock, and with some special resemblances perhaps to Conrad's Eurocentred Latin American ironist, Martin Decoud. Borges's most 'satiric Touch', as Swift might have said, is at the expense of the novel-form, without which he could not have existed as a writer, but whose essential expansiveness he subverts. His six-page story 'The Duel' opens with the observation that Henry James 'might have devoted to it a hundred or so pages of tender irony, enriched by complex and painstakingly ambiguous dialogues'. Borges's stories are notoriously brief, and he has hinted that behind his elaborate (and elaborately intertextual) enterprise of abridging works of potentially vast extent to miniature proportions there also lies a yearning for the economy and immediacy of oral speech:

The composition of vast books is a laborious and impoverishing extravagance. To go on for five hundred pages developing an idea whose perfect oral exposition is possible in a few minutes! A better course of procedure is to pretend that these books already exist, and then to offer a résumé, a commentary.

The claim will seem at least as paradoxical as Kenner's account of Lewis. Borges's words may seem to aspire to the condition of the spoken word, but they point also to some of the most characteristic features of learned and literary satire: the reduction by boiled-down paraphrase, the mock-commentary, the vital dependence on pre-existing texts and commentaries. Borges is as strongly given as Swift to complicated acts of parody, and as comically or quizzically fascinated by the intertextual predicaments of others: his Averroes, in the story discussed by Sturrock, wrote his commentary on Aristotle, whom he had to read in 'the translation of a translation', like the modern critic in Swift who reads and cites Longinus in an English 'Translated from *Boileau*'s Translation'. Swift is an author Borges admires, and a model or partial model for more than one of his stories. Not the Swift of the bardic curses of *Traulus* or *The Legion Club*, with their drumming incantations of insult, but the author of *A Tale of a Tub*, of *Gulliver's Travels*, of *A Modest Proposal* : parodies, commentaries on themselves, parodies of commentaries, abstracts or résumés of universal knowledge, learned explorations of infinite sequence and permutation, accounts of quests for the Great Book in the Library of Babel. Swift wrote in uncompromising rejection, Borges with a cagey ironic tolerance, of the divagations of the human intellect. But Borges's stories would not have their present form without the tradition of learned prose satire that runs from Rabelais and Cervantes to Swift and Sterne and Nabokov, uniting in its later phases with the novel-form.

The essays in this book were collected as an act of homage to the late Robert C. Elliott, and first appeared in the *Yearbook of English Studies*, 14 (1984), as one of its series of Special Numbers on particular themes. Other volumes of the *Yearbook* have dealt or will deal with American Literature, Theatrical Literature, Literature and its Audience, Heroes and the Heroic, Colonial and Imperial Themes, Anglo-French Literary Relations, and Literary Periodicals. The volume on Satire is the only one dedicated to a particular scholar. Many of its contributors were friends of Elliott and all are, in an essential sense, his students.

Robert C. Elliott
1914–1981

ALVIN KERNAN

Princeton University

Although there is no immediate danger of unanimity of opinion on the subject of satire, it does seem arguable that there are large agreements among those who deal with this subject, and that the state of the art is probably in advance of that of lyric. . . . the real proof has come in a series of excellent books that have appeared in a period of about two decades. The many studies that might be named have given us understanding of the origins of satire, of the satirist's world and method, of the literary resources drawn on, of recurrent elements, of the psychology of the satiric writer and reader, and of the values entwined in this most curious art.

These words of Earl Miner's in a recent article, 'The Restoration, Age of Faith, Age of Satire', are heartening as a reminder that even in a time when there seems to be too much literary criticism and no way of settling its endless disagreements, it can have a cumulative and a positive effect. Heartening, too, in reminding us of the large and central part Robert Elliott played in making it possible for Earl Miner to write those words; and a fitting memorial of this good friend and great scholar, to whom this volume is dedicated, can well be a description of his work in making satire at least partially if not totally ours.

I first got to know Bob Elliott in the stacks of the Sterling Library at Yale in the middle 1950s when we were both working on books on satire. My own study, which later became *The Cankered Muse*, was an attempt to work out the particular shape and definition of satire in Elizabethan England, while Bob's work, which later became *The Power of Satire*, was an investigation of both the formal structure of satire and its relationship to certain social imperatives. We got to know each other because we were both searching along the same tracks and frequently found that when a particular book was not in the stacks it was on the shelves of the other's study. In this odd way we began to corroborate each other's judgement on the bibliography, and gradually we isolated a number of remarkable pieces of recent criticism which made it possible to think of satire in a way which advanced upon the one great English monument of the criticism of satire, Dryden's *Discourse Concerning Satire*.

The piece on which our attention first centred was an essay, '*Satura Tota Nostra Est*', written by the classicist George Lincoln Hendrickson in 1927, which disentangled the almost limitless references of the word 'satiric' from the particular formal poetic structure of the Roman satire of Horace and Juvenal. When in doubt about Hendrickson's meanings, we were extraordinarily fortunate in being able to question him over lunch at Branford College, where he in his nineties was an Emeritus Fellow, Bob was a visiting fellow from Ohio State University, and I as the youngest member of the fellowship was performing the duties required of someone in that situation. I was always fascinated, I remember, as was Bob, by the fact that Professor Hendrickson regularly wrapped his butter up in a napkin and took it back to his room with him after the meal. We never dared ask him what he did with the butter, and the Master of the College, Norman Buck, on being queried, only responded like the practising satirist he was, 'Lincoln always was tight'. At the same time, there was at Yale and ready for discussion a young classicist, William Anderson, who continued Hendrickson's work in a long series of articles exploring the nature of Roman satire. Or, still on the same ground, we could cross the street to Davenport College and question Maynard Mack about his famous article, 'The Muse of Satire', in which he had established (working primarily with Pope) that the satirist, rather than expressing himself directly in his satire, worked through one of several principal satiric personae.

Bob Elliott was particularly interested in a 1912 article by Fred Norris Robinson, 'Satirists and Enchanters in Early Irish Literature', which described in marvellous detail the functions of satire in a primitive society, and the kinds of control exercised on it. But the majority of the works we exchanged and discussed were, in keeping with the critical spirit of the times, formalist in their orientation, and tended towards the isolation of particular literary works properly called satire and the exploration of their structural characteristics, especially their style. Prominent among these books was David Worcester's *The Art of Satire*, in which he treats satire as 'the engine of anger', rather than its direct expression, and categorizes the various rhetorical strategies which satirists traditionally use to make their writing both acceptable and effective. Similarly there were Ellen Douglass Leyburn's articles, which explored the frequent use of the beast fable in satire and eventuated in her book, *Satiric Allegory: Mirror of Man* (1956), and two remarkable articles by Mary Claire Randolph 'The Medical Concept in English Renaissance Satiric Theory' (1941) and 'The Structural Design of the Formal Verse Satire' (1942), in which she established the fundamental A–B structural opposition in satire of the ideal and the actual that has provided a foundation for most studies of satire since that time. Finally, Bob Elliott and I both found endlessly suggestive an article of Northrop Frye's, 'The Nature of Satire', which had first appeared in 1944 and then in a revised form, as 'The Mythos of Winter: Irony and Satire', in *Anatomy of Criticism* in 1957. Frye was exciting, as he always is, not only for his ability to summarize the iconography of satire, its characteristic perversion and distortion of the primary symbols of unity and amity among men, but also because he placed satire prominently in a total literary structure. In his overall scheme of literature, satire along with irony became one of the four major literary myths, appearing at a definite point in the development of a particular literary system, and sharply distinguished, despite lines of continuity, from tragedy on one hand and romance on the other.

These articles have all been reprinted in Ronald Paulson's *Satire: Modern Essays in Criticism*, unfortunately now out of print, where anyone who cares to look at them can see the way in which they pulled satire out of the vague general mass of literature and sub-literary activity and made it sharply and objectively real, a genre with definite boundaries and formal properties. This probably sounds very old-fashioned by now, when such literary objects are being regularly deconstructed, but I can testify to the genuine excitement with which Bob Elliott and I saw satire in these writings emerging clearly as a Wimsattian verbal icon from a great bibliographical swirl that contained such diverse materials as Aretino and Aristophanes, Freud on wit and Bergson on comedy, Lucian's dialogues, the flyting contests of the Eskimos, *The Dunciad*, and *Nineteen Eighty-Four*.

Ronald Paulson was later to contribute to and capitalize on this clear definition by putting much of western satire into a firm historical order in his two books, *The Fictions of Satire* (1967), and *Satire and the Novel in Eighteenth-Century England* (1967), while I tried to follow out the formal properties of satire in *The Cankered Muse* (1959) and *The Plot of Satire* (1965). But it was Bob Elliott who saw and fully realized in *The Power of Satire: Magic, Ritual, Art* (1960) the critical opportunity that a firm grasp of the satiric object offered. He refused to settle for some particular satirist, or the satiric writing of a single period, or even for western satire, but ranged out to deal with the satires of Arabia and of primitive tribes, with the satiric poetry of pre-historic Ireland and twentieth-century fascism. He took full advantage of earlier formal definitions of the satiric art, and his book includes some splendid close analysis of the structure of *Timon of Athens*, *Le Misanthrope*, and *Gulliver's Travels*, but he always reaches out beyond the works themselves to explain just why satire, whether in the form of curse or mock-epic, takes the particular shapes that it so regularly does. What he finally saw, and made us see so effectively, is that satire, like any other work of art, exists in a society which strongly influences its rhetorical strategies. This social setting was, he perceived and demonstrated, particularly important for satire which has a very dangerous power, aggression, not reformation as had previously been argued, as its primary motive. All societies, therefore, because they feared aggression so greatly and so rightly, had developed strong controls over its expression in life and in art. The controls ranged, Elliott saw with his characteristic anthropological wide view, from censorship and libel laws to myths that told of wrongful curses returning on the curser's head, and they dictated a number of the characteristic strategies of literary satire. Wit, the beast fable, the innocent persona, the emphatic assertions that satire tells the literal truth, the constant protestations that no particular men but wrong-doing are attacked, these are all, Elliott saw, literary or linguistic forms of social restraints imposed on the powerful aggressive force of satire as it developed from a magical force with power literally to harm its object, to ritual, and ultimately to an art which still evokes some of the old primitive fears associated with 'hard attack'. Society, he concludes,

has doubtless been wise, in its old pragmatic way, to suspect the satirist. Whether he is an enchanter wielding the ambiguous power of magic, or whether he is a 'mere' poet, his relation to society will necessarily be problematic. He is of society in the sense that his art must be grounded in his experience as social man; but he must also be apart, as he struggles to achieve aesthetic distance. His practice is often sanative, as he proclaims; but it may be revolutionary in ways that society cannot possibly approve, and in ways that may not be clear even to the satirist.

In subsequent years, after moving from Ohio State to the University of California at San Diego where he was a member, suitably, of a Department of Literature, not of English alone, Elliott's attention turned to the other, more positive side of satire, the ideal social order against which the satirist regularly measures the failings of his depraved world. This interest resulted in several articles, brought together in a book, *The Shape of Utopia: Studies in a Literary Genre* (1970). Here, again following his anthropological bent, Elliott traced the movement from myths of a Golden Age through Saturnalian rituals to Utopian literature, and showed in a variety of ways the continuing involvement of satire with the great dream of human freedom and happiness. Satire seems to him to be the necessary perpetual shadow of the world of gold, entering its ritual celebrations in the form of licensed attack on the repressive order, haunting its desire for perfection, and carrying its bright image over into its own dark scenes of mock-epic and mock-utopia.

After this Elliott's scholarly attention turned elsewhere, but before he was finished with satire he wrote the entry on satire for the fifteenth edition of *The Encylopedia Britannica, Macropaedia*, Volume XVI, which summarizes his own work and that of others of his generation. The article stands as the best short version we have of what now seems to be the accepted view of the art of satire, and that satire can command several pages in the *Macropaedia* rather than being a brief entry in the *Micropaedia*, which is where the old view of satire as an inferior art form would have located it, is largely the result of the work of the man who wrote the article.

Elliott's writings stand at the centre of the criticism of satire in his time but his work was always, he insisted, only part of a larger project in which the nature of satire was elaborated and explored in a number of other fine books, among which must be mentioned Edward W. Rosenheim's *Swift and the Satirist's Art* (1963) and Matthew Hodgart's *Satire* (1969), and which still continues in recent writing like Michael Seidel's *The Satiric Inheritance: Rabelais to Sterne* (1979). The entire project now stands at risk, of course, as various new kinds of criticism deconstruct not only single works of literature but critical formulations of individual genres like satire, and even literature itself. But Elliott has protected his view of satire from these decontructions by his social orientation, for his definition never relies entirely on the formal characteristics of satire but pushes back beyond them to show their involvement with a continuing social activity, the management of attack and aggression. If satire be not an absolute reality, but a socially constructed activity and art form, then the construction as he defined it is not the work of a few critics but of society itself trying over long periods of time in many ways to shape meaningfully one of the most persistent *données* of human life. Literary satire, he told us, is but one record of society's continuous positive attempt to make a satisfactory human world out of the materials it has to work with, which is where the emphasis finally must be in literary studies.

It is a pleasure to be able to record that before he died so suddenly in 1981 Bob Elliott had the satisfaction of realizing, as few critics ever can, that his writings on satire had entered into the mainstream of critical understanding. The place was right, the meeting of the English Institute in Cambridge, Massachusetts, in the early fall of 1978. The speaker was right, Harry Levin, the magnificent summarizer of large literary scenes and trends; and the topic was perfect, 'The Wages of Satire'. We sat together for the last time, and as Levin, without by now needing to cite sources, wove together one after another 'fact' about satire, we exchanged the names of writers and works we had discussed twenty-five years earlier in Sterling Library and those who had written since that time in a way which made believable Levin's main argument: that it was no longer acceptable to think of satire as a minor, shapeless, and destructive form of writing. As Levin put it, citing exactly the right name, 'for unqualified belief in the power of satire, we should have to turn back — as Robert C. Elliott does in his interesting book of that name — to a primitive state of mind which believed as strongly in curses as in blessings'.

Aristophanic Satire

STEPHEN HALLIWELL

Corpus Christi College, Cambridge

'No-one will contend that the corrupt and abominable manners of the times in which Aristophanes wrote, did not fully warrant the severity of his satire.' This somewhat stark judgement from the pen of Richard Cumberland, grandson of Richard Bentley, represents an application to Aristophanes, and to the genre of Old Comedy to which he belonged, of the traditional defence of satire as a moral force against the corruption of the age.[1] Even in the ancient world we find attempts of this kind to justify what might otherwise appear to be an offensive element of personal lampoon and scurrility in the work of Aristophanes. Thus the Roman satirist Horace looked back to the poets of Old Comedy as chastisers of criminals and reprobates, while Quintilian described the genre as 'pre-eminent in the censure of vice'.[2] This attitude has been perpetuated by many later writers, and even a repudiation of it as spirited as George Grote's in his *History of Greece* has failed to destroy its currency.[3] That 'Aristophanes is a moral and political reformer' can still be asserted with unargued confidence.[4]

Ostensible support for the moralistic view of Aristophanic satire is certainly to be found in some of the poet's own pronouncements about his functions: passages such as *Acharnians*, lines 630–58, where Aristophanes describes himself as a purveyor of true and just admonishment to the Athenians; or *Wasps*, lines 1029–43, where he presents his satire of the politician Cleon, and of other targets, as a campaign to purify the city and fight for the people's interests. But the apologetics of satirists who purport to work 'for Truth's defence' cannot always be taken at face value. Aristophanes's claims to a serious purpose not only need to be assessed in context, with careful attention to the tone of the rhetoric with which they are usually expressed, but must also be measured against the details of his practice. Moreover, any general interpretation of the satirical element in Old Comedy must take into account the implications of the genre's cultural setting, and it is to this topic that I turn first.[5]

---

[1] Essay no. 135 in *The British Essayists*, with prefaces by R. Lynam and others, 30 vols (London, 1827), XXX, 322–27 (p. 323), and see M. L. Clarke, *Greek Studies in England 1700–1830* (Cambridge, 1945), pp. 152–53 and 156. Cumberland was something of an amateur, but many scholars have taken a similar line: for example, Porson's view, cited by Clarke (p. 156).

[2] Horace, *Satires*, 1.4.1–5; Quintilian, 10.165.

[3] *A History of Greece*, new edition, 10 vols (London, 1888), VII, 15–17.

[4] Gilbert Highet, *The Anatomy of Satire* (Princeton, New Jersey, 1962), p. 27.

[5] For the purposes of this essay I have restricted myself to the satire of individuals, and excluded Aristophanes's treatment of general categories such as women and foreigners.

Ancient comedy was regularly associated, both in its circumstances of production and in its pervasive values, with festivity, and this association is particularly strong in the case of Athenian Old Comedy. The term 'comedy' itself derives from the festive custom of the *kōmos*, an intoxicated, noisy, and irreverent carousal, in which boisterous elements were none the less held together by a framework of convention. A standard ingredient of the *kōmos*, and of kindred practices, was the abuse of bystanders, or a general mockery of those outside the solidarity of the celebrating group. The type of Greek festival in which a whole city took part was, in certain respects, just a *kōmos* writ large, and it is this broadest kind of festive abandon, in which some release from normal restraints was permissible, that provides the essential background to the spirit of Old Comedy in Athens.

In his *Laws* (637), Plato makes the Spartan Megillus refer in a tone of puritanical offence to the drunkenness which typified festivals of Dionysus at Athens and elsewhere; and in particular Megillus alludes to the activities of 'men on wagons', who represented a custom of what might be termed folk satire, whereby public entertainment was provided by the frank abuse of citizens. The comic poet's licence of free speech, which allowed him both humorous obscenity and the right of personal insult with impunity, was an institutional development from the more diffuse manifestations of *Festesfreude* which must have had a popular history stretching back far beyond the introduction of dramatic performances into Athenian festivals. The most obvious parallel from later times to the spirit of the Dionysiac festivals at which Aristophanes's plays were staged is the European Carnival, especially after its integration into the Christian calendar, when it acquired the significance of a last fling of sensuality before the deprivation of Lent.[6]

There have been attempts, however, to connect Old Comedy more specifically with the traditions of Greek festivals and folk practices. I shall pick out two for brief mention. In the ancient world there existed a belief that Old Comedy had grown out of customs of folk justice of the charivari type, whereby the depraved victims were subjected to a ritual of public opprobrium as a form of shameful punishment. In fact there is no evidence to support this theory, which was invented or conjectured to lend plausibility to the kind of moralistic justification of scurrility to which I have already referred. More recently much has been made of the view that Old Comedy was derived from phallic ritual, particularly by the so-called Cambridge school of anthropologist-classicists.[7] But it is misguided to try to understand Aristophanic comedy, and especially its satirical aspects, in the terms of ritual. Even the fundamental premise of a link between comedy and phallic ritual is uncertain: Aristotle asserts it (*Poetics*, 6. 1449a. 10–13), but probably

---

[6] See, for example, P. Burke, *Popular Culture in Early Modern Europe* (London, 1978), Chapter 7.
[7] See, especially, F. M. Cornford, *The Origin of Attic Comedy* (London, 1914), and for decisive criticisms, A. W. Pickard-Cambridge, *Dithyramb Tragedy and Comedy* (Oxford, 1927), pp. 329–49 (this section is omitted in the revised edition by T. B. L. Webster (Oxford, 1962)).

largely on the grounds of the obscenity common to the two activities. The wearing of a phallic costume by some, but probably not all, comic actors may indicate only a general affinity with Dionysiac festivity, not a specific ritual antecedent. More importantly, putatively religious origins will not necessarily give us the key to the developed artistic genre. To Aristophanes, in the revised parabasis of *Clouds* (ll. 537–39), the actor's phallus is no more than a comic cliché, something to make the boys in the audience laugh. And when we do find elements of phallic ritual, or of other practices of ritual abuse, in Aristophanes, they are dramatically introduced in the same way as any other activities from Athenian life.[8]

Aristophanic satire is to be interpreted, then, in the broad context of 'a festival in a season of licence', as George Meredith put it, but not as a special derivation from ritual.[9] The festive experience of the satire was, at any rate, certainly not religious. What was involved for both the poet and his audience was a release from the normal obligation to heed the restraints and subordinations of social hierarchy, according to which power and prestige belonged to the rich, the politically influential, and those prominent in other ways.[10] Comic satire was therefore the expression of a spirit of unbridled freedom of speech, and this fact consorts ill with the idea of responsible criticism motivated by serious standards. Moreover, comedy's privilege was axiomatically exceptional not only in the positive enjoyment of freedom from restrictions, but also in its implicit impotence, in its inability to exert a practical influence on social and political life.[11] Athenian society, with its typical Greek sensitivity to personal honour and reputation, and consequently to ridicule and insults, could not have tolerated, and indeed celebrated, the privileges of comic satire unless there had existed a general recognition of the conventions which separated the festivals from the normal life of the city.

An essential factor in this separation was the limitation of comic performances to only two major occasions each year, with the possibility of a lesser performance at a small local festival. When, therefore, a critic compares Aristophanes's treatment of Socrates in *Clouds* to 'a series of satirical shows on television, regularly attacking the same person', he overlooks the important distinction between a form of popular satire which does, and one which does not, enjoy repeated and therefore cumulative access to its public.[12] It

---

[8] The most important cases are *Acharnians*, ll. 237–79 (a phallic procession) and *Frogs*, 316–459, on which see pp. 15–16 below.

[9] *An Essay on Comedy*, edited by Lane Cooper (New York and London, 1972), p. 79. On Meredith's attitude to Aristophanes, see also Gillian Beer, *Meredith: A Change of Masks* (London, 1970), pp. 119, 196, 200.

[10] On the Aristophanic ethos of self-assertion against the forces of authority, see K. J. Dover, *Aristophanic Comedy* (Berkeley and Los Angeles, 1972), pp. 31–41.

[11] For some observations on Aristophanes's lack of influence, see H. Lloyd Stow, 'Aristophanes' Influence upon Public Opinion', *The Classical Journal*, 38 (1942), 83–92. The claim of S. C. Humphreys (*Anthropology and the Greeks* (London, 1978), p. 229), that in Old Comedy 'the power of public opinion is deliberately harnessed as a force of social control', is extravagant, and would require substantiation of a kind which it cannot be given.

[12] Alan Sommerstein, in *Aristophanes: The Knights etc.*, translated by David Barrett and Alan H. Sommerstein (Harmondsworth, 1978), p. 9.

may be conveniently added here that the time-scale of productions of Old Comedy meant that poets were not usually in a position to cultivate the kind of topicality on which the work of popular satirists in the mass media so heavily depends. Certainly the observable practice of Aristophanes shows a concentration on the broader and less ephemeral features of contemporary Athens. Even at its apparently most personal, Aristophanic satire tends to touch on aspects of social life which were of general and permanent interest to the Athenian audience. I hope that this will be borne out by parts of my analysis of the chief techniques of satire employed in the plays, to which I now turn.

It is appropriate to begin the analysis by looking at perhaps the most striking of the modes of Aristophanic satire, the direct impersonation of individuals, since we will here encounter in an immediate form several issues which are raised by the subject as a whole. A preliminary question concerning impersonation is whether it was normal to present a visually recognizable image or caricature of the individual. It is relevant here to consider the fact that realistic portraiture was still very rare in Greek art during Aristophanes's lifetime; it was only in the fourth century and the subsequent Hellenistic period that the style developed extensively.[13] Classical Greek art tended, rather, to portray individuals in a generalized or idealized form. A passage in Aristophanes's *Knights* (ll. 230–33) none the less seems to imply that portrait masks could be used in the theatre, but I believe it has been correctly argued that this passage is chiefly designed to prepare for the humour of a horrendous, yet supposedly inadequate, presentation of Cleon, alias the Paphlagonian slave.[14] What Aristophanes's reference to a 'likeness' of Cleon suggests is that impersonated characters in comedy would normally carry an appropriate mask; but the nature of personal sculpture in this period establishes that for Greek eyes this would not need to entail a precise copy of facial features. It should be added that visual caricature by its very nature depends on a close familiarity with the target's appearance, and it is doubtful whether this condition could always have been satisfied for Aristophanes's mass audiences.

This general argument can be substantiated by the evidence of the surviving plays. It is noticeable that in a majority of cases of satirical impersonation there is in the text no indication at all of any individual portrayal or caricature in the mask, and this fact must be taken in conjunction with an undoubtedly strong tendency for Aristophanes to make verbal references to his specific visual effects. What we do find, however, in several instances, are signs that a character is masked or costumed in accordance with a comic stereotype. Thus both Agathon and Cleisthenes in *Women at the Thesmophoria* are evidently given exaggeratedly feminine looks (see ll. 97–98,

[13] See G. M. A. Richter, *The Portraits of the Greeks* (London, 1965).
[14] See K. J. Dover, 'Portrait Masks in Aristophanes', in *Komoidotragemata: Studies in Honour of W. J. W. Koster* (Amsterdam, 1967), pp. 16–28.

136–52, 191–92, 575), and the whole treatment of their roles suggests that it
is the type, not a particular likeness, which the audience is expected to
appreciate.[15] In contrast, there is no trace in the text of anything satirical in
the appearance of Euripides in the same play. More remarkable, in view of
ancient references to his ugliness, is the apparent lack of an individual
caricature of Socrates's appearance in *Clouds*. It is likely in fact that Socrates
was presented simply in a way consonant with the play's general picture of
philosophers as dirty, pale faced, poorly fed, and short of clothing. Even if
some of these features were themselves derived from Aristophanes's own
observation of Socrates, this would not alter the generalizing tendency of the
satirical technique.[16]

If these remarks on the appearance of impersonated characters are on the
right lines, then they point the way towards a wider thesis about this area of
satire. I suggest that Aristophanes's fundamental procedure in most cases is
not to focus on particular features or traits, but rather to turn the nominally
real individual into an exaggerated and easily recognizable type. The
person's identity, and some of his associations, form the basis for a structure
of more or less fictional characterization in terms which can be appreciated
by a large popular audience, whether or not they have a detailed acquaintance with the particular target. This is not to deny Aristophanes's own close
familiarity with some of the people he brings into his plays, nor to ignore the
possibility of a higher degree of individualization in certain cases, but only to
argue that the main thrust of this type of satire is towards the simplification
and exaggeration of salient characteristics, and ultimately towards the
assimilation of the individual to a generalized or typical comic conception.

To illustrate the mechanics of the technique I shall take the treatment of
the military General, Lamachus, in *Acharnians*. It is a common observation
that Lamachus is the first braggart soldier in European comedy, and the fact
that we should recognize him as such, despite his real identity, is significant
for the manner in which Aristophanes has turned him into something
fictionally larger than his real self.[17] The first audience of *Acharnians* contained a large number of citizen soldiers, and it was Aristophanes's aim in
debasing a well-known General to appeal to their suppressed feelings of
cynicism towards their leaders: the festival experience of release from normal
inhibitions has a special force where escape from rigorous military discipline
is concerned. Aristophanes's presentation of Lamachus is not merely
denigratory; it draws implicitly on a sense of his real status.

---

[15] For the stereotyped comic conception involved, see K. J. Dover, *Greek Homosexuality* (London, 1978),
pp. 144–45.
[16] That a portrait mask was used for Socrates has recently been reasserted by Martha Nussbaum,
'Aristophanes and Socrates on Learning Practical Wisdom', in *Aristophanes: Essays in Interpretation*, edited
by J. Henderson (Cambridge, 1980), pp. 43–97 (p. 71). But she relies on a doctrinaire interpretation of
what is in any case probably a worthless anecdote in Arrian, and she ignores the lack of references in the
text.
[17] For an earlier hint of the braggart soldier, see Archilochus, Fragment 114, in *Iambi et Elegi Graeci*,
edited by M. L. West, 2 vols (Oxford, 1971), I, 45.

Just before the General first appears (*Acharnians*, l. 566) he is invoked by part of the chorus in terms which set into motion a procedure of burlesque exaggeration: 'Hail Lamachus! You whose eyes flash with lightning! | Appear and come to our rescue, hero of the Gorgon crest!' This is in fact parody of a religious prayer, and the overdone language is combined in the original with the dochmiac metre, a rhythm peculiarly associated with moments of tension or heightened emotion in tragedy. When Lamachus does step out to answer the call, Aristophanes transforms the contemporary General by his very costume into a ridiculously inflated embodiment of conceited military prowess. His crest and shield are absurdly large, and lines 591–92 suggest that his comic phallus is prominent. Much attention is drawn to this costume both in this scene and in the later one where Lamachus arms for war (ll. 1097–1142). The outfit is shown up as a shell of inflated pride and mock bellicosity. The comic 'hero', Dicaeopolis, openly flouts the general whom in real life he, or his like, would have to treat with respect. And in the play's finale we hear and see how Lamachus's prowess turns out to be illusory, as, after a humiliating failure, he is brought back on stage to the accompaniment of cries of distress which deliberately remind us of the dénouement of a tragedy.

The blend of hyperbole and fantastic burlesque in the ridicule of Lamachus means that we can hardly expect to be able to reduce the treatment of him to the terms of sober or serious criticism. There seems little doubt that Lamachus was in fact an able and respected military leader, and it is hard to believe that Aristophanes was attempting to convince his audience otherwise. Even if we suppose what is far from certain, that Lamachus was the proponent of an aggressive war policy, Aristophanes cannot have expected this in itself to make him unpopular, since it is presupposed elsewhere in *Acharnians* that the general mood in Athens was in favour of the continuation of war. One reason why Aristophanes has picked Lamachus out as the epitome of the officer class is the etymology of his name, which means something like 'very belligerent'. But this fortuitous factor, which gives material for a number of puns, is evidently not to be taken very seriously.

This is not, however, to argue that the burlesquing of Lamachus is necessarily good-natured. To judge the tone precisely is very difficult, but it is at least clear that its force is more that of abuse and deflation than of measured or coherent criticism. The satirical effect is developed mainly in terms of the disparity between the self-esteeming and pompous behaviour of Lamachus and the picture of his supposedly true nature which is presented assertively by Dicaeopolis and eventually vindicated by the action of the play. The cumulative degradation of the General may allow the conclusion that Aristophanes is using his fiction to evoke a kind of *Schadenfreude*, but that is a very different matter from either attributing a committed point of view to the author himself, or regarding the satire as a directly personal attack on

Lamachus. We can see from the lack of any real individuality in the portrayal of Lamachus that he is the target of a generalized cynicism about military leaders, and we can find at *Peace*, lines 1172–90, a description of the blustering officer precisely as a type conceived by popular sentiment. The festival is a time for the comic poet to give uninhibited expression to such collective attitudes. Outside the festival, cynicism must be kept in check and subordinated to a recognition of political realities.

I believe that Lamachus is representative of the individuals impersonated in Aristophanes, though the precise way in which a figure is built around a central conception varies. The Euripides who appears in three of the surviving plays, for example, is a fictional character created out of the material of his own plays. To most Athenians Euripides was a playwright and nothing more; to make a comic personality of him, Aristophanes needs to exploit the notion that a poet's work reflects his own nature, and to transform stylistic and dramatic features of the former into traits of the latter. Those who believe that this was both intended and received as if it were serious biography hold an unjustifiably low opinion of the intelligence of Aristophanes and his audience. In the case of the Socrates of *Clouds*, who furnishes probably the most debated issue in the history of Aristophanic criticism, it has often been recognized that Aristophanes attributes to the philosopher somewhat indiscriminately a whole cluster of features which make up a generalized and prejudiced picture of 'the intellectual type'.

Unfortunately this point has sometimes been obscured by confusion with the question of how far Aristophanes himself was familiar with the details of Socrates's life and teaching: a question which is certainly intriguing, but which is independent of the satirical techniques used to create the dramatic character of Socrates.[18] A number of specific connexions between the contents of *Clouds* and what we know of the real Socrates do not affect the broadly stereotypic manner in which Aristophanes presents his philosopher.[19] The play's emphasis on a *school* of intellectuals, which can be represented as well by the personified Unjust Argument as by Socrates himself, intimates Aristophanes's greater concern with the popular view of philosophers as a class than with any particular individual. It is for this reason that the surface of *Clouds* inevitably seems somewhat opaque to those who would like to discern the comic poet's personal views behind it. We need not believe that Aristophanes was an admirer of Socrates, but to conclude

---

[18] For a classical statement of the generic characterization of Socrates in *Clouds*, see Lessing's *Hamburgische Dramaturgie*, edited by K. L. Berghahn (Stuttgart, 1981), § 91, pp. 458–62. I have tried to suggest that this is perfectly compatible with Aristophanes's own familiarity with the real Socrates, for which see Nussbaum's article, cited above. But Nussbaum assumes, quite wrongly in my view, that Socrates was a figure whom Aristophanes's audience 'all knew so well' (p. 71), and this, together with a philosophical analysis which is too heavy for the texture of the play, yields a distorted interpretation.

[19] I should note that by 'stereotypic' I do not intend to subscribe to the belief in a set of traditional and fixed comic character types, as put forward, for example, by Cornford in Chapters 7–8. For trenchant criticism of this theory, see L. Breitholtz, *Die dorische Farce im griechischen Mutterland* (Uppsala, 1960), Chapter 3, and especially pp. 95–101 on Socrates.

with Hazlitt that he has treated the philosopher 'most scurvily both as to wit and argument' would be to read the play with an educated sensitivity which is quite alien to its festive irresponsibility.[20]

What I have so far been arguing for can be roughly summarized under three headings: first, the prevalence of a satirical irreverence which is to be understood as the expression of the distinctive festival ethos and licence for free speech, rather than as the declaration of an allegiance to serious standards or the cause of truth; secondly, a tendency towards treating individuals in such a way as to render them clear embodiments of typical characteristics, and particularly of popular conceptions of certain classes of people; and finally, and largely as a consequence of the two preceding points, the difficulty and inappropriateness of reading Aristophanic satire in terms of a personal authorial commitment.

All three of these contentions can be sustained when we shift attention from the impersonatory mode to the much more diffuse body of material which comprises hundreds of personal gibes and references scattered more or less incidentally throughout the plays. It is the copiousness and range of this collection of satirical jokes which has perhaps more than anything else been responsible for the view of Aristophanes as an exposer and scourge of vice, folly, and personal weakness. There has often, however, been an arbitrary inconsistency in this attitude: for while the major targets of Aristophanic satire, such as Euripides and Socrates, have been defended against their treatment in comedy, most of the lesser targets, many of whom mean little to us, have been rather blandly assumed to deserve whatever may be suggested about them in the plays. But if we can observe a considerable degree of distortion and even fiction in the presentation of figures about whom we do have knowledge from other sources, then we should be all the more cautious about accepting what is satirically imputed to butts for whom comedy is the only or the primary source.

It is in fact possible to raise doubts on purely internal grounds about the truthfulness of many Aristophanic jokes. The case of Cleonymus exemplifies this well. Cleonymus is the target of a long series of gibes, over more than a decade, and in many of these it is asserted or implied that he had thrown away his shield in battle. Had such an act of cowardice been proved, or probably even just widely believed, Cleonymus would have been barred from political life; yet it is clear from Aristophanes's own references to him that he had a political career of some importance, and this is confirmed by independent evidence. The insulting and degrading force of Aristophanes's image of Cleonymus is evident, but to treat it as historically reliable is unwise. While, however, it is necessary to take a similarly critical attitude to many other sets of jokes, it is more important to understand why it is in general naïve to look for truth in this type of satire. Against this naïvety two

---

[20] *The Complete Works of William Hazlitt*, edited by P. P. Howe, 21 vols (London, 1930–34), VI, 28.

aspects of comic technique need to be stressed. The first is the dramatic
context and character of most of the utterances in which personal gibes and
insults are contained. It is a rudimentary requirement of the dramatic nature
of the utterances that any satirical motivation or animus must seem to belong
to the speaker. Although Aristophanes shows little concern for integrating
jokes into his dramatic speech with much sophistication, their normal
justification derives from the feelings of his characters. Consequently, the
distinctive feature of this kind of satire is its affinity with the wit and abuse of
ordinary conversation; and its characteristic range of tone is therefore ribald,
spiteful, and irreverent.

A representative instance may be taken from the passage in *Women at the
Thesmophoria*, where Euripides has just shaved his kinsman to facilitate his
impersonation of a woman: *Euripides* (passing a mirror) 'Can you see
yourself?'; *Kinsman* 'Good God no! I can see Cleisthenes!' (l. 235). The gibe
picks up the standard suggestion that Cleisthenes is an effeminate homosexual, a role in which he will appear later in the play (ll. 574–654). But the
blend of disgust at his own appearance, and vulgar cynicism about that of
Cleisthenes, with which Euripides's kinsman makes the remark, renders the
question of what truth there is in the satire a rather pointless one. This is above
all *comic* satire, in which the pleasure of frank abuse justifies itself. To look for
moral force in such short references is simply to miss the humour of them.

The second aspect of comic technique which I would emphasize is a
tendency, akin to that on which I earlier commented, to reduce individual
butts to an easily grasped and simplified conception of ridiculous or disap-
proved behaviour. This reductivism both appeals to widely shared attitudes
(often to popular prejudices) and by its very nature militates against a just or
accurate appraisal of personal characteristics. When at *Peace*, line 395, the
chorus ask Hermes to side with their effort for peace ('If you loathe Peisander's
crests and eyebrows') what we have is a satirical vignette of the blustering
military commander of Lamachus's type: the presentation is here, of course,
much more compressed, with just the merest indication of the stock attributes
of pompousness and superciliousness, but the underlying conception is the
same. In both cases the question of how truly the individual embodies the type
is lost beneath the comic appeal and the blunt cynicism of the type itself. A
limited analogy could be drawn between this feature of Aristophanic satire
and the patterns of ridicule and invective used by Greek orators in political
controversy and forensic dispute.[21] But the orator is at least limited by the
pressures of relevance and practical persuasion; the comic poet has a free rein,
and need not fear a reply.

The corollary of this, however, as I suggested earlier, is that the poet cannot
expect to influence his audience's beliefs in a direct way, and also that the
content of his satire cannot always be regarded as having the same status as

---

[21] See K. J. Dover, *Greek Popular Morality in the Time of Plato and Aristotle* (Oxford, 1974), pp. 30–33.

ordinary claims and propositions. The point can be illustrated by *Women in the Assembly*, lines 102–03, where Praxagora tells her female companions that their false beards will ensure that they go undetected in the men's political assembly: 'At least, nobody has noticed that Agyrrhius borrows Pronomus's beard. Yet Agyrrhius used to be a woman!' Agyrrhius was a leading politician at this date, and Praxagora is imputing to him both a natural effeminacy and a previous period of passive homosexuality, with Pronomus probably representing his lover. Some may think it likely that Aristophanes knew of a relationship between these two men (such matters were not wholly private at Athens), but it hardly matters whether he did. For most of his audience the point of the joke would be self-explanatory, since it was a stock piece of popular cynicism to suppose that entry to a political career was gained through one's sexual availability as an adolescent. Indeed, this idea appears in its generalized form only a few lines later in this same passage, at lines 112–13. If the Athenians tended to believe their own cynicism on this subject, which there is no way of telling, then no doubt they believed the worst of Agyrrhius. But whether or not they did, the gibe against the politican is meant to be abusive and to gratify popular sentiment, not to be informative.

The three features which I have predicated of Aristophanic satire in general (independence of a commitment to serious values, a tendency towards stereotyping, and an appeal to popular attitudes which makes the author's point of view hard to discern) can be found in a concentrated and heightened form in a number of choral odes that can be loosely described as satirical interludes. The fact that these odes are more or less independent of dramatic context allows the gratuitous nature of the festive emotions to be manifested in them with particular clarity.[22] Moreover, the use of the collective choral voice can be exploited to underline the broad and popular character of the sentiments expressed and invited by the satire. These odes characteristically involve a reliance on simple primitive urges, as well as a frankness which evidently requires no apology. The world is wishfully manipulated, just as it is on a large dramatic scale in most of Aristophanes's plays. Thus, explicitly imaginary situations are conjured up (*Acharnians*, ll. 1150–73; *Plutus*, ll. 302–15), and tales are told of bizarre and distant places (*Birds*, ll. 1470–93, 1553–64, 1694–705). Some odes toy in a blunt way with the thought of a victim's physical discomfiture (*Acharnians*, ll. 840–41, 1165–72; *Plutus*, l. 305), or even his death (*Acharnians*, ll. 1150–51; *Knights*, ll. 973–76). And the attraction is obvious of a society from which enemies and undesirables are excluded (*Acharnians*, ll. 836–59; *Frogs*, ll. 354–71, 1491–99).

Perhaps the most interesting of these odes for my purposes is *Frogs*, lines 416–30, even though this is the only one of its type to form an episode within the drama. But the fact that at this point in *Frogs* Aristophanes is actually

---

[22] I find the attempt of C. Moulton ('The Lyric of Insult and Abuse in Aristophanes', *Museum Helveticum*, 36 (1979), 23–46), to show that some of these odes are subtly related to the themes of their plays, very far fetched.

dramatizing a festival, involving moreover a chorus who are engaging in licensed festive mockery, allows him to treat the ode as an effectively free-standing piece of satire. This is marked especially by the gratuitous way in which the chorus launch themselves into the song at lines 416–17 with an invitation to the actors to 'join us in our ridicule of Archedemus'. As this invitation also emphasizes, the communal spirit of the song is explicit. The chorus is an anonymous festive group; they have no special point of view, and anyone can join them who, like Dionysus and Xanthias, is infected by their celebration. Although their song forms part of a religious occasion, the content of it is not at all religious. The chorus pick out three prominent Athenians and subject them to uninhibited insults: the politician Archedemus is accused of not being a legal citizen (a stock allegation of political slander); the son of Cleisthenes is portrayed as mourning the death of an imaginary homosexual lover (the father's old comic reputation being thus handed on to the son); and the wealthy but profligate Callias is obscenely charged with fighting his own sexual battles at a time when the city is fighting for its survival.

Although there is some linguistic sophistication in the song, in the form of puns and other wordplay, the essential gibes are easily intelligible, and require nothing more than a willingness to enjoy the spirit of deliberate and uninhibited rudeness. To choose how strictly to believe the particular imputations is no part of a proper response to this ode. The fact that the celebrating chorus are, in a sense, in a world of their own would be very clear to an audience who could see their merry dance, patterned to the iambic rhythms of popular song. What is so significant about this passage of *Frogs* is that Aristophanes has blended together, so that they become indistinguishable, the specific festival portrayed within the play and the general character of his own brand of choral satire. The mood of this song is emblematic of Aristophanes's relation to his own festive context.

I have now attempted to show, with a necessarily high degree of selectivity, how the techniques and practices of Aristophanic satire are based not on the premise of a didactic or edifying function for the poet's work, but on the conventions and presuppositions of a special festive freedom of speech, which is insulated from some of the normal requirements of social and political life in the city. This line of argument might be thought, however, to give rise to certain paradoxes, on which I wish to make some observations. The most obvious paradox was mentioned in my introduction, where I noticed that Aristophanes himself lays claim to a seriousness and truthfulness which I have been trying to deny him. The poet's professions about his educative functions are made in the special section of his plays where the chorus address themselves directly to the audience on his behalf, the parabasis.

It is certainly clear that if Aristophanes did regard his satire as serving a political or moral purpose, we should expect this to be confirmed in the parabasis, in which there are no necessary dramatic constraints on his relation to his audience. That this expectation is fulfilled in the surviving plays has often been asserted. According to Gilbert Highet, for example, the parabasis is used to focus the audience's attention 'on the central message of the play'.[23] This is, however, an extravagant claim, and it can be demonstrated that in most of the parabases there is no obvious match between the chorus's statements and the main themes of the play.[24] It does not follow from this, of course, that Aristophanes's general justifications of his satire are not seriously meant, nor that the possibility of independently committed satire within the parabasis is ruled out. But there are good reasons none the less for doubting such seriousness or commitment.

A great deal of the personal ridicule to be found in the parabases follows similar patterns to those I have already tried to establish. This is most evident for the abuse of rival poets which occurs in several plays, especially *Knights* and *Clouds*. Here we are dealing with something intimately connected to the competitive circumstances in which the plays were first produced. But the satire which expresses professional rivalry has to justify itself ultimately in comic terms. We can see this clearly in Aristophanes's portrait of Cratinus (*Knights*, ll. 526–36) as a predecessor whose career had gone into decline: Cratinus's career had indeed begun long before that of Aristophanes, but it was not yet over, for he was competing at the same festival as *Knights*. What distinguishes this, however, from the usual satirical techniques employed in the dramatic scenes and speech of the plays is an element that can best be described as rhetorical, and it is this factor which is crucial for an understanding of the Aristophanic parabasis.

The fact of direct audience-address in the parabasis makes the chorus's status, or the poet's status where the chorus speak on his behalf, analogous to that of the public speaker in a political assembly or a court of law. Aristophanes exploits this analogy most fundamentally by adopting the manner and the discursive argumentation of public rhetoric. Satirical elements in the parabasis are therefore characteristically set in a framework of argument: they are used to illustrate or support the case which the chorus purport to urge on the audience, whether this concerns the poet's rivals or some topic from the general life of the city. Moreover, there is a special connexion between the rhetorical style of the parabasis and the claims which Aristophanes makes for the usefulness of his satire to the Athenians, for such claims to be benefiting the city and combating its enemies are a standard feature of public oratory, as used both by the proponents of political causes and by forensic advocates in those cases which involve the public interest. It is particularly clear, then, in such passages as *Acharnians*, lines 630–58, and *Wasps*, lines 1029–43, that Aristophanes is striking the posture of the city's adviser and defender. But the question remains: how seriously?

---

[23] *The Anatomy of Satire*, p. 28.
[24] See Dover, *Aristophanic Comedy*, pp. 51–53. *Knights* is a significant instance, since the play is the most political of the surviving eleven, yet its parabasis steers almost entirely clear of the issues of the drama.

To answer this question fully would require detailed criticism of individual parabases, but I can here only briefly indicate my contention that the typical rhetoric of the Aristophanic parabasis is intended to be understood as amusingly exaggerated and artificial. Two passages may be picked out to support this. The first is *Wasps*, lines 1029–43, already mentioned, where Aristophanes describes the campaign which he boasts he has been waging since the beginning of his career against the major enemies of Athens, especially the politician Cleon. It is interesting that immediately before this passage Aristophanes denies that he has used his supposed power as a comic poet for pursuit of his private interests: this disclaimer is modelled on another standard device of the public orator.

But the positive side of the poet's argument is presented through a colourful mixture of allegory and mock heroics. Aristophanes himself is compared to Heracles, and his enemy Cleon is transformed into a monster of Gargantuan proportions. Although there are elements in the picture of the monster which allude to real features of Cleon's political life (his clique of supporters and his formidable rhetorical delivery), the most noticeable aspect of the whole description (ll. 1031–35) is the way in which it reduces Cleon to a collection of frightful or repellent physical features. Its force, in other words, is essentially abusive and debasing, and the small ingredient of intelligible political allegory is swamped beneath the accumulation of offensive details. It is significant that Cleon is indeed identified only as the monster, and not by his real name, which would clearly detract from the inflated tone of the comic fiction.

What we encounter here, then, in a purported account of Aristophanes's career, is a fine illustration of the characteristically denigratory thrust of his satire. The framework of a speciously serious argument is the mere vehicle for an attack whose technique and rationale have to be understood in terms of the genre's licence for scurrile entertainment. We should not allow the assumption that Aristophanes personally loathed Cleon to persuade us that this passage from *Wasps* offers anything that could be regarded as genuinely political. When Aristophanes suggests, at line 1036, that he has refused bribes to silence him, the pretence that comedy is part of the world of real politics simply sustains the braggadocio of the whole passage: there is no more substance to it than there is to the suggestion at *Acharnians*, lines 652–54, that the Spartans are offering peace to Athens in order to steal Aristophanes from her.

It is a telling fact that the argument at *Wasps*, lines 1029–43, is designed to lead up to Aristophanes's complaints about the Athenians' failure in the previous year to appreciate the comic originality of *Clouds*: the pseudo-political claims for the poet's satire are ultimately subordinated to his artistic pride, and we may well think that this represents his true priorities. The point is confirmed by a passage from *Clouds* (ll. 545–59), where Aristophanes combines a boast about the innovative qualities of his own satire with an attack on the triteness of his rivals'. As in the parabasis of *Wasps*, there is a pretence of real political achievement in the poet's career. Aristophanes describes how he had struck Cleon in the stomach and knocked him to the ground, but had then forborne to jump on him. This image, taken from Greek wrestling, implies that in his major satire, *Knights*, on the political leader, Aristophanes had won a victory over Cleon, and also that he had been too condescending to finish off the fight. The first of these propositions is a deliberate and humorous fiction: the success of *Knights* had been purely theatrical, and we know that it had no impact on Cleon's real political stature. The second proposition is more revealing, for it represents, if in a slightly embellished form, what mattered most to Aristophanes: his artistic originality. The comic poet's claim to offer his audience something new and clever every year (ll. 547–48) is proof that his values are not those of the truly committed satirist.

I hope now to have gone some way towards resolving the paradox of Aristophanes's own professions of a serious function within the life of his city. Two further paradoxes which might be thought to emerge from my account of his satirical practice can be taken closely together. I have argued that Old Comedy was effectively insulated, by its festive context and its traditions, from impinging in an influential way on social or political reality. It may seem that my argument goes against the grain of two of the distinguishing marks of Aristophanes's work: the explicit and mordant quality of his treatment of individuals, and the apparently constant concern of his plays with themes of major social and political importance to his audience. It has been the view of many readers of Aristophanes that the only conceivable justification of such strong habits of vilification could be a moralistic purpose, and it is consequently assumed that the poet's victims must have deserved all they got: an echo of such thinking can be heard in the quotation from Richard Cumberland with which I began. But to reason in this fashion is to assimilate Aristophanes too easily to the traditions, and the self-image, of later European satire, and to miss the significance of the genre's original context.

It is a desperate task to try to bring Aristophanes somehow into line with the standards of ages which have put so much emphasis on decorum, and any straightforward version of the moralistic argument falls not only on the grounds of historical naïvety, but also because of the patently gratuitous nature of so much of the personal abuse in his plays. It would be no more reasonable, however, to conclude that Aristophanes was himself irresponsible and malevolent in the exercise of his talent, for this too would be to apply inappropriate standards. The kind of irresponsibility which my own argument has attempted to attribute to Old Comedy is not a matter of the evasion of standards, but rather an institutionalized and culturally sanctioned exemption from them. Given the normal Greek notion of ridicule as a serious and powerful weapon in relations with one's enemies, it is not surprising that a licence for uninhibited ridicule should have produced comic material which will seem badly in need of justification to those who do not really believe in the pleasures of satire.

But even for those who can acknowledge the coarse and cynical vigour of Aristophanes, a sense of the original festive context remains indispensable for a proper appreciation of his satire. Here a comparison may be instructive. It is not difficult to see why Shelley, who had read the comic poet in the Greek, should have tried to derive some inspiration from Aristophanes for his satire on the trial of Queen Caroline in 1820, *Oedipus Tyrannus or Swellfoot the Tyrant*. Shelley combines a general Aristophanic ethos of scabrous explicitness with a vivid repertoire of dramatic imagery which also owes something to the English tradition of political cartoons. But Shelley's work was not only an expression of personal disgust; it was also a potential influence on the real political world of public opinion. A threat of prosecution brought the withdrawal of the book. In sharp contrast to this, Shelley's main Aristophanic model, *Knights*, was not only tolerated by the Athenians, but won the public honour of first prize at its festival.[25] Whatever we may conjecture that Aristophanes himself put into the play from his own animus against Cleon, the satirical charge was effectively dispersed in performance, without seriously impinging on the city's democratic politics.

It remains true, of course, that Old Comedy was engaged with important aspects of Athenian society, though perhaps rather more selectively than has sometimes been realized. But to understand the nature of this engagement we must avoid the facile application of ideas borrowed from other times and cultures, and we must work up from the secure foundation of an awareness of the special relation, in the festive context, between the poets of Old Comedy and their public. If we wish to try to recover the personal voice of Aristophanes behind his satire, we can do so only by a difficult and critical process of discrimination.

[25] Some attempts were made to put legal curbs on the freedom of Old Comedy, but none had much impact. The idea that the decline of the genre was due to legal restrictions is a myth.

Rough Music: Some Early Invectives and Flytings

DOUGLAS GRAY

Lady Margaret Hall, Oxford

R. C. Elliott's *The Power of Satire*, with its emphasis on the importance of the ancient connexion of satire with magic and its cogent demonstration of the extreme complexity of the nature of satire, was an important landmark for students of medieval literature, for it, together with Alvin Kernan's *The Cankered Muse*, suggested a framework within which much of the satire written between Juvenal and Dryden could be seriously investigated. Histories of English satire had usually either ignored early satire or had dismissed it as 'mere invective' or 'primitive': at best a clumsy and awkward precursor of the polished formal satire of the neo-Classical revival. In fact, throughout the Middle Ages 'the satiric' was pervasive, and found expression in a variety of forms, ranging from the elegant literary satire of Chaucer (almost unique in being able to catch a genuinely Horatian tone) to examples of coarse, popular, and sometimes sub-literary satire. It is with the latter end of the spectrum that this article is concerned, and in particular with its more literary expression in the flytings of Dunbar and Skelton.

Appropriately, it seems that the noun 'invective' is first attested in English in Skelton's *The Garland of Laurel* (where it is linked with Juvenal), and that the word 'fliting' or 'flyting' ('contention, wrangling; scolding, rebuking') first appears in its specifically literary sense in Dunbar's exchange with Kennedy. This sense is defined by *OED* as 'poetical invective; chiefly, a kind of contest practised by the Scottish poets of the 16th century, in which two persons assailed each other alternately with tirades of abusive verse'. Dunbar and Kennedy do just this, but what happens in even such an apparently simple dramatic invective form as the flyting is rather more interesting than the dictionary's bald definition suggests. Some remarks of W. H. Auden draw attention to a number of elements in the flyting. After lamenting that 'flyting seems to have vanished as a studied literary art and only to survive in the impromptu exchanges of truckdrivers and cabdrivers', he continues:

The comic effect arises from the contradiction between the insulting nature of what is said which appears to indicate a passionate relation of hostility and aggression, and the calculated skill of verbal invention which indicates that the protagonists are not thinking about each other but about language and their pleasure in employing it inventively. A man who is really passionately angry is speechless and can only express his anger by physical violence. Playful anger is intrinsically comic because, of all emotions, anger is the least compatible with play.[1]

[1] 'Notes on the Comic', in *The Dyer's Hand and Other Essays* (London, 1963), p. 383.

That the flyting is an art form, that it is essentially rhetorical, and that it involves (in a quite complicated way) an element of play and of 'acting' are, as we shall see, all points of central importance. There are, however, other aspects equally interesting, which emerge when we set flytings and other invectives against their background of popular satire, of those 'homely taunts' which Dryden himself mentions in his historical survey of ancient satire. From his point of view, such forms are 'the underwood of satire rather than the timber trees', but, it must be said, they have been thick on the ground for a very long time. As Dryden rather nicely puts it:

If we take satire in the general signification of the word . . . for an invective, 'tis certain that it is almost as old as verse; and though hymns, which are the praises of God, may be allow'd to have been before it, yet the defamation of others was not long after it. After God had curs'd Adam and Eve in Paradise, the husband and wife excus'd themselves by laying the blame on one another.[2]

Perhaps we may think of such popular satire (involving 'homely taunts', 'the defamation of others', etc.) as a kind of continuing ground bass underlying all the varied elaborations and experiments of more self-consciously literary satirists.

A number of preliminary points may be made quickly. First, such satire is by no means always as playful as Auden's remarks might suggest. Early satire often puts into practice the advice on polemic given in the *Protagoras* (339E), that one's opponent should reel 'as one punched by a good boxer'; a hefty blow beneath the belt is more characteristic of it than a delicate rapier thrust. And, sometimes encouraged by the common etymological association of 'satire' with 'satyr', it is often rough, harsh, and abrasive in rhythm, diction, and thought: 'like the Porcupine, | That shoots sharpe quils out in each angry line' (in Joseph Hall's *Virgidemiarum*, v.3.1). Elliott's pages on the connexion with magic are illuminating here. He gives us a mass of evidence from a number of cultures of a deep-rooted fear of the harm, whether physical or psychical, that can ensue from satire. In early Celtic literature, satires, which are virtually magical spells, are said to have had physical effects (producing blisters on the cheek of a victim, blighting the whole of Leinster, etc.),[3] and Icelandic literature has much evidence of the terrible effects of calumniation through lampoons (*níðvísur* : *níð* is a form of ridicule which represents a person as a figure of universal contempt, often with an obscene element which gives it a defamatory and poisonous sting, whether it is expressed in words only (*tunguníð*) or by carving (*tréníð*)).[4] Even in the seventeenth century, a traveller records that in Iceland 'the wound given by

---

[2] 'Discourse Concerning the Original and Progress of Satire', *The Poetical Works of Dryden*, edited by George R. Noyes, revised edition (Boston, 1950), p. 294.

[3] See especially F. N. Robinson, 'Satirists and Enchanters in Early Irish Literature', in *Studies in the History of Religion Presented to C. H. Toy*, edited by D. G. Lyon and G. F. Moore (New York, 1912), pp. 95–130.

[4] See F. Ström, '*Níð, ergi* and Old Norse Moral Attitudes' (Dorothea Coke Memorial Lecture, 1973 (London, 1974)).

a Mad-Dog' is 'scarce more dangerous than their venemous Satyrs', and tells a story he had heard of an Icelandic student at Copenhagen being terrified of the malignant effect of a satire made by one of his fellow countrymen.[5] All this is reflected in those various stories of death being caused by a satirist: Archilochus, Hipponax, Dafydd ap Gwilym, and others. Not surprisingly, satirists, as Elliott showed, are often presented as railers or malcontents, figures such as Thersites, Bricriu, Loki, Kay, or perhaps, in the twentieth century, Lenny Bruce. This stereotype of the satirist seems to lie behind Gavin Douglas's reference to the literary quarrel between Poggio and Valla:

> And Poggius stude with mony girne and grone
> On Laurence Valla spittand and cryand, fy!
> (*The Palice of Honour*, l. 1232)

Secondly, this fear of the power of the satirist's words has a social dimension. This too is widespread. E. E. Evans-Pritchard remarks that in Africa song is a weapon of power. Not only can it be used to lampoon one's enemies, but 'it serves also as an organ of law, in the wide sense of the word as a body of binding sanctions, in that it chastises the man who has offended public opinion'.[6] Popular satire has a normative function, which plays a part in ensuring the coherence of the social group, a function which is notably effective in societies with a highly developed communal sense of 'honour' and 'shame'.[7] There is of course considerable variety here, both in the intensity of the ridicule (ranging from a desire to destroy or drive out the victim to a kind of social 'letting off steam')[8] and in the nature of the 'norms' (sometimes law 'in the wide sense of the word', sometimes popular prejudice, sometimes a kind of rough justice which might encourage wise men to learn from the harm of fools, as the proverb has it).

Thirdly, popular satire involves or implies some kind of 'performance'. It is usually an oral performance, and a public one; sometimes it is dramatic or quasi-dramatic. Such satire often has an expressive quality (rather like the 'performative utterances' of J. L. Austin) which is not always immediately obvious on the printed page.[9] To understand its effect, we have to try to reconstruct a context of performance, in which performer(s), satirical words and/or representation, and audience all play interrelated roles: a performance which in the words of a modern folklorist 'is an active part of the social drama, reflecting in a small way the ever-present existence of conflict in

---

[5] Isaac de la Peyrère, *Relation de l'Islande* (1644), translated in Churchill's *Voyages*, Volume II (1704), pp. 437–38.
[6] *The Position of Women in Primitive Society and Other Essays in Social Anthropology* (London, 1965), p. 168.
[7] See Elliott, pp. 67–87 (with references), and, among a number of recent anthropological studies, J. du Boulay, *Portrait of a Greek Mountain Village* (Oxford, 1974), pp. 181–87.
[8] A good example of this latter is the song of derision (exchanged between the women of a tribe and their men who had returned empty-handed from a raid) translated in B. Mitcalfe, *Poetry of the Maori* (Hamilton, New Zealand), pp. 37–38.
[9] See J. L. Austin, *Philosophical Papers* (Oxford, 1961), p. 222 (cited by Emrys Jones, *Scenic Form in Shakespeare* (Oxford, 1971), p. 91). He is discussing utterances (like saying 'I do' in a marriage ceremony) which lead us to say that the speaker is '*doing* something rather than merely *saying* something'.

everyday life'.[10] Even in *narratives* of verbal conflict, a collector has found that 'the speaker re-enacts his own part, and that of his opponent, with an intensity of feeling and expression that stands out in an otherwise taciturn discourse', and that these descriptions of conflicts move towards a dramatic climax, sometimes the emotional release of the spoken insult.[11] And indeed, in our discussions of even the most literary satire we find ourselves talking of the satirist's relationship with an *audience*, of how he manipulates his 'voices' or his 'person', of how he enlists his audience's sympathy, of how it must share with him 'commitment to certain intellectual and moral standards that validate his attacks on aberration' (as Elliott puts it in his *Encyclopedia Britannica* article).

It is time to turn to some brief examples of traditional popular satirical forms. In Chapter 39 of *The Mayor of Casterbridge*, Hardy gives us a vivid description of a 'satirical mummery', the 'skimmington' or 'skimmity ride' procession to the houses of those who have offended (or who are thought by some to have offended) the community: 'two images on a donkey, back to back, their elbows tied to one another's! She's facing the head, and he's facing the tail'. It is accompanied by much noise: 'roars of sarcastic laughter' and 'rude music' ('the din of cleavers, tongs, tambourines, kits, crouds, hum-strums, serpents, rams'-horns, and other historical kinds of music'). The satire has an immediate emotional and physical effect on one of the victims; Lucetta (who, unlike Farfrae, has not been got out of the way) recognizes herself and falls to the floor, and 'remained convulsed on the carpet in the paroxysms of an epileptic seizure'. Satirical performances of this kind have been recorded in many areas of England and Europe in a variety of closely-related forms and under a variety of names: in some English counties, the 'wooset' or the 'ooser', or simply 'riding' (or riding the stang, the pole, etc.); elsewhere as the French *charivari*, the *cencerrada* ('ringing of cowbells'), or the *vito* (because the rapid steps of the dancers recall the dance of St Vitus) of southern Spain.[12] Some descriptions sound even more brutal than Hardy's 'skimmity'; in the Devonshire 'Stag-Hunt', for instance, a man with a painted face and antlers was pursued by a 'leaping, howling hunt' of men to the house of the adulterers, where, with the aid of a bladder of ox blood, the 'kill' finally took place.[13]

It is impossible to say how ancient the practice is. In England, the first really detailed description is in Butler's *Hudibras* (later illustrated by Hogarth), but it seems very likely that the custom is an old one; in France it is clearly attested

[10] R. D. Abrahams, 'Introductory Remarks to a Rhetorical Theory of Folklore', *Journal of American Folklore*, 81 (1968), 143–57.
[11] M. J. Lovelace, '"We had Words": Narratives of Verbal Conflicts', *Lore and Language*, 3 (1979), 29–37.
[12] There is a large literature on this: articles with very full references are those of E. P. Thompson, '"Rough Music": Le Charivari anglais', *Annales*, 27 (1972), 285–312, and J.-C. Margolin and C. Marcel-Dubois in *Les Fêtes de la Renaissance*, edited by J. Jacquot and E. Konigson, 3 vols (Paris, 1956–75), III, 577–601, 603–15. For further English examples, see R. A. Firor, *Folkways in Thomas Hardy* (Philadelphia, 1931), pp. 58, 238–42, and E. C. Cawte, *Ritual Animal Disguise* (Cambridge, 1978), pp. 109, 192–93; for European, V. Alford, 'Rough Music or Charivari', *Folklore*, 70 (1959), 505–18; for Spanish, J. A. Pitt-Rivers, *The People of the Sierra* (London, 1954), Chapter 11.
[13] See T. Brown, *Folklore*, 63 (1952), 104–09.

in the Middle Ages.[14] Both forms and functions seem to have been flexible. The practice is used to punish a variety of offences (adultery, seduction, the marriage of a widower with a young girl, wife-beating or husband-beating, etc.), usually those that are regarded as examples of shameless behaviour or flagrant immorality. There is often a 'legal' and normative aspect to it: the punishment is sometimes organized after secret discussion and debate. It is a public proclamation of shame, an 'outburst of aggressive ridicule', that gives expression to what had previously been thought or said only in private. It is a form of ritualized hostility, which can vary in tone, from a carnivalesque boisterousness to something which 'stops just short of lynching' (in one part of Spain it was called *la pandorga* 'the mobbing up'). The effect on the victim of this latter sort may be permanent (a shame which it is felt can never be lived down) and may lead to complete ostracism, exile, or even death.[15]

From our point of view, two common elements are of particular interest. One is that of dramatic *performance* (which needs to be organized: see *The Mayor of Casterbridge*) with an audience. The mimic quality is sometimes reflected in imitations of the tone of voice of the victims, or in the life-likeness of the images (which may remind us of the ancient magic power of satire — it is a kind of *tréníðr*). The whole thing is a sort of street theatre, which in its own rough way is doing what Dryden recommends to the satirist (in his 'Discourse'), to 'make a man appear a fool, a blockhead or a knave'. The other constant element of the 'performative utterance' is the 'rough music' (called sometimes in German *Katzenmusik*). In *Hudibras* the mock triumphal procession is accompanied by a great din of horns, pans, dogs, boys, kettle-drums, and bagpipes. Other descriptions list ladles and skimmers, bells, and 'cows' horns, frying-pans, warming-pans, and tea-kettles, drummed on with a large key; iron pot-lids, used as cymbals; fire-shovels and tongs rattled together; tin and wooden pails drummed on with iron pokers or marrow-bones — in fact, any implement with which a loud, harsh, and discordant sound can be produced'.[16] It is a kind of 'anti-music', which expresses mimetically both the discord and disharmony caused by the offenders, and the harshness of satire as public ridicule. The burlesque 'symphony' is similar to that associated with the grotesque and capering devils on the medieval stage: in *Le Jeu d'Adam*, when the devils carry Adam and Eve to Hell, they dance, make a great smoke, and 'shall shout to each other in their joy; and they shall bang their cauldrons and kettles together so that they can

[14] *Hudibras*, edited by J. S. Wilders (Oxford, 1967), pp. 142–45. For French medieval examples, see E. K. Chambers, *The Medieval Stage*, 2 vols (Oxford, 1903) I, 153 (it is found, for instance, in the *Roman de Fauvel*). I wonder if something like it may lie behind the ME phrase 'my bell shall be rung' (B. J. Whiting, *Proberbs, Sentences and Proverbial Phrases . . . before 1500* (Cambridge, Massachusetts, 1968), B 233) which is used by Chaucer's Criseyde (*TC*, 5. 1061–62) when she ponders how her shame will be spread throughout the world.

[15] See E. P. Thompson, p. 290; Pitt-Rivers, pp. 171–77. In its innocuous form it appears characteristically as a rowdy and noisy wedding celebration (for example, nowadays, in the fastening of tin cans on cars); see R. Bernheimer, *Wild Men in the Middle Ages* (Cambridge, Massachusetts, 1952), pp. 166–71.

[16] *The Book of Days*, edited by R. Chambers, 2 vols (London and Edinburgh, 1869), II, 510–11.

be heard outside'.[17] And in the skimmington the instruments were also supported by vocal 'anti-music' ('shouts, yells, hisses, cries of shame'), and with the hue and cry sometimes came 'ditties and ballads' (*Hudibras*) or other forms of 'old doggrel yelled out by those who are skimmity riding'.[18]

'Old doggrel' is often a feature of those 'homely taunts' which, though publicly uttered, are not part of an elaborate performance like the skimmington. C. R. Baskervill, in his study of the Elizabethan jig, quotes a libellous 'ryme' of 1584 which Anne Wrigglesworth of Islip was accused of making:

> Yf I had as faire a face as John Willms
>   his daughter Elzabeth hasse,
> Then wold I were a taudrie lace as Goodman
>   bolts daughter Marie dosse;
> And if I had as mutche money in my pursse
>   as Cadmans daughter Margaret hasse,
> Then wold I have a basterd lesse
> Then Butlers mayde Helen hasse.

Here the jingling 'doggrel' rhythm in combination with a kind of mock syllogistic structure makes an oddly effective taunt. Anne Wrigglesworth pleaded that though she had said the rhyme she had not 'made' it, and certainly, as Baskervill says, it seems to be a formula into which various names could be fitted. Its purpose, public ridicule, is similar to that of the more spectacular *charivari*: 'To be made the hero of comic ballads hawked and sung about the streets . . . was regarded as the natural penalty of becoming ridiculous or notorious.'[19] Yet again we have an example of the power of the satirist when he 'names' a victim.

A similar effect is sometimes achieved by the widespread practice of 'naming' a person by a satirical nickname. Examples from Andalusia studied by Pitt-Rivers (pp. 160–69) show the working of a community's sanctions: the names are bestowed not by a particular neighbour but by the community as a whole. But again we find a variety of tone and a variety of response (traditional nicknames handed down from generation to generation are accepted without complaint, but new and ugly ones cause intense pain, and are imputed by the victims to 'envy' rather than to any kind of 'law'). Again, public ridicule is often the end: 'To hear one's nickname sung in the *Carnaval* by the anonymous mocking voices of the pueblo must indeed have meant humiliation.' Satirical nicknames have, of course, constantly

---

[17] *Medieval French Plays*, translated by R. Axton and John Stevens (Oxford, 1971), pp. 35–36. In the Chester *Harrowing of Hell*, when Christ enters Hell, a stage direction instructs the devils to make a clamour or a loud sound of things striking together. See also M. Bakhtin, *Rabelais and his World*, translated by H. Iswolsky (Cambridge, Massachusetts, 1968), p. 266.

[18] *EDD*, from F. T. Elworthy, *A West Somerset Word Book* (1866). The example runs: 'Now [Jimsy Hart], if thee disn mend thy manners, | The skin of thy ass we'll zend to the tanner's: | And if the tanner, he on'l tan un well, | We'll hang un pon a nail in hell; | And if the nail beginth to crack, | We'll hang un 'pon the devil's back; | And if the devil urnth away, | We'll hang un there another day.' Compare the example given in Chambers's *Book of Days* (used by a herald in a 'riding the stang' procession).

[19] *The Elizabethan Jig* (Chicago, 1929), pp. 66–67.

been given to social and ethnic groups as well as to individuals (compare the medieval French *godon* (that is, 'God damn') for English soldiers, or the eighteenth-century English names for an Irishman: 'boglander', 'dear joy', 'teague', etc.).

Comparable to these are the short rhymed 'taunts' known as *blasons populaires*, traditional witticisms now usually directed against a village and its inhabitants or a rival school:

> Helmsdale is a dirty place,
> A dirty set of people,
> Herring heads at every door
> And a church without a steeple.[20]

Such *blasons* have, in performance, the social function of affirming the solidarity of the group; in a way, defence as well as attack may be involved. Perhaps it is worth recalling this when we read their nearest equivalent in medieval English literature, those abusive poems against the Scots or the Flemings. The idea behind the *blason populaire* can sometimes find literary expression in elegant form. Dunbar's 'Dregy' sets within a witty parody of the Office for the Dead a satirical contrast between the delights of (court) life in Edinburgh and the austerities of Stirling. Rabelais finds in 'blazoning' an invitation to rhetorical hyperbole, and constructs from traditional sayings of the 'saoul comme un Anglais'-type an amazing edifice in which 'praise and abuse are merged into an indissoluble unity.'[21]

The element of competition in the *blason populaire*, whether implicit or explicit (to the taunt 'Totley bugs, | Water clogs, Water porridge and hardly that', the boys of Totley would reply 'Dore bugs, | Water clogs | Eating out o' swill-tubs | Up a ladder and down a wall, | A penny loaf will serve you all') leads to our final type of popular satire, that which involves some kind of verbal contest.[22] Verbal duels survive not only in children's games (the exchange of cries of derision or of mocking verses) but, in some societies, among adults in forms that range from those which depend on insinuation and innuendo to those like the public knockabout game of 'the Dozens', played by American blacks, in which 'a crowd gathers expectantly and eggs on the rivals as they exchange insults and invective'. They are found in a variety of cultures (from the Highlands of Scotland to the coasts of Greenland, where the aim of the Eskimo 'nithsong' was to vindicate oneself by making one's opponent the laughing stock of the community) and over as wide a span of time (from verbal duels in the Indian epic, the songs of mutual derision sung by men and women in ancient Greek festivals, formal contests in invective and vituperation in pre-Islamic Arabia, to the flyting of Loki

---

[20] See J. R. Scott, 'A Description . . . of the Rhymed *blason populaire* Tradition in England', *Lore and Language*, 2 (1975), 9–23 (with many references).
[21] Bakhtin, p. 429.
[22] The quotation is from Scott, p. 20.

with the gods in the Eddic *Lokasenna* and beyond).[23] Even such a specialized form as the duel between two poets is found in the *Frogs* of Aristophanes, in the exchange between Aeschylus and Euripides. In some of the ancient duels the power of the word and a connexion with magic or with cosmological wisdom are evident. This is especially the case with exchanges of riddles (as between Oðinn and the giant Vafðrúðnir); there are a number of stories in which defeat in a riddle contest results in death. Perhaps we have an attenuated echo of this in the encounter between the devil and the virgin in the fifteenth-century ballad (Child, No. 1):

> 'What ys hyer than ys [the] tre?
> What ys dypper than ys the see?' . . .
>
> 'Hewene ys heyer than ys the tre,
> Helle ys dypper than ys the see.'

where the elements of 'game', wisdom, and supernatural danger are all mingled.[24]

In medieval literature it is generally the element of game which predominates. The *Pèlerinage de Charlemagne* describes the *gabs* exchanged by the peers, where taunt is combined with vaunt in a wild release of verbal energy and fantasy: 'Let king Hugo lend me his horn [says Roland] and I will stand outside the town and blow so hard that the gates will fly off the hinges. And if the king attacks me I will spin him round so fast that his ermine cloak will vanish and his moustache catch fire.'[25] And the convention of boasting and scoffing continues in the exchanges of heralds at tournaments. Indeed our English literary flytings seem to be almost as closely related to the tradition of burlesque or mock tournaments as to the formal poetic debates with which they have sometimes been compared. These mock tournaments occur not only in fiction (as in *The Tournament of Tottenham* or the battle between the Tailor and the Soutar in Dunbar's 'Fasternis Evin in Hell'), but also in life.[26] The *Journal d'un bourgeois de Paris*, for instance, describes an 'entertainment' in that city in 1425: 'Four blind men wearing armour and each carrying a club were put into an enclosure in which there was also a strong pig. This they were to have if they could kill it. They fought this very odd battle, giving each other tremendous blows with the clubs.'[27]

---

[23] See O. I. Romanov, 'Donship in a Mexican-American Community in Texas', *American Anthropologist*, NS, 62 (1960), 966–76 (p. 972); Elliott, pp. 73–74 (and references); James Ross, 'A Classification of Gaelic Folk-Song', *Scottish Studies*, 1 (1857), 119–21; F. W. Hodge, *Handbook of American Indians*, 2 Parts (Washington, 1910), II, 77; J. Huizinga, *Homo Ludens*, English translation (London, 1949), pp. 66–71; F. B. J. Kuiper, 'The Ancient Aryan Verbal Contest', *Indo-Iranian Journal*, 4 (1960), 217–81.
[24] F. J. Child, *The English and Scottish Popular Ballads*, 5 vols (Boston, Massachusetts, 1882–98). For riddles, see Huizinga, pp. 106–18; *Encyclopaedia of Religion and Ethics (ERE)*, edited by J. Hastings, 13 vols (London, 1908–26), s.v. 'Riddles'; M. W. Beckwith, 'Hawaian Riddling', *American Anthropologist*, 24 (1922), 311–31. In an exchange in the *Kalevala* (Runo 3), Väinämöinen worsts Joukahainen and by his verbal magic imprisons him in a swamp.
[25] Huizinga (p. 70), paraphrasing from line 471 (see E. Koschwitz's edition (Leipzig, 1923), pp. 27–29).
[26] See *The Poems of William Dunbar*, edited by James Kinsley (Oxford, 1979), No. 52 (compare p. 340 for other comic brawls and mock-tournaments).
[27] *A Parisian Journal 1405–1449*, translated by J. Shirley (Oxford, 1968), pp. 205–06.

In England popular flyting continued after the Middle Ages, although we usually have only brief references. It sometimes went into 'jigs' (for example, 'a jigge of two principall Clownes, each gibing the other', a pattern which has survived into modern times) or ballads involving domestic debates or dialogues of neighbours and gossips. It was associated with particular callings. By the sixteenth century fishwives were already notorious, and in the seventeenth century there are ballads with titles such as 'The Bloody Battle at Billingsgate, Beginning with a scolding bout between two young Fish-women, Doll and Kate'.[28] Its most famous survival was in the 'water wit' of the Thames watermen and travellers. *The London Spy* gives a number of examples; a 'scoundrel crew of Lambeth gardeners' begins:

'You couple of treacherous sons of Bridewell. How dare you show your ugly faces upon the River of Thames, and to fright the Queen's swans from holding their heads above water?' to which our well-fed pilot . . . replied, 'You lousy starved crew of worm-pickers and snail-catchers. You offspring of a pumpkin, who can't afford butter to your cabbage, or bacon to your sprouts. Hold your tongue, you radish-mongers, or I'll whet my needle and sew your lips together.'[29]

Later exchanges with boats containing women, and a 'parcel of City shop-keepers', show that the art of the 'water dialect' consisted not only in a tirade of exaggerated abuse but in fitting it to the nature, appearance, or calling of the adversaries. Dr Johnson scored a notable victory in one of these exchanges by replying to 'some coarse raillery': 'Sir, your wife, under pretence of keeping a bawdy-house, is a receiver of stolen goods.'[30]

What emerges from these various examples is surely that popular satire; though it may be crudely abrasive, is not always simple or straightforward. It gives us further evidence of the complex and rather mysterious nature of satire itself. Although many of our examples have clearly had some kind of normative function in a community, they cannot be neatly explained (or explained away) in simple functionalist terms. There is often a destructive and negative element. Sanctions and norms may be being enforced, but often brutally, at the cost of great personal hurt. One cannot avoid the suspicion that sometimes the satire may arise from 'envy' (tellingly associated, in traditional iconography, with serpents coming from the mouth), from a desire to destroy, or at the very least from the hope of vexing somebody.

Satire has its dark side, the malignant power of *nið*. On the other hand, there is an element of 'game' and of creativity. There is, for instance, widespread evidence of enjoyment and delight among the participants in the 'work' of making satire. An observer of one African lampooning episode, in which women sang obscene songs against an offender, remarks that he had

---

[28] See Baskervill, pp. 68–71, 74, 167–69; compare *The Tongue Combatants*, a prose flyting (1684), R. J. Roberts, *The Book Collector*, 17 (1968), p. 217.

[29] *The London Spy*, edited by A. L. Hayward (London, 1927), p. 118.

[30] Boswell, *Life of Johnson*, edited by R. W. Chapman, corrected by J. D. Fleeman (Oxford, 1970), p. 1084. Boswell records that it was thought to be at least equal in excellence to 'the admirable scolding of Timon of Athens'.

'never seen them so spirited', that 'mixed with what seemed genuine amusement there was much uncontrolled, abandoned laughter', and a suggestion of 'consciously kicking over the traces'.[31] The emotional release 'did them some good', in the words of the old wife Maggie in Scott's *Antiquary* (Chapter 39: 'I think maybe a flyte wi' the auld housekeeper at Monkbarns, or Miss Grizel, would do me some gude'). This sense of exhilaration is sometimes part of a carnival spirit that delights in kicking over the traces, in inversion, travesty, obscenity, in an anarchic fantasy which is at once subversive and creative. This is sometimes transformed into an extraordinary energy of language, a kind of rhetorical élan which generates hyperbole or surrealist fantasy, and is 'sublime in the use of profanity'.[32] In a verbal duel there may sometimes be an ambiguity about this heightened language of abuse: virulent, but yet in a strange way almost affectionate, as if the adversaries enjoyed a kind of 'joking relationship'. And, finally, there is some evidence of the way in which good satire transforms a particular event or person into something much larger and more universal, of that imaginative quality, which T. S. Eliot praised in Jonson, of *creating* the objects of satire rather than simply 'hitting them off'.

The wider European literary background of the flytings of Dunbar and Skelton has been discussed in some detail, and there is no point in rehearsing that material (the *sirventes* and the *tenso* of the Troubadours, the literary quarrels of Italian humanists, etc.) once again.[33] It is, however, worth remarking that although much has been lost there survive a number of satirical poems written in English before the end of the fifteenth century which in one way or another are relevant to our study of the later flytings and invectives.[34] Dunbar's violent and eloquent attack on Donald Oure and Skelton's poems against the Scots and Dundas and Albany have some obvious antecedents in those verses which attack ethnic groups, Scots, Englishmen, or Flemings. One of Minot's songs plays nice variations on the refrain 'War ye with the Scottes, for thai er ful of gile', vaunts that Bannockburn has been avenged at Halidon Hill, and proceeds to taunt the Scots with rhetorical question ('Whare er ye, Skottes of Sant Johnes toune?') and direct address, using scornful alliterating 'nicknames':

---

[31] M. M. Green, quoted in R. Finnegan, *Oral Literature in Africa* (Oxford, 1970), p. 278.
[32] Mark Twain, *Life on the Mississippi* (see the discussion in W. F. Thompson, 'Frontier Tall Talk', *American Speech*, 9 (1934), 187–99). On obscenity, see E. E. Evans-Pritchard, 'Some Collective Expressions of Obscenity in Africa', reprinted in *The Position of Women*, pp. 76–101; *ERE* s.v. 'cursing' has other examples of ritual, affectionate, and joking uses. 'Joking relationships' (normally involving kinship) have been much discussed; see A. R. Radcliffe-Brown, *Structure and Function in Primitive Society* (London, 1952), pp. 90–116; D. F. Thomson, *American Anthropologist*, NS, 37 (1935), 460–90.
[33] See R. Brotanek, *Untersuchungen über das Leben und die Dichtungen Alexander Montgomeries* (Vienna and Leipzig, 1896), pp. 97–103; H. M. Ayres, '*Theodulus* in Scots', *MP*, 15 (1917–18), 539–48; I. S. Ross, *William Dunbar* (Leiden, 1981), pp. 185–86; A. R. Heiserman, *Skelton and Satire* (Chicago, 1961), pp. 283–85.
[34] See the general study by J. Peter, *Complaint and Satire in Early English Literature* (Oxford, 1956); R. M. Wilson, *The Lost Literature of Medieval England* (London, 1952), Chapter 10.

> Rughfute riveling, now kindels thi care,
> Berebag with this boste, thi biging es bare,
> Fals wretche and forsworn, whider wiltou fare?[35]

From the Scottish side comes the song 'Mayedenes of Engelande, sare may ye morne', recorded in the *Brut*. Its refrains ('with hevalogh', 'with rombylogh') seem to echo watermen's or sailor's songs, and are apparently a scornful allusion to Edward II's preference for water travel.

Although the chronicler Fabyan was writing long after Bannockburn and the composition of this song, his remarks that it was performed and that it was one of several are quite likely to be correct; it was, he says, 'sungyn in daunces in carolis of the maydens and mynstrellys of Scotlande, to the reproofe and dysdayne of Englysshe men, with diverse other which I over passe'.[36] He elsewhere gives another example of the 'dyverse truffys, roundys and songys' made by the Scots, 'in despyte of the Englysh men', which the *Brut* says was fastened as 'a bille' on the church doors of 'Seint Peres toward Stangate' (a common way of publishing satirical or seditious material):

> Longe beerdys hartles
> Paynted hoodys wytles
> Gay cotis graceles
> Maykyth Englande thryfteles.[37]

I 'overpass' the surviving examples of 'the many rymes of the Flemmynges' in order to linger momentarily over some invectives against named persons.[38] Sometimes these are unpopular figures of political importance such as the Duke of Suffolk (murdered in 1450). One poem which celebrates his arrest opens with a crowing exaltation: 'Now is the fox drevin to hole! hoo to hym, hoo, hoo!' The remainder does not quite live up to this promise, but makes something of the image of the (almost completed) hunt, and makes merry at the expense of Suffolk under the nickname of Jack Napys (the clog and chain in his badge suggesting a tame ape). Another celebrates his death in a mock Office for the Dead (with the refrain 'for Jac Napes soule, Placebo and Dirige').[39] Neither, of course, show the slightest sympathy for him. Sometimes more obscure individuals are the targets, such as the otherwise unknown 'Jon Clerke' of Torrington in Devon, or the Mayor of Cambridge, on whose gate in 1418 was fixed a 'schedule':

> Looke out here Maire with thie pilled pate
> And see wich a scrowe is set on thie gate
> Warning thee of hard happes.[40]

---

[35] *Historical Poems of the XIVth and XVth Centuries*, edited by R. H. Robbins (New York, 1959), No. 9.
[36] See Wilson, pp. 212–13; *Historical Poems*, p. 262.
[37] Wilson, p. 197 (the use of stereotyped formulae to build up a cumulative pattern is found in the more general satirical poems on the 'abuses of the age' (see *Historical Poems*, No. 56)).
[38] For examples, see *Historical Poems*, Nos 28, 29, 30.
[39] *Historical Poems*, Nos. 75, 76.
[40] Jon Clarke appears in a carol, see R. L. Greene, *The Early English Carols*, second edition (Oxford, 1977), No. 393.1; for the Mayor, see Wilson, pp. 199–200.

The description of similar threatening verses against William Paston (also posted publicly) as 'certeyns Englysh billes rymed in partye' perhaps suggests a similar doggerel form.[41] There survives a snippet of a Thames watermen's song (alluded to by Skelton in *The Bowge of Court*) for John Norman (1453), a Lord Mayor who instead of going by land to take his charge went by boat: 'Rowe the bote Norman, rowe to thy lemman.' The chronicle's remark, 'and so forth with a longe processe', may suggest what Udall in the sixteenth century calls 'a ragmans rewe', 'a long jeste that railleth on any persone by name, or toucheth a bodyes honestee somewhat nere'.[42]

There are also examples of more sophisticated forms of satire. A verse on 'rich Alan, the bald man' is in the form of a mock epitaph, later used by both Dunbar and Skelton.[43] Some of the invectives against women occasionally generate a rhetorical exhilaration in which the sheer power of language begins to take over.[44] One splendid piece of fantasy, which consists of a list of *impossibilia* followed by a triumphant refrain ('than put in a woman your trust and confidence'), rises to a surrealist conclusion:

> Whan crabbis tak wodcokes in forestes and parkes,
> And haris ben taken with swetnes of snaylis,
> And camelles with ther here tak swalowes and perchis,
> And myse mowe corn with wafeyyng of ther taylis,
> Whan dukkes of the dunghill sek the blod of Haylis,
> Whan shrewd wyffes to ther husbondes do non offens —
> Than put in a woman your trust and confidence.

> > (*Secular Lyrics*, No. 114)

A similar sense of excitement sometimes occurs in the deliberate 'reversals' of conventional descriptions of personal beauty. Here, indeed, there is a pair of complementary poems (in MS Rawl. poet. 36) which almost suggests a flyting. The lady's verse letter gives an unflattering account of her lover:

> Youre manly visage, shortly to declare,
> Your forehed, mouth, and nose so flatte,
> In short conclusyon, best lykened to an hare
> Of alle lyvyng thynges, save only a catte.

He replies in kind, pausing to criticise her style ('The ynglysch of Chaucere was nat in youre mynd'), but his description of her ugliness has a fantastic hyperbole:

> Youre camusyd nose, with nose-thryllys brode,
> Unto the chyrch a noble instrument
> To quenche tapers brennyng afore the rood.

> > (*Secular Lyrics*, Nos 208, 209)

which is sustained until the letter's obscene ending.

---

[41] *Paston Letters and Papers of the XVth Century*, edited by N. Davis, Volume I (Oxford, 1971), p. 7; compare Wilson (pp. 200–02) for similar lampoons.

[42] See Wilson, p. 204. Udall is translating Erasmus's *Fescennina carmina*; see Baskervill, pp. 22–23; *OED* s.v. 'ragman roll', 'rigmarole'; Whiting, R9.

[43] *Secular Lyrics of the XIVth and XVth Centuries*, edited by R. H. Robbins (Oxford, 1952), No. 124.

[44] See the last stanza of *Secular Lyrics*, No. 211.

Another source for our meagre information on popular satire is the medieval drama.[45] Here we sometimes find experiments with fantastic speech put in the mouths of ranting and threatening tyrants like Herod, or Pilate (for example, at the beginning of the Towneley *Processus Talentorum*), or the idolators in the Digby *Mary Magdalene*, or sometimes the torturers of Christ.[46] The scene outside Paradise when Adam and Eve excuse themselves by laying the blame on each other is given an extended treatment by the York dramatist, and some later scenes of domestic disharmony are virtually small flytings (the exchanges, for instance, between Noah and his wife or between Mak and Gyll). In the Chester *Adoration of the Shepherds* there is an extended scene of flyting by Gartius, the shepherds' boy, a Thersites-like railer and boaster, against his masters. Rough abuse quickly turns into a physical wrestling match.

In Scotland the evidence has survived in an even more fragmentary form, and there is the added complication that it is extremely difficult to date some of the satirical pieces with any certainty. However, poems like *The Gyre Carling*, Roull's *Cursing*, and especially Henryson's *Sum Practysis of Medecyne* show that Dunbar's satirical genius did not flower in an empty desert.[47] *Sum Practysis* is a wild and flamboyant attack on an (unnamed) opponent in the form of a mock prescription to cure malice. The ingredients include laxatives, excrement, and some delightfully fantastic items like 'fyve unce of ane fle wing' or 'sevin sobbis of ane selche [seal]'. It is a deliberately crude piece of invective intended to make an opponent reel as from a boxer's blow: it concludes,

> It is ane mirk mirrour
> Ane uthir manis erss.

The use of alliteration for satiric emphasis or for a rhetorical 'cumulative' effect is more frequent in fifteenth-century English poetry than is sometimes realized, but in Scotland, where the tradition of purely alliterative poetry seems to have long survived, it is an even more distinctive part of the satirist's rough music. One heavy-handed attack on women begins

> O wicket wemen, wilful, and variable,
> Richt fals, feckle, fell, and frivolus,
> Dowgit, dispytful, dour, and dissavable . . .

and continues remorselessly thus for twenty lines (*Secular Lyrics*, No. 212). Fortunately, the best satirical poets (Henryson, Douglas (in the Prologue to Book VIII of his *Eneydos*), and Dunbar) are rather more artful.

---

[45] See, for example, A. Nicholl, *Masks, Mimes and Miracles* (London, 1931), pp. 185–86.
[46] On the way in which the torturers make use of rhyming nonsense and incantatory questions in the manner of childrens' games, see R. Woolf, *The English Mystery Plays* (London, 1972), p. 255.
[47] On these, see T. Turville-Petre, *The Alliterative Revival* (Cambridge, 1977), pp. 117–19; on Henryson's poem, see also the notes in *The Poems of Robert Henryson*, edited by D. Fox (Oxford, 1981), pp. 475–87, and Douglas Gray, *Robert Henryson* (Leiden, 1979), pp. 244–49.

It is perhaps not surprising that 'The Flyting of Dunbar and Kennedie' does not seem to have aroused much enthusiasm among scholarly commentators: Dunbar's most recent editor, James Kinsley (see Poem No. 23) and his most recent critic, Ian Ross, are almost alone in doing justice to it. It is neglected partly because it has the abrasive crudity of much popular satire, and partly because it is a minor work of an extremely talented satirist, who seems to have had an almost instinctive control of the satirical forms and registers available to him. Yet a number of the characteristics of Dunbar's more obviously sophisticated satires — his superb range and control of language, his gift for creating a fantastic or nightmarish 'scene', a kind of satirical 'speaking picture', (as in the 'Fenyeit Freir of Tungland') — can be clearly seen in the 'Flyting'. The work presents difficulties, most obviously some intractable linguistic ones in the ultra-colloquial element in its vocabulary, but also difficulties of a contextual kind. The 'Flyting' may, as Kinsley says, 'have been developed in a series of attacks and counter-attacks circulated in manuscript at court; it may, at least in its final form, have been recited before the king as a stylized duel in verse'. It is difficult, too, since the detailed context of personal relationships has been lost, to catch the exact nuances and tones. It seems to be a 'game' (later, at least, Dunbar refers to 'gud maister Walter Kennedy' in 'The Lament for the Makars'), but presumably is the kind of game which is played 'for real'. It certainly seems to demand some kind of 'performance'.

The 'Flyting', as we have it, begins with a brief introduction by Dunbar, in which, in the traditional manner of satirists, he claims that he writes in self-defence, against a slight '(ane thing . . . compild | In generale'). It is cleverly done. A remark on the proud way Kennedy and Quintin (apparently a kind of 'second' in the duel, as Schir Johne the Ros is for Dunbar) have 'styled' themselves leads into a threat of their fate if they should dare to make 'of mannace ony myntyng | In speciall':

> Howbeit with bost thair breistis wer als bendit
> As Lucifer that fra the hevin discendit,
> Hell suld nocht hyd thair harnis fra harmis hynting.

Having placed his opponents among the proud progeny of Lucifer, Dunbar's imagination begins to run wildly on the apocalyptic vengeance that he will bring upon them:

> The erd sould trymbill, the firmament sould schaik,
>   And all the air in vennaum suddane stink,
> And all the divillis of hell for redour quaik,
>   To heir quhat I suld wryt with pen and ynk:
>   For and I flyt, sum sege for schame sould sink,
> The se sould birn, the mone sould thoill ecclippis,
> Rochis sould ryfe, the warld sould hald no grippis,
>   Sa loud of cair the commoun bell sould clynk.

It is probably true that, as Kinsley says, 'the bathos of Dunbar's climax shows his burlesque intention at the outset' (p. 287). I wonder, however, if the reference is at the same time a more pointed one. Dunbar goes on to insist that he would be 'wondir laith . . . to be ane baird', and he not only clearly associates bards with flyting, but regularly uses 'bard' as a term of abuse (ll. 49, 63, 96, 120, 183, 208, 244). There is evidence that there was a medieval Gaelic tradition of flyting, and that 'bards', as *The Buke of the Howlat* puts it, 'bitterlye could ban'. It has been suggested that the Middle Scots flyting came from this Celtic tradition, but there does not seem to me to be any conclusive evidence to support the theory. Perhaps, rather, Dunbar is here making fun of the wild 'skimble-skamble stuff' that he associates with Highland bards (see l. 107, 'sic eloquence as thay in Erschry use'). It is, nevertheless, a memorably overdrawn statement of the power of flyting ('to gar me ryme and rais the Feynd with flytting'), and a vaunt (a kind of *bēot* or *gab*) of Dunbar's own skill in that dark art. By continuously insisting that he does not wish to engage in it, and by emphasizing his moral disapproval of it ('incres of sorrow, sklander and evill name'), he succeeds in stressing both his own virtue (responding to 'thair bakbytting') and the power of *nið*. It will bring public shame upon his adversaries; he will 'throw all cuntreis and kinrikis thame proclame'. With this resounding threat the introduction is brought to a conclusion. At the beginning of the performance Dunbar has, with a deliberately uncertain balance of 'game' and 'earnest', established two of the satirical roles he may be minded to play: that of the outraged man of virtue, forced to defend his honour, and that of the wild bard with his magical powers.

Kennedy responds (ll. 25–48) in the manner of a rival herald or a rival challenger. With much abuse he demands that Dunbar should beg for mercy. His threats are accompanied by the rough music of insistent alliteration ('dirtin Dumbar', 'mandrag, mymmerkin', 'dirtfast dearch', 'fantastik fule', 'skaldit skaitbird', etc.), and the abusive imagery of popular polemic ('Ignorant elf, aip, owll irregular'). Like a good satirist he begins to create the figure he means to destroy: he elaborates on Dunbar's puny, dwarfish, and monstrous appearance and on his Thersites-like railing character; this graduate is 'maid maister bot in mows'. Kennedy's reference to his own 'laureat lettres', in contrast to 'thy ryming, rebald, and thy rowis', not only introduces a literary note which reminds us that this is, *inter alia*, a competition in the art of using words, but also a *topos* of this form of invective: that style is the man and that bad style reveals his true inner nature exactly as his external ugly appearance does (as Dunbar says later, in proverbial vein, 'thy frawart phisnomy | Dois manifest thy malice to all men'). Kennedy brings this 'round' to a nice climax with his own vaunt, demanding that Dunbar accept meekly a physical punishment in recompense (playing quite carefully with the boundary between Auden's paradoxical 'playful anger' and the real physical violence in which the flyting of the Chester shepherds ends):

> Se sone thow mak my commissar amendis,
> And lat him lay sax leichis on thy lendis

> Meikly in recompansing of thi scorne,
> Or throw sall ban the tyme that thow wes borne.

Dunbar's long reply (ll. 49–248) begins with an extraordinary tirade of invective:

> Iersche brybour baird, vyle beggar with thy brattis,
> Cuntbittin crawdoun Kennedy, coward of kynd . . .

in which abuse is hurled at Kennedy's appearance, Highland stock, behaviour, and general lack of any sort of virtue. The challenge to combat is eagerly taken up, but the weapons are not to be those of formal physical duels; here the appropriate form for the lash of satire is that used for whipping a cur:

> With ane doig leich I schepe to gar the schout
> And nowther to the tak knyfe, swerd nor aix.

Allusions (no doubt libellous) to incidents in Kennedey's life are interspersed with jeers at his Highland appearance (for example, he wears a kilt; compare ll. 104, 119) and poverty. Kennedy's eloquence has a Highland poverty also; it is upended with an ingeniously crude taunt:

> Thow hes full littill feill of fair indyte:
> I tak on me ane pair of Lowthiane hippis
> Sall fairar Inglis mak, and mair parfyte,
> Than thow can blabbar with thy Carrik lippis.

The fantastic rhetorical hyperboles provoked by the task of describing Kennedy's ugliness show the surrealist side of Dunbar's imagination. One passage, which suggests that he is so misshapen that the torturers of a number of well-known saints must have taken various pieces of his physiognomy, culminates in the extraordinary image:

> The gallowis gaipis eftir thy graceles gruntill ['snout']
> As thow wald for ane haggeis, hungry gled.

The visual and imaginative shock of this is certainly a blow to make an opponent reel, but it is worth noting that the lines also show that the rough music of a good flyting has its continuities, reprises, and variations as well as much spontaneous clatter. Images of Kennedy as a lean and hungry Highlander eager for what Dunbar seems to think of as the poorest fare, of him looking like a rough, hungry, predatory bird (see l. 56: 'Revin, raggit ruke'), and of him looking like suitable food for the gallows (see the nickname 'widdefow' (gallow's bird) in l. 101, and, later, ll. 127, 141, 175–76), have already been woven into the texture, and are here triumphantly fused. The joyous creation of an absurd, grotesque figure as his opponent and victim leads Dunbar into extended elaboration of the rhetorical 'circumstances', and, as in 'The Fenyeit Freir', into the devising of 'speaking pictures' and dramatic scenes. Kennedy he imagines living like a reiver in a dilapidated lepers' house, with his 'quene', stealing hens ('thow plukkis the pultre and scho pullis of the penis'):

> And quehn thow heiris ane guse cry in the glenis
> Thow thinks it swetar than sacrand bell of sound.

From this pastoral scene of petty outlawry, Dunbar returns to the 'gryslie peteous port' of his opponent, and produces a splendidly bizarre variation on the usual stereotypes of ugliness. 'Thow lazarus, thow laithly lene tramort' (putrefying corpse), he says, and elaborates the picture of the corpse ('hiddowis, haw and holkit is thyne ee') come from the grave to haunt men and, like the macabre figures in 'The Three Living and the Three Dead' or 'The Dance of Death', to terrify them ('they gane it garris us think that we mon de'). This 'hungert heland gaist' that Dunbar conjures up in order to conjure away is a figure of fantasy ('Thy rigbane rattillis and thy ribbis on raw', 'Thy laithly lymis ar lene as ony treis'), but it is tempting to speculate whether Dunbar has, in the manner of later caricaturists, seized on one physical trait (a gaunt and thin figure?) and exaggerated it so as 'to grasp the perfect deformity and thus reveal the very essence of a personality'.[48] Further allegations of an unsavoury and scatological nature ('thy hostand hippis lattis nevir thy hos go dry') follow, to prepare us for a final scene of public ridicule set in the streets of Edinburgh. Dunbar imagines the effect that would be caused by the appearance of this uncouth creature, with wisps of straw hanging out from his worn boots. Cleverly, he involves his audience in the scorn:

> Cum thow agane to skar *us* with thy strais,
> *We* sall gar scale our sculis all the to scorne
> And stane the up the calsay quhair thow gais.

And as the scene warms up, with the boys pouring out like bees, it becomes a fantastic 'mobbing-up', with Kennedy fleeing like an owl ('lyk ane howlat chest with crawis'), pursued by dogs and shouts of abuse as if it were an unrehearsed skimmington. Its 'rough music' concludes with the cries, baskets, and tubs of the fishwives:

> Than rynis thow doun the gait with gild of boyis
> And all the toun tykis hingand in thy heilis;
> Of laidis and lownis thair rysis sic ane noyis . . .

> Fische wyvis cryis, Fy! and castis doun skillis and skeilis,
> Sum claschis the, sum cloddis the on the cutis.

Finally, Dunbar himself brings it to an amazing crescendo of abuse with a spectacular display of internal rhyming:

> Loun lyk Mahoun, be boun me till obey,
> Theif, or in greif mischeif sall the betyd;
> Cry grace, tykis face, or I the chece and fley;
> Oule, rare and yowle — I sall defowll thy pryd.

---

[48] Annibale Carracci, quoted by E. H. Gombrich and E. Kris, *Caricature* (Harmondsworth, 1940), p. 12.

After such a performance it is almost inevitable that Kennedy's final section should seem rather flat and long-winded. It gets off to a good start:

> Dathane deivillis sone and dragone dispitous,
> Abironis birth and bred with Beliall,
> Wod werwoif, worme and scorpion vennemous,
> Lucifers laid, fowll feyindis face infernall . . .

and moves rapidly into an attack on Dunbar's forbears, notorious for their treachery (may we hazard the guess that Dunbar perhaps prided himself on his ancestry?). However, it lacks the wild enthusiasm of Dunbar. Moreover, too much of the central section is defensive, attempting rather laboriously to refute points made by Dunbar. Much of this is eloquent, notably in the defence of Kennedy's own writing and of Gaelic ('it was the gud langage of this land'), and sometimes shows a nice control of varying tone, but it does not often have the outraged vehemence that Skelton knows how to put into such passages. Towards the end it becomes more lively, with Dunbar-like abuse (he is described as 'a crabbit, scabbit, evill facit messan tyke, | A schit but wit, schyre and injurius') and allusions to disreputable episodes. There is a certain splendour in the elaborate way he rejects his opponent's charges of 'shitting' by describing for three stanzas the dangers which Dunbar's presence caused on shipboard:

> Thow schot, and was not sekir of thy tayle,
> Beschate the stere, the compas and the glas; . . .
> Thow spewit and kest out mony a lathly lomp
> Fastar than all the marynaris coud pomp.

And the final five stanzas are given over to an immense list of abusive names (devils, giants, tyrants, traitors) applied in one way or another to Dunbar, spiced with some Latin phrases at the expense of the unfortunate cleric, as if Kennedy is determined, in true Celtic manner, to 'rhyme' Dunbar down to hell:

> Prickit, wickit, convickit lamp *Lollardorum*
> Defamyt, blamyt, schamyt *primas paganorum.*
> Out, out, I schout, apon that snowt that snevillis;
> Tale tellare, rebellare, induellar wyth the devillis,
> Spynk, sink wyth stynk *ad Tertara termagorum.*

From this sustained example of literary flyting a number of points of literary interest have emerged. Perhaps the most important, and the most surprising, is that though it is 'rough music' it really is a kind of music. It demands careful control, of register, tone, imagery, and 'argument'. For there is a structure of rhetorical argument which is played off against an imitation of the haphazard sequences of colloquial flyting, just as there is a pleasing disparity between the elaborate literary stanza form and the demotic rhythms and vocabulary of abuse. We find this again in the flyting of Skelton, who is perhaps in touch with an even greater variety of satirical and linguistic techniques than Dunbar. Among his satirical poems there are a number of invectives (notably the verses against the Scots, Dundas 'that Scottish ass' who alleged that Englishmen had tails, and, later, against Albany) which are obviously related to the tradition we have been discussing. However, space will permit only a few notes on his poems against Garnesche.[49] These are similar to the exchange between Dunbar and Kennedy, although here we have only one side of the flyting surviving. It is sometimes claimed that Skelton's flyting had its origin in the Scottish tradition, but there is no certain evidence for this: the similarities are close, but not close enough to be called echoes, and, as we have seen, there was a widespread tradition of various sorts of invective in England before Skelton. It continued to flourish in his lifetime. There is a particularly interesting reference in a poem recorded in the 'Great Chronicle', an invective against John Grumbold, a 'disciple' of the hated Dudley and Empson (who fell in 1509). At one point the author exclaims that neither he nor any man in England could discover and describe Grumbold's 'dedys serpentyne': even Skelton, Cornishe, More, or Chaucer if he were alive,

> Cowde not in metyr half thy shame spelle
> Nor yit thy falshod half declare or telle.

But, he continues, it would be a pity for poets of such fame to spend their time about 'soo vyle a thyng': it would be more 'accordyng' if

> such as put lewd maters in wrytyng
> In dogerell ryme, of Cok Wattys janglyng
> Shuld blaze the faytis of the, swynish of kyynd,
> And in most rudenes to bryng they vyce to myynd.[50]

We do not have the works of 'Frankleyn or Ryngeley, if they were lyvyng | Or Henry Glasberd', whom he mentions as able to 'blaze' the 'armys' of Grumbold, but it is yet another piece of evidence for the existence of a thriving tradition of popular verse. And, although it is undoubtedly right to place Skelton among the 'serious' satirical poets, he too, if he thought it 'accordyng', was prepared to 'blaze' vices and follies 'in dogerell ryme'.

The poems against Garnesche are four closely related pieces, the first two 'in metyr', the last two in 'Skeltonics'. As in the case of Dunbar and Kennedy, there is much that we do not know. As far as the context goes, all we know is that Skelton claims to be defending himself against the challenge of Master Garnesche, 'rudely revilying me in the kynges noble hall', a phrase which could well suggest some sort of public (oral?) challenge, and, perhaps, a similar kind of reply. Nor do we know anything certain of the personal relations between Skelton and this courtier, a gentleman-usher and a knight. In the first piece, Skelton formally 'receives' the challenge and taunts the

[49] See *The Poetical Works of John Skelton*, edited by A. Dyce, 2 vols (London, 1843), I, 116–31.
[50] *The Great Chronicle of London*, edited by A. H. Thomas and I. D. Thornley (London, 1938), pp. 361–62.

challenger with a burlesque catalogue of the names of knights from romances, most of them either or both Saracens and markedly unsuccessful. His challenger, whom he calls Sir Satrapas and (a nickname?) Sir Chesten, is clearly not in the tradition of noble chivalric heroes. He is also singularly ugly, and again we have to remain uncertain whether this is all pure fantasy or whether the caricaturist has been at work, exaggerating one or more features (hairiness? a large nose?). He is also proud, like Saracen giants, and, as we know, pride comes before a fall. By the final stanza a splendid creation has emerged, in part the ranting ugly Saracen, in part the fantastic burlesque knight in the style of Sir Thopas:[51]

> I sey, ye solem Sarson, alle blake ys your ble;
>   As a glede glowynge, your ien glyster as glasse,
> Rowlynge in yower holow hede, ugly to see;
>   Your tethe teintyd with tawny your semely snowte doth passe,
>   Howkyd as an hawkys beke, lyke Syr Topyas.

The final lines,

> Boldly bend you to batell, and buske your selfe to save:
> Chalenge your selfe for a fole, call me no more knave,

make a good conclusion, because they are in effect a defiant answer to the earlier repeated refrain, which was always in the form of a taunting question:

> But sey me yet, Syr Satropas, what auctoryte ye have
> In your chalenge, Syr Chesten, to calle me a knave?

There is a simple argumentative structure involved ('since you have challenged me, tell me what authority you have to call me knave?') and the elements are rearranged. Skelton is very much in control, moving easily from register to register, setting slang words ('teggys') beside strings of fantastic names and titles ('Syr capten of Catywade, catacumbas of Cayre'), his scorn emphasized both by the constant alliteration and by the repetition of the 'polite' forms of address 'ye', 'your', and 'Syr'. Although he makes it clear that he is dealing with a fool and a knave, his taunting rejection of the challenge has a certain self-possession and even dignity (mirrored in the word 'auctoryte'). We are a long way from the Celtic enchanter whom Dunbar and Kennedy conjure up.

In the second piece, of identical form and length, addressed to Garnesche and his associate, 'gresy gorbelyd Godfrey', the tone becomes sharper, with angrily insistent short phrases:

> How may I your mokery mekely tollerate,
>   Your gronynge, your grontynge, your groinynge lyke a swyne?

---

[51] The alliterative formula and similes of the first two lines are probably parodic echoes of those of popular romances. On the continuing interest in Thopas, see J. A. Burrow, 'Sir Thopas in the 16th Century', in *Middle English Studies Presented to Norman Davis*, edited by D. Gray and E. G. Stanley (Oxford, 1983), pp. 69–91.

The refrain here emphasizes the similarity of Garnesche with the ranting idolatrous tyrants of the mystery plays:

> Ye cappyd Cayface copious, your paltoke on your pate,
> Thow ye prate lyke prowde Pylate, be ware yet of chek mate.

The similarity seems to be threefold: in manner of speech ('copious', 'prate'), in appearance ('cappyd' may suggest headgear bizarrely like a Jewish cap; 'paltoke', which usually means 'doublet', may be a joke at the expense of some (fashionable?) hat like a vast turban), and finally in being defeated by the forces of righteousness. Garnesche is developed into a grotesque parody of the courtier, or, rather, of the hanger-on round court ('ye hobble very homly before the kynges borde', 'your moth etyn mokkysh maneres', etc.), while the remark that his face shines 'like a greased boot' is shown later, in a passage on his career as a page, to be satirically appropriate.[52] A phrase from a popular song, 'Huf a galante', is hurled at him with some deliberation, for the text of it which survives is a sharp attack on overdressed braggarts, with their empty purses and very ragged finery.[53] The burlesquing of chivalric challengers and encounters continues (this challenger contrived once to break his head with his own sword, called, like Roland's, Durendal) with lists of knights and a cry used to urge contestants to engage in the fray: 'Baile, baile at yow bothe, frantyke folys!' It culminates in the last stanza:

> Gup, gorbellyd Godfrey, gup, Garnysche, gaudy fole!
> To turney or to tante with me ye ar to fare to seke:
> For thes twayne whypslovens calle for a coke-stole.

And Skelton's fantastic imagination begins to run wild, with a reference to a monster with a man's face, three huge teeth, and eyes like a goat, and a dreadful, if inevitable, pun on his adversary's name: 'Thow mantycore, ye marmoset, garnyshte lyke a Greke'.

The third piece is a reply to a 'lewde letter', and for this he turns (with satirical decorum) to his own marvellously inventive and dynamic version of demotic 'dogerell ryme'.[54] It is all headily abusive with a Rabelaisian zest, but there is an underlying structure and control. Skelton carefully creates two opposed characters: himself as the outraged laureate poet and Garnesche as a mad, raving knave and would-be courtier. Disreputable episodes from his life, as a kitchen page ('a greasy knight') and as a young squire and unsuccessful amoroso, are described or alluded to (in one case with startling colloquial abruptness: 'pay Stokys hys fyve pownd'). A formal 'blazon' of his ugly face,

> But now, gawdy, gresy Garnesche,
> Your face I wyse to varnyshe

[52] There is a background of 'estates' satire here, concerned with the 'miseries of the courtiers' life' (the title of a famous fifteenth-century example by Aeneas Sylvius, used in the *Eclogues* of Skelton's contemporary, Barclay).
[53] *Historical Poems*, No. 52.
[54] See J. Norton-Smith, 'The Origins of Skeltonics', *Essays in Criticism*, 23 (1973), 57–62.

> So suerly yt xall nat tarnishe.[55]
> Thow a Sarsens hed ye bere,
> Row and full of lowsy here,
> As hevery man wele seethe,
> Ful of grett knavys tethe,
> In a felde of grene peson,

is linked with his lack of wit, and his crude railing and 'lewd' use of English. Skelton works up to a veritable satirical bombardment:

> Now, Garnyche, garde thy gummys;
> My serpentins and my gunnys
> Agenst ye now I b[e]nde

and there follows a salvo of eleven lines of abusive name-calling with every item prefixed by the offensive 'thou': 'Thou tode, thow scorpyone, | Thow bawdy babyone'. Typically, this flamboyant display of 'rough music' is concluded by a splendidly precise verbal image:

> Tyburne thou me assynyd,
> Where thou xulddst have bene shrynyd.

'Shrined' momentarily suggests the picture of the knavish body of Garnesche placed between the posts of the gallows like a saint in his shrine.[56]

The final piece continues these themes and techniques, with a still more elaborate 'blazon', and a very fervent defence of the laureate poet and his eloquence.[57] New variations are used. There is a clever pedantic-sounding correction of Garnesche:

> Thow seyst I callyd the a pecok:
> Thow liist, I callyd the a wodcoke;
> For thow hast a long snowte

(and, moreover, because the woodcock was notable not only for its long bill and large eyes but for its stupidity: it gave its name to fools who were easily gulled). This is quickly turned into a crude taunt:

> I wold sum manys bake ink horne
> W[e]r thi nose spectacle case;
> Yt wold garnyche w(e)ll thy face.

[55] I suspect that Skelton is playing here on various senses of the verb 'varnish' (see *OED*: 'paint over, coat with varnish', 'give a glossy appearance to' (associated in Chaucer's *Reeve's Tale* with drunkenness), 'embellish, adorn'). The 'Saracen's Head' of course became a traditional *blason* (*OED*, 'Saracen', example from 1510).

[56] There is, I think, also a play on the sense of 'shrine' as 'to venerate a person as a saint', 'to canonize'. Skelton has already used the word (l. 47 of this poem) of Garnesche's tatty clothes: 'In dud frese ye war schrynyd.'

[57] Again, as in the Dunbar poem, ugliness of appearance, manners, and language are intimately connected, but there is a more humanist note when Skelton works into his 'blazon' the topic of 'true nobility', against the 'disparagement' of Garnesche:
> Thow claimist the jentyll, thow art a curre;
> Haroldis they know thy cote armur:
> Thow thou be a jantyll man borne,
> Yet jentylnes in the ys thred bare worne;
> Haroldes from honour may the devors,
> For harlottes hawnte thyn hatefull cors.

Finally, Skelton defends himself against the charge of captious railing ('I rayle to the soche as thow art'), and enlists the 'famous poettes saturicall' of antiquity as a supporting chorus. A proverb, not tragedies, however, is more appropriate for the instruction of such a knave: 'Pride gothe before and schame commyth after.' It all ends with a marvellous whirl: a mock-prayer that Garnesche may be preserved from the gallows, an insouciant agreement with his request that he should be let 'go pley', and a fervent statement of readiness against further scribbling:

> Scrybbyl thow, scrybyll thow, rayle or wryght,
> Wryght what thow wylte, I xall the aquyte.

After Skelton's day, the Scottish sixteenth-century poet Alexander Montgomerie still knew how to use the flyting as 'a studied literary form'.[58] And, although later satirical poets aspiring to elegance in their attacks on 'scribblers' did not favour it, W. H. Auden's remark that it has vanished is not quite true. Apart from its continued life in popular satire, it has kept on surfacing, perhaps predictably, in *performance*, in some quite studied and literary scenes in plays, from the 'jealousy duet' of *The Beggar's Opera* to *Who's Afraid of Virginia Woolf?*. A brief example has recently been heard on the London stage, in Ligeti's opera, *Le Grand Macabre*. But my long 'processe' deserves to be brought to its end by Vladimir and Estragon in *Waiting for Godot*:

Vla.	Moron!
Est.	That's the idea, let's abuse each other.
	They turn, increase the space between them, turn again and face each other.
Vla.	Moron!
Est.	Vermin!
Vla.	Abortion!
Est.	Morpion!
Vla.	Sewer-rat!
Est.	Curate!
Vla.	Cretin!
Est.	(*with finality*) Crritic!
Vla.	Oh!
	He wilts, vanquished, and turns away.

[58] 'The Flyting of Montgomerie and Polwart', *Poems of Alexander Montgomerie*, Supplementary Volume, edited by G. Stevenson, STS, 59 (Edinburgh and London, 1910), pp. 130–89.

Chaucer's *Sir Thopas* and *La Prise de Nuevile*

J. A. BURROW

University of Bristol

In her chapter on *Sir Thopas* in *Sources and Analogues of Chaucer's Canterbury Tales*, L. H. Loomis concentrated on identifying among the mass of Middle English metrical romances the particular objects of Chaucer's imitation. But the sources and analogues of *Sir Thopas* are not to be looked for only in *Guy of Warwick* and its congeners; Chaucer's poem is itself a burlesque, and it may therefore also be compared with other medieval burlesques. This other set of literary relations, however, has attracted little attention from scholars. Loomis dismisses that side of the family in a single sentence: *Sir Thopas*, she asserts, 'follows no previous pattern of burlesque or parody, either social or literary'.[1]

Chaucer could read English, French, Latin, Italian, and also possibly Flemish and Spanish; so a survey of all the burlesque or parodistic writings that he might have known would be a laborious task. The present discussion is confined to one French text, the thirteenth-century *Prise de Nuevile*. Loomis herself draws attention to this poem, in a footnote to the sentence quoted above, as one of three 'medieval French burlesques on the *chansons de geste* or the romances of chivalry' which, 'though analogous in parodistic spirit to *Thopas*, differ from it entirely in style and substance'; but it may be doubted whether she had read *La Prise de Nuevile*, for she speaks of it as inedited, evidently following the authority she cites: a volume of the *Histoire littéraire de la France* published in 1856.[2] Since then the poem has in fact been edited twice, by A. Scheler in his *Trouvères belges*, Nouvelle Série (Louvain, 1879), and by A. Jeanroy and H. Guy in their *Chansons et dits artésiens du XIIIᵉ siècle* (Bordeaux, 1898). In any case, Loomis's description of *La Prise de Nuevile* as differing entirely in style and substance from *Sir Thopas* cannot be accepted, unless she simply means that the French poem is not a burlesque of Middle English romances, which goes without saying. The truth is that *La Prise de Nuevile* resembles Chaucer's poem closely in several respects, and is quite enough in itself to cast doubt on Loomis's assertion (barely credible, in any case) that *Sir Thopas* 'follows no previous pattern of burlesque or parody'.

---

[1] *Sources and Analogues of Chaucer's Canterbury Tales*, edited by W. F. Bryan and Germain Dempster (London, 1941), p. 486.

[2] The other texts mentioned by Loomis are *Audigier*, a scatological *chanson de geste*, most recently edited by O. Jordogne, *Moyen Age*, 66 (1960), 495–526, and *Dit d'aventures*, edited by G. S. Trébutien (Paris, 1835). The latter has no relevance to *Sir Thopas*.

Since *La Prise de Nuevile* is little known and rather hard to come by, a description is necessary.[3] The poem survives in only one manuscript, B.N. MS français 12615 (Noailles), where it forms part of a series of moral and satirical poems, all edited by Jeanroy and Guy, and dated by them between 1248 and 1280.[4] Many of these pieces refer specifically to affairs in Arras, the great industrial and commercial centre in Artois; and it seems clear that *La Prise de Nuevile* was composed there, for an audience acquainted with local people and places.[5] It is a comic poem of 173 alexandrine lines, divided into monorhymed *laisses* in the manner of a *chanson de geste*. It describes how 'more than sixty' Flemings (later wildly augmented to three thousand) assemble in the industrial quarter of Arras and set out to 'assault the castle of Neuville'. The language of the piece is a most peculiar form of Northern French, exhibiting numerous phonetic, lexical, and grammatical abnormalities, and incorporating a number of Flemish words. The author's intention was presumably to represent the absurd French spoken by Flemish guest-workers in Arras: 'ce lourd patois dont, à coup sûr, les Artésiens s'amusaient en hommes qui se piquent de correction et recherchent l'élégance'.[6]

The poem, in Scheler's edition, opens as follows:

> Siggeur, ore scoutés, que Deus vos sot amis,
> Van rui de sinte glore, qui en de croc fou mis.
> Assés l'avés oït van Gerbert, van Gerin,
> Van Willaume d'Orenge, qui vait de cief haiclin,
> Van conte de Bouloigne, van conte Hoillequin,
> Et van Fromont de Lens, van son fil Fromondin,
> Van Karlemaine d'Ais, van son pere Paipin;
> Mais jo dira biaus mos qui bien dot estre en prins;
> Li ver i stront bien fat, il ne sont pas frurins,
> Ains sont de bons estuires, si com dist les escrins.
> Ce fu van rovison, qui de tans fu suerins,
> Que d'alusete cante van soir et van matin.
> Le los ele est kiie, ce fu à put estins,
> Pour aler sour Noevile le custel asalir.

---

[3] See also the account in Marie Ungureanu, *Société et littérature bourgeoises d'Arras au XIIe et XIIIe siècles* (Arras, 1955), pp. 145–48. I am much indebted to this excellent book. A. Guesnon brings local knowledge to bear in his discussion of the poem in *Moyen Age*, second series, 4 (1900), 131–37.

[4] *Chansons et dits artésiens*, p. 11. Guesnon suggests that 1280 is too late a terminus.

[5] The action of the poem evidently takes place in the industrial quarter of Arras, where Flemings worked in the cloth trade. *Flamengherie* (l. 119) seems to mean 'Flemish quarter'. Several of the personal names mentioned in the poem have been traced in Arras documents by Guesnon (pp. 134–35). *Purte de Meulens* (l. 55) is a gate in Arras. *Custel de Noevile* is probably the castle of Eustache de Neuville, outside Arras (Guesnon, p. 134). Ungureanu (p. 147) sees this as a stronghold to which the town patricians (*useriers*, l. 71) might have retired in face of a rising of the commons.

[6] *Chansons et dits artésiens*, p. 27. Jeanroy and Guy analyse the language of the poem on pages 30–31, following Scheler, *Trouvères belges*, p. 353. The Flemish expressions are as follows: definite article *de* (passim) and *van* (ll. 2, 30, 164); possessive pronouns *min* (ll. 34, 45, 54, etc.) and *sin* ('his', ll. 74, 75, 82, etc.); *van* in a variety of prepositional functions, mostly equivalent to French *de* (passim); *war* for 'where' (ll. 96, 135); *here* and *vrouwe* as male and female titles of respect (ll. 44, 53); and *sinte* for 'saint' (ll. 2, 30, 113, 131, 159, 160, 164). See, for all these, A. Lubben, *Mittelniederdeutsches Handwörterbuch* (Norden, 1888). The only complete Flemish sentence is 'War se gane' (l. 135), glossed by editors 'Where are they going?' (I am indebted to Dr Frank Shaw for his help with Flemish).

(My lords, now listen, and may God be your friend, the king of heavenly glory who was put on the cross. You have heard much of Gerbert and of Garin, of William of Orange, who goes with head bowed, of the Count of Boulogne and of Count Hoillequin, of Fromont of Lens and his son Fromondin, of Charlemagne of Aix and his father Pepin; but I shall speak fine words which should be much prized. The verses will be well made; they are not feeble. They concern a good story, just as the book tells it. It was at rogation time, when the weather was calm, and when the lark sings at evening and morning. The host is summoned, in an evil hour, to go against Neuville to take the castle by storm.)

In these lines the splendid muster-roll of heroes from the *chansons de geste* and the jongleuresque promise of a 'bons estuires' are belied by the dreadful French in which they are couched.[7] The very first sentence has two Flemish intruders (*van*, here used as a definitive article, and *de*, in 'de croc', also a definite article), as well as a sprinkling of unArtesian forms (*siggeur, scoutés, sot, rui, sinte,* and *croc*). These linguistic features indicate at once to the reader that this is to be, as Scheler succinctly puts it, 'un texte dont la cacologie fait le mérite'.

The 'good story' itself is easily summarized, for it consists of nothing more than the preliminaries to an assault which never takes place. The Flemings assemble in response to a call to arms. Their leader, Simon Banin, vows to uphold the honour of the weavers in the coming battle. This heroic utterance is followed by two more speeches, delivered by Bauduins Makesai and Willaume Mordenare. Banin then commands his men to return to their houses and arm themselves 'a wise de valier' (in knightly fashion). The central section of the poem, which follows (ll. 73–162), is devoted to three scenes of arming, elaborated in the formulaic manner of the *chansons de geste*.[8] Bauduins Makesai, having donned his armour and mounted his steed, unfortunately knocks himself out on the lintel of his own gateway, thus confirming the forebodings of his faithful wife Gommeline. The young lad Oitin, 'un farlet ù moult ot cortosie' (l. 117), takes an affecting leave of his sweetheart, 'Wissebel le blonde', who gives him an embroidered purse full of spices to comfort him in the wars.[9] Finally, the 'sage home Liépin' dons a hauberk, girds on his sword, mounts his good steed Walopin, and with a pious prayer rides to the gathering. The Flemings are now assembled; but just as they are setting off, God performs a great miracle:

---

[7] Garin le Loherain and his son Gerbert de Metz are heroes of the Lorraine cycle of *chansons de geste*; William of Orange has a cycle of his own; the Count of Boulogne represents the cycle of Godfrey of Boulogne; Count Hoillequin is perhaps the mysterious Hellequin, or Hurlewain, leader of 'le maisnie Hellekin'; Fromont of Lens (Lens in Artois, which explains why Bauduins Makesai claims him as kinsman, ll. 44–45) and his son Fromondin are adversaries of the Lorrainers in the Lorraine cycle; Pepin and his son Charlemagne rule France in many *chansons de geste*.

[8] For analysis of arming scenes in *chansons de geste*, see J. Rychner, *La Chanson de geste: Essai sur l'art épique des jongleurs* (Geneva, 1955), pp. 132–38.

[9] The spices are *skitoval* or zedoary (Chaucer's *cetewale, Thopas,* l. 761, also *Miller's Tale*, l. 3207), *canouele* or cinnamon, *drugie* or comfits, *graus d'escoufle* — possibly cloves (French *clou de girofle*, Chaucer's *clowe-gylofre, Thopas,* l. 762), and *nos mosquellie* or nutmeg (*Thopas,* l. 763). The exact point of introducing such spices into the burlesque is not clear in either *Nuevile* or *Thopas,* but the coincidence deserves note.

Un esfoudre de ciel i va la jour kiant,
Et Wautier Nainmeri, qui fat de bon sargant,
Il porte un lariflume van de ven desploant,
Et Grardin le kiiere, qui l'aloit tulelant —
Deus, com sont à masaise orendroit no cergant!
Hue van Castelain il leut un fain si grant
Il leüst bien mengnié en moille tro pain blanc.

(A thunderbolt came falling from the sky that day; and Wautier Nainmeri, the good soldier, he who carried the banner unfurled to the breeze, and also Grardin the town-crier, who was going to the wars at his side [?] — my God! how worried our soldiers now were. Hue van Castelain got so hungry that he could have eaten three white loaves in soup.)

These lines, the last in the text as preserved in the Paris manuscript, present several difficulties of interpretation.[10] On any interpretation, however, they bring the poem to a sudden and most unexpected halt. Scheler marks the poem 'inachevé', but Jeanroy and Guy observe that the manuscript lends no support to this supposition: 'Cette plaisanterie ne pouvait, du reste, se prolonger indéfiniment'.[11]

The main points of similarity between this peculiar piece and Chaucer's *Sir Thopas* can be tabulated as follows:

(a) Both poets describe the unheroic doings of Flemish townsfolk in a metre and manner associated, in their respective vernaculars, with heroism and adventure.

(b) The language of both is to a considerable degree deliberately 'cacological'. Like the Flemish French of *La Prise de Nueville*, the idiom of popular poetry adopted in *Sir Thopas* exhibits many features calculated to offend readers who 'se piquent de correction et recherchent l'élégance'.

(c) Both poems begin with minstrelesque appeals for attention ('Siggeur, ore scoutés', 'Listeth, lordes') and promises of good things to come.

(d) Both include a catalogue of heroes drawn from the kind of poem which they imitate (*Nuevile*, ll. 3–7; *Thopas*, ll. 897–900).

(e) Both devote a disproportionate amount of space to descriptions of the preliminaries of battle: vows (*Nuevile*, ll. 29–40, 42–46, 51–62, 70–72; *Thopas*, ll. 817–26, 872–74) and armings (*Nuevile*, ll. 75–91, 120–27, 149–52; *Thopas*, ll. 851–87).

(f) Both end abruptly and inconclusively, before the promised battle has been reached.

These points of similarity are not specific enough to prove that the English poet knew *La Prise de Nuevile*, though he certainly could have done so, for he himself had travelled 'in Flaundres, in Artoys, and Pycardie', like the Squire

---

[10] Scheler and Jeanroy/Guy take the obscure word *tulelant* (read by the latter *tuletant*) to introduce a speech. This occupies line 171 only in Jeanroy/Guy, lines 171–73 in Scheler. I take the word as a typical distortion of *turelant* 'tourneying' (compare *Le Moniage Guillaume*, second redaction, ll. 2715, 2719). Line 171 then refers loosely to the discomfiture of soldiers such as Wautier and Grardin. See also Guesnon (p. 136). I cannot explain why the thunderbolt makes Hue hungry.

[11] *Chansons et dits artésiens*, p. 97.

on the Canterbury pilgrimage, and his wife's family came from neighbouring Hainaut.[12] At the least, however, *La Prise de Nuevile* must be taken, *pace* Loomis, as representing a 'previous pattern of burlesque or parody' which is of immediate relevance to *Sir Thopas*.

Comparison of the two poems may begin with their endings. Burlesque commonly gets its comic effects by mixing incongruous ingredients from two contrasting worlds, one high and the other low. Shock tactics such as these tend to yield diminishing returns. Hence most burlesques get their best effects early on, before the joke has begun to seem laboured and predictable. One may therefore sympathize with the Artesian poet if he did indeed, as Jeanroy and Guy suggest, break *La Prise de Nuevile* off once his points were made. 'Cette plaisanterie ne pouvait . . . se prolonger indéfiniment.' Yet Chaucer undoubtedly hit upon a more artistic solution to the problem. Like the Knight's interruption of the *Monk's Tale*, Harry Bailly's interruption of *Sir Thopas* saves the author from the necessity of prolonging indefinitely a tale which has already well and truly made its point, and at the same time provides the opportunity for a spirited episode in the Canterbury drama. It is an exemplary instance of artistic economy:

> 'Namoore of this, for Goddes dignitee,'
> Quod oure Hooste, 'for thou makest me
> So wery of thy verray lewednesse
> That, also wisly God my soule blesse,
> Myne eres aken of thy drasty speche.'   (VII.919)[13]

By comparison, the end of *La Prise de Nuevile* cannot fail to appear 'inachevé'.

The rest of this essay will be concerned with a more general point of comparison between the two poems: what I shall call the 'direction' of their comedy. Burleque is not the same thing as satire, and there seems no reason in principle why its bringing together of high and low should not result in a pure and motiveless comedy of incongruity. In practice, however, readers seem to need to know which of the two worlds is to be understood as the main target of the comedy. It is as if the joke requires direction. Quite apart from any premeditated satirical intention on the author's part, such directedness must be taken as an internal or formal requirement of the genre: a principle of its ballistics, one might say. However, direction is not always easy to determine; and in the case of both *La Prise de Nuevile* and *Sir Thopas* good judges may be found taking refuge in the suggestion, hopefully offered, that the joke works both ways, against high *and* low. Thus F. N. Robinson, in his standard edition of Chaucer, speaks of *Sir Thopas* as 'a twofold satire, literary and social' (p. 12), meaning that the poem is directed against both the 'high' world of romance and the low bourgeois hero. In the same way, Jeanroy and

---

[12] See M. M. Crow and C. C. Olson, *Chaucer Life-Records* (Oxford, 1966), pp. 31 (Artois and Picardy), 44–46, 48, 51 (Flanders), 69 (the Roets of Hainaut).
[13] Quotations are from *The Works of Geoffrey Chaucer*, edited by F. N. Robinson, second edition (Boston, Massachusetts, 1957).

Guy see *La Prise de Nuevile* as a literary satire aimed at both the 'lourd patois' of the Flemings and the lofty manner of the *chansons de geste*; and Ungureanu takes a similar view: 'Il est difficile de dire si en appliquant le style épique au récit d'un soulèvement ouvrier, le poète a voulu railler l'épopée ou les ouvriers; peut-être les deux!'[14]

'Peut-être les deux!' The conclusion is hardly satisfactory. One cannot expect that, in the normally free and fanciful process of burlesque invention, all the jokes will end up facing the same way; and there may well be cases where the traffic seems equally thick in both directions. But this is not so in either *Sir Thopas* or *La Prise de Nuevile*. Comparison between the two poems helps to show, I think, that in each the comedy has its own dominant (though not exclusive) direction: in *La Prise de Nuevile* against the low world of the Flemings, in *Sir Thopas* against the 'high' world of the English romances.

The high world in *La Prise de Nuevile* is that of the *chansons de geste*. This is represented in the poem by its characteristic metre (the epic *laisse*) and the associated formulaic style, by its epic heroes (Gerbert and the rest), by actions typical of such heroes (vow, arming, muster, siege), and by the appropriate qualities and sentiments (courage and loyalty in the men, foreboding and grief in the women). It is a delicate matter to decide how far such features form the target of the joke in a burlesque, especially for modern readers over-accustomed to the 'send-up'. If other works by the author in question are known, these may provide a control by suggesting likelihoods one way or the other, as Chaucer's works do for *Sir Thopas*; but no such evidence is available in the case of the anonymous *Nuevile*. Nor does literary history help in this case. Although *chanson de geste* was already in the thirteenth century an ancient form, there is no good reason to suppose that it would have been regarded in Arras at that time as obsolete or ridiculous.[15] One must therefore look in the text itself for positive signs that the high heroic world is being debunked: deliberate exaggerations and distortions which turn imitation into parody. In *La Prise de Nuevile*, however, the imitation of features from the *chansons de geste* seems in general quite straightforward (barring, of course, the application of them to low subjects), and the selection of features to imitate shows no particular bias towards those which a thirteenth-century Artesian poet might be supposed to have found ridiculous. Perhaps the writer may be said to 'railler l'épopée' when he takes from the *chansons de geste* the form *Biauliant/Belliant* (ll. 30, 164) for Bethlehem, and when he refers to God as *rui amant* (ll. 29, 163), an expression

---

[14] *Chansons et dits artésiens*, pp. 27–28; *Société et littérature bourgeoises*, p. 147.
[15] Most of the surviving manuscript copies of *chansons de geste* were written in the thirteenth or fourteenth centuries. All nine copies of *La Prise d'Orange*, for instance, are dated between the middle of the thirteenth century and the middle of the fourteenth (edited by C. Régnier, second edition (Paris, 1969), pp. 7–10). The Arras poet Jehan Bodel wrote a serious *chanson de geste*, *La Chanson des Saxons*. Ungureanu (p. 114) argues that this must be early, because epic was a 'genre déjà démodé à Arras dans la seconde moitié du XIIIe siècle'; but to prove this she cites only the evidence of *La Prise de Nuevile* itself and *Audigier*, which begs the present question.

derived by popular etymology from *raement* 'redeemer' and found in *La Prise d'Orange*.[16] More certainly, the third and fourth *laisses* make a joke at the expense of the old heroic poems when they show two warriors both speaking 'first' on the same occasion (ll. 41, 50), an amnesiac touch which recalls the curious disjunctions of time characteristic of traditional formulaic narrative.

Yet the poet's epic style does not yield many such identifiable cacologies. Indeed, he shows real command of the techniques of the assonantal *laisse*. His verses are, as he claims, 'bien fat'. The twelve-syllable lines are divided by caesura into two hemistiches of six (or seven) syllables each in the accepted fashion; and the hemistiches exhibit traditional phrases, varied in the second hemistich to conform to varying assonances, just as Rychner describes.[17] Compare, for instance, the following lines referring to God:

> Van rui de sinte glore, / qui en de croc fou mis (l. 2)
>
> Van rui de sinte glore / qui nasqui Biauliant (l. 30)
>
> A, Diu pere de glore, / Sinte Mare d'amie (l. 131)
>
> A! Deus piere de glore, / qui en de croc fu mis (l. 157)
>
> Van rui de sinte glore / qui nasqui Belliant (l. 164)

Flemish abnormalities apart, these lines could come from a true *chanson de geste*. Lines 2b and 157b are exactly matched by *La Prise d'Orange*, line 562b ('qui en la croiz fus mis'). Lines 30b and 164b adapt the description of Christ to a different assonance much as in *La Prise d'Orange*, line 500: 'Et de la Virge fus nez en Belleant'.[18] A similar technique is to vary just the last word of a formula, thus:

> Here Fromont de Lens, / qui tant ot le cors fier,
> Fu le cousin larmain / min parastre Wautier (l. 44)
>
> Vrouwe Eisse, vo nante, / qui tant ot le cors gent,
> Fu cousine larmaine / min parastre Hersent (l. 53)

It is perfectly clear, in any case, that most of the jokes in *La Prise de Nuevile*, at the linguistic level, are directed not at the *chanson de geste* but at the Flemings and their 'lourd patois'. To them must be attributed, not only the occasional Flemish word, but also most of the many distorted forms of French words: distortions which often admit into the poem echoes from the lower depths, as when Gommeline 'se prist à porpisser' (for *porpenser*, l. 95) or when Liépin declares his faith in a miracle 'de cul fin' (for *coeur*, l. 161). *La Prise de Nuevile* never descends to the level of the other burlesque epic cited by Loomis, *Audigier*, where the scatological baseness of the low world is indeed

---

[16] *Belleant* may be found in *Gerbert de Metz* (l. 771) and *La Prise d'Orange* (l. 500). For *roi amant*, see *La Prise d'Orange* (l. 464) and Régnier's note.
[17] *La Chanson de geste*, pp. 139–53.
[18] The similarities of 2b to 157b and of 30b to 164b draw attention to the fact that the seventh and eighth *laisses* return to the assonances of the first and second, as if beginning a cycle again. The sequence is: *i / an / ié / en / é/ i.e // i / an.*

'beneath all up to that sunk to', in Joyce's words. *La Prise de Nuevile* is not, except linguistically, a very broad burlesque. Its Flemings do not use cakes as shields, or bear barrels in their coats of arms, or, like Audigier's father, use their lances against spiders' webs. The narrative is not fantastic. Yet the absurdity of the Flemings, to which the linguistic features decisively point, appears throughout. Their highest ambition, as portrayed here, is to gain a place on the body which controlled the cloth industry (ll. 46, 59), or else, more boldly, to count among the twelve *échevins* or aldermen who governed Arras (ll. 40, 72). They eat 'good Flemish cheese' (l. 56), wear clogs instead of spurs (l. 155), and even, in one case, carry a bill-hook into battle (l. 126).

With Chaucer's *Sir Thopas* in mind, we may take the arming of Bauduins Makesai (ll. 75–91) as an example of what could be called the 'satire' on the Flemish weavers. After having his horse Baielart saddled, Bauduins dons his aketon or quilted coat and his iron cap, and girds his good sword Salouwart by his left side. Apart from the evident incongruity of the heroic names of horse and sword, there is nothing absurd here.[19] However, the aketon was in the thirteenth century worn as main body armour chiefly by footsoldiers, not mounted knights;[20] and it is when he comes to mount his horse that Makesai's failure to sustain the 'wise de valier' becomes most evident:

> Une seile batiere fist Maquesai porter,
> Il saut sor Baielart, qu'à d'estré ne sot grés,
> D'un cordele de lins fu se .ii. piés loé;
> Je vo dira por coi, se savoir de volés:
> S'aucon mousart venoit qui le volot horter,
> Maquesai ne porot sans se queval varser.   (l. 86)

(Maquesai caused a *siele batiere* to be brought, and he leapt up onto Baielart without using the stirrup. His two feet were bound together with a linen cord; and I will tell you why, if you wish to know: If any wretch came along and wished to strike him, Maquesai could not fall without taking his horse with him.)

Leaping into the saddle without using the stirrups is correct heroic behaviour; but the *siele batiere* spoils the effect, whether it is a saddle built up to prevent the rider falling off, or else, worse still, some kind of device to help him up in the first place.[21] The same aid is employed by Liépin later (l. 153); and, like Maquesai, Liépin also takes the precaution (unparalleled, surely, in the best knightly circles) of having his feet tied together under the horse's belly (l. 154). The poet's straightfaced explanation of this prudent arrangement brings the arming scene to a dryly bathetic conclusion: 'Maquesai ne

---

[19] Ungureanu takes *Baielart* as a form of *Bayard*, the name of the fairy horse of the hero of the epic *Renaut de Montauban* (p. 147). She is wrong to suggest (p. 147) that Makesai girds his sword on the incorrect side: see, for example, *La Chanson de Roland* (l. 3143).

[20] See C. Blair, *European Armour* (London, 1958), p. 33. As Blair's evidence shows, such quilted coats were worn for defence, despite Ungureanu (p. 147).

[21] Jeanroy and Guy refer to Godefroy, who takes the phrase (found only in *Nuevile*) to refer to a saddle with built-up saddle-bows 'destinées à affermir le cavalier'. Scheler, in his note, prefers Ste-Palaye's suggestion of a mounting-stool. The latter interpretation is supported by the parallel line (*Nuevile*, l. 153): 'Par un sele batiere sali sour Walopin'.

porot sans se queval varser'. Here as elsewhere, the intention is clearly to 'railler les ouvriers'. The attempts of the Flemish weavers to act and speak 'a wise de valier' and so enter the heroic world of the *chansons de geste* are continually frustrated. Their language, their limited ambitions, their cautious approach to horses: such things betray a congenital incapacity for high deeds of chivalry.

Thirteenth-century Arras and fourteenth-century London were both towns in which Flemings generally occupied low positions in a 'bourgeois' hierarchy whose upper ranks merged with the aristocracy; and Chaucer certainly belonged to that same upper bourgeoisie whose attitudes *La Prise de Nuevile* appears to reflect. It would therefore not be surprising if the burlesque jokes in *Sir Thopas* took the same mainly downward direction as they do in *La Prise de Nuevile*. Such was, indeed, the conclusion arrived at by J. M. Manly, without reference to *La Prise de Nuevile*, in a well-known essay published in 1928:

Undoubtedly [Chaucer's] contemporaries would have recognized immediately that he was writing a burlesque romance, but they would not necessarily have concluded that he was satirizing romances as a form of literature. Would not their attention rather have been fixed upon the subject of the burlesque itself and upon the ridiculous figure presented by Chaucer's romantic hero? Accustomed as they undoubtedly were to poke fun, mingled with not a little resentment, at the efforts of the Flemish *bourgeoisie* to ape the manners of the English and French aristocracy, and with their new-found wealth to compete in dress, in manners, and in exploits on the battlefield with the ancient chivalry of France and England, would they not have recognized unhesitatingly that the object of satire was the ridiculous pretentiousness of these Flemings?[22]

Like Banin, Maquesai, and the rest, the hero of *Sir Thopas* is indeed a Flemish townsman:

> Yborn he was in fer contree,
> In Flaundres, al biyonde the see,
> At Poperyng, in the place.   (l. 718)

There is a double bathos here: first from the 'fer contree' to 'Flaundres', a country which no fourteenth-century Londoner could have regarded as either remote or romantic, and then from Flanders to Poperinge, whose name, like the many Flemish names in *La Prise de Nuevile*, strikes a further discordant note. We might expect these lines to establish, as Manly believes they do, a clear direction for the jokes which follow. Yet the fact is that, in the rest of *Sir Thopas*, we find not a single specifically Flemish feature of any sort. The name Thopas itself, whatever its precise significance, is not Flemish; and, although its bearer is undoubtedly ridiculous, Manly fails to show that he is ridiculous in any distinctively Flemish fashion. The sexual jokes which many readers have detected point in no recognizable direction; and the

---

[22] '*Sir Thopas*: A Satire', *Essays and Studies*, 13 (1928), 52–73 (pp. 59–60).

hero's reluctance to encounter anything more threatening than 'bukke and hare' is simply a time-honoured burlesque joke. Cowardice was not a monopoly of the Flemings.

The chief 'Flemish' feature which Manly sees in *Sir Thopas*, however, is their 'ridiculous pretentiousness'. The hero, according to him, displays the 'bourgeois tastes of the newly rich', 'apes the manners of the aristocracy', and makes ludicrous blunders in the process. But there is nothing *distinctively* Flemish here, as there is in *La Prise de Nuevile*; and in any case Manly's identification of 'bourgeois' absurdities in Chaucer's poem proves to be far from reliable. Sir Thopas certainly does fall short of knightly excellence in several respects; but his deficiencies do not add up to a portrait of specifically bourgeois (let alone Flemish) ineptitude. Thus the sports of wrestling and archery (ll. 739–41), as Manly himself observes, belong in medieval literature to the yeomen; and a sturdy yeoman, however incongruous he may be in a romance of chivalry, is not the same thing as a bourgeois Fleming. Elsewhere Manly sees pretentious absurdities where none exist. This is particularly the case in his discussion of the arming of Sir Thopas (pp. 70–71). We have already seen that the arming of Bauduins Makesai in *La Prise de Nuevile* plainly exhibits the Flemish weaver's failure to master the 'wise de valier' to which he aspires. He uses a *siele batiere* and has his feet tied together for greater security in the saddle. Manly sees similar absurdities throughout the arming of Sir Thopas. Thus, after quoting *Sir Thopas*, lines 860–68, he observes:

The aketon was not worn by a knight under his armour, but was a padded jacket with plates of metal sewed on it and was specifically the defensive armour of the common foot-soldier. It was therefore an absurdity that the knight should don an aketon; a double absurdity that he should put on over it a haubergeoun; a triple absurdity that over these should be worn a 'fyn hawberk' (p. 70).

But caution is necessary here. Bauduins Makesai does indeed fall short of full knightly kit, as I suggested earlier, in wearing an aketon as his sole body armour, in the manner of a footsoldier; but to wear it, as Thopas does, under other armour, appears to have been normal practice in the best circles. A recent authority defines the aketon as 'a plain quilted coat usually worn under the armour'. It was also, as the same authority shows, normal practice to wear a chainmail shirt or haubergeoun under one's plate armour or hawberk.[23] Manly's way of reading the tale yields demonstrably false results here.

Unlike *La Prise de Nuevile*, *Sir Thopas* seems not to offer any single consistent 'low' world which can be reconstructed and identified, as Manly attempts to do. In any case, comparison of the two poems, and in particular of their language and style, strongly suggests that the main target of Chaucer's

---

[23] Blair, *European Armour*, pp. 33, 55–61. Further evidence against Manly's reading of the arming scene will be presented in my notes to *Sir Thopas* in the forthcoming third edition of Robinson's *Chaucer*.

burlesque is to be looked for in a different direction. These are both texts 'dont la cacologie fait le mérite'; but Chaucer's joke is not at all the same as the Artesian poet's. In *La Prise de Nuevile* the imitation of the style and diction of the *chanson de geste* shows no identifiable bias towards features which might have been regarded as ugly or absurd: uglinesses and absurdities in the language of this poem belong, not to the high epic world, but to the low world of the 'Flamengherie'. In *Sir Thopas*, the case is quite the contrary. Chaucer makes no attempt to suggest any 'lourd patois' for his Flemish hero; but his imitation of the English romance manner, unlike that of the French epic in *La Prise de Nuevile*, shows a marked bias, which all scholars have recognized, towards features which Chaucer certainly did regard as ugly or absurd. The cacology, in fact, here belongs not to the low world of the Flemings but to the 'high' world of the English romances.

Manly is right to reject the notion that Chaucer was 'satirizing romances as a form of literature'. The object of the joke is not romance itself, but the popular English varieties of romance: old poems such as *Guy of Warwick* and *Bevis of Hampton*, and recent derivatives such as *Lybeaus Desconus* and *Sir Launfal*. Loomis and other scholars have amply demonstrated that Chaucer goes out of his way to imitate the diction and style of such romances; and it is these deliberate departures from the poet's normal usage, here as in *La Prise de Nuevile*, which signal the main direction of the burlesque joke. Following this lead, we can find in the poem other, non-linguistic, jokes at the expense of the 'geestours' and their tales. The long description of the arming of Sir Thopas, for instance, is to be taken as displaying poetic rather than knightly incompetence. Every item in the passage is said, so easily said, to be outstanding in its kind. The hero eats fine ginger (l. 854), wears fine linen and a fine hawberk (ll. 858, 863), and carries a spear of fine wood (l. 881). Such repetitions, in Chaucer, are rarely accidental. In this case they reflect upon the indiscriminate lavishness of popular romance. Nor can the length of the description be justified. As the Host says to Chaucer, when he interrupts the tale: 'Thou doost noght elles but despendest tyme' (l. 931). Parts of *Sir Thopas* waste time in pointless particularities; and other parts save it, to equally bad effect ('Sire Thopas fil in love-longynge'). The jerky and unbalanced progress of the story implies, in the author of *Troilus and Criseyde*, a profound dissatisfaction with the pacing of the narrative in *Guy of Warwick* and the rest.

Because in Chaucer's poem the high world of romance is thus represented in a low form, the burlesque distinction between the grand and the petty, so clear-cut in *La Prise de Nuevile*, becomes blurred here. Also, as we have seen, Chaucer's low world is itself not clearly identifiable in the way Manly suggests. Consequently, whereas in *La Prise de Nuevile* almost all the jokes can be understood in terms of *chanson de geste* on the one hand and *Flamengherie* on the other, in *Sir Thopas* there are many jokes which have no identifiable 'target'. Why, for instance, does the hero have 'lippes rede as rose', like a woman? The absurdity is characteristic neither of Flemings nor of heroes such as Guy of Warwick. This seems to be simply free-wheeling fun, of a sort common in burlesque. However, comparison with *La Prise de Nuevile* does help to establish the *main* direction of the joke in Chaucer's poem. Unlike *Nuevile*, it is essentially a literary burlesque. The comparison also shows that Chaucer can hardly be said to have 'followed no previous pattern of burlesque or parody'.

Jonson and Anger

IAN DONALDSON

The Australian National University

We often praise, and sometimes invent, in others the qualities we most value in ourselves. Jonson's poem 'To the Memory of My Beloved, the Author, Mr William Shakespeare, and What He Hath Left Us' is a moving and generous tribute to Shakespeare's genius; yet the figure which the poem conjures into existence seems at moments to bear less resemblance to Shakespeare than to Jonson himself:

> Shine forth, thou Starre of *Poets*, and with rage,
> Or influence, chide, or cheere the drooping Stage.   (l. 77)

Who else but Jonson would have pictured a stellified Shakespeare not merely cheering but chiding and raging at the present generation of playwrights from his exalted position in the heavens? Who else but Jonson, meditating the full significance of Shakespeare's name, would have praised

> . . . his well torned, and true-filed lines:
> In each of which, he seemes to shake a Lance,
> As brandish't at the eyes of Ignorance?   (l. 68)[1]

What animates the writings of the dead poet (Jonson implies), what makes him himself, what shakes the spear, is a deep vexation at human stupidity; Shakespeare has become the angry antagonist of his audience, threatening to hurl his laboured lines like missiles at their stupid heads. It is a powerful image in its way, yet it scarcely evokes the character of Shakespeare as we think we perceive it through his works. What it does evoke are the tone and temperament of Jonson himself; the Jonson who (as 'Horace') was alleged in Dekker's *Satiromastix* to 'fling epigrams, embleames, or play-speeches' about him 'lyke hayle stones'; the Jonson who feared that his *Epigrams* would be thought to 'hurle inke, and wit, | As mad-men stones: not caring whom they hit'; the Jonson who saw writing as analogous to the martial arts (frequent repetition of one's former work, he advised, is a helpful exercise: 'as in throwing a Dart, or Javelin, wee force back our armes, to make our loose the stronger').[2] It also evokes the Jonson of 'Come leave the

---

[1] *Ungathered Verse*, 26. All quotations are from *Ben Jonson*, edited by C. H. Herford and P. and E. Simpson, 11 vols (Oxford, 1925–52); i/j and u/v regularized. The best accounts of the poem are by T. J. B. Spencer, 'Ben Jonson on his beloved, The Author, Mr William Shakespeare', in *Elizabethan Theatre IV*, edited by G. R. Hibbard (London, 1974), pp. 22–40; and Richard S. Peterson, *Imitation and Praise in the Poems of Ben Jonson* (New Haven and London, 1981), pp. 158–94.

[2] Thomas Dekker, *Satiromastix*, v. 2. 384–85, edited by Josiah H. Penniman (Boston and London, 1913); Jonson, *Epigrams*, 1. 5; *Discoveries*, l. 1715.

lothed Stage' and of the 'Apologetical Dialogue' to *Poetaster*, in which the character of 'the Author' (possibly represented on stage by Jonson himself) appears at the end of the play to rebuke his enemies and describe what he could do to them if only he chose to try:

> They know, I dare
> To spurne, or baffull 'hem; or squirt their eyes
> With inke, or urine: or I could doe worse,
> Arm'd with Archilochus fury, write *Iambicks*,
> Should make the desperate lashers hang themselves.
> Rime 'hem to death, as they doe *Irish* rats
> In drumming tunes. Or, living, I could stampe
> Their foreheads with those deepe, and publike brands,
> That the whole company of *Barber-Surgeons*
> Should not take off, with all their art, and playsters.
> (*Poetaster*, 'To the Reader', l. 158)

Writing is conceived of here as an act of aggression, and poetry itself as a potent weapon, a force that has the power to kill; Jonson's pen has become a brand, just as Shakespeare's line becomes a lance. It is a remarkable, exhilarating, and uncomfortable passage, fuelled by anger, curiously unmodulated and unsmiling despite its reckless forays into derisive humour, accumulating a disconcerting power through its very intensity and excess. To have heard Jonson himself declaiming the lines in the theatre must have been an alarming experience.

   Robert C. Elliott quoted these lines from the 'Apologetical Dialogue' at the outset of his book *The Power of Satire*, the first two chapters of which 'are in effect a gloss on Jonson's threat', learnedly tracing the ancient traditions of lethal invective which the passage recalls. Archilochus, whose scornful iambics (according to legend) had driven his victims, Lycambes and his daughter Neobule, to suicide, had become a notable exemplar for satirists. Like a magical curse, a satirical utterance (it was comfortingly maintained) might literally kill those against whom it was directed.[3] In invoking this unamiable tradition, Jonson reveals an aspect of his own temperament and genius about which modern criticism has chosen on the whole to remain silent. We hear more nowadays of Jonson's rationality, self-containment, and moral composure than of his anger and excess. Yet contemporary witnesses spoke in other terms. 'He is passionately kynde and angry', wrote William Drummond of Hawthornden about Jonson in 1619, 'carelesse either to gaine or keep, Vindicative, but if he be well answered, at himself'.[4] Jonson's anger may well have been intimately related not merely to his kindness and to his self-assertiveness (as Drummond suggests) but also, in a complex way, to his creative power. I want to suggest that anger meant a great deal to Jonson, both morally and creatively, and that it is a major

---

[3] *The Power of Satire: Magic, Ritual, Art* (Princeton, New Jersey, 1960).
[4] *Conversations with Drummond*, l. 687.

source of energy throughout much of his work: energy which Jonson himself seems at times to have regarded, however, with ambivalence, and which he was not always able fully to direct and control.

Anger is not always thought of as a creative emotion; often it is regarded as equally inhibiting to art and to social intercourse. 'Indignation isn't a creative force', declared E. M. Forster roundly in his working notes for *Aspects of the Novel*; '"Come, you're cross, and what for", we exclaim'.[5] In Forster's *Howard's End*, one recalls, 'the outer life of "telegrams and anger"' is seen as inimical to the inner life of artistic imagination and endeavour. Jonson's own view of anger is very different, and it has once again the weight of a long tradition behind it:

> O, these so ignorant Monsters! light, as proud,
> Who can behold their Manners, and not clowd-
> Like upon them lighten? If nature could
> Not make a verse; Anger; or laughter would.

In these lines from 'An Epistle to a Friend to Persuade Him to the Wars' (*Underwood*, 15, l. 59) Jonson suggests that anger, like laughter, is not merely a moral but also an artistic force, helping actually to shape his verse, to bring it into being. Jonson is here echoing Juvenal: 'si natura negat, facit indignatio versum' ('if nature denies me, indignation makes my verse').[6] Here again the classical source seems to correspond to something in Jonson's own nature.

The notion of anger as a creative force occurs once more in the Epistle Dedicatory to the Universities of Oxford and Cambridge which Jonson prefixed to the quarto edition of *Volpone* in 1607. Here Jonson outlines the abuses in contemporary manners and letters which have raised him to his 'present indignation', an indignation which (it is implied) operates as a powerful creative stimulus: provoked to wrath, Jonson is also provoked to utterance and to art. Poetry herself, says Jonson, will assist him against his enemies:

Shee shall out of just rage incite her servants (who are *genus irritabile*) to spoute inke in their faces, that shall eate, farder then their marrow, into their fames; and not *Cinnamus* the barber, with his arte, shall be able to take out the brands, but they shall live, and bee read, till the wretches dye, as things worst deserving of themselves in chiefe, and then of all mankind.   (l. 138)

Like many other writers of satire, Jonson insists that the animus of his writing is not personal but is in some way bestowed from without; it comes from Poetry herself: Jonson is merely an agent, a servant, to her 'just rage'. Yet like the 'Apologetical Dialogue' to *Poetaster*, which at several points it

---

[5] *Aspects of the Novel and Related Writings*, The Abinger edition of E. M. Forster, edited by Oliver Stallybrass, Volume XII (London, 1974), p. 128. Forster was passing judgement on *Gulliver's Travels*.
[6] Juvenal, *Satires*, 1.79. Jonson's 'or laughter', as Gordon William points out to me, simultaneously acknowledges the more genial traditions of Horatian satire.

resembles, the passage seems powerfully and personally felt. Jonson again visualizes his writing as an act of aggression. The angry poet will spout corrosive ink into the faces of his adversaries, sear them with brands to the very quick. Those adversaries are themselves represented as aggressive and dangerous men, who 'care not whose living faces they intrench, with their petulant styles' (l. 73): their 'styles' being not merely their manner of writing but also, more literally, the pens with which they write. The Roman *stilus* was a sharp metal instrument with which a writer might defend himself in more ways than one.[7] The literary battle seems full of menace. It is a strange introduction to one of the world's greatest comedies, even if we glimpse subliminally an odd affinity between the justice which Jonson wishes to mete out upon his enemies and the justice which Volpone himself fears after he has been thwarted in his attempted rape of Celia: 'I doe feele the brand | Hissing already, at my fore-head' (III.8.17).

The dramatist Peter Barnes, who has worked closely with several of Jonson's plays in the theatre, once said that he pictured Jonson's characters 'either being perpetually angry, or perpetually drunk; in the sense that they continuously reveal themselves'.[8] Barnes's comment nicely catches that passionate, headlong, self-revealing quality of many of Jonson's dramatic characters; a quality that is also at times to be glimpsed, in a different form, in Jonson's discursive writing and in his non-dramatic verse. Anger is, however, a complex emotion, morally, psychologically, and (not least) creatively, and it is necessary to distinguish between some of the several ways in which Jonson regards and exploits it throughout his writing. The tragedies form a convenient starting-point.

II

In Jonson's tragedies, anger is depicted as a powerful retributive force which slowly builds in intensity throughout the action of the plays until it reaches flashpoint, precipitating the downfall of the protagonists. Like the creative anger which animates poets, this force is seen as impersonal, irresistible, bestowed from without; essentially, it is a moral force, which may seem indeed at time like a manifestation of the divine will. In *Sejanus*, characters such as Arruntius, Agrippina, and Drusus show their anger (Drusus most notably when he strikes Sejanus at the end of the first act of that play) and this anger is offered to us as a kind of guarantee of their moral integrity (Sejanus himself experiences anger, but thinks it politic to conceal the emotion: 'Wrath, cover'd, carryes fate', he says quietly to himself after Drusus has struck him (1.568)). Heaven itself may be angry with the political corruption of Rome; yet, as Arruntius complains, heaven seems puzzlingly slow to act:

---

[7] See Horace, *Satires*, II. 1. 39–46 (and *Satiromastix*, I. 2. 297–301).
[8] 'Ben Jonson and the Modern Stage', a debate between Irving Wardle, Peter Barnes, Terry Hands, Jonathan Hammond, and Colin Blakely, *Gambit*, 6, No. 22 (1972), 5–30 (p. 17).

> Still, do'st thou suffer heav'n? will no flame
> No heate of sinne make thy just wrath to boile
> In thy distemp'red bosome, and ore-flow
> The pitchy blazes of impietie,
> Kindled beneath thy throne? Still canst thou sleepe,
> Patient, while vice doth make an antique face
> At thy drad power, and blow dust, and smoke
> Into thy nostrils? Jove, will nothing wake thee?   (IV.259)

Heaven finally shows its 'just wrath' in the fifth act of the play. In the midst of Sejanus's sacrifices to '*Great mother* Fortune', the goddess ominously averts her face, to the terror of the Flamen:

> Yet! heav'n, be appeas'd.
> And be all tokens false, or void, that speake
> Thy present wrath.   (V.188)

Tacitus had explained Sejanus's ascendancy as the result of heaven's anger against Rome.[9] Jonson, though following Tacitus closely, varies this idea: heaven's anger is instead directed against Sejanus.

Yet the wrath that finally destroys Sejanus is not associated primarily with heaven or with the morally virtuous characters of the play or even with Tiberius, whose personal feelings are kept well out of view. Sejanus falls victim instead to the 'wild furie' and 'popular rage' (V.769, 776) of the people of Rome, by whom he is savagely dismembered. In one sense of course the anger of the mob is warranted, by the conduct of Sejanus, by the signal from the goddess Fortune, and by the authority of Tiberius's letter. Yet Jonson also allows us to see this popular anger as a wild and destructive force, indiscriminate in its operation, abruptly possessing the mob like a brief madness and departing with equal abruptness, leaving them puzzled and regretful over their actions. The innocent as well as the guilty suffer: Sejanus's daughter is raped, and then strangled along with her equally blameless brother. Anger is no longer a creative force, no longer a property of the morally percipient. Instead, it is like the blind frenzy which possesses the women of Thebes in *The Bacchae*, driving them on to dismember Pentheus. Nowhere else in Jonson's work is anger presented in so violent and terrifying a form.

Catiline (1611) presents a pattern in some ways curiously similar to that of *Sejanus* (1603). Anger is once more the principal guiding and controlling emotion, which is to bring about the downfall of the protagonist. This time, however, the anger is more clearly seen to derive from, and be approved by, heaven. Like Arruntius in *Sejanus*, Cicero in the third act of *Catiline* wonders how heaven manages to hold back its wrath:

> Is there a heaven? and gods? and can it be
> They should so slowly heare, so slowly see!
> Hath Jove no thunder? or is Jove become

---

[9] Tacitus, *The Annals*, IV. 1.

> Stupide as thou art? o neere-wretched *Rome*
> When both thy *Senate*, and thy gods doe sleepe,
> And neither thine, nor their owne states doe keepe!
> What will awake thee, heaven? what can excite
> Thine anger, if this practice be too light? (III.235)

'Hath Jove no thunder?' Later in the act, heaven makes a direct response to this question; the stage-direction reads, '*It thunders, and lightens violently on the sodaine*'.[10] 'Heare', says Cato,

> The gods
> Grow angrie with your patience. 'Tis their care,
> And must be yours, that guiltie men escape not.
> As crimes doe grow, justice should rouse it selfe. (III.836)

Unlike the fearful senators (who '*passe by, quaking and trembling*') Cato boldly interprets this thunder as a signal for political action:

> Doe; urge thine anger, still: good heaven, and just.
> Tell guiltie men, what powers are above them.
> In such a confidence of wickednesse,
> 'Twas time, they should know something fit to feare. (IV.24)

This heavenly anger finds its earthly agent in Cicero. 'H'has strove to emulate this mornings thunder, | With his prodigious rhetoricke', says Catiline sarcastically later in the act (IV.464), as Cicero draws to the close of another massive rhetorical attack upon Catiline and his conspirators. Sidney in his *Apology for Poetry* had spoken of the way in which Cicero in his great Senate speeches drove out Catiline 'as it were with a thunderbolt of eloquence'.[11] Jonson gives this figure a more literal application, and in so doing associates Cicero's speeches in an obvious way with the wrath of heaven.

The divine anger is contrasted with other kinds of morally unjustified or trivial anger shown by other characters in the play: with Cethegus's impotent anger against the gods, for example (V.603), or the tantrums of Fulvia, which the conspirator Quintus Curius finds erotically stimulating:[12]

---

[10] Earlier in the play (I. 488), Catiline has appealed in vain for a clap of thunder to mark the conspirators' sacrament of blood. Though the thunderclap during Cicero's Senate speeches appears to be Jonson's invention, the historical Cicero mentions *fulminum iactus*, the fall of thunderbolts, as one of several portents occurring during his consulship and apparently presaging the Catilinian conspiracy (*In Catilinam*, 3. 8). The appeal to heaven and the thundering response may have been a Jacobean stage convention (compare Vindice in *The Revenger's Tragedy*, IV. 2. 198: 'Is there no thunder left, or is't kept up | In stock for heavier vengeance? There it goes! [*Thunder sounds*]'; compare v. 3. 41–47, and *Othello*, V. 2. 237–38), having its origin in ancient beliefs about the significance of thunder. The convention is found as late as Shaw's *Heartbreak House*: 'Is there no thunder in heaven?', asks Captain Shotover rhetorically at the end of the first act, and is answered by falling bombs at the end of Act three. Jonson expresses scorn for stage thunder in the prologue to *Every Man in His Humor*, ll. 19–20. Thunder is often spoken of in *Sejanus* (II. 205; III. 122–23; IV. 336–39, 409, etc.) but never heard. For fears and superstitions about thunder in Jonson's own day, see Keith Thomas, *Religion and the Decline of Magic* (Harmondsworth, 1973), especially pp. 32, 33, 134, 747, 759.
[11] Edited by Geoffrey Shepherd (London, 1965), p. 138. H. D. Jocelyn points out to me that Cicero in turn had referred to Demosthenes's thunderbolts of eloquence, *Letters to Atticus*, Ia etc. Compare *Discoveries*, ll. 2560–63.
[12] Compare Propertius, *Elegies*, III. 8 (etc.). Deliro and Fallace in *Every Man Out of His Humour* (IV. 2. 11–15, etc.) are another Jonsonian couple who find anger sexually exciting.

> I would have my love
> Angrie, sometimes, to sweeten off the rest
> Of her behaviour.   (II.327)

Fulvia's physician instructs Fulvia's servant Galla to anger Fulvia for 'exercise':

Fulvia   How! Do's he bid you
                    To anger me for exercise?

Galla   Not to anger you,
                    But stirre your bloud a little: There's difference
                    Betweene luke-warme, and boyling, madame.   (II.21)

This mild stirring of the blood is contrasted with the true anger which stirs such men as Cato and Cicero to the defence of Rome. During the fifth act of the play, Caesar attempts to persuade the Senate that it behoves them to refrain from anger while prosecuting Catiline. Anger, argues Caesar, might be expected of 'Poore pettie states', but not of those 'that are | Head of the world, and live in that seene height, | All mankind knows their actions':

> They must nor favour, hate, and least be angrie:
> For what with others is call'd anger, there,
> Is crueltie, and pride.   (v.466)

Jonson allows us to see the deviousness of this plea. The anger that drives Cicero is divinely urged and sanctioned, and legally and politically warranted by the extreme crisis of the state. Yet this anger stands in a sense outside Cicero. It is not self-interested anger, nor does it limit his capacity for even-handed judgement. It is quite unlike the anger of the mob who dismember Sejanus. It is indeed quite unlike anger as it usually shows itself; and Cicero is able to say in a surprising paradox at the end of the play, 'Justice is never angrie' (v.599). What drives Cicero on is a force which is in an ultimate sense cool, disinterested, assured, divinely authorized: an anger which is 'never angrie'.

For all the care with which this paradox is proposed, Jonson is on tricky ground here. The notion of Cicero's noble and disinterested anger and of his rhetoric rumbling at the conspirators like thunder from heaven is not altogether convincing or attractive in human terms, and the audiences who expressed their dissatisfaction at the original performance of the piece may have been daunted not merely by the sheer length of Cicero's tirades but also by a certain naïvety of concept at the heart of the play. Once again it is noticeable that Jonson is excited by the idea of rhetoric as a destructive force, a thunderbolt which will destroy the enemies of Rome. Cicero's speeches are like Shakespeare's lance, brandished at the eyes of Ignorance, or Jonson's own hissing brand, flourished at the enemies of Poetry. Evidently Jonson's audiences were less attracted to this notion than he was. They left the theatre.

III

Not the least remarkable of Jonson's qualities as a writer, however, was his readiness to experiment with certain themes and ideas in both comic and tragic contexts.[13] The notion of rhetoric as a destructive thunderbolt recurs a number of times in Jonson's comic writing, where it is the more comfortable for being clearly seen as a comic hyperbole. Ovid in *Poetaster*, playing the part of Jupiter, humorously turns upon Julia, his Juno:

> We tell thee, thou anger'st us, cot-queane; and we will
> Thunder thee in peeces, for thy cot-queanitie.

Crispinus   Another good jest.   (IV.5.124)

Subtle, at the opening of *The Alchemist*, is to threaten Face in similar terms:

> I'll thunder you, in peeces. I will teach you
> How to beware, to tempt a *furie*' againe
> That carries tempest in his hand, and voice.   (I.1.60)

And Mosca in *Volpone* urges on the lawyer Voltore with the same figure:

> Mercury sit upon your thundering tongue,
> Or the *French* Hercules, and make your language
> As conquering as his club, to beate along,
> (As with a tempest) flat, our adversaries.   (IV.4.21)

'As conquering as his club': the notion is characteristically Jonsonian.

Jonas Barish has shown how Jonson in *Bartholomew Fair* (1614) returns in a spirit of apparent levity to themes and ideas which he had treated with full seriousness three years earlier in the ill-fated *Catiline*, and how in particular Justice Adam Overdo in *Bartholomew Fair* at moments recalls, and appears almost to parody, the figure of Cicero in *Catiline*.[14] Perhaps it is worth noting in this context one further fact about Overdo: namely, his anger. Disguised as a fool in order to spy out the 'enormities' of Bartholomew Fair, Overdo is disconcerted to hear the members of the watch discussing the terrible temper of the Justice of the fairground: Adam Overdo.

Haggis But he will burne blew, and swell like a bile (God blesse us) an' he be angry.

Bristle I, and hee will be angry too, when him list, that's more: and when hee is angry, be it right or wrong; hee has the Law on's side, ever. I marke that too.

Overdo I will be more tender hereafter. I see compassion may become a *Justice*, though it be a weakness, I confesse; and neerer a vice, then a vertue.   (IV.1.77)

Despite these penitent resolutions, Overdo cannot resist the temptation, as the play proceeds, to resume the role of the angry moralist: of a Cicero (one might say) or a Ben Jonson: 'It is time, to take Enormity by the fore head, and brand it; for, I have discover'd enough' (V.5.125). The comic minefield

---

[13] See Ian Donaldson, 'Jonson and the Moralists', in *Two Renaissance Mythmakers*, edited by Alvin Kernan (Baltimore and London, 1977), pp. 146–64.
[14] *Ben Jonson and the Language of Prose Comedy* (Cambridge, Massachusetts, 1960), pp. 212–13.

through which Jonson leads us here is clearly one which he himself knows well enough.

Adam Overdo is not of course the only angry character of *Bartholomew Fair*. Anger is the great informing idea in that play, driving the characters forwards and awry in much the same fashion that love and enchantment drive the characters of *A Midsummer Night's Dream*. The boldness of Jonson's conception is in having not just one angry person in the comedy but many, who cannon and collide in dazzling sequences and combinations. Humphrey Wasp, 'child of wrath, and heyre of anger' (II.6.146), buzzes in perpetual irritation from the first act to the last, assaults the Justice in the fairground, loses his ward, Bartholomew Cokes (who in turn loses two purses, his hat and cloak, his bride-to-be, and much else besides), loses his temper, and is finally disgraced. Zeal-of-the-Land Busy stalks wrathfully through the fair, overturning the stalls of gingerbread and angrily denouncing the iniquities of the puppet-show (somewhat daringly, Jonson recalls the overturning of the tables of the money-changers in the temple, one of the rare episodes in the gospels in which Christ is shown in anger: 'His disciples remembered that it was written, The zeal of thine house shall eat me up', John 2.17). Knockem and Quarlous — the names declare them ('you must not quarrell with Master *Quarlous*', 1.3.48) —angrily come to blows. Alice the punk angrily beats Justice Overdo's wife. Ursula the pig-woman displays an angry spirit which earns her the name of 'Mother o' the *Furies*'.

Quarrelling is the favourite activity of the play, a pastime, a way of life. In the fourth act of the play the quarrelling formalizes itself into the game of 'Vapours', in which it is incumbent upon each player to contradict the previous speaker, *'whether it concern'd him, or no'*. Knockem, Northern, Puppy, Cutting, Whit, Wasp, Edgworth, and Quarlous are the (not altogether sober) challengers in this game, in which the spirit of contention, now feigned, now real, reigns supreme.

Wasp   I have no reason, nor I will hear of no reason, nor I will looke for no reason, and he is an Asse, that either knowes any, or lookes for't from me.

Cutting   Yes, in some sense you may have reason, Sir.

Wasp   I, in some sense, I care not if I grant you.

Whit   Pardon mee, thou ougsht to grant him nothing, in no shensh, if dou doe love dy shelfe, angry man.

Wasp   Why then, I doe grant him nothing; and I have no sense.

Cutting   'Tis true, thou hast no sense indeed.

Wasp   S'lid, but I have sense, now I thinke on't better, and I will grant him any thing, doe you see?

Knockem   He is i' the right, and do's utter a sufficient vapour.

Cutting   Nay, it is no sufficient vapour, neither, I deny that.

Knockem   Then it is a sweet vapour.

Cutting   It may be a sweet vapour.

Wasp   Nay, it is no sweet vapour, neither, Sir, it stinkes, and I'le stand to't.

Whit   Yes, I tink it dosh shtinke, Captaine. All vapour dosh stinke.

Cutting   By your leave, it may, Sir.

Wasp   I, by my leave, it may stinke, I know that.

Whit   Pardon me, thou knowesht nothing, it cannot by thy leave, angry man.

Wasp   How can it not?

Knockem   Nay, never question him, for he is i' the right.

Whit   Yesh, I am i' de right, I confesh it, so ish de little man too.

Wasp   I'le have nothing confest, that concernes mee. I am not i' the right, nor never was i' the right, nor never will be i' the right, while I am in my right minde.   (IV.4.42)

The game ends in total confusion: '*They fall by the ears*', runs the stage-direction; Edgworth steals the wedding licence from Wasp's box, Cutting and Quarlous begin to quarrel, then '*They draw all, and fight*' (IV. 4.115, 144). The watch come in to make their arrests, and Wasp turns upon them angrily: 'Cannot a man quarrell in quietnesse? But he must be put out on't by you?' (IV.4.168). Quarrelling has become so much the norm amongst this company that an interruption to a quarrel seems like an incivility. The contentiousness of the entire gathering is parodied in the puppet show which concludes the play, in which the puppets, like the humans, '*quarrell and fall together by the eares*' (V.4.334), and the figures of Damon and Pythias, legendary for their placid friendship, are depicted by the puppets in a new and angry character:

> Though hourely they quarrell thus, and roare each with other,
>   they fight you no more, then do's brother with brother.
> But friendly together, at the next man they meet,
>   they let fly their anger, as here you might see't.   (V.4.282)

The idea that friendship may sometimes be no more than a mutual agreement to redirect hostilities is a very Jonsonian one.

Bartholomew Fair is seen nowadays as a more serious play than once it was, and the comedy indeed shows Jonson's continued preoccupation with certain problems which engaged him in *Sejanus* and *Catiline*: in particular, with problems relating to the exercise of moral authority and to the kinds of passions which people in authority, and people under the authority of others, may often feel. *Bartholomew Fair* is a comedy much concerned with the dangers of misdirected and excessive anger. In the prologue to the play, Jonson reminds King James that the self-righteous wrath of Puritans such as Zeal-of-the-Land Busy has long bothered the kingdom:

> And such like rage, whereof the petulant wayes
> Your selfe have knowne, and have bin vext with long.   (l. 6)

Yet it is equally important to see that *Bartholomew Fair* represents a major break with one of the central assumptions of the tragedies and of the satirical comedies: the assumption that moral wisdom necessarily expresses itself through righteous anger. Anger in *Bartholomew Fair* is a wholly ridiculous emotion, an emotion that constantly inhibits and perverts true judgement. The play is closer in spirit to *Every Man In His Humour*, in which the coolly jovial Justice Clement is shown to have a moral percipience denied to the warmly indignant Elder Knowell.

One final point needs to be made about anger in *Bartholomew Fair*: that it is in a curious way enjoyable, a principal source of the play's great comic energies. 'Though a quarrel in the street is a thing to be hated, the energies displayed in it are fine', wrote Keats.[15] Jonson would not have been so explicit about the matter, but we may sense in his play a similar ambivalence. Anger is seen as a divisive emotion, yet also oddly enough as a sociable one: many of the play's characters come to the fair precisely in order to enjoy the exhilaration of a public quarrel. The same paradox may be felt elsewhere in Jonson's comedies. The quarrelling of Face and Subtle in *The Alchemist*, for instance, leads ultimately to the break-up for the 'venter *tripartite*', yet it serves also for a time as a bonding activity, which both men seem rather to enjoy. Subtle's reputed gifts in quarrelling, like his reputed gifts in alchemy, have furthermore an attractive power: Kastril, who has travelled from the country to London precisely in order to learn the mysteries of quarrelling, delightedly enrols as apprentice to this virtuoso in the art of anger. By the end of the play the 'angrie Boy' is to find another master, Lovewit, who dazzles and converts him with a brilliant display of expert quarrelling:

> Gods light!
> This is a fine old Boy, as ere I saw! . . .
> 'Slight, thou art not hide-bound! thou art a *Jovy*' Boy!   (v.5. 132, 144)

Lovewit is jovial ('*Jovy*') not merely in his merriment, but also in his capacity for Jove-like anger. The anger of Subtle, Lovewit, and Kastril himself is of course mere play-acting, anger devoid of true moral cause or substance; yet Jonson allows us, too, to enjoy the great spill of energy that comes from these verbal encounters.

IV

In Jonson's non-dramatic verse, anger is once more a frequent source of excitement, yet seldom in so genial a way as in the comedies. It is through anger that Jonson in his satires most commonly expresses a sense of moral outrage. Yet often he seems less aware than he is in the comedies of the perils and limitations of the emotion he exploits, and his 'angry' poems at times take large poetic risks. 'To Captain Hungry' (*Epigrams*, 107) gives some sense of the characteristic method. Its subject is a cashiered soldier who invents stories about campaigns in which he has fought and military secrets to which he is privy in order to win himself a free meal from his listeners:

---

[15] *The Letters of John Keats 1814–1821*, edited by H. E. Rollins, 2 vols (Cambridge, Massachusetts), ii, 80.

> Doe what you come for, Captayne, with your newes;
>   That's, sit, and eate: doe not my eares abuse.
> I oft looke on false coyne, to know't from true:
>   Not that I love it, more, then I will you.
> Tell the grosse *Dutch* those grosser tales of yours,
>   How great you were with their two Emperours;
> And yet are with their Princes: Fill them full
>   Of your *Moravian* horse, *Venetian* bull.

In these opening lines Jonson creates a dramatic relationship between himself and the captain. He taunts, teases, and provokes the captain, until after twenty lines or so he gets a reaction — which draws his further scorn:

> Nay, now you puffe, tuske, and draw up your chin,
>   Twirle the poore chaine you run a feasting in.
> Come, be not angrie, you are Hungry; eate;
>   Doe what you come for, Captayne, There's your meate.

The very injunction *not* to be angry (as so often in these cases) is of course a further provocation to anger; yet Jonson is also implying that his victim is incapable of feeling any emotion other than hunger; he is, he has become, 'Captain Hungry', the name defining the limits and possibilities of his character; he can never be more nor less than this. 'Hungry' can never be 'angrie': the two words mockingly chime. A true soldier, it is implied, feels true anger, as does a true poet; Jonson allows us to feel and to enjoy the current of real anger that charges his lines, and to contrast this anger with the moral, emotional, and physical impotence of his victim.

This notion of a reputed anger abruptly dwindling on closer inspection is one which is familiar from Jonson's comedies: one thinks of the feigned wrath of Downright in *Every Man in His Humour*, and of Daw and La Foole in *The Silent Woman*. *Hot Anger Soon Cold* is the significant title of a (now lost) play which Jonson wrote for Henslowe. In *Bartholomew Fair*, Ursula spars with Knockem the horse-courser in very much the same terms as Jonson does with Captain Hungry:

Never tuske, nor twirle your dibble, good *Jordane*, I know what you'll take to a very drop. Though you be Captaine o' the Roarers, and fight well at the case of pis-pots, you shall not fright me with your Lyon-chap, sir, nor your tuskes; you angry? you are hungry: come, a pig's head will stop your mouth, and stay your stomacke, at all times. (II.3.47)[16]

Knockem's apparent anger is no more than hunger; his tusks (like Captain Hungry's) are for eating, not fighting; he has a stomach for food but not for valour. But the speech also of course humorously reveals something about Ursula, and it is no real surprise that at the end of the play the two of them are content to troop off together to Justice Overdo's for supper, to stop their mouths and stay their stomachs. In the comedies, Jonson expertly controls

---

[16] The humourous equation of anger and hunger occurs again in *For the Honour of Wales*, ll. 133–36.

reflexive ironies of this kind: accusations rebound upon accusers, angry
denunciations tell us as much about the denouncers as about the victims.
Anger, like alcohol, is a great exposer of character, as Peter Barnes's
comment (already quoted) suggests. One of the problems about anger in
satiric verse is that, unless handled and varied with consummate skill (as in,
say, *An Epistle to Dr Arbuthnot*), it may reveal the character of the satirist as
nakedly as that of the victim, prompting us perhaps to speculate about the
reasons for his passion: 'Come, you're cross, and what for?'

Jonson in his satiric verse rarely practises the arts of coolness, indirection,
and anonymity; instead, he is usually passionately, indignantly visible (as it
were) in the centre of his poems, laying about him with vigour and anger; his
poems aim to raise the emotional temperature. It is significant that he should
choose, for example, in one of his better-known poems (*Ungathered Verse*, 34)
to *expostulate* with Inigo Jones, arguing heatedly and directly with the victim
for over a hundred lines. Powerful and energetic though the poem is, it may
also seem to be curiously lacking in modulation and variety; Jonson's anger
seems almost to get the better of him. In a shorter poem to Inigo Jones
(*Ungathered Verse*, 36), Jonson ostensibly tries a different technique:

> Sir Inigo doth feare it as I heare
> (And labours to seem worthy of that feare)
> That I should wryte upon him some sharp verse,
> Able to eat into his bones and pierce
> The Marrow! Wretch, I quitt thee of thy paine
> Thou'rt too ambitious: and dost fear in vain!
> The Lybian Lion hunts noe butter flyes,
> He makes the Camell and dull Ass his prize.
> If thou be soe desyrous to be read,
> Seek out some hungry painter, that for bread
> With rotten chalk, or Cole upon a wall,
> Will well designe thee, to be viewd of all
> That sit upon the Comon Draught: or Strand!
> Thy Forehead is too narrow for my Brand.

Jonson begins by talking about Jones in the third person, but within five
lines he is addressing him contemptuously face to face, and the pretence of
equable indifference rapidly drops away. The poem rests upon the paradox
that Jones is, and is not, worth bothering about. Nothing will induce Jonson
to write a 'sharp verse' upon Jones, yet this declaration rapidly becomes the
sharp verse that Jonson will not, yet does, write. Jonson plants his brand
upon the forehead he professes to ignore. 'I never thought an angry person
valiant', declares Lovel in *The New Inn* (iv.4.64), and Jonson himself seems
to struggle for a similar loftiness of spirit, yet the actual energies of the verse
tell another tale. The poem is closely modelled upon one of Martial's
epigrams (12.61), and it is from Martial in particular that this notion of
branding derives. Cinnamus the barber, whose acquaintance we have
already made, appears in another of Martial's epigrams, written in reply to a
critic of Martial's poems: 'But if the heat of my wrath sets a brand upon you,

that will remain and cling to you and be read all over the town, and Cinnamus, for all his cunning skill, will not efface the marks' (6.64).[17] To Jonson (who had himself been branded on the thumb in 1598 for killing a fellow-actor) the notion seems to have had a peculiar force. Satire and physical violence are closely associated in his mind. Both may be generated by moral anger, by heat. The pain inflicted by satire is analogous to that inflicted by branding, but more searing, more shameful, more deeply enduring.

V

To a later writer such as John Dryden, this kind of angry satirical writing no longer seemed possible or appropriate. To pass from Jonson's writing to Dryden's is to enter quite another world, to encounter verse satire written with new sensibilities and new sophistication. Though in many ways he greatly admired him, Dryden believed that Jonson belonged to a coarser, rougher age, 'When men were dull, and conversation low'. Neither Jonson nor any of his great contemporaries, thought Dryden, was able thoroughly to satisfy the more refined and sophisticated tastes of Restoration society, 'an age more gallant than the last'.

> None of 'em, no not *Jonson*, in his height
> Could pass, without allowing grains for weight.
> Think it not envy that these truths are told,
> Our Poet's not malicious, though he's bold.
> 'Tis not to brand 'em that their faults are shown,
> But, by their errours, to excuse his own.[18]

''Tis not to brand 'em': part of the change of sensibility is signalled by this new gentlemanliness in the tone of assessment which Dryden here adopts, courteous for all its firmness. A poem such as *Mac Flecknoe* reveals the affinities between Jonson and Dryden and also their radical differences on the matter of poetic anger. Jonson's attacks on Captain Hungry and Inigo Jones are scornful and direct; he addresses them by name and title: the attacks appear to come, as it were, straight from himself. Dryden's methods are quite different; his poem is more impersonal and less direct. Dryden himself is nowhere to be found in it; he is elsewhere, aloof, paring his fingernails. It is Flecknoe, not Dryden, who appears to undo Thomas Shadwell, but he is allowed to do so innocently, unwittingly, in the process of praising Shadwell, whom he sees as his natural successor and heir to the Kingdom of Nonsense.

---

[17] Translation by W. C. A. Ker in the Loeb *Martial Epigrams*, revised edition (London and Cambridge, Massachusetts, 1968). Runaway slaves were branded in this manner (see, for example, Petronius, *Satyricon*, 103); for the literary application of the notion, see Horace, *Satires*, 1. 4. 1–5.
[18] 'Epilogue' to the Second Part of *The Conquest of Granada* (1672), in *The Poems of John Dryden*, edited by James Kinsley, 4 vols (Oxford, 1958), 1, 134.

Dryden aggrandizes in order to deflate, but he deflates by means of an irony at once more delicate and more pervasive than Jonson's. Above all, Dryden's wit is cool, urbane, delighted, running at quite a different poetic temperature from that of Jonson. About Shadwell he implies two things in particular: that he attempts to practise satire of the rough and vigorous kind of Ben Jonson, his admired master; and that in Shadwell's hands such satire becomes at once indiscriminate and ineffectual, unlike that of Jonson himself:

> Where did his [Jonson's] wit on learning fix a brand,
> And rail at Arts he did not understand?   (l. 177)

Shadwell is presented as angry but impotent, malicious but toothless ('Thy inoffensive Satyrs never bite'), and Dryden's own satire bites all the more sharply because of the way in which he retains his artistic coolness and apparent unconcern.

Dryden's chosen weapon was not the brand; he chose sharper, colder, instruments which would dispatch his victims more deftly, seeing

a vast difference betwixt the slovenly butchering of a man, and the fineness of stroke that separates the head from the body, and leaves it standing in its place. A man may be capable, as Jack Ketch's wife said of his servant, of a plain piece of work, a bare hanging; but to make a malefactor die sweetly was only belonging to her husband.[19]

Throughout his *Discourse Concerning the Original and Progress of Satire* Dryden is exercised by a problem which never seriously bothers Ben Jonson: namely, how to reconcile the conflicting demands of truth and plain-dealing with those of good manners, good humour, and a Christian consideration for the feelings of others; how to combine the force of Juvenal with the civility of Horace.[20] Anger in a poet is no longer for Dryden a mark of special grace, anger in a victim no longer a sign of satirical success: 'If a *Poem* have a *Genius*, it will force its own reception in the World. For there's a sweetness in good Verse, which Tickles even while it Hurts: And, no man can be heartily angry with him, who pleases him against his will.'[21]

To Jonson, anger (at its best) was a great creative and moral force, derived if not from heaven then from a passionate perception of the nature of virtue and wickedness, right and wrong, a force which animated the statesman, the rhetorician, the soldier, the poet, a force which could purge or save the state at times of moral crisis. Like all great forces, it was also potentially dangerous, and open to abuse. It could be trivialized and indulged in for improper reasons, reduced to a directionless yet mildly thrilling game.

---

[19] *A Discourse Concerning the Original and Progress of Satire* (1693), in *Of Dramatic Poesy and Other Critical Essays*, edited by George Watson, 2 vols (London and New York, 1962), II, 71–155 (p. 137).
[20] John Dennis: 'There is in *Horace* almost every where an agreeable Mixture of good Sense, and of true Pleasantry, so that he has every where the principal Qualities of an excellent Comick Poet. And there is almost every where in *Juvenal*, Anger, Indignation, Rage, Disdain, and the violent Emotions and vehement Style of Tragedy' ('To Matthew Prior, Esq; upon the Roman Satirists', *Critical Works*, edited by E. N. Hooker, 2 vols (Baltimore, 1943), II, 218–19).
[21] *Absalom and Achitophel*, 'To the Reader' (*Poems*, I, 215).

Charlatans might pretend to possess this force, as they pretended to other arts and powers; yet true anger would always in the end expose and drive out false. Of the humorous aspects of anger, and of the risks besetting the angry moralist, Jonson was certainly keenly aware, as the practice of his comedies reveals. Yet in comparison with a later writer such as Dryden, Jonson is bothered relatively little by the possibility that anger may be seen as churlish or perilously self-revealing; about the tactics of anger he seems relatively fearless and unreflective. Dryden's attitude is subtly but significantly different from Jonson's: he views anger warily, uneasily, as a powerful but socially disruptive force. The time is not far off when Addison and Budgell will counsel readers of *The Spectator* to suppress all anger in argument and discussion ('no one values your Anger, which only preys upon its Master'), and Lord Chesterfield will commend to his son a similar policy of severe social restraint:

> The principal of these things is the mastery of one's temper, and that coolness of mind, and serenity of countenance, which hinder us from discovering, by words, actions, or even looks, those passions or sentiments by which we are inwardly moved or agitated, and the discovery of which gives cooler and abler people such infinite advantages over us, not only in great business, but in all the most common occurrences of life. A man who does not possess himself enough to hear disagreeable things without visible marks of anger and change of countenance, is at the mercy of every artful knave or pert coxcomb.[22]

It is not altogether a matter of coincidence that Jonson's reputation went into sharp decline in the eighteenth century; his writing, as Stuart Tave has shown, did not readily display those qualities of amiability, benevolence, and good humour which many readers of the period were disposed to seek.[23] We are still to some extent the heirs of many of the social and literary assumptions of that century, and it is worth recalling the impact made upon those assumptions in not-so-distant times by a play bearing the provocative title *Look Back in Anger*: a play which prompted in some quarters the Forsterian response that anger is not a creative force. Despite the impact of this play and the changes in the English theatre which it helped to bring about, Jonson may still seem to be in some ways too unrestrained, too hot-blooded, too uncivil a writer to be comfortably accommodated to the present English theatrical tradition and the social assumptions which it reflects: a situation which Jonson himself would have viewed with profound dismay, and quite possibly with anger.

---

[22] *The Spectator*, edited by Donald F. Bond, 5 vols (Oxford, 1965), II, 275 (no. 197); *Lord Chesterfield's Letters to his Son and Others*, introduced by R. K. Root (London and New York, 1929), p. 103.
[23] Stuart M. Tave, *The Amiable Humorist* (Chicago and London, 1960).

Voices of the Satirist: John Donne

ARNOLD STEIN

University of Illinois at Urbana-Champaign

The subject I propose will include some of Donne's imaginative uses of the 'self' as these are projected by narrator and persona. My chief attention will be directed towards the character of the satirist and his 'voices', but my essay is not on the *Satires* as a body of work. Instead, I shall try to develop some observations that begin in the *Satires* by relating these matters to Donne's practice in other poems; finally, I shall try to follow parts of the subject into the religious prose. Works I shall not try to bring into the compass of my discussion are *Metempsychosis*, *Ignatius His Conclave*, and the *Anniversaries*.

In 1947 and 1948 Robert Elliott and I were colleagues and at the beginnings of a long friendship. There was much earnest conversation between us: his interest in satire was just putting down strong roots, mine had briefly flowered and begun to fade. I have returned to the general subject as if to renew an old conversation and to say some things that would not have occurred to me then.

The narrator of Satire I is a theatrical image of the youthful Donne, a scholar among his books conferring with God and the Muses and at first severely lecturing a familiar intruder on the personal faults which make his convivial invitation unacceptable. Once the narrator decides to emerge from his study, for reasons which satisfy him and are pronounced as judgement, though the reader may well be surprised, the narrator chiefly reports what he sees and hears. In so far as he has sinned against his 'conscience' by leaving the companionship of his studies (described with mannered and ambiguous mockery), he will deserve the discomforts of the expedition and pay for his implied intellectual restlessness. In effect, however, this Horatian self-inclusion seems aimless and simply disappears. If he feels any guilt in having decided to go, we are left to infer that, uncertainly, and to attribute to personal feeling some of the intensity with which he observes. Objects and actions dominate the flow of attention. And yet there he is, seeing but never seen.

On the other hand, as narrator he presides over a loose and rambling account that follows the fortuitous, though luck is on his side when he finds a last episode appropriate to concluding such a story, with the companion confined to bed 'constantly a while'. The narrator's own introductory lecture, for the most part turned outward in moral severity, goes on for nearly half the poem and demonstrates that he was right in advance, in everything but the sentimental morality which at the last authorized the sudden judgement to accept the invitation. Yet the reality of the street will leap from the immediacy of descriptive anticipation to the more fully charged immediacy of enactment. And further, what happens in the street will provide opportunities not present in the lecture (one may ask, why not?) for indulging in extended digressions. These awaken, as from slumbering inertness, objects and thoughts which are suddenly brought to notice in a casually spontaneous way that seems to focus only in movement and perhaps not to remember the things it has made briefly vivid in passing.

The device of satiric comparison bears an unmistakable Juvenalian stamp, but Donne has enlarged the device: it is now more mannered, can carry more messages, and can mock itself as well as the objects casually thrown up. The confinement of the study, and its mental and physical programme of education for death, would seem to have stored up for release a considerable mass awaiting expression, with not a few ripples of artful excess. As persona the narrator satisfies himself in describing the comic world of the street, and his imagining ear quickens in producing his companion's breathless and affected speech carried to the edge of verisimilitude, where it delights, not less for being set beside his own precise marksmanship of witty rejoinders that ought to destroy but are (deliberately) wasted on his companion.[1]

The companion and the persona are small figures brilliantly illustrated; the narrator is a large figure who can divide himself into the persona (1) who speaks the first fifty lines, (2) who then records in different voices what he sees and hears, and (3) who also speaks self-characterizing replies in dialogue. That large figure moves in shadows, terse, garrulous, acting out his ignoring of an obvious initial mistake but not really touched by this, and not quite identifiable. Behind him is the poet who is responsible for the narrator and all else; he moves in and out of still deeper shadows. I surmise that friends hearing Donne read the poem aloud and change his voice to play the parts, or friends reading the poem themselves in a personal manuscript and imagining his voices, as we must do, would have noted all I have mentioned and more, not as a puzzle to be solved but as a delightful interplay of parts in movement.

What I want to emphasize in the example of Satire 1 may be referred, though not without qualification, to the other satires. I mean the uses of persona, narrator, and the author himself, their related separatenesses and near identities. To these I should add the casual air of exposition and its easy form, and the ways in which the sense of a governing design is forestalled.

Donne's instincts and skills as a poet came together early. No one else interested in Roman elegies or satires had the sureness of hand and eye to convert old models into original English poems so flowering in their present

[1] An exception is 'He droopt' of line 87.

that they seemed fully rooted there. If Homer taught poets how to lie properly, and Ben Jonson taught English poets how to borrow, Donne showed how the right poet might conquer and rule. To speak of satires only, and that briefly, what Donne most wanted was the tradition for licensed freedom of movement. As Roman satire developed into a consciously distinct genre, the satirist enjoyed a free disregard for the standards of economy and decorum obeyed in other genres. He could manage his art whether angry or amused, whether carried away by the strength of his feelings or weaving at leisure his threads of varied laughter. Nor was the exact epigrammatic turn embarrassed by the veering, crammed digression, nor the tirade by the proximity of a subtle gesture.

As the epic poet had his Muse and the privilege of soaring aloft, the satirist had the right to turn his feelings directly outward in response to the follies and vices of the times. His authority derived from his power to hold, to entertain variously, and to produce telling recognitions of the rightness and wrongness of what he presented. The figure of the satirist himself might, like Horace, draw inspiration from the great example of Socrates, teaching by urbane indirectness and using his personal presence to reach beyond himself towards recognizable truths. Or, like Persius and Juvenal, the satirist might seem to owe his very existence to the urgency of certain issues for which he was an impelled spokesman. A familiar vehicle of his speech may be described, to borrow the words of Donne, as 'Metaphoricall and Similitudinarie Reasons . . . made rather for illustrations, then for argument or answer'.[2] Such a satirist is less an orator than a *vates* with special gifts for disabusing the present, one in whom the attributes of personality are few or vague but moral character is paramount.

Donne creates his own satiric spokesmen, and he seems to have had a discerning eye for precedents and suggestions that would suit his own temper and purposes. In addition to the Roman examples there were the prophets of scriptural tradition, 'which made of two | One law, and did unite'.[3] Some of their tones may be heard in moments of Satires III, IV, V, the *Anniversaries*, and the religious prose. Then there were speakers in the native tradition: Langland, Skelton, the Spenser of *Mother Hubberds Tale* and *Colin Clouts Come Home Again*, Martin Marprelate, and soon the railing figure who would become the malcontent on the stage, and that figure dear to the hearts of Englishmen well before he answered to the name of 'plain dealer'. Most of these satiric speakers are bound by a general obligation, more than personal, to speak out against the ills that affront them. Their methods and aims differ, but not their obligation to speak out. Though the use of disguise might invoke the harmless pleasures of fable and bow to the laws of prudence while exploiting a further dimension of unacknowledged reference, and though lively entertainment might attract the curious (as in Martin Marprelate's

[2] *Biathanatos*, p. 109. I use the edition of 1648.
[3] 'A Litanie', l. 66.

bold success) or perhaps divert the less rigorous guardians of authority, these speakers were all alike in that they were expressing themselves from positions outside the established order of custom or good taste, and also from positions outside some of the larger and more powerful institutions, as the Church or the Court. It will not distort matters too much, especially in regard to Donne, if we use the modern term and call them 'alienated'.

The satiric spokesmen Donne employs are outsiders, whether angry or disengaged, or both more and less; or both and at the same time earnest seekers, as of true religion. They furnish considerable and varied amusement but they are not themselves actively amused. They do not smile or enter into the fooling as pretended equals, to achieve the special comic triumphs available only from the inside, as by a Touchstone or a Falstaff. Their agility of mind does not choose to move in that direction; they prefer a certain distance most favourable to their power of inventive observation. Their agility lies within the compass of aroused singlemindedness, with no apparent concern for what can be seen or said by means of grace, pliancy, and peripheral vision. They are not brilliant *and* obtuse like the spokesman of Marvell's 'The Mower against Gardens'. Their power and flaws and concentrated point of view are all to be recognized by friends and connoisseurs. Behind their masterful expression there is a prior law to which they are responding, but it is a law which seems to be imposed by chance, for they are themselves forced to speak out because of what they meet or are led into. But the law is there: they attack, but only because they are defending neglected truths (Satire III is an exception in that the speaker initiates his mental expedition). All the satiric spokesmen act as if they are entirely in charge, but the poet knows better and permits brief openings through which we may glimpse parts in movement.

I have been piecing together a kind of composite character, as it were, but Donne does not make or or give himself an easily identifiable character as do earlier and later professional satirists. Nothing in the classical and native precedents quite corresponds to Donne's use of satiric spokesmen. He invents the art of related separatenesses and near identities potential in the inherited looseness of form. By long reading we may perhaps hope to recognize parts of the actual person his friends knew. But we can hardly be sure that we judge accurately even obvious disguises and exaggerations: their occasional, ephemeral, and particular meanings flaunting the literal and the oblique, perhaps pretending unintentional (or deliberate) slips, and so on. Still, though we come late and are not the readers he had in mind, we can see some things with reasonable assurance, like the varying gap between the assumed narrating voice and the other voices of the poet on record. We can see and hear enough to recognize his originality and something of the character of his practice.

He often employs the contrivance of a staged voice, no doubt tuned a little strangely both to amuse intimates and to establish a distinct style against which he can register changes of person and meet changes in the flow and side-currents of material. What is written *was* written by the poet, but the narrator is free to overrule the regulations and illusions of time. For the narrating voice may choose to retell matters from what seems to be an actual place in time (though with modest room for moving about), but the narrator also creates at will the sense that he is himself there in an imagined present and is in person describing, acting, and responding. He is both in position and moving; he is discontinuously and at once, with finely adjusted interstices, poet, narrator, and persona.

If some of the preceding analysis would seem to be more appropriate to the intricate achievements of famous poems in the *Songs and Sonnets*, I have pointed in the right direction, though perhaps more emphatically than the immediate subject required. In the *Songs and Sonnets* Donne can do whatever he learned in writing the *Satires* and of course can do more. That satiric skills are not lacking in the lyrics and deserve special attention I acknowledge, and pass on to other examples that will furnish more yielding and clearer demonstrations of what I have set out to discuss.

In Elegy xvi (Grierson), 'On his Mistris', the direct address of lyric and many circumstances lead us to believe that the speaker is the poet in his own person.[4] He represents himself as speaking to his mistress, though he is writing to her, and *on* her, as well. His immediate aim is to dissuade her from accompanying him, disguised as a page, and to persuade her to accept their parting in ways that will augur best his return to her. The materials of argument intertwine, and his image of her takes shape while he seems intent on the practical subject. There are other indirectnesses, for all movements and changes of voice are adjusted to a personal argument based upon a central position which never moves, that of professing his love and his dependence upon her. The changes of voice, however, are extreme and abrupt, in method resembling the ways of a satiric narrator though the intent is that of a lover. The opening, 'By our first strange and fatall interview', invokes the intimately-shared tender memories, the threats and dangers felt together and separately, and the oaths which come to the point of the period, looking backward and forward, by being unsworn. Then the next fourteen lines present the persuasions of a lover's praise, on varied levels and mixed with prudent advice on the limits of love and the dangers of life. Against the brief celebration of her person the following seventeen lines bring forward the ugly probabilities of the foreign world, in suggested scenes that draw upon satiric skills but are applied to a practical purpose. The last fourteen lines have as their centrepiece, among other negative injunctions, the dream she is told not to have, presented with commanding immediacy in a feminine voice intended as hers. The dream is a powerful warning to her against morbid imagining; to him it may be something else.

---

[4] Citations are from *The Elegies and The Songs and Sonnets*, edited by Helen Gardner (Oxford, 1965).

Throughout, the speaker's identity is constant, but after the introductory passage his deepest feelings break the surface in brief moments that do not clarify the purpose of their emergence. Expressions that seem to pause or stray from their context, as the religious intimations of a last 'strange and fatall interview', create a kind of crosscurrent that affects the assurance of his argument, of that 'masculine persuasive force' directed at her. Yet these expressions nevertheless do reinforce the central position of a speaker professing his love and dependence upon her; they murmur love's assurance at a deeper level that cannot be declared, the weight of his own distress reaching towards her while saying other things. They provide the punctuation of religious assurance, marking an ultimate comfort before and beyond the imminent realities of travel. Her presence in England strengthens his will to return, and 'oh, if thou dye before, | From other lands my soule towards thee shall soare'. England like other places, but for her more fitting, is only a 'gallerie'

> To walk in expectation, till from thence
> Our greate King call thee into his presence.

The perils of staying and going, and the deeper shadows in which the fact of human helplessness is ever present, threaten lovers and can be noticed, but are not to be discussed. The final couplet echoes the real possibility of separation by death:

> Augure mee better chance, except dreade Jove
> Think it enough for mee, to'have had thy love.

This concluding gesture of conditional resignation does not blur his identity as lover, but it exposes an uncertainty and personal appeal under the 'masculine' persuasion. It is a rare moment in early Donne, that of using himself in circumstances which represent general helplessness and provide an exit line left open against the organized forcefulness and containment of what has been written. It resembles in part the ending of 'A Valediction: of my Name in the Window':

> Neere death inflicts this lethargie,
> And this I murmure in my sleepe;
> Impute this idle talke, to that I goe,
> For dying men talke often so.

In Elegy ix (Grierson), 'The Autumnall', the poet takes up the proposition that the best beauty in women is that of the autumn years. His argument pretends to be general, though the 'one *Autumnall* face' of the second line sounds more like sudden conviction than the citation of evidence. Yet the person for whom we think the argument is made remains to one side, veiled in 'here', 'this', and 'her', but she is permitted to read her character in the diplomatic wit of the poet, and how he 'acts', and in what he expects her own wit to understand. As in the preceding example, the speaker is the poet himself, but what he says involves his own 'acting', to convince the lady of the most important truth of his personal admiration.

The praise that celebrates autumnal beauty shows that it can rise above the obvious difficulties of the theme to say some things of superior resonance, as 'Here where still Evening is; not noone, nor night', and the delicately mocking grace of the last lines:

> may still
> My love descend, and journey down the hill,
> Not panting after growing beauties, so,
> I shall ebbe on with them, who home-ward goe.

But the main body of the poem is an expectable succession of hyperboles and witty inventions intended more to amuse than convince. Also expectable is the introduction of difficulties to be surmounted, but Donne turns these in his own way, as if they were the uncompromising evidence of sincerity to vouch for the easier hyperboles. The wrinkles of middle age do not go unregarded, but they are ostentatiously transformed by the cosmetic imagination. On the other hand, the 'Winter-faces' must not even be named, though unsparingly described for several lines by hyperboles drawn from a quite different exchequer: 'Name not these living Deaths-heads unto mee'. Only spring and summer comparisons are to be admitted, except in the final lines, which now assimilate the flow of time into the praise, after having carefully made previous items depend on the implicit arresting of time.

In the steady succession of witty turns Donne manages to introduce a different movement, of more extended illustrative points, and a shift in tone. These come after the joke that wine in June 'enrages blood' but 'comes seasonabliest, when our tast | And appetite to other things, is past'. The blood of later years will be not enraged but pleasingly warmed for 'other things', and the veiled phrasing, after the extended bridge of speculation on why the Lydian Platan tree was loved, becomes less polite and more 'liberal': if the tree *were* young then its youth was blessed 'with ages glory, Barren-nesse' (Mrs Herbert had ten children by her first husband). After this the lady is treated to the relatively long tirade that excludes 'Winter-faces', in which the poet is acting the part of one who protests too much, as he produces hyperboles that suggest he may owe as much to personal revulsion as to wit.

The poem is a minor but useful example of Donne creating parts and voices for a character not acknowledged to be present, and the satire on 'Winter-faces' mocks the speaker, whatever else it does. At this point, having looked at two poems in which the poet is the ostensible speaker expounding his theme from a definite position (within the compass of which he can still create some flexibility of movement), we are almost ready to take up Satire III, which differs from its companions and may be illustrated by the example of our two elegies. First, however, I want to comment on another poem, a verse letter to a man, his good friend Sir Henry Wotton.

'Sir, more then kisses, letters mingle Soules' turns quickly to its theme, that life is a voyage and that we cannot avoid the dangers and defilement represented by the country, the court, and the town. What shall we do? Freely-moving analytical descriptions put aside arctic and tropical regions to arrive at the temperate zone and then the 'knottie riddle' that each possible choice is worst equally. By now geography has been centred in man himself, and a new image of the first chaos reinforces the 'riddle' as it begins a new range of exploratory analysis. The development is free, neither strictly ordered nor digressive, illustrating the conditions and human consequences of choice of place, and ending with a summary judgement:

> I thinke if men, which in these places live
> Durst looke for themselves, and themselves, retrive,
> They would like strangers greet themselves, seeing then
> Utopian youth, growne old Italian.   (l.43)[5]

That pessimistic judgement brings the choice of place to a dead end and is transitional to the way out of the problem. The answers are illustrated by images that summarize well-known arguments; they mean: know yourself, be content, make the hard right choice, do not compromise, avoid the cure of adding 'correctives', simply 'purge the bad'. The prescription contains other items, however, which are less easily transcribed from the honoured advice of moral traditions. They involve the necessity of moving in the right way while standing still in the right way ('continuance maketh hell'), both 'closely':

> Bee thine owne Palace, or the world's thy Gaole.
> And in the worlds sea, do not like corke sleepe
> Upon the waters face; nor in the deepe
> Sinke like a lead without a line: but as
> Fishes glide, leaving no print where they passe,
> Nor making sound, so, closely thy course goe;
> Let men dispute, whether thou breathe, or no.

The images return to the 'worlds sea' (on a deliberately small scale), and the wrong extremes of the earlier frigid and tropical zones are remembered by the rejected examples of cork or lead. The disabilities of the temperate zones, and their choice of country, court, town, are replaced by the world of water; there the emblematic fish and their self-contained movements, inaudible, and leaving no trace, furnish an example of undefiled life in, but not of, the world.

Still, what the concealment really means and does will not be stated, nor what for human beings the practical equivalent of water might be. This truth is not like that in Satire III. It has not been reached by the determined efforts of open ascension; it is not plainly there on a hill for anyone to see but has been discovered as an alternative to prominent realities which cannot change their nature. This truth is retrieved by a kind of rescue operation, that of turning to a power within human nature, and is attained through a

---

[5] *The Satires, Epigrams and Verse Letters*, edited by W. Milgate (Oxford, 1967).

state of 'brave' inconspicuousness. It is not an answer of energetically willed movement but of minimal, self-contained, self-directed movement, separate not social, creating an internal environment as answer to the insoluble problems of choosing an external environment. Does Donne or Wotton yearn for the freedom of ideal inconspicuousness, or is that answer a side-glance at a familiar affectation, or recurring impulse, of men busy at getting on in the world, their lack of privacy not in their own command but part of the cost of enjoying a position; and a side-glance at rivals and spies and the practical need of meeting certain external dangers by being as inconspicuous as possible?

Donne is pleasing a friend, overcoming 'absence' and 'the tediousnesse of my life' by writing a letter. Otherwise, as he begins by saying, 'I could ideate nothing'. Letters may be written in actual or willed solitude, but the other person is felt to be present, the anticipated listener to a monologue imagined as conversation. So too there may be silences and gaps which will also be understood, and other privileges in the communications between friends. Donne is in addition tacitly entering a kind of communal enterprise, making his contribution to a set question concerning human choice.[6] His own identity is fixed and single, sealed by the rhyming signature and by the identity of the person addressed. The problem he engages in the main body of the letter, and his chosen ways in and out of the problem, present no dramatic persona. Instead, the speaker is one thinking-and-feeling person who is an image of the poet as he writes, and yet not to be mistaken for an unposed picture of the man in his ordinary affairs of daily life. Except for the opening and conclusion, 'I' appears only once, the 'I thinke' which tells what 'Utopian youth' may discover. Who would wish to receive this as a remark of personal opinion that may compliment the 'I' and 'you' of an elevated private conversation? I believe Wotton would read as we may read, and see that the friend writing rises to the great possibility of the period, and speaking as inspired poet creates a momentous parable.

The concluding lines are all praise, attributing the lessons just 'said over' as ones learned from Wotton himself, 'whom . . . I throughly love'. If these are at all echoes from the live talk between friends, Wotton will recognize them, part of what has been written must then remain an entirely personal message, unless other friends have heard or will hear the same things from Wotton, or he chooses to explicate parts of the poem to others. But in any case the life of the example held up to view is that of the actual man whose 'actions are authors', the sentence Donne wrote for Edward Herbert.[7] Wotton has travelled in Germany, France, and Italy (in 'Countries, Courts, Towns'), 'And brought home that faith, which you carried forth'. He has been able simply to 'purge the bad', to 'dwell' in himself like the snail, and

[6] See Milgate's note, pp. 225–26.
[7] 'To Sir Edward Herbert, at Julyers', l. 49.

like gliding fishes keep his own course 'closely'. Wotton illustrates what in its context of Satire III may sound like an elliptical precept: 'Keep the truth which thou has found.' The 'truth', like Wotton's 'faith', is religious but also represents, at least in the Wotton Donne knew, an essential integrity of life. We may find the useful comment when Walton retells what John Hales reported of Wotton's conversation shortly before his death: 'In this voyage I have oft met with . . . many troubles of mind and temptations to evil. And yet, though I have been and am a man compass'd about with humane frailties, Almighty God hath by his grace prevented me from making shipwreck of faith and a good Conscience.'[8]

Though the speaker of Satire III does not declare his identity, trusted readers (like Wotton) would certainly have recognized the autobiographical resemblances to the serious young man who could not ask his own father about truth and, unlike Wotton, did not have a settled religious faith to carry forth and bring home, but had to seek. The voyage in search will not discover a hard truth realized by such conditions as dwelling within oneself, so that all other residence is indifferent: the kind a wise traveller makes the best of, a truth by which the select few may govern their lives. The seeking is itself now part of a common truth available to all, as it is not in the letter to Wotton, and the dwelling is the true church, never named. Though the best decision will seem to involve some inevitable compromise between the visible militant church and the triumphant church in heaven, yet the accepted necessity of seeking shows the mark already there of a conscientious reformist, an individual who is intent on discriminating between good and bad in his own reason and motives. The development is changeable, as in the other satires, with a long introduction, passages of swift mobility, extreme compression, and easy expansion, but the momentum and purpose of the argument are sustained. The style accommodates a passionate seeker, identifying himself with a cause and yet not less able to command the satirist's privilege of standing back to describe and 'purge the bad'.

In the letter to Wotton, the hard-eyed critical examination of the human scene is more tightly drawn, but both poems share the same cold view of what is presented to be rejected. As the problem of the letter is engaged, there is no place for any sense of optimistic warmth until it is time for the answers; then the imperatives of advice have a more personal speaker behind them, but full warmth is reserved for the final praise of Wotton, whose personal life demonstrates that the solving answers are indeed possible. In contrast, the satire is often personal in its language. Some of the answers are presented as near and easy, and the speaker sympathetically tries to encourage other seekers even when he calls them 'Foole and wretch'. Though his questions roughly expose the folly and vice they challenge, these are questions that

---

[8] *Lives*, The World's Classics (London, 1927), p. 149.

point towards answers helpful to the ignorant and misled, and the direct advice conveys a sense of personal relationship between speaker and listener: 'aske thy father . . . beleeve mee this . . . doubt wisely . . . Yet strive so, that . . . Thy Soule rest . . . . Keepe the truth which thou has found'. Indeed, as the speaker gives advice he often sounds less like one who is in full possession of the answers he administers than like one who is also describing and encouraging himself.

In the letter to Wotton the issue of where and how to live in the world is rigorously driven to a narrow opening for which there is not direct preparation, but the effective rigour of the argument at last depends on an implied prior acceptance, that of an underlying desire to know the world and to act as well as possible in it. That desire is never directly challenged and purged, though even Wotton may have experienced his doubts, as the evidence that leads towards a standard rejection of the world took shape. Since the third satire confronts the problems of seeking true religion, and the governing purpose must be individual salvation, the difficulties and the answer will be different. Wotton is a rare hero but a secular one. Admiring friends might choose to 'dispute', conscious of the hyperbole and its philosophical and religious references to the good life and the good death, 'whether thou breathe, or no'. But religious trepidation and holy fear are excluded from the controlling wisdom which proves itself by the right kind of self-government, rejection, and internalizing.

In the third satire there are many things to be rejected: everything included in knowing and fearing the world, the flesh, and the devil, and what they represent. The world gets most obvious attention: 'mans lawes' when preferred to God's in a corruption of the ancient 'earths honour', or the deception, when God's laws are accepted under the sponsorship of the secondary laws of habit and custom, or when the authority of kings and theologians is passively followed in matters that concern the soul's own salvation. Choosing the true church is beset by the interference of laws and customs, and by the external conditions of historical time and place, as well as by the superficial vagaries of human taste and reasoning.

As we receive the answers of salvation, however, there are difficulties that cannot be handled with the robust assurance of intellectual detachment that examines and solves the set problems in the letter to Wotton. The goal of salvation is understood to be certain, the external enemies are clearly describable, the defence of doubt is plain and dignified, but the process of attaining the goal, by seeking, doubting, striving, keeping, is less clear in itself than in its necessary conflict with the forces that would deflect it. There are abrupt turns, and open unnegotiated places in the discourse, and these are further perplexed by the varying degrees to which the speaker himself seems to enter and act in what he says, not assuming an unmoved station or formal mask for presenting the issues, but expressing the doubts, hopes, and convictions with a sense of personal urgency. Do we trust the argument, as

Donne elsewhere advises, or the speaker adding his own testimony?[9] For the act of crucial choice is to be made under conditions of rational objectivity:

> but unmoved thou
> Of force must one, and forc'd but one allow;
> And the right.

Salvation is related to the right choice for the right reasons, without agitating other fine questions on the subject. There is no admitted option of piecing together one's own church, and since there is no authorized divine permission to do so, the laws and customs of time, place, and power (those external agents resisted and ridiculed elsewhere) combine to enforce one side of the necessity of choice. Is the argument making a tactical retreat, or is the poet weaving the ironies that show him 'unmoved' in his understanding while forced to obey combinations of power that do not singly stay within their proper 'bounds', and are too intricate for purging all that may be bad, though one can take a stand against the worst?

The choice of how one is to live one's earthly life and prepare one's spiritual life cannot be made in ignorance of the effects and the causes of choosing. If one is personally obliged to take action, it would be an affected extravagance of wit to say that every church is worst equally. If he has found the truth he must keep it; he cannot do the same with his doubt. Asking one's father is a suggestive act of faith, and a philosophical judgement on the existence and on the attributes of a first cause; there is no surviving primitive church, but classical and modern scepticism offered advice on accepting the practical compromises with time, place, and power. Furthermore, there are the scriptural precepts and experiential knowledge concerning the human 'bounds' imposed by time and death. Even to will comes short of the required assent of spiritual action: 'therefore now doe'. The speaker understands and dissociates himself from the common faults that lie in premature action, but he must accept his own 'bounds' (not part of the discussion) for the time that can be allotted to doubting wisely.

The concluding extended image summarizes the issue in so far as it concerns making the right choice and resisting the excesses of power and its human agents:

> As streames are, Power is; those blest flowers that dwell
> At the rough streames calme head, thrive and prove well,
> But having left their roots, and themselves given
> To the streames tyrannous rage, alas, are driven
> Through mills, and rocks, and woods; 'and at last, almost
> Consum'd in going, in the sea are lost.[10]

---

[9] *Biathanatos*, p. 19.
[10] Milgate, l. 103. The final couplet adds a comment which affects both the image and the passage from line 89: 'So perish Soules, which more chuse mens unjust | Power from God claym'd, then God himselfe to trust'.

The 'blest flowers' are the happy souls that dwell in true religion, at the 'calme head' of the source of all power. But what the flowers can 'now doe' is limited by the 'Similitudinarie Reasons' of the image. They cannot dwell and move, like the snail of the letter to Wotton, or 'glide . . . closely' like the fishes, or live and act with integrity. They are more like souls in the heavenly paradise than the striving souls with whom Donne appears to identify his own seeking. If the rough stream symbolizes no other connexion with the 'worlds sea' than the 'tyrannous rage' of human power, then God and the 'blest flowers' can dwell only at the calm source; just power derived from God cannot venture into the secular stream, and the good have no place to go in the living world, and no good to do for themselves or others. They are released from the human necessity (and choice) of acting.

The brilliant singlemindedness of the image resembles the spirit of the argument that until it turned found countries, courts, towns, and the little world represented by man all corrupt and corrupting, and seemed to lead to the traditional answer of rejecting the deceptions of the world by rejecting the world. In conclusion Donne resumes one authentic voice of the satirist and scourges the kind of life that depends upon the favour of kings and their favourites. That life provides an ever-shining mark for God and man; one knows the names and histories of the successful victims. Yet those who manage to stay close to the source while it is calm, or who are knowing and lucky in mastering the destructive currents, may be thought by others and by themselves to 'thrive and prove well'. It is an angry image and carries the emphasis, or judgement, or unrestrained feeling of a last word. It says less than the larger argument of the poem, but in its allegorical movements admits more than the image proposes.

As for the poet himself, he knew the problems of the subject and knew how to arrive at more than one answer. He will praise the model of Wotton's life, but the way that triumph emerges from the threats enclosing moral existence (not to mention political existence in the last years of Elizabeth's reign) singles out the heroic achievement that may still suggest a resemblance to the personal escape.[11] If purging the bad should prove insufficient, the final remedy would still have in reserve the old prescription of rejecting the world and the withdrawal to the assurance of nothing but religious faith. Wotton served King James honourably in the courts, theatres, and undersea world of diplomacy, did well and less well, and retired to his final post at Eton with some trouble of conscience and a damaged estate caused by the King's unpaid debts. Ben Jonson is said, in the conversations Drummond took notes on, to have had 'by heart' Wotton's poem on 'The Character of a Happy Life', and Wotton wrote, when Somerset fell from favour: 'Learn to swim and not to wade | For the hearts of kings are deep.'

---

[11] Wotton's poem, 'The Character of a Happy Life', arranges both active and defensive virtues to define the happy life as the possession of personal freedom and the command of one's desires, but it pays its respect to the good fortune of 'having nothing' which may attract false friends or powerful enemies.

As for Donne, he will not settle his own life by the kind of eloquent decisiveness which a satiric voice can produce. Even as he wrote Satire III he aspired to an honourable career under the sponsorship of secular power. He knew enough of what Wotton knew, and could imagine the rest, and the alternatives. He also commanded the eloquent anger and the privileged voice of a satiric outsider.

I now turn to some brief consideration of satiric voice and what it represents in the religious prose. My starting point will be the familiar observation that Dr Donne writes as a 'conservative' insider who has accepted the many obligations of his position in the Church of England. The man writing the *Devotions upon Emergent Occasions*, making a book of his anticipated death, is the author and actor staging himself as he writes. He exhibits a remarkable freedom to move within a fixed position, circumscribed by faith and doctrine and by the ruling phenomena expected to attend one who may, or possibly may not, be dying. Thus he can turn around the passionate human cry: why to me, why not to someone else?

We scarce heare of any man *preferred*, but wee thinke of our selves, that wee might very well have beene that *Man*; Why might not I have beene that *Man*, that is carried to his *grave* now? Could I fit my selfe, to *stand*, or *sit* in any Mans *place*, and not to lie in any mans *grave*? I may lacke much of the *good parts* of the meanest, but I lack nothing of the *mortality* of the weakest; They may have acquired better *abilities* than I, but I was borne to as many *infirmities* as they. To be an *incumbent* by lying down in a *grave*, to be a *Doctor* by teaching *Mortification* by *Example*, by *dying*, though I may have *seniors*, others may be *elder* than I, yet I have proceeded apace in a good *University*, and gone a great way in a little time, by the furtherance of a vehement *fever*; and whomsoever these *Bells* bring to the ground to day, if hee and I had beene compared yesterday, perchance I should have been thought likelier to come to this preferment, then, than he.[12]

Like gallows humour at its best, the performance is playing to the audience that will be there to savour the precarious relish. The author is speaking in his own person, but that person is responding to the special constrictions and liberties of one who is ready to leave and is practising his farewells to life, enjoying the unique privilege of saying what only one in his position can say with such convincing and unsettling authority. Even the common deliberateness of some of the wit, uncharacteristic of Donne, exploits with a sure hand what a public audience will most want, and while the moment of drama lasts even those individuals of refined taste and judgement may find themselves feeling what their unseen neighbours feel. The author is speaking in his own person, but his mind is playing and is like a persona, one that shows no signs of understanding its real intention, that of preparing to leave this interlude and all the prominently displayed opportunities of the position and its moment. In the following Devotion Donne will

---

[12] Meditation 16. I quote from Anthony Raspa's edition of *Devotions upon Emergent Occasions* (Montreal and London, 1975), pp. 82–83.

welcome the answer from without (reality untainted by any suspicion of his own mental collaboration), and in responding to his own condition in another man's he spontaneously turns from himself to pray for the soul of his unknown dying neighbour. In the act he is indeed loving his neighbour as himself, and the self is different, not reduced but transformed. (To trundle forward some heavy wit of my own: I call attention to that mental triumph in the art of concealed self-containment and inconspicuousness, the emblematic fish of the letter to Wotton.)

Looked at so, the example quickly goes beyond the usual purposes of satire, but I mean chiefly to illustrate the points of similarity in Donne's resourceful uses of self and persona, and the differences when the voice is that of an *insider* who speaks from a fixed position, not to intimates but to others who have a common share in what is being ridiculed or affirmed.

Another instance to consider is one written before Donne took orders; he is writing as a polemicist but an extraordinary one, whose position does not prevent some intricate satirical charity and some touches of personal identification with the case he is dismantling:

And it falls out very often, that some one Father, of strong reputation and authority in his time, doth snatch and swallow some probable interpretation of Scripture: and then digesting it into his Homilies, and applying it in dehortations, and encouragements, as the occasions and diseases of his Auditory, or his age require, and imagining thereupon delightfull and figurative insinuations, and setting it to the Musique of his stile, (as every man which is accustomed to these Meditations, shall often finde in himselfe such a spirituall wantonnesse, and devout straying into such delicacies), that sense which was but probable, growes necessary, and those who succeed, had rather enjoyed his wit, then vexe their owne; as often times we are loathe to change or leave off a counterfeit stone, by reason of the well setting thereof. (*Biathanatos*, pp. 206–07)

He describes the probable genesis of 'some probable interpretation of Scripture', mixing the styles of fable, history, and parable. 'And it falls out very often' becomes a story of once upon a time. But the unspecified time and person are historicized by the Father's 'authority in his time' and by his individual response to special needs, the spiritual 'diseases' of his congregation 'or his age'. The circumstances are like the fact of one specific time to the Father; as presented, they are recognizable as often recurring, and therefore the example might seem to reflect a general law of history. The issue, however, is that of an 'interpretation of Scripture', and the Father's response to special needs outside himself is reported in a neutral voice that expresses no judgement of the accuracy of these facts. What is clear and emphatic is that the Father, moved by the urgency of personal desire, takes and applies the opportunity offered by the external circumstances. That which was 'but probable, growes necessary', and others may read in the parable their own inclinations when they meditate and write or when they read what they enjoy. Aesthetic delight, though believed to be authorized by the Holy Ghost in Scripture, is not immune to habitual distrust elsewhere; examples of inspired human piety notwithstanding, any opponent who writes very well may be charged, in a style calculated to embarrass, with 'spirituall wantonness, and devout straying into such delicacies'.

It follows that secular writing is not less subject to the deceptions wrought by human responses to beauty and expressiveness. One may observe too much put in or left out, as in the case of a probable image that becomes necessary when it interprets power at the end of Satire III. The critic and the writer are not the same person at the same time, and the meeting of external and internal influences is not always clearly separable and identifiable in one's own story. Here, while mocking and exposing as if he stands outside, Donne also draws on his own experience in imagining. One may ask: does the story he tells bear any prophetic resemblances to the individual formation and growth of certain favourite points of emphasis he will keep returning to in the pulpit? He seems to have an eye on his own ways of thinking in images that precede and may seem to dominate the turns of thought. His justly famous eloquence can do many things, and among them, especially in prose, can set a line of thought 'to the Musique of his stile'.

It is the engagement of the narrator in what he says that changes his dominant position as critical observer. On the one hand, he tells the story and the process of development in ways that clearly expose and invalidate the sequence, but the voice that presents matters with the resolute objectivity of a satiric outsider does not remain critical and distant; it moves into the account as well. For this is no simple folly or vice. A good man is carried away by his own good intentions and by abilities which are part of his natural endowment, but as one sincerely dedicated to God's service his endowment cannot be ascribed to nature alone and condemned as perverse. Nor can his response to a probable present urgency be condemned. The Father speaking and writing is susceptible to the errors of trusting his own experience, keeping the truth he has found, and sharing, to the best of his ability, his experience with others. The case is complex enough to represent as parable one kind of intellectual predicament, the unrecognized dilemma. To recreate the case while exposing the human susceptibilities, Donne invents a mimesis and enters into what he tells, creating the voice of a secret double who imitates, with some deliberate histrionics, Donne's own voice and consciousness. The mistaken Father and all who resemble him are part of a community of well-meaning sinners and otherwise imperfect men, and the satirist is also a member, though here a critical one.

When he himself needs to *act* in the service of God and man, he may put aside the finer questions of error and frankly counter one kind of dangerous present susceptibility with a desirable one deemed in need of being fortified (he does not hesitate to add practical 'Correctives' where it would not do simply to 'purge the bad'). One may hear him following happily in the steps of the mistaken Father, at least so far as to respond to his own judgement of the present condition of the age and to the 'diseases' of his own listeners:

I would always raise your hearts, and dilate your hearts, to a holy Joy, to a joy in the Holy Ghost. There may be a just feare, that men do not grieve enough for their sinnes; but there may bee a just jealousie, and suspition too, that they may fall into inordinate griefe, and diffidence of Gods mercy; And God hath reserved us to such times, as being the later times, give us even the dregs and lees of misery to drinke. For, God hath not onely let loose into the world a new spirituall disease; which is, an equality, and an indifferency, which religion our children, or our servants, or our companions professe . . . but God hath accompanied, and complicated almost all our bodily diseases of these times, with an extraordinary sadnesse, a predominant melancholy, a faintnesse of heart, a chearlessnesse, a joylesnesse of spirit, and therefore I returne often to this endeavor of raising your hearts, dilating your hearts with a holy Joy, Joy in the holy Ghost, for *Under the shadow of his wings*, you may, you should, *rejoyce*.[13]

In the pulpit Donne is a thoughtful master of the occasion, the time, the place, and the general character of the congregation he expected when he chose his text and prepared his sermon. He is acutely sensitive to the needs of his listeners and to the responses he intends to evoke, and to their placement in the discourse. At the same time, among other conflicts of interest and conscience he would need to reconcile, is the concept of his office as one that made him the narrator, secretary, and vicar of the word and spirit of God. In sermons, as he wrote to the Countess of Montgomery with the copy of a sermon she had requested, the 'Spirit of God that dictates them in the speaker or writer, and is present in his tongue or hand, meets himself again (as we meet our selves in a glass) in the eies and eares and hearts of the hearers and readers'. That spirit 'makes a writing and a speaking equall means to edification'. But Donne also wrote in the same letter, 'I know what dead carkasses things written are, in respect of things spoken' (*Sermons*, II, 179). He is an orator and spiritual guide who acts with a commitment to the primacy of the word spoken or imagined as spoken. He is conscious of the effects in the pulpit of his own voice, person, and character. He can also use his own authority as a sinner, though he does not dull the effect by overuse.[14]

As for satire, the Roman Church is usually good for 'holy scorne' and can furnish listeners with the respite of a diverting elation: which feeling Donne knows how to exercise and how to turn to a spiritual benefit.

We have not leasure to speake of the abuse of prayer in the Roman Church; where they wil antidate and postdate their prayers; Say to morrows prayers to day, and to dayes prayers to morrow, if they have other uses and employments of the due time

---

[13] *The Sermons of John Donne*, edited by G. R. Potter and E. M. Simpson, 10 vols (Berkeley, 1953–62), VII, 68–69.
[14] The basic position is that of a general understanding which Donne does not often dwell upon directly. For example, here is a direct statement: 'I preach but the sense of Gods indignation upon mine own soul, in a conscience of mine own sins, I impute nothing to another, that I confesse not of my selfe, I call none of you to confession to me, I doe but confesse my self to God, and you' (*Sermons*, II, 52–53). And another: 'I am in St. *Pauls quorum, quorum ego sum minimus*, the least of them that have been sent; and when I consider my infirmities, I am in his *quorum*, in another commission, another way, *Quorum ego maximus*; the greatest of them' (II, 248).

betweene; where they will trade, and make merchandise of prayers by way of exchange, My man shall fast for me, and I will pray for my man; or my Atturney, and Proxy shall pray for us both, at my charge; nay, where they will play for prayers, and the loser must pray for both.

The entertainment at the expense of distant enemies leads quickly to 'a sad consideration', the 'weaknesses of the strongest devotions in time of Prayer'. Donne offers himself in a memorable scene of one failing 'to make a Prayer a right Prayer':

I throw my selfe downe in my Chamber . . . I neglect God and his Angels, for the noise of a Flie, for the ratling of a Coach, for the whining of a doore; I talke on, in the same posture of praying; Eyes lifted up; knees bowed down. . . . A memory of yesterdays pleasures, a feare of to morrows dangers, a straw under my knee, a noise in mine eare, a light in mine eye, an any thing, a nothing, a fancy, a Chimera in my braine, troubles me in my prayer.   (*Sermons*, VII, 264–65)

The first sermon preached before King Charles was one that Donne plainly regarded as the challenge of a special opportunity. The sermon is a masterpiece of sustained diplomatic eloquence, spiritual 'edification' in harmony with conservative political philosophy, reassuring the new King, advising him with delicate indirectness, demonstrating allegiance by castigating declared enemies and clearly recognizable faults and by making law, obedience, faith, and peace the optimistic answer for the righteous. The Roman enemy from without is handled at unusual length as representative of real danger to the foundations of church, state, and family; the tone, however, is for the most part that of patient patriotic reasonableness.[15] The sharpest ridicule is reserved for traditional enemies within, suspicious dissatisfied citizens and public officials who do not serve the laws of the state with loyal disregard for other interests. It is proper to suspect the motives of one's own actions, but citizens who busy themselves with the actions of their superiors, which lie beyond their compass of understanding, will lose their personal peace and turn trifles into extravagant rumours of corruption and destruction. If 'I know not why it is done', it is like applying the ignorant answer of *witchcraft* 'to thinke it is done for *Money*'. On the other hand, 'if the *Magistrate* stops his Eares with *Wooll*, (with staple bribes, profitable bribes) and with *Cyvet* in his wooll, (perfumes of pleasure and preferment in his bribes) . . . . so must wee ever exhort the *Magistrate*, That hee would plucke

---

[15] Donne was quite aware of the political 'bounds' of satire against the Roman Church, and when some kinds of emphasis would be undiplomatic. James was intent on the policy of a Spanish marriage and Charles was to marry a French princess. In a long personal (but tactful) letter to Sir Thomas Roe, Donne enclosed a sermon preached and printed by order of King James. He would have liked to enclose another, in which 'I was left more to mine owne liberty', but this would have been 'Indiscretion', for the copy 'is as yet in his Majesties hand, and, I know not whether he will . . . command it to be printed' (apparently he did not). As for the Spanish business: 'many men, measuringe publique actions, with private affections, have been scandalized and have admitted suspicions of a tepidnes in very high places. Some civill acts, in favor of the Papists, have been with some precipitation over-dangerously mis-applyed too . . . I know to be sory for some things that are donne, (that is, sorry that our tymes are overtaken with a necessity to do them) proceeds of true zeale; but to conclude the worst upon the first degree of ill, is a distillinge with too hot a fire' (*Complete Poetry and Selected Prose*, edited by John Hayward (London, 1929), p. 477).

his hand out of his pocket, and forget what is there, and execute the Lawes committed to him' (*Sermons*, VI, 259, 244–45).

Donne delivered many 'occasional' sermons and they reflect serious efforts, but his general view, often repeated, is disapproving. The basis of his criticism is such that he could not have simply ignored his own hard judgement. I assume that he needed to reconcile his actions to himself, and could do so, by drawing upon those reasons which harmonize the complex obligations of a public position of spiritual leadership. For instance, there is the kind of charity, invoked in the sermon to Charles, which maintains peace within the family, 'though not by an exquisite performing of all duties, yet by a mutuall support of one anothers infirmities'.[16] I quote an impressive judgement on the dangers that may be inferred from the practice of occasional sermons, and this is from the sermon Donne delivered, by invitation, to a meeting of the Virginia Company:

Birds that are kept in cages may learne some Notes, which they should never have sung in the Woods or Fields; but yet they may forget their naturall Notes too. *Preachers* that binde themselves alwaies to *Cities* and *Courts*, and *great Auditories*, may learne new Notes; they may become *occasionall* Preachers, and make the emergent affaires of the time, their *Text*, and the humors of the hearers their *Bible*; but they may loose their Naturall Notes, both the *simplicitie*, and the *boldnesse* that belongs to the Preaching of the *Gospell*: both their power upon lowe understandings to raise them, and upon high affections to humble them. They may thinke that their errand is but to knocke at the doore, to delight the eare, and not to search the House, to ransacke the conscience.   (*Sermons*, IV, 276–77)

The sermon follows a lavish banquet, but the financial and other news is bad. Donne does not choose to 'ransacke the conscience', but he does not ignore 'the emergent affaires of the time'; he preaches the sustained high message of his text, but with brief glances, tactful, dignified, and encouraging, to raise and humble their religious, social, and financial hopes in the colonial enterprise. The 'diseases' of this auditory are well ministered to. In the words of an early sermon, the preacher becomes

Carmen musicum, a musical and harmonious charmer, to settle and compose the soul again in a reposed confidence, and in a delight in God . . . he shall have a pleasant voice, that is, to preach first sincerely (for a preaching to serve turns and humors, cannot, at least should not please any) but then it is to preach acceptably, seasonably, with a spiritual delight, to a discreet and rectified congregation, that by way of such a holy delight, they may receive the more profit.   (*Sermons*, II, 166–67)[17]

---

[16] *Sermons*, VI, 255. On the other hand, 'there is no *Peace* where there is no *Obedience*' (p. 254), and '*Obedience* to lawfull Authoritie, is alwayes an *Essentiall* part of Religion' (p. 258). Reasons of state may also prudently advise and reinforce the charity due all members of a family: 'As *States* subsist in part, by keeping their weakenesses from being known, so it is the quiet of *Families*, to have their *Chauncerie*, and their *Parliament* within doores, and to compose and determine all emergent differences there' (p. 259).
[17] The description seems to fit his sermon to the Virginia Company better than his declaration there of 'the *simplicitie*, and the *boldnesse* that belongs to the Preaching of the *Gospell*'. One may admire the sermon, as I do, and yet think the boldness there in part belongs to another school, as when he ends by explaining how an old oratorical device worked and the 'contrary way' he has taken: 'all this while [I] have seem'd to tell you what should be done by you, I have, indeed but told the Congregation what hath beene done already . . . do still, as you have done hitherto' (*Sermons*, IV, 281).

'And in this voice they [preachers] are *musicum carmen*, a love-song . . . in proposing the love of God to man.' In another voice they are 'a Trumpet, to awaken with terror', to sound the alarm, the battle (with ourselves, the world, 'with powers and principalities, yea into a wrastling with God himself and his Justice'), but also to sound 'the Parle . . . and so to come to treaties and capitulations for peace', and thus to the voice of the 'love-song' (*Sermons*, II, 166, 169–70).

In another early sermon Donne delivers the 'Rule' that God 'employs' the common and particular 'affections' of those who serve him. St Paul, 'who had been so vehement a persecutor, had ever his thoughts exercised upon that . . . he suffers most, he makes most mention of his suffering of any of the Apostles'. And Solomon, 'whose disposition was amorous . . . conveyes all his loving approaches and applications to God, and all Gods gracious answers to his amorous soul, into songs, and Epithalamions, and meditations upon contracts, and marriages' (*Sermons*, I, 237). Donne put his early career behind him, but not all his 'affections', which God could employ. He was not 'a bitter and satyricall preacher', like the Jeremiah he freely interprets as a man who finds himself to be a trumpet voice preaching 'heavy Doctrin, and therfore his Auditory hated him' (*Sermons*, II, 52–53). Among Donne's 'affections' were those of the satirist, and the amorous disposition of the love poet, and he could mingle both strains in the love song of a poem. As a preacher he has both more and much less liberty (under God, church, and state) in the use of his 'affections'. The satiric voice has limited but still frequent and interesting employment.

The sinner speaking for himself to God commands an art and resources not suitable to the satirist, but the voice is one which speaks out most distinctively only in certain of Donne's religious poems. There, poet, narrator, and persona represent levels of consciousness in the tripartite soul of a religious supplicant. In the sermons he is a representative sinner at work, committed to the 'edification' and good of his listeners. Even when he speaks with the voice of 'a Trumpet, to awaken with terror' or 'to ransacke the conscience', that voice will not extend beyond its episodic function. Whatever his personal dissatisfactions and anxieties, which will also find their moments of expression, Donne assumes that he addresses, even while he is purging and shaping it, 'a discreet and rectified congregation' whom he may best serve by preaching 'acceptably, seasonably'. In addition to his spiritual gifts and discipline, he has the trained genius of a great orator, diplomat, and poet able to work with and within the laws of his art. Under James and Charles he is a master of 'discretion', a virtue that grows and comes to embrace a number of related values in his judgement.

To conclude: I have chosen to emphasize a few of the limiting complications of the preacher as satirist, and I have suggested that there are some new advantages as well. There is much more to be said on the subject, as, for instance: Donne's own ways of trumpeting 'heavy Doctrin'; the decorum with which he touches live issues of the day without engaging them too far; his use of the ability to produce the cutting expressions than can separate a congregation into individual sinners; his art of rational ridicule, as of 'others' and their folly, to elevate self-esteem in order to bring it down with a bruise worth remembering; his art of exact observations and of making brief scenes that enliven and vary the discourse for the moment, but will bring home to the listener the sense, comparative and transferable, that the concrete matters he smiles at are less real than the moral and spiritual issues they punctuate.

The Art of Violence in Rochester's Satire

KEN ROBINSON

University of Newcastle upon Tyne

Rochester's poetry is often violent. Its iconoclasm preys upon traditions and expectations, reducing the fair Chloris of pastoral idealism to a masturbating pig-girl or the brave Greeks at the seige of Troy to sexual aggressors. And it shatters the dictates of social nicety by mentioning the unmentionable, be it premature ejaculation, a smock soiled with excrement, or a penis smoking with menstrual blood. This iconoclasm is not gratuitous. In the lyric 'By all love's soft, yet mighty powers', for example, it sets in motion a controlled collision of pragmatism and idealism in which a materialistic acceptance of the world as it is jostles uneasily with idealistic disillusionment. It is both a piece of common-sensical advice to 'take to cleanly sinning' with the aid of 'paper . . . behind | And spunges for before' and an outcry that 'Love has pitched his mansion in | The place of excrement'. The repulsion is not explicit — there is no outburst of 'Celia shits'; it is felt in the texture of the phrases 'fuck in time of flowers' and 'smock beshit' which disturb the mellifluous calm of their stanza:

> By all love's soft, yet mighty powers,
>   It is a thing unfit
> That men should fuck in time of flowers,
>   Or when the smock's beshit,

and in the fractured idealism of the beginning of the second stanza: 'Fair nasty nymph, be clean and kind.'[1] This witty parody of an earlier and more romantic tradition's praise of cruelly fair mistresses both depreciates Phyllis's standards of hygiene and casts a longing eye at a conception of woman in which foul linen is inconceivable.

Such iconoclastic recoil does not present itself as tortured. Rochester's poem is 'mannerly obscene', not because like Sedley's wit it 'can stir nature up by springs unseen | And without forcing blushes, warm the Queen', but because its violence is wittily contained.[2] Its dismay at woman's bodily processes is at least partially offset by the note of pragmatism, and kept in check by the poem's pervasive irony. But for all the lyric's control, the violence is not neutralized. 'By all love's soft, yet mighty powers' shares with much of Rochester's poetry a kaleidoscopic effect which establishes one tone

---

[1] *The Complete Poems of John Wilmot, Earl of Rochester*, edited by David Vieth (New Haven, Connecticut, 1968), p. 139. All quotations from Rochester's poetry are from this edition, with page numbers cited.
[2] 'An Allusion to Horace', p. 123.

only to shift suddenly to another and another. It encourages the reader to expect a mild complaint within the conventions of romantic poetry only to modulate to violent distaste and then to a more constructive tone, and so on. Often the *coup de grâce* of the effect comes when the poem's apparent note of completion is undermined, leaving the reader with competing perspectives which the poem as a whole does not resolve but holds in suspension. In 'By all love's soft, yet mighty powers' the teasing ambivalence of 'fresh' in the final stanza hints that there might be some question about the male speaker's own 'spotless flames':

> If thou wouldst have me true, be wise
> And take to cleanly sinning;
> None but fresh lovers' pricks can rise
> At Phyllis in foul linen. (p. 139)

In 'Grecian Kindness' a tone of masculine brutality is similarly disrupted when the Greeks unexpectedly display compassion, lulling their punks asleep. Whether such subversion operates or not, the kaleidoscopic variations in mood yield a controlled instability of tone which allows violent elements in the poetry (like the repulsion of 'By all love's soft, yet mighty powers') to retain their potency. By contrast, the cruelty of Dryden's famous lines on Shaftesbury and his son in *Absalom and Achitophel*,

> Got, while his Soul did hudled Notions try;
> And born a shapeless Lump, like Anarchy,

is subservient to the poem's dominant reasonableness.[3] If the mask of urbanity slips in these lines, the effect is calculated and momentary. Once the reader has been allowed to glimpse the strength of feeling that the mask conceals, balance is restored. The ferment of Rochester's violence can make the artistic control of a poem seem precarious. When Sir Carr Scroope is attacked in terms similar to Dryden's,

> A lump deformed and shapeless wert thou born,
> Begot in love's despite and nature's scorn,

the succeeding lines do not domesticate the portrait's vehemence.[4] They offer to turn it to comic advantage but leave a residual violence so strong that it seems to defy efforts to contain it. The poetry derives a peculiar strength from wit under stress.

It may seem odd to begin a paper on Rochester's satire by discussing one of his lyrics (albeit a lyric that approaches satire), but it is a convenient way to stress at the outset that violence is not the sole province of the satires, and to focus the fragile relationship that exists in the satires with which this paper will be especially concerned: between violence or cruelty on one side and rational and artistic restraint on the other. I shall deal not with the witty

---

[3] *The Poems of John Dryden*, edited by James Kinsley, 4 vols (Oxford, 1958), I, 221.
[4] 'On the Supposed Author of a Late Poem in Defence of Satyr', p. 133.

conversational venom of 'An Allusion to Horace' and 'A Letter from Artemesia in the Town to Chloe in the Country', in which reputations die at every word, but with the less temperate instances of satiric cruelty in Rochester's work, with his invective moments, lampoons, impromptus, and epigrams. Here the satire seems to embody spontaneous violence that tests to breaking point the strategies of containment. According to Gilbert Burnet, Rochester believed that 'a man could not write [satire] with life, unless he were heated by Revenge'.[5] I shall explore the way that more extreme moments of violent feeling could be carried through into poetry without dilution or artistic incoherence.

John Chalker has argued that Augustan satire provides a proper framework within which its violence can be experienced and that in so doing it serves positive and affirmative ends.[6] Others have stressed the moral basis of such affirmation. Mary Claire Randolph's bipartite theory, for example, describes the classical alliance of negative and normative elements in formal verse satire, an alliance the Augustans recognized.[7] The emphasis upon affirmation is common coin amongst those who discuss Rochester's period; but it is not much help when we approach his own satire. There is more than a grain of truth in Tom Brown's judgement that 'reforming the Age was none of his Province'.[8] If we want to find analogues for the frameworks within which Rochester's violence finds expression, we must turn not to formal verse satire but to more primitive modes, modes which no-one has done more to define than Robert C. Elliott.

As Rochester's remarks to Burnett show, his satire has its roots in the vindictive, combative, and territorially aggressive urges which find direct expression in, for example, the Arabian *hija*, the *glam dicind* of the Irish satirists, or the vituperations of Archilochus.[9] In each of these forms satire was at its most potent, assuming magical power to disfigure and to kill. Way beyond the disappearance of belief in the magic of rhyming men to death, satirists remained convinced that they could still brand their victims with social stigma; or at the very least they saw in the invective a mode of expression for extreme anger. Elliott cites the modern example of Hugh MacDiarmid, who sees himself as 'carrying on (newly applied in vastly changed circumstances) the ancient bardic traditions of a very intricate and scholarly poetry, and with it the bardic powers of savage satire and invective' (p. 28). In Rochester's own time (in which the belief in magic was in its death throes) his friend and disciple John Oldham was similarly applying the traditions of Archilochus and Ovid's *Ibis* to the circumstances of

---

[5] *Some Passages of the Life and Death of John, Earl of Rochester* (1680), p. 26.

[6] *Violence in Augustan Literature* (London, 1975), pp. 23–24.

[7] 'The Structural Design of the Formal Verse Satire', *PQ*, 21 (1942), 368–84 (pp. 369–75); and Howard D. Weinbrot, *The Formal Strain: Studies in Augustan Imitation and Satire* (Chicago, 1969), pp. 59–75.

[8] See *Rochester: The Critical Heritage*, edited by David Farley-Hills (London, 1972), p. 176.

[9] See Robert C. Elliott, *The Power of Satire: Magic, Ritual, Art* (Princeton, New Jersey 1960), pp. 3–99. I am indebted to Professor Elliott in much that follows.

Restoration London. And in the same period titles such as *Ratts Rhimed to Death: or the Rump Parliament Hang'd in the Shambles* (1660) or *Rome Rhym'd to Death* (1683) tell their own story.[10]

Thomas Drant's notion that 'satire' derived from the Arabic for a butcher's cleaver might be fanciful but it catches something of the malefic extremes of the invective.[11] But as Dryden reminds us, butchery is not enough. There is 'a vast difference betwixt the slovenly butchering of a man, and the fineness of a stroke that separates the head from the body, and leaves it standing in its place'.[12] The examples of Oldham and MacDiarmid illustrate that one of the ways in which invective can be artful lies in the scholarly adaptation of ancient modes. Oldham wrote vitriolically not because he couldn't help it but because he chose to. Like MacDiarmid's, his is an invective both scholarly and carefully worked:

> And I go always arm'd for my defence,
> To punish, and revenge an Insolence.
> I wear my Pen, as others do their Sword,
> To each affronting Sot, I meet, the Word
> Is *Satisfaction*: strait to Thrusts I go,
> And pointed Satyr runs him through and through.

As if to pre-empt any objection that such stuff is mere rant, Oldham draws attention to the mode in which he is writing, the mode of Archilochus and Ovid:

> Torn, mangled and expos'd to Scorn, and Shame,
> I mean to hang, and Gibbet up thy Name.
> If thou to live in Satyr, so much thirst,
> Enjoy thy Wish, and Fame, till Envy burst,
> Renown'd, as he, whom banish'd *Ovid* curst:
> Or he, whom old *Archilochus* so stung
> In Verse, that he for shame, and madness hung:
> Deathless in Infamy, do thou so live,
> And let my Rage, like his, to Haltars drive.[13]

Their example licenses violently retributive verse. Similarly, MacDiarmid's invective depends in part on the reader's recognition of its roots. As Elliott puts it, 'the language might be that of Aithirne the Importunate — or a *defixio* of the fourth century B.C.' (p. 28). In both cases the reader's awareness of adherence to a mode ensures that the violence is seen as not raw but controlled.

---

[10] Rochester's name was associated with *Rome Rhym'd to Death* in which 'On Rome's Pardons' appeared. For a discussion of the poem's authorship, see *Complete Poems* pp. 219–20 and David Vieth, *Attribution in Restoration Poetry: A Study of Rochester's 'Poems' of 1680* (New Haven, Connecticut, 1963), pp. 353–62 and 474–77.

[11] *Medicinable Morall* (1566), sig. A4ᵛ. Quoted in P. K. Elkin, *The Augustan Defence of Satire* (Oxford, 1973), p. 27.

[12] *Of Dramatic Poesy and Other Critical Essays*, edited by George Watson, 2 vols (London, 1962), II, 137.

[13] *The Works of John Oldham*, in 4 parts (1686), II, 132. Subsequent quotations are from this edition unless otherwise stated.

Writing in such a way involves a high level of self-conscious artistry. Where the self-consciousness is felt as part of the texture of the poetry, as in Oldham's lines above, the effect is a curiously mannered expression which can easily run to melodrama or to self-parody. But the self-consciousness can be hidden, as in MacDiarmid's case, and then the primary impact is vehemence, even though the reader may recognize that the poem is a contribution to a mode. Similar tones are present in Rochester's poetry, in, for example, the comically self-conscious diatribe against his penis in 'The Imperfect Enjoyment' and in the disturbing cruelty of the last thirty-three lines of 'A Ramble in St James's Park'. In the first the mannered excess of Oldham's lines is replaced by a comedy that by the end of the poem is at breaking strain. The tone modulates into foetid disgust of such strength that it threatens to break loose from the containing framework of comic dispraise:

> Thou treacherous, base deserter of my flame,
> False to my passion, fatal to my fame,
> Through what mistaken magic dost thou prove
> So true to lewdness, so untrue to love?
> What oyster-cinder-beggar-common whore
> Didst thou e'er fail in all thy life before?
> When vice, disease, and scandal lead the way,
> With what officious haste dost thou obey!
> Like a rude, roaring hector in the streets
> Who scuffles, cuffs, and justles all he meets,
> But if his King or country claim his aid,
> The rakehell villain shrinks and hides his head;
> Ev'n so thy brutal valour is displayed,
> Breaks every stew, does each small whore invade,
> But when great Love the onset does command,
> Base recreant to thy prince, thou dar'st not stand.
> Worst part of me, and henceforth hated most,
> Through all the town a common fucking post,
> On whom each whore relieves her tingling cunt
> As hogs on gates do rub themselves and grunt,
> Mayst thou to ravenous chancres be a prey,
> Or in consuming weepings waste away;
> May strangury and stone thy days attend;
> May'st thou ne'er piss, who didst refuse to spend
> When all my joys did on false thee depend.
> And may ten thousand abler pricks agree
> To do the wronged Corinna right for thee.   (pp. 39–40)

This is a prime instance of the mercurial change of mood that breeds inquietude of tone. Comparable pieces from the period (like the bawdy 'Base mettell hanger by your Master's Thigh!')[14] are uniform in texture; they show nothing of the violent self-disgust that erupts with the image of the fucking-post. Rochester orchestrates the different tones available to him in

---

[14] Attributed to Rochester in several manuscripts (see *Complete Poems*, p. 224). For a text, see *The Penguin Book of Restoration Verse*, edited by Harold Love (Harmondsworth, 1968), p. 84.

the invective, shifting suddenly from tongue-in-cheek expostulation to quite uncomic and forceful repugnance. Once the violent image is complete the poem modulates into a more formulaic handling of the mode and a less fervid tone. Something of the earlier note of comic dispraise re-enters the poem in these concluding lines, but it vies for supremacy with residual aggression. The result is a feeling of violence only just restrained.

In the case of 'A Ramble in St James's Park' it is only necessary to compare the following lines,

> May stinking vapours choke your womb
> Such as the men you dote upon!
> May your depravèd appetite,
> That could in whiffling fools delight,
> Beget such frenzies in your mind
> You may go mad for the north wind,
> And fixing all your hopes upon't
> To have him bluster in your cunt,
> Turn up your longing arse t'th'air
> And perish in a wild despair!   (p. 45)

with lines from Oldham's 'Satyr upon a Woman' to see just how much Rochester could rival Oldham in malediction:

> First, for her Beauties, which the Mischief brought,
> May she affected, they be borrow'd thought,
> By her own hand, not that of Nature wrought:
> Her Credit, Honour, Portion, Health, and those
> Prove light, and frail, as her broke Faith, and Vows.
> Some base unnam'd Disease, her Carkass foul,
> And make her Body ugly, as her Soul.
> Cankers, and Ulcers eat her, till she be,
> Shun'd like Infection, loath'd like Infamy.   (*Works*, I, 145)

Both passages pile curse on curse in a fury mitigated only by a recognition that this is a mode. Part of the immediate texture of Oldham's lines, the recognition works beneath the surface in Rochester's verses, rendering them less stable. They build to a climax of cruelty that verges on the gratuitous:

> But my revenge will best be timed
> When she is married that is limed.
> In that most lamentable state
> I'll make her feel my scorn and hate:
> Pelt her with scandals, truth or lies,
> And her poor cur with jealousies,
> Till I have torn him from her breech,
> While she whines like a dog-drawn bitch.   (p. 45)

Like the gratuitous violence that Claude Rawson has explored in Swift's writings, the image of the howling unsatisfied bitch, its sexual partner ripped from it in the act of coition, breaks suddenly and brutally upon the reader.[15]

---

[15] See *Gulliver and the Gentle Reader: Studies in Swift and Our Time* (London and Boston, 1973), pp. 33–59.

Its power resides in its startling vividness (supported by the aggressive stress on 'torn') which quickly gives way to a more controlled vindictiveness in the poem's coda, in which Rochester voices the 'mocking, supremely self-confident tone' that is part of the formulaic of the invective:[16]

> Loathed and despised, kicked out o' th' Town
> Into some dirty hole alone,
> To chew the cud of misery
> And know she owes it all to me.
>   And may no woman better thrive
>   That dares prophane the cunt I swive!   (pp.45–46)

Whereas such an explosion tends in Swift's work to enact an unexpected freedom from a conscious moral purpose,[17] in Rochester's image it is not moral purpose but the sense of mannerly writing within the invective mode that is almost destroyed. The satire's veneer of self-control is momentarily fractured.

I have described the cruelty of the eruptive lines from 'A Ramble in St James's Park' as almost gratuitous, not out of academic caution but because even at this point there is an underlying control. Werner Jaeger has pointed out that the Strassburg Fragment (97A) of Archilochus is 'dictated by a hatred which is *justified*, or which Archilochus believes to be justified'.[18] As he and others have emphasized, the justification lies in a sense of moral vocation. Although Rochester's poem seeks to exact personal revenge rather than moral retribution, his curses nevertheless stand in need of some sort of justification. They should not, for example, be in excess of the injury that they answer. Aimed at a retaliatory 'eye-for-an-eye' attack, their defence lies in their appropriateness as mirroring-punishments. A mirroring-punishment is 'one in which a notion of "aptness" or "appropriateness" is expressed by partial associative detail reminiscent or indirectly descriptive of the offence'.[19] Rochester himself draws attention to the aptness of his imprecations:

> May stinking vapours choke your womb
> Such as the men you dote upon!   (p. 45)

If a reader did not know the rest of the poem it would be possible to read off Corinna's crime from these lines: infidelity with a variety of unsavoury men. Whereas in their purest form mirroring-punishments are amusingly apt, transplanted to the invective their humour becomes splenetic. In Rochester's invective moments their violence can be so arresting that the reader's awareness of appropriateness is thrust into abeyance. Such is the case with

---

[16] Elliott, p. 14.
[17] See Rawson, p. 35.
[18] *Paedeia: The Ideals of Greek Culture*, translated by Gilbert Highet, 2 vols (Oxford, 1946), I, 121. Quoted in Elliott, p. 11.
[19] See Trevor N. Saunders, 'Talionic and Mirroring Punishments in Greek Culture', *Polis*, 4 (1981), 1–16 (p. 1).

the image of the 'dog-drawn bitch'. Although its power feels to be independent of the criterion of aptness, it does mirror Corinna's offence. Just as Rochester experiences sexual resentment because he has been supplanted in her favours, so, if the curse were to bear fruit, she would suffer sexual anguish as her lover was ripped from her. The impression of gratuitousness is deliberate. At a distance we can say that the poem never loses coherence, but to *experience* it is to taste a cruelty momentarily liberated from artistic restraint.

Rochester's lampoons also embody a delicate balance between wit and brutality, and they too have close similarities with more primitive forms of satire, forms like the Eskimo drum-song in which combatants settle grievances not with fists or weapons but with words. Each seeks both to wound his adversary by direct verbal onslaught and to worst him indirectly by winning the audience's approbation for his well-turned barbs or his subtle manipulation of the formulaic and traditions of the contest. Rochester's verse-combats with Sheffield and Sir Carr Scroope are the Restoration equivalent of this form. The contretemps with Scroope, for example, seems to have been born with Rochester's swipe at 'the purblind Knight' in his 'Allusion to Horace' (p. 126). The hit drew from Scroope his 'In Defence of Satyr' which, stinging Rochester, produced in its turn 'On the Supposed Author of a Late Poem in Defence of Satyr'. Scroope parried with 'Rail on, poor feeble scribbler, speak of me' and backed out of the contest, leaving Rochester to administer the final blows in 'The Mock Song' and 'On Poet Ninny'. Like the Eskimo drum-song or the insults of the negro 'dozens' convention,[20] Rochester's contributions to this paper war aim at controlled violence in a public arena, controlled enough to stay this side of inchoate fury but not so controlled as to lose its edge of personal cruelty.

It is characteristic of such flyting that it should be, or seem to be, improvised, strongly rhythmic, relentlessly (and scurrilously) personal, and often parodic.[21] Despite being pondered, Rochester's verse hostilities with Sheffield and Scroope share these qualities. All have an extempore feel, whether it is designed to catch the torrentous flow of abuse or grows out of the simply effective parody of 'I swive as well as others do'. And the violence of the attacks makes itself felt in the strong rhythmic beat of lines such as

> Bursting with pride, the loathed impostume swells;
> Prick him, he sheds his venom straight, and smells,   (p. 142)

from 'My Lord All-Pride', or

> Crushed by that just contempt his follies bring
> On his crazed head, the vermin fain would sting,   (p. 141)

from 'On Poet Ninny', whose every stress is the verbal equivalent of a deftly administered physical blow. Together these qualities feed the cruelty of the

[20] See Elliott, pp. 70–74.
[21] See Gilbert Highet, *The Anatomy of Satire* (Princeton, New Jersey, 1962), p. 152.

lampoons, making it seem likely to assert itself at the expense of art without
ever doing so; for gratuitous violence would be an admission of defeat. One
sure way of winning the contest was so to anger an opponent that he was
reduced to incoherent rage or to physical aggression.

The appeal to an audience necessitates artistic strategies different from
those in the invective. Being splenetic was not the only way in which the
invective's curses differed from the mirroring-punishment in its proper form.
Hephaestus's revenge for the adultery of Aphrodite with Ares is a paradigm
mirroring-punishment. Hephaestus, knowing that the lovers plan to meet in
his absence, puts invisible and unbreakable bonds around his bed which are
tightened when Aphrodite and Ares are in each other's arms so that no
movement is possible. The gods who form Hephaestus's immediate audience laugh an 'unextinguish'd laughter' in recognition of the aptness of this
device.[22] Their laughter is, as a recent critic puts it, 'festive, ebullient, and
sustained . . . . [It] appears to emanate from glorious fulness of being'.[23] The
humour of the closing lines of 'A Ramble in St James's Park' is by contrast
dark. The outcome when Homer's gods enjoy Hephaestus's joke together is
the levy of a recognized fine; but Rochester's invective laughter makes no
such call on an accepted code of values. In the invective the satirist is, in
Oldham's words, 'Both Witness, Judge, and Executioner' (*Works*, I, 141).
The cruel amusement is his alone to relish: his audience can only appreciate
its appropriateness as evidence of witty control within a mode. In the
lampoon written as part of a satiric contest, public approval or enjoyment is
itself a form of violence. One of Rochester's most common tactics of cruelty
in such poetry is quasi-objectivity. He will suggest that his opponent is self-
evidently ridiculous, that, for example, God acted as a satirist when he
created Sir Carr Scroope, or that

> Men gaze upon thee as a hideous sight,
> And cry, 'There goes the melancholy knight!' (p. 142)

The ironically self-condemnatory monologue or letter, like 'A Very
Heroical Epistle in Answer to Ephelia', is another form of the same strategy,
as, too, is the presentation of a victim as a type or paradigm in the manner of
the Theophrastan character. Both 'On Poet Ninny' and 'My Lord All-Pride'
approximate to the character, as a comparison of the latter with Oldham's
'Character of a Certain Ugly Old P——' will show.

> Against his stars the coxcomb ever strives,
> And to be something they forbid, contrives.
> With a red nose, splay foot, and goggle eye,
> A ploughman's looby mien, face all awry,
> With stinking breath, and every loathsome mark,
> The Punchinello sets up for a spark. (p. 143)

---

[22] See Saunders, pp. 3–4.
[23] J. S. Cunningham, 'On Earth as it Laughs in Heaven: Mirth and the "Frigorifick Wisdom"', in
Augustan Worlds: Essays in Honour of A. R. Humphreys, edited by J. C. Hilson, M. M. B. Jones, and J. R.
Watson (Leicester, 1978), pp. 131–51, (pp. 134–35).

He's one of the *Grotesques* of the *Universe*, whom the grand *Artist* drew only (as *Painters* do uncouth ugly *Shapes*) to fill up the empty *Spaces* and *Cantons* of this great *Frame*. He's *Man anagrammatiz'd*: A *Mandrake* has more of *Humane Shape*: His *Face* carries *Libel* and *Lampoon* in't. *Nature* at its *Composition* wrote *Burlesque*, and shew'd him how far she could out-do *Art* in *Grimace*. I wonder 'tis not hir'd by the *Play-houses* to draw *Antick Vizards* by. Without doubt he was made to be laugh'd at, and design'd for the *Scaramuchio of Mankind*.[24]

If Rochester's onslaught on Sheffield influenced Oldham's portrait of ugliness it was because the younger poet recognized its affinities with the character. On the basis of such quasi-objective sketches Rochester could claim explicitly to speak for his audience:

> All pride and ugliness! Oh, how we loathe
> A nauseous creature so composed of both!   (p. 141)

These witty claims on public agreement embody an aggressive generality that Scroope could not match. His epigram on Rochester is simply personal abuse:

> Rail on, poor feeble scribbler, speak of me
> In as bad terms as the world speaks of thee.
> Sit swelling in thy hole like a vexed toad,
> And full of pox and malice, spit abroad.
> Thous canst blast no man's fame with thy ill word:
> Thy pen is full as harmless as thy sword.   (p. 132)

Scroope seems to offer to speak for the world, but the manœuvre fails. When Scroope attacks Rochester as 'full of pox' he means it literally; but when Rochester conjures up a figure full of contradictions the emphasis is upon the imaginative truth of his portrait supported by a combative pattern of antithesis:

> A lump deformed and shapeless were thou born,
> Begot in love's despite and nature's scorn,
> And art grown up the most ungraceful wight,
> Harsh to the ear, and hideous to the sight;
> Yet love's thy business, beauty thy delight.   (p. 133)

It is perhaps small wonder that Scroope should have quit the battlefield leaving Rochester to maraud at will.

Although for tactical reasons the violence of the lampoons is never allowed to seem gratuitous, it is turbulent. The poetry enacts a running conflict between malevolence and the various strategies of restraint. The last quotation provides a fine example of this conflict in action. Its lines are meant to serve the satiric argument that Scroope is a walking contradiction, born ugly but affecting beauty; but their abuse is so unremitting that the argument is displaced until the final line. Despite the triplet, the first four

---

[24] *The Works of John Oldham*, in 4 parts (1684), IV, 112–13.

lines operate as a closed unit whose completion is sealed by heavily alliterative stress. If the last line of the triplet reasserts restraint, it also feels to be tagged on, not because there is a failure of art but as an embodiment of controlled instability. The line does not muzzle but momentarily redirects the passage's cruelty, which remains to erupt again.

On the face of it Rochester's impromptu 'Here's Monmouth the witty' might appear to be as simply savage (and probably not as artful) as Scroope's epigram:

> Here's Monmouth the witty,
> And Lauderdale the pretty,
> And Frazier, that learned physician;
> But above all the rest,
> Here's the Duke for a jest,
> And the King for a grand politician.   (p. 135)

To pronounce publicly that a man is not witty or that he is ugly, that a doctor is unskilled, or that a king is politically inept is to indulge in one of the crudest forms of verbal violence, whether the attack is direct or indirect. But Rochester's lines are not quite so straightforward. The impromptu presents a very different method of containing satiric cruelty, though it retains the instability of tone of the invectives and lampoons. The difference lies in the nature of the impromptu. To respond to it in general is to appreciate a triumph against the odds over those forces of poetic darkness, metrical clumsiness, and inarticulacy which threaten to make spontaneous composition deviate from sense. To respond to Rochester's impromptu is to recognize the difficulty of marshalling a series of discreet hits at individuals within a regular pattern of rhymed verse without the gibes becoming self-contained, and doing it extempore (it does not matter whether the lines were actually extempore; it is enough that they should feel to be). The difficulty is all the greater because of the deadly accuracy of Rochester's barbs. They seem designed primarily to wound rather than to accommodate the demands of the verse; and yet they are held together not in loosely connected couplets but in a pattern of rhyme and ironic transition which suggest a pondered control without jeopardizing the impromptu quality. Encompassed in extempore verse, the savagery of Rochester's hits is offset by improvisatory skill and ingenuity. The result of this recipe is a teasing ambivalence of tone, extempore ingenuity and potent satire competing for the poem's focus.

Thomas Hearne records that Charles and several courtiers 'being in company, my lord Rochester, upon the king's request, made the following verses [the impromptu]'.[25] Whereas in the satiric combat with Scroope opponent and audience were sharply demarcated, in the case of 'Here's Monmouth the witty' Charles and the rest were simultaneously audience

---

[25] *Reliquiae Hearniae: The Remains of Thomas Hearne, M.A.*, edited by Philip Bliss; 3 vols (London, 1869), I, 119.

and victims. We might imagine them unsure whether to be amused or affronted. The impromptu hovers between cruelly-precise attack and witty insolence. As Giles Jacob put it, Rochester 'had a peculiar Talent of mixing his Wit with Malice, and fitting both with such apt words, that Men were tempted to be pleased with them', even in this case the victims.[26]

The famous impromptu satire on Charles II also uses ambivalence to contain its violence:

> God bless our good and gracious King,
> ~~Whose promise none relies on;~~
> Who never said a foolish thing,
> Nor ever did a wise one.   (p. 134)

For Matthew Hodgart these lines exemplify the epigram. They are 'a civilised form of the primitive lampoon-satire, which aims magically at the destruction of the victim: it is civilized in so far as it uses the elegant forms of sophisticated verse but remains cruel at heart'.[27] This is true up to a point. Certainly there is cruelty: it grows out of characteristically Rochesterian ironic reversal, ostensible praise alternating with blame. But unlike the destructive bathos of lines (p. 56) from 'Signior Dildo' ('That pattern of virtue, Her Grace of Cleveland, | Has swallowed more pricks than the ocean has sand'), the impromptu does not allow its reduction to ruffle the smooth movement of its verse. Its cruelty is firmly balanced by a playful and bantering surface.

This bantering element does not fit Hodgart's view of the epigram. It is the product of a verse movement that, far from using 'the elegant forms of sophisticated verse', is closer to Sternhold's and Hopkins's widely despised metrical version of the Psalms. One anecdote about the impromptu's composition claims that 'the King praising the translation of the Psalms, says my Lord Rochester, "An't please your majesty, I'll show you presently how they run"'.[28] There is no need to accept the anecdote to see its significance. Rochester parodies the regular stress of the Sternhold and Hopkins translation,

> The Lord of hosts doth us defend,
> He is our strength and tow'r;
> On Jacob's God we do depend,
> And on his mighty pow'r,   (46.11)[29]

to create a lighter, more playful texture than a more mellifluous verse form would have allowed. This texture is central to the poem's ambivalence. It both forms an appropriate vehicle for the savage cat-and-mouse game of

---

[26] *The Poetical Register: Or, The Lives and Characters of All the English Poets*, 2 vols (1723), II, 231.
[27] *Satire* (London, 1969), p. 160.
[28] See *Complete Poems*, p. 134.
[29] *The Whole Book of Psalms, Collected into English Metre by Thomas Sternhold, John Hopkins, and Others* (Cambridge, 1751), sig. C1ᵛ.

praise and blame and suggests that the impromptu might be a *jeu d'esprit*. Sedley's 'To Cloe' is a much better example of the form of epigram described by Hodgart. Despite its artful orchestration of an elegiac admonitory tone, it leaves no room for doubt that it is trained at the ageing ugliness that underlies Cloe's affected beauty:

> Leave off thy Paint, Perfumes, and youthful Dress,
> And Nature's failing Honesty confess;
> Double we see those Faults which Art wou'd mend,
> Plain downright Ugliness wou'd less offend.[30]

There is no equivalent in Rochester's verses for the ugliness that, as sound echoes sense, blots the final line of Sedley's poem. If there had been the ambivalence would have been resolved.

There is nothing equivocal about the epigram on Cary Frazier: it is clearly designed to murder a reputation:

> Her father gave her dildoes six;
>   Her mother made 'em up a score;
> But she loves nought but living pricks,
>   And swears by God she'll frig no more.   (p. 137)

and yet it lacks the turbulent violence of the lampoons on Sheffield and Scroope. The epigram's violence is remarkable not because its energy is disruptive but because its cruelty is so calculated. If the attack's wit embodies rational control, that wit is dedicated to single-minded malevolence. But for all the epigram's stable tone, it uses a form of the iconoclastic thwarting of expectation associated with Rochesterian ambivalence. Expectations are not induced and then exploded; instead they are implied as expected alternatives representing positives which never materialize. So when Cary rejects the transvalued sexual training of her upbringing (turning from dildoes to phalluses) she does not, as might have been expected, prefer normal to onanistic, natural to artificial satisfaction, or at least she does not simply do so. There is nothing generous in her lust, for the connexion through rhyme of 'dildoes six' and 'living pricks' has the force of making dildoes and pricks interchangeable. Dildoes are inanimate pricks or (to be more faithful to the macabre cruelty of Rochester's gibe) *dead* pricks; and *living* pricks are *living* dildoes. With a viciousness that is held in check only by the wit that focuses it, Rochester is suggesting that Cary does not need artificial aids as they are normally understood because her consorts serve her as human dildoes. Swear as she might that she will frig no more, she will in a sense ironically continue to do so. Whereas the impromptus can get away with satiric assassination by means of the suggestion that they are not unequivocally committed to violence, the epigram requires its reader to take a connoisseur's delight in cruelty. Fundamental to that delight is a

---

[30] *The Poetical and Dramatic Works of Sir Charles Sedley*, edited by V. De Sola Pinto, 2 vols (London, 1928), I, 54.

recognition that the cruelty operates at the limits of what can be made acceptable through wit.

The attack on Cary Frazier harbours a strong strain of resentment at her reduction of men to dildoes. To some extent all satire expresses some similar emotion or attitude which is normally, as in the epigram, subservient to the satire's task of correction or revenge. But in my final example the expression of disillusionment and disgust is no less central to the poem's effect than its eruptive satire. 'To Mrs Willis' is as violent in its retraction from Sue Willis as it is in its assault upon her; and in both respects the poem treads a tightrope over the seething torrents of raw vehemence. Its mock-invocation epitomizes its precarious balance:

> Whom that I may describe throughout,
>   Assist me, bawdy powers;
> I'll write upon a double clout,
>   And dip my pen in flowers.   (p. 138)

The bawdy picture of writing in menstrual blood on a sanitary towel carries such a charge of repulsion that it tests to breaking point the device of parodic invocation. Almost too great to be restrained, the disgust spills over from Willis herself to the fact of menstruation in all women in a reaction much like that in 'By all love's soft, yet mighty powers'. Both poems display a Hamlet-like proclivity to generalize under the pressure of extreme disenchantment, a tendency which acts as a seismographic record of the emotional turmoil which puts the wit of 'On Mrs Willis' under increasing tension.

If we put the invocation back into context, it becomes clear that the disgust is all the stronger for being directed, too, at Rochester himself. The characteristic explosion of expectations at the poem's opening defines the nature of this self-dissatisfaction:

> Against the charms our ballocks have
>   How weak all human skill is,
> Since they can make a man a slave
>   To such a bitch as Willis!   (p. 137)

What promises to be male conceit turns out to be a forceful lament at man's inability to rein his sexual drives, an inability that enslaves him 'to such a bitch as Willis'. The gap between expected pride in male potency and the actual and loathsome world of subjection to Willis generates a resentment aimed both at man himself and the woman he cannot resist. The poem as a whole charts not just the expression of this turbulent disillusionment but the battle to contain it.

The movement of the first stanza, from civilized wit to vehement complaint, establishes the poem's pattern; but whereas at this stage disruptive passions are held in check by wit, by the poem's end the restraint has run thin. The final stanza is the culmination of a relentless stripping away of the façade that Sue Willis presented to her public. First, Rochester lays bare the truth that lies beneath the face she turns upon the world in general; then he turns to the truth hidden behind her appearance as a prostitute; and finally he reveals the nasty physical facts of the last two lines with their gross literalization of the metaphor of Willis's cunt as a sewer:

> Bawdy in thoughts, precise in words,
>   Ill-natured though a whore,
> Her belly is a bag of turds,
>   And her cunt a common shore.   (p. 138)

With the narrowing of focus comes a crescendo of disgust whose destructive effect is felt in the poem's structure. The structural cohesion that has had to withstand growing pressure stanza by stanza almost collapses in the last lines. The shocking coda is linked to the antithetical opening of its stanza by the flimsiest of threads, in fact by rhyme alone. If it were not for that thread the repulsion from Willis, from the association of sexual and excremental functions in women in general, and from man's susceptibility to Willis and women like her would be completely gratuitous. As it is the disgust is felt as gratuitous and spontaneous even though it is carefully contrived.

One of the most remarkable qualities of the onslaughts on both Sue Willis and Cary Frazier is their moral neutrality. It might be supposed, for example, that the subversion of normal parental attitudes by Cary's parents would have moral implications, but the experience of the epigram is a dissolution rather than espousal of moral positives. The positive of generous lust fails to establish itself just as much as that of proper parental guidance on sexual matters. The vacuum created by witholding moral norms that might (in the poem's own terms) have been expected is filled by the violence of resentful pugnacity. 'On Cary Frazier' and 'On Mrs Willis' are a far cry from the affirmative violence that John Chalker finds characteristic of Augustan satire. They are neither moral in the normal sense nor moral by virtue of releasing violence to a positive end. Their neutrality is broadly representative of all the satire that I have been examining. The invectives share nothing of Archilochus's sense of moral mission, and the battles with Sheffield and Scroope appeal not to the moral but the artistic sense of their audience. And the ambivalence of the impromptus precludes a moral perspective.

This neutrality is closely related to the more general uncertainty about morals in Rochester's work. The kaleidoscopic ambivalence that is shared by poems as various as 'By all love's soft, yet mighty powers', 'Grecian Kindness', and the impromptus is not confined to those pieces. It is there too in, for example, the lyric 'All my past life is mine no more', which can be read as either a lament at man's lot in a deterministic universe or a cunning excuse for inconstancy. These poems, and others like them, express a scepticism not unlike Montaigne's but crucially different in one respect. For Montaigne scepticism led to a trust in the Church's authority; for Rochester it led nowhere, unless it was to a sense of insoluble dilemma. In this cul-de-sac, as in the world of Rochester's fictional representative, Dorimant, manners replaced morals. There was a categorical imperative to maintain rational self-control, or at least to present a mask of self-control to the world. Rochester's poetry obeys this imperative, but it does not always project unruffled urbanity. Whether it is in the poetry explored in this paper or in the metaphysical turmoil of 'A Satyr against Reason and Mankind', his satire can present a dynamic tension between extreme violence and wit. It is a measure of his honesty as a poet that he should portray this tension; and it is a measure of his control that it could take such a variety of forms.

Oldham, Pope, and Restoration Satire

RAMAN SELDEN

University of Durham

It is the fate of writers whose reputation lies below the first rank to suffer from false comparisons and to fall between the lines of tradition which critics lay down. The poetry of John Oldham has not been given the attention it deserves, partly because his distinctive qualities have not been properly recognized, and partly because no modern edition has yet appeared.[1] The standing of Rochester has risen recently, following the work of David Vieth and others. The relaxation of censorship and the fascinations of materialism and libertinism have contributed to Rochester's sudden rise in the critical stakes. Oldham will not benefit much from these cultural predispositions. It is now possible to publish Oldham's impressive Rochesterian poems, 'Sardanapalus' and 'Upon the Author of the Play Call'd Sodom'. However, the poems which are most characteristic are the Juvenalian satires (*Satyrs Upon the Jesuits*), the *Imitations* (of Horace's Satire 1.9, Boileau VIII, and Juvenal III and XIII), the Pindariques (notably *Upon the Works of Ben Johnson*), and the satires relating to poets and poetry (*A Letter from the Country to a Friend in Town*, 'Upon a Bookseller', 'An Allusion to Martial', 'A Satyr Address'd to a Friend', and the 'Spencer' satire). Any rehabilitation of Oldham requires a thorough reconsideration of his place in the tradition of Augustan satire. A careful examination of Pope's relationship to Oldham reveals a greater number of connexions and similarities between the two poets than one might expect. On the other hand, it would be wrong to compare them on the basis of a narrowly Augustan reading of Oldham's poetry. We should not simply regard Oldham as a primitive Augustan, but should recognize that he was writing within a Restoration poetic which was much richer and more heterogeneous than the usual period generalizations suggest.

Two substantial accounts of Oldham place him quite differently in relation to the traditions of verse satire. Paul Korshin stresses the 'old-fashioned' side of Oldham's work, especially his development of the harsh satire of the Elizabethan tradition as continued in the satires of Cleveland. In his view, Oldham is 'a philosophical rebel who, in his zeal for purifying the temple of its pollutions, makes a substantial contribution to the evolution of the poetics of dissent'.[2] Korshin concedes that in his later work he came to

---

[1] The Oxford annotated edition edited by Harold Brooks (with my collaboration) is at present in press. Quotations from Oldham in this essay will be from the MS of that edition.
[2] From *Concord to Dissent: Major Themes in English Poetic Theory 1640–1700* (Menston, Yorkshire, 1973), p. 147. Howard D. Weinbrot adopts a similar view of Oldham in his *Alexander Pope and the Traditions of Formal Verse Satire* (Princeton, New Jersey, 1982), pp. 10–11, 26, 83.

recognize 'the value of moderation and disinterestedness in social dissent'.
Rachel Trickett's valuable account places much greater emphasis upon
Oldham's Augustan credentials. Her special concern for the evolution of the
autobiographical persona of the satirist inevitably draws attention to Oldham's later 'Horatian' tendencies. She compares his poems about the role of
the satirist and about the trials of a poet's existence with Pope's: 'Oldham's
attempts at this were much simpler and clumsier than Pope's, but Pope was
to be its supreme master, and no one blended again so perfectly magnilo-
quent public exhortation and the quicksilver moods of the individual mind.'[3]
Judged on this ground, Oldham is naturally seen as a pioneer and experi-
menter.

Between the extremes of Elizabethan satirist *redivivus* and Augustan
satirist *primitivus* lies a terrain which remains to be defined. A reading of
Oldham requires a consideration of at least four distinct poetic contexts: the
tradition of 'rough' satire, which flourished between Cleveland and the
1680s; the neo-Classical line of Jonson, Cowley, and Waller; the vogue of
heroic drama; and the poetry of the Court Wits. While there was certainly a
shift in Oldham's development away from the poetics of 'rough' satire, there
was also a continuous process of reworking and recombining these lines.

The style of Cleveland was still viable in the Restoration period, as a
glance at the *Poems on Affairs of State* reveals. The following lines from
Cleveland's *The Rebell Scot* evidently anticipate Oldham's manner:

> He that saw Hell in's melancholie dreame,
> And in the twilight of his Fancy's theame,
> Scar'd from his sinnes, repented in a fright,
> Had he view'd Scotland, had turn'd Proselite.
> A Land where one may pray with curst intent,
> O may they never suffer banishment!
> Had *Cain* been *Scot*, God would have chang'd his doome,
> Not forc'd him wander, but confin'd him home.
> Like Jewes they spread, and as Infection flie,
> As if the Divell had Ubiquitie.   (l. 57)[4]

The same use of satiric hyperbole can be found in Oldham's *Satyrs Upon the
Jesuits*:

> When God his stock of wrath on *Egypt* spent,
> To make a stubborn Land and King repent,
> Sparing the rest, he had this one Plague [the Jesuits] sent;
> For this alone his People had been quit,
> And *Pharoah* circumcis'd a Proselyte.   (*Satyr II*, l. 15)

Oldham outdoes Cleveland in this type of rhetoric by building up an effect of
witty exaggeration, making each couplet outdo the former couplet in
outrageous fancy:

[3] *The Honest Muse: A Study in Augustan Verse* (London, 1967), p. 102.
[4] *The Poems*, edited by B. Morris and E. Withington (London, 1967), p. 30.

> When the first Traitor *Cain* (too good to be
> Thought Patron of this black Fraternity)
> His bloudy Tragedy of old design'd,   ⎫
> One death alone quench'd his revengeful mind, ⎬
> Content with but a quarter of Mankind: ⎭
> Had he been *Jesuit*, had he but put on
> Their savage cruelty, the rest had gone:
> His hand had sent old *Adam* after too,
> And forc'd the Godhead to create anew.   (*Satyr* II, l. 105)

One of the most popular poems of 1660, Robert Wild's *Iter Boreale*, lampoons the expelled Rump Parliament with a Clevelandesque gusto which anticipates some of Oldham's vigour. The following passage describes the activities of John Lambert's 'under-devils', Quakers and 'New Lights', who drove priests from their livings:

> The priests ordained to exorcise those elves
> Were voted devils and cast out themselves —
> Bible, or Alcoran, all's one to them;
> Religion serves but for a stratagem —
> The holy charms these adders did not heed;
> Churches themselves did sanctuary need.   (l. 188)[5]

Wild, John Ayloffe, Andrew Marvell, and John Oldham follow Cleveland, but mitigate that obscurity and harshness of expression which the Elizabethans believed were authorized by the Roman satirist Persius. The theoretical statements of Oldham, Shadwell, and others about satiric style retain the rhetoric of the older tradition, but their satiric *practice* reflects the modifying pressures of Restoration Classicism.[6] However, Oldham never completely abandoned the 'rough' manner of the *Jesuits*. The following lines on the pangs of guilty consciences occur in his imitation of Juvenal's thirteenth satire, written in his mature period:

> Believ't, they suffer greater Punishment
> Than *Rome*'s Inquisitor's could e'er invent:
> Nor all the Tortures, Racks, and Cruelties,
> Which ancient Persecutors could devise,
> Nor all, that *Fox* his Bloody Records tell,   ⎫
> Can match what *Bradshaw*, and *Ravilliac* feel, ⎬
> Who in their Breasts carry about their Hell. ⎭   (l. 322)

It is also true that Oldham's reputation during the Augustan period was based upon his Juvenalian credentials.[7]

Oldham's importance in the development of neo-Classical poetics in the tradition of Jonson, Denham, Waller, and Cowley has been highlighted by Harold Brooks's article on the 'Imitation' and by Rachel Trickett.[8] While he

---

[5] *Anthology of Poems on Affairs of State*, edited by G. de F. Lord (New Haven and London, 1975), pp. 10–11.
[6] See my 'Juvenal and Restoration Modes of Translation', *MLR*, 68 (1973), 481–93.
[7] See Weinbrot, pp. 117–20.
[8] Brooks, 'The "Imitation" . . . before the age of Pope', *RES*, 25 (1949), 124–40.

never aimed at a neo-Classical 'correctness' in prosody,[9] Oldham extended
the scope of Imitation beyond Rochester's practice, not only by sustaining
the modernization of the classical model but also by emulating Ben Jonson's
special talent for finding colloquial equivalents for Latin idioms. The
following account of the crowded streets of London in *Juvenal III* anticipates
Pope's and especially Swift's manner:

> Thick Crowds in every Place you must charge thro,
> And storm your Passage, wheresoe're you go:
> While Tides of Followers behind you throng,
> And, pressing on your heels, shove you along:
> One with a Board, or Rafter hits your Head,
> Another with his Elbow bores your side;
> Some tread upon your Corns, perhaps in sport,
> Mean while your Legs are cas'd all o're with Dirt.   (l. 377)

In his imitation of Horace's satire on the bore, Oldham brilliantly transfuses
the idiom and reference of Etherege's and Wycherley's comedies into the
satirist's complaints and the tedious discourse of the bore, who

> Names every Wench, that passes through the Park,
> How much she is allow'd, and who the Spark,
> That keeps her: points, who lately got a Clap,
> And who at the *Groom-Porters* had ill hap
> Three nights ago in play with such a Lord   (l. 31)

The favourite haunts of the Court Wits, Hyde Park and the Groom Porter's
(where gambling took place), evoke a contemporary London life-style
known to Oldham partly through the drama and partly through the poetry
of the Wits themselves.[10]

The extent of Rochester's influence on Oldham has been disputed.[11]
Oldham's tribute to Rochester in *Bion*, even if one allows for the artificiality
of obituary verse and the influence of the Greek original, cannot be ignored:
'If I am reckon'd not unblest in Song, | 'Tis what I owe to thy all-teaching
tongue' (l. 191). Under the influence of Rochester and his circle, Oldham
wrote a number of poems in which he developed the persona of the rake.
'Sardanapalus' emulates the obscene wit of Rochester's court lampoons,
while 'Upon the Author of the Play call'd Sodom' reverses the attack by
using the imagery of obscenity against the writer of an obscene play (thought
to be Rochester at the time). In the *Satyr against Vertue* and *A Dithyrambique on
Drinking* ('Suppos'd to be spoken by Rochester at the Guinny-club'), Oldham developed his most distinctive literary device, the unreliable persona.

[9] Taking the first hundred lines of two early and two later poems, we find that there is no significant
change in the number of 'imperfect' rhymes: *Jesuits I* (17), *Jesuits II* (22), *Juvenal III* (26), *Juvenal XIII* (18).
[10] See Pepys, 1 January 1667/6, and J. H. Wilson, *The Court Wits of the Restoration* (Princeton, New Jersey,
1948), p. 12,
[11] See Dustin H. Griffin, *Satires Against Man: The Poems of Rochester* (Berkeley, Los Angeles, and London,
1973), p. 257; Korshin, p. 145; H. F. Brooks, 'The Poems of John Oldham', in *Restoration Literature: Critical
Approaches*, edited by H. Love (London, 1972), pp. 177–203 (pp. 190–91); and David M. Vieth, *Attribution
in Restoration Poetry: A Study of Rochester's Poems of 1680* (New Haven and London, 1963), pp. 185–86.

Much of the dramatic vitality of the *Jesuits* derives from this use of the rakish or villainous speaker, whose arguments against religion, virtue, and reason, put with all the rhetorical force of the Juvenalian satirist, explode in his own face. The earlier Rochesterian poems belong to the ancient tradition of the 'Paradoxical Encomium', while the *Jesuits* use the device Harold Brooks has called 'self-incriminating monologue'.[12] However, in Oldham's practice, both narrative forms employ a dramatically-distanced and unreliable persona. The device permits Oldham to exploit his talent for rhetorical exaggeration and wit of incongruity. Thomas Wood, in his elegy on Oldham, sums this up well when he describes Oldham as a poet 'That Vice could praise, and Vertue too disgrace; | The first *Excess* of Wit that e'er did please'. In this, he learnt something from Butler's *To the Happy Memory of the Most Renowned Du-Vall* (1671),[13] and Rochester's 'A Very Heroical Epistle in Answer to Ephelia', 'The Disabled Debauchee', and perhaps the character of Corinna in *A Letter from Artemisia . . . to Chloe*. Rochester's debauchee, 'Forc'd from the pleasing billows of debauch | On the dull shore of lazy temperance', resembles Oldham's Rochesterian 'Court-hector', who mocks the 'lazy Ease' of the virtuous in heaven and argues that men were misled into virtue in 'the World's rude untaught Infancy' before it reached the 'Manhood and Discretion of Debauchery'.[14]

Three of the poems we have been discussing each explore, in half-ironical, half-celebratory fashion, a different aspect of the cult of Rochester and his circle: the *Satyr against Vertue* treats the libertine antinomian outlook; *A Dithyrambique* deals with the vogue of Dionysiac intoxication, and 'Sardanapalus' impersonates the celebrant of sexual triumph.[15]

The appeal to Oldham of Rochester's poetry did not lie in its materialist philosophy or its libertinism. Oldham's impersonations of Rochester's rakish manner are dramatic experiments, or, in the case of 'Sardanapalus', an exercise in fashionable wit. However, in 'Sodom' Oldham successfully combines Juvenalian rant with Rochesterian obscenity in a poem of imaginative daring. The poem proceeds through a series of related conceits: the author is 'clapt with *Poetry*'; his brains are like ulcers dropping foul matter; his Muse has the '*Flowers*'. 'Nature', declares Oldham, 'made'

> Thy Tongue a *Clitoris*, thy Mouth a *Cunt.*
> How well a *Dildoe* would that place become,
> To gag it up, and make't for ever dumb!   (l. 31)

Oldham proceeds to imagine a scene in which the impotent obscenity of the play he is attacking is used by a prostitute for an appropriately vain stimulus to lust:

[12] See H. K. Miller, 'The Paradoxical Encomium with Special Reference to its Vogue in England from 1600 to 1800', *MP*, 52 (1956), 145–78; Brooks, 'Poems of Oldham', p. 193.
[13] See Brooks, 'Poems of Oldham', pp. 190–91.
[14] Rochester is quoted from *The Complete Poems*, edited by David M. Vieth (New Haven and London, 1968).
[15] I owe these descriptions to Harold Brooks.

> When Suburb-Prentice comes to hire Delight,
> And wants Incentives to dull Appetite,
> There *Punk*, perhaps, may thy brave works rehearse,
> Frigging the senseless thing with Hand and Verse.   (l. 41)

This is something of both Rochester's intensity of disgust and Oldham's favourite style of heroic rant; it represents a successful fusion of Rochester's and Dryden's satiric voices.

Oldham's interest in the varieties of rhetorical exaggeration that can be expressed through personae was fed by a number of available styles: the standard Juvenalian voice is tempered by the irony of Butler, the savage wit of Rochester, the sublimity of Pindarique verse, and the rather factitious sublimity of the heroic plays. Oldham's use of irony appears much less subtle than Butler's, but the dramatic energy is much greater. Oldham, who was never able to maintain himelf in London (apart from a brief and unsuccessful sojourn in a Clerkenwell garret) noticeably avoids the sophistication of libel and lampoon typical of the Court Wits. His *dirae*, 'A Satyr upon a Woman' and 'Upon a Bookseller', avoid direct attack upon a named individual; even when adopting the mask of Archilochus (in the second poem), Oldham's interest is neither merely personal nor moral, but poetic:

> Thou, who with spurious Nonsence durst profane
> The genuin Issue of a Poet's brain,
> May'st thou hereafter never deal in Verse,
> But what hoarse Bellmen in their Walks rehearse   (l. 62)

The Pindarique elevation and mock religious idiom combined with the indignant rhetoric remind one forcibly of Rochester ('And may no woman better thrive | That dares profane the cunt I swive' ('A Ramble in St James's Park', l. 165)).

Pope's remark, recorded by Spence, that Oldham 'has strong rage, but 'tis too much like Billingsgate', has remained the view of many critics.[16] James Sutherland considers Oldham 'harsh, masculine, satirical, and severely limited in his sensitiveness . . . he moves with a kind of clumsy buoyancy, tumbling over his feet and talking all the while as he goes'.[17] This catches something of the 'aristocratic' disdain which gives some of Pope's satires their superior tone. Dryden's generous elegy recognizes the validity of Oldham's roughness in satire; there is no social undertone to his appraisal of Oldham's vehement style:

> A noble Error, and but seldom made,
> When Poets are by too much force betray'd.   (l. 17)[18]

Pope's view of Oldham was bound to be less sympathetic. It was his ambition to be the first 'correct' poet, following the programme of stylistic

[16] Joseph Spence, *Observations, Anecdotes, and Characters of Books and Men*, edited by James M. Osborn (London, 1966), § 473.
[17] *English Literature of the Late 17th Century* (London, 1969), p. 164.
[18] 'To the Memory of Mr Oldham', l. 17. Quoted from *Poems and Fables*, edited by James Kinsley (London and New York, 1962).

retrenchment put forward by the polite circle of Granville, Garth, Congreve, Walsh, and others in the 1690s. Granville had declared that at the Restoration 'The Muse ran mad, to see her exil'd Lord' and in the theatre the heroes 'scarce cou'd speak one reasonable Word'.[19] Son of a nonconformist minister, always dependent on schoolmastering or tutoring for a living (except in the last months of his life), and carefully non-political in his patriotic attacks on the Jesuits, Oldham acquired little of the Augustan poet's social poise, ideological sophistication, refinement of wit.[20]

Pope's youthful imitations reflect a keen interest in the old cavaliers and the Court Wits, especially Cowley, Waller, Rochester, and Dorset. Spence records (§ 473) that, in Pope's view, Rochester 'had much more delicacy and more knowledge' than Oldham, and that Dorset was even more delicate. Nevertheless, Rochester's 'Upon Nothing', imitated in Pope's 'On Silence', has strong affinities with Oldham's satires of ironic reversal. Pope's translations of Ovid and Statius also have some connexions with Oldham. In them, Pope has developed that controlled Longinian sublimity which allows the decorous exhibition of passion in a dramatized context. Sapho's frustrated love (in 'Sapho to Phaon') and Oedipus's curses upon his sons (in Pope's version of *Thebaid* 1) are expressed in a passionate rhetoric which resembles Oldham's in his translation of Ovid's *Byblis* and his *Jesuits*. Compare Pope's Sapho,

> But when its way th'impetuous Passion found,
> I rend my Tresses, and my Breast I wound,
> I rave, then weep, I curse, and then complain,
> Now swell to Rage, now melt in Tears again.   (l. 129)[21]

with Oldham's Byblis:

> What pains, what raging pains I undergo:
> Ah me! I rave! what tempests shake my breast?
> And where? O where will this distraction rest?   (l. 133)

We know that in 1700 Pope bought a copy of Oldham's works, in which he made a list of the 'most remarkable Works in this Author': the fourth of the Satires upon the Jesuits, *Satyr against Vertue*, the imitations of Horace's *Ars Poetica* and of Horace's satire on the bore (1.9), and the Morwent ode.[22] Pope's choice lends support to the view that he was interested in several aspects of Oldham's poetry and not merely in the more obviously Augustan poems (none of the 'autobiographical' poems are listed by Pope). Pope borrowed many phrases and hints from Oldham, but only one or two are from the five named poems. It is possible, however, to discern a more general significance in his stated preferences. The freshness and topicality of the two

[19] 'An Essay upon Unnatural Flights in Poetry', *Poems on Several Occasions* (1712), p. 176.
[20] See Brooks, 'Poems of Oldham', pp. 180–81.
[21] Pope is quoted from the one-volume Twickenham edition of the poems, edited by John Butt (London, 1963).
[22] See H. F. Brooks's bibliography of Oldham, *Proceedings of the Oxford Bibliographical Society*, 5, 1 (1936), revised (Kraus Reprint, Nendeln, Liechtenstein, 1969), p. 28.

imitations clearly influenced Pope's own practice. In the *Essay on Criticism*
Pope pays tribute to Roscommon, whose translation of Horace's *Ars Poetica*
was used by Oldham in his version. Pope evidently did not include Oldham
among those writers who afflict Horace 'in Wrong *Translations*'. When Pope
writes, 'Some to *Conceit* alone their Taste confine, | And glitt'ring Thoughts
struck out at ev'ry Line' (l. 289), he may be echoing Oldham's version of the
Ars Poetica, where Oldham criticizes those who 'Are proud, when here and
there a glittering line | Does through the mass of their coarse rubbish shine'
(l. 24): Oldham's Horace, when he sees a 'happy thought' among the 'filthy
trash' written by an 'incorrigible sot', confesses 'I vex to see't | And wonder
how (the Devil!) he came by't' (l. 579). Pope echoes this in the *Epistle to Dr
Arbuthnot*: when we see the editors of Shakespeare and Milton preserved like
forms in amber, we 'wonder how the Devil they got there?' (l. 172).[23]
Oldham was certainly in Pope's mind when, in the *Essay on Criticism*, he
wrote of the poets who persist in their scribbling, 'Ev'n to the Dregs and
Squeezings of the *Brain*' (l. 607). In *Jesuits II*, Oldham's satirist tells how God
thought fit 'To scourge this latter and more sinful age | With all the dregs and
squeesings of his rage' (l. 24). The total transformation of the borrowing is
characteristic of Pope.

Pope's choice of the Morwent ode is surprising. This elegy on the death of
Oldham's bosom friend at college, Charles Morwent, was written at Shipton
Moyne before Oldham's mature period in Croydon. Like two other early
poems, 'To Madam L. E.' and 'On the Death of Mrs Katherine Kingscote',
it derives from the complimentary verse of Cowley and Waller. The
metaphysical tradition is also strongly present, as the frequent echoes of
Donne and Cleveland testify. Pope's admiration for the poem is best
understood in the context of F. R. Leavis's discussion of the 'Line of Wit',
which, he argues, descends to Pope through Marvell and Carew rather than
through the more orthodox line of Cowley, Waller, and Dryden.[24] Leavis is
surely wrong in believing that the metaphysical conceit bypasses the early
Augustan poetic tradition: the panegyrics of Waller and the early poetry of
Dryden (the Lord Hastings elegy, and *Annus Mirabilis*) show how the
metaphysical conceit could be naturalized in the elegant harmonies of
Augustan verse. The vogue of Cowley's Pindarique odes was still at its
height when Oldham wrote the Morwent Ode. The controlled sublimity
and the tempered Donnean hyperboles of this first important poem are
impressive. Harold Brooks rightly says, of Stanza 21, that 'the style looks
back to the earlier and more living phases of the metaphysical tradition'.[25]
The same was said by Leavis of Pope's 'Elegy to the Memory of an
Unfortunate Lady'. The following lines from the thirty-fourth stanza of the
Morwent ode might well have appealed to the Pope of the 'Elegy':

[23] See also Butler, *Hudibras*, II.3.564: 'how the Devil you come by't'.
[24] *Revaluation: Tradition and Development in English Poetry* (London, 1936), pp. 10–36.
[25] 'Poems of Oldham', p. 187.

> Thy Soul which hasten'd now to be enlarg'd,
>   And of its grosser Load discharg'd,
>   Began to act above its wonted rate,
> And gave a Praelude of its next unbody'd State.
>   So dying Tapers near their Fall,
>   When their own Lustre lights their Funeral,
> Contract their Strength into one brighter Fire,
> And in that Blaze triumphantly expire.   (l. 617)

Oldham here uses that characteristically neo-Classical version of the neo-Platonic idiom (brought to perfection in Cowley's Pindariques) which gives the conceit an Augustan weight and explicitness. One might justly compare the passage with the lines from Pope's 'Elegy' which attracted Leavis's special admiration:

> From these [dull souls] perhaps (ere nature bade her die)
> Fate snatch'd her early to the pitying sky.
> As into air the purer spirits flow,
> And sep'rate from their kindred dregs below;
> So flew the soul to its congenial place,
> Nor left one virtue to redeem her Race.   (l. 23)

Pope's own best known Pindarique, on St Cecilia's Day, describes the power of music in metaphysical fashion: 'Our Joys below it can improve, | And antedate the Bliss above' (l. 122). Oldham's lines on the delights of an amorous dream are evidently the source of Pope's best phrase: 'Not dying Saints enjoy such Extasies, | When they in Vision antedate their Bliss' ('The Dream', l. 73).

While it is true that Pope's mock-heroics owe something to the Restoration poetry of irony to which Oldham's *Satyr against Vertue* belongs, his selection of the poem for special praise is somewhat unexpected; the irony of Oldham's poem is both cruder and less controlled than Pope's. While Pope's ironic praise of dulness is stablized by the consistent inversion of values, Oldham's attack on virtue is complicated by his desire to dramatize the libertine outlook of Rochester. His 'Apology', appended to the published version, and his 'Counterpart to the Satyr Against Vertue', published in the *Remains* (1683), only emphasize the instability of the first poem's irony. A successful impersonation of Rochester inevitably leaves to the reader the task of determining a point of view. Defoe's Moll Flanders presents the reader with a similar problem. Pope's use of irony always depends on a strong presumption of shared values which prevents the loss of control that otherwise might arise in the more subtle cases (the *Epistle to Augustus*, for example).

Before attempting a general assessment of the relationship between Oldham and Pope as satirists, it is worth noting that Oldham's versions of classical pastorals were well respected in his day (his translation of Virgil's Eclogue VIII was included in Dryden's *Miscellany Poems* in 1684). It is not surprising that Pope saw something to admire in this group of poems. The

Twickenham editor and earlier editors have noted a substantial number of parallels, almost all linking Pope's 'Winter' and Oldham's *Bion* (based on Theocritus's third idyll). Pope's 'Winter' is a complex and highly sophisticated web of allusions to and echoes from a wide range of pastoral poems. It is often difficult to identify definite sources in this type of highly conventional verse, but there are signs that one of Oldham's best passages, in which he adds something of his own to Theocritus, was carefully assimilated by Pope:[26]

> Sad *Echo* too does in deep silence moan,
> Since thou art mute, since thou art speechless grown: . . .
> Trees drop their Leaves to dress thy Funeral,
> And all their Fruit before its *Autumn* fall:
> Each Flower fades, and hangs its wither'd head,
> And scorns to thrive, or live, now thou art dead:
> The bleating Flocks no more their Udders fill,
> The painful Bees neglect their wonted toil:
> Alas! what boots it now their Hives to store
> With the rich spoils of every plunder'd Flower,
> When thou, that wast all sweetness, art no more?   (ll. 60, 64)

The first line seems to have given the hint for Pope's 'In hollow Caves sweet Echo silent lies' (l. 41), which is developed into four lines that are quite beyond Oldham's powers. The third line of the above quotation seems to have been expanded by Pope into a richer conceit: 'Now hung with Pearls the dropping Trees appear, | Their faded Honours scatter'd on her Bier.' (l. 31). The next couplet in Pope may also be partly influenced by Oldham's lines 66–67 ('Each Flower fades . . . now thou art dead'): 'See, where on Earth the flow'ry Glories lye, | With her they flourish'd, and with her they dye.' The last four lines of the Oldham passage are compressed by Pope into a single couplet: 'Th'industrious Bees neglect their Golden Store; | Fair *Daphne*'s dead, and Sweetness is no more!' (l. 51). Neatly appropriating the rhyme-word, Pope 'improves' the epithet ('painful' bees is inelegant!) and infuses a poetic heightening by adding periphrasis ('Golden Store' for 'Hives'), and by lightly personifying 'Sweetness'. One other passage in *Bion*, 'Fair *Galatea* too laments thy death, | Laments the ceasing of thy tuneful breath' (l. 115), is imitated in 'Winter': 'The balmy *Zephyrs*, silent since her Death, | Lament the Ceasing of a sweeter Breath' (l. 49). Characteristically, Pope gives the borrowing point by making 'balmy *Zephyrs*' do the lamenting, thus adding a nice cosmic hyperbole. Finally, Pope picked up one of Oldham's best phrases (not derived from anything in the Latin) from his version of Eclogue VIII; Alpheus hopes to win Daphnis by the power of magic: 'Charms in her wonted Course can stop the Moon' (l. 103). Pope's *Temple of Fame* has, on its 'Eastern Front', statues of magicians and astronomers: 'These stop'd the Moon' (l. 101).

[26] Other parallels are between 'Summer', l. 84, and *Bion*, l. 40; 'Winter', l. 21, and *Bion*, refrain; 'Winter', ll. 39–40, and *Bion*, ll. 25, 27–28.

Pope's reading of Oldham's whole range of satiric writing was more thorough than most critics have realized. His allusive method makes it difficult to pinpoint precise borrowings or to be certain which sources among several possible are being tapped in specific instances. *An Essay on Man* has many passages which resemble ideas and expressions in Oldham's *Boileau VIII*. Some of these may simply reflect a common response to the French original, but it is hard to believe that Pope's reading of Oldham has not entered into the poem's system.[27] The following example is representative. Pope's lines on 'reasoning Pride' ('All quit their sphere, and rush into the skies. | . . . Men would be Angels' (1.124)) resemble Oldham's portrait of man, who 'puft with pride', aspires to Godhead: 'The Skies and Stars his properties must seem, | And turn-spit Angels tread the spheres for him' (l. 74).

Pope's stated admiration of the *Satyr Against Vertue* and *Jesuits IV* reminds us that Oldham was important to him as a satirist of ironic reversal. Several masterpieces of Augustan satire belong to this category. The programme of the Scriblerus Club is summed up in Pope's remarks in *An Essay on Criticism*:

Of all the Causes which conspire to blind
Man's erring Judgement, and misguide the Mind,
What the weak Head with strongest Byass rules,
Is *Pride*, the *never-failing Vice of Fools* . . .
Pride, where Wit fails, steps in to our Defence,
And fills up all the *mighty Void* of *Sense!*   (ll. 201, 209)

Nature abhors a vacuum, and, in the absence of 'Sense', spurious forms of 'Wit' take its place. The Augustan poet usually deals with deviant activities of pride by ironically impersonating or praising them. Butler, Buckhurst, and Rochester, in the Restoration period, worked their ironies by slyly setting off their satiric portraits against a background of assumed neo-Classical and courtly values. David Vieth has pointed out the extent to which these writers anticipated the type of satire Pope perfected in *The Dunciad*: 'The satire operates by ironically replacing traditional norms with their direct contraries: the poet appears to praise what he censures.'[28] Oldham's *Satyr Against Vertue* with its ironic praise of vice belongs to this kind. The *Dithyrambique*, Oldham's other mock-Pindaric impersonation of Rochester, ironically attacks reason and praises the divine frenzy of the drinker. The speaker says adieu to 'poor tott'ring Reason':

I've something brisker now to Govern me,
A more exalted noble Faculty,
Above thy Logick and vain boasted Pedantry.   (l. 94)

[27] Other parallels are between *An Essay on Man*, 1.68 and *Boileau VIII*, l. 69; *EM*, II.16 and *B8*, l. 90; *EM*, II.13–17 and *B8*, ll. 348–55; *EM*, IV.220 and *B8*, ll. 140, 150–51. There is also a resemblance between *An Essay on Man* and Oldham's 'A Satyr Touching Nobility' (based on Boileau v), for example between *EM*, 207–08, and 'Nobility', l. 117. Maynard Mack establishes other links between *An Essay on Man* and Oldham: see Twickenham edition, IV, 243n., and IV, 24n.
[28] *Attribution in Restoration Poetry*, p. 105.

Pope employs the same irony in *The Dunciad*, when he describes Cibber's repose upon the goddess's lap: 'Then raptures high the seat of Sense o'erflow, | Which only heads refin'd from Reason know' (III.5). 'Rochester' compares his drunken state to 'the Rage young Prophets feel' when 'They rave and stagger, and are mad like me'. Similarly, 'A slip-shod Sibyl' leads Cibber, 'In lofty madness meditating song' (III.15–16).

False wit is the topic of Dryden's and Pope's finest satires, and parody of the divine cosmic order is their central trope. Cowley's *Davideis* and Pindarique odes were the major sources of neo-Classically-honed cosmic 'enthusiasm'. Pope's *Dunciad* draws on a number of sources of the sublime, from Genesis to Milton's *Paradise Lost*. The manner and forms of reversal have been studied frequently.[29] It has not been noticed, however, that Oldham's poetry offered Pope a full inventory of the topoi associated with false wit.

Oldham develops the metaphor of poetic creation in his Pindarique ode in praise of Jonson. Just as Pope gives us, in *An Essay on Man*, an ideal of cosmic harmony which is reversed in *The Dunciad*, so Oldham presents Jonson's poetry as the true creation of genius. Before Jonson, the theatre

> . . . groan'd under a wretched Anarchy of wit.
> Unform'd and void was then it's Poesy,
> Only some preexisting matter we
>   Perhaps could see
>   That might foretel what was to be:
>   A rude and undigested lump it lay,
> Like the old Chaos ere the birth of light and day,
> Till thy brave Genius like a new Creator came,
>   And undertook the mighty frame . . .
>
> No sooner did thy Soul with active force and fire
>   The dull and heavy mass inspire,
>   But straight throwout it let us see
>   Proportion, order, harmony,
> And every part did to the whole agree,
> And strait appear'd a beauteous new-made World of Poetry.

> (ll. 32, 46)

Pope's Dulness, 'the great Anarch', and her chief dunce, Cibber, the 'Anti-Christ of wit', bring in the reign of 'Chaos' and 'blot out Order, and extinguish Light' (*Dunciad*, IV.13–14). The Cowleian idiom is there in Oldham's poem in a form especially open to satiric appropriation. Pope himself sometimes uses the style of Pindarique enthusiasm when writing of poetic creation, for example in his account of Virgil in the *Essay on Criticism*. Virgil, in 'his boundless Mind', 'design'd' his epic on the model of nature, but finding '*Nature* and *Homer* . . . the *same*', he 'checks the bold Design', and follows the ancient rules (ll. 130–40). The same idiom is used when Oldham praises Jonson: 'Nature and Art, together met and joyn'd, | Made up the

---

[29] See especially A. L. Williams, *Pope's 'Dunciad': A Study of its Meaning* (London, 1955), and Tony Tanner, 'Reason and the Grotesque: Pope's *Dunciad*', *Critical Quarterly*, 7 (1965), 145–60.

character of thy great mind' (l. 76). Pope probably picked up a phrase from Oldham's description of the artist's laborious composition of a 'matchlesse Piece'. Before it is finished, 'Long he contrives and weighs the *bold design*' (l. 214, my emphasis). Pope's paradox, that Nature and Homer are the same, is paralleled in Oldham's Pindarique ode, 'The Praise of Homer': 'We scarce discern where Thou, or Nature best has drawn' (l. 31).

The rich eclecticism of Dryden's satiric style included a strong element of Juvenalian vehemence. His translations of the Roman poet reveal his relish for the clash of heroic and vulgar discourses.[30] His apparently equivocal assessment of Oldham in the elegy probably reflects his partial attraction to the Billingsgate element in Oldham's satires. An amusing note in *The Dunciad* contrasts Dryden's unabashed obscenity in *MacFlecknoe* with Pope's more dignified procedure in Book II: 'but our author is more grave, and . . . tosses about his Dung with an air of Majesty' (*Dunciad Variorum* (1729), II.71n). Nevertheless, Pope too found a place for the 'strong rage' of Restoration satire. Earl Miner remarks on the surprising extent of eighteenth-century taste for the 'louder writings' of Butler, Cotton, and Oldham; he adds: 'It seems that the age of correctness sometimes liked the least correct things from the age of incorrectness.'[31]

Rachel Trickett draws attention to Oldham's development of the Horatian autobiographical persona, the voice of the 'Honest Muse', in his 'Letter from the Country to a Friend in Town', in which he confesses his addiction to scribbling.[32] His manner, one should add, resembles Pope's when he attacks the poets who 'rave, recite, and madden round the land' (*Epistle to Dr Arbuthnot*, l. 6), or when, having promised friends 'to rhyme no more', he wakes next morning 'in a raging fit' (*Imitations*, Epistle 1.6.178). Oldham describes how, when he feels 'the raving fit', like one 'in *Bedlam*', 'I run stark mad in Rhime'. When 'in a freakish Trance' his resolution weakens, Oldham cannot bear to quit his 'beloved Mistress, Poetry': 'Rich, or a Beggar, free, or in the Fleet, | What ere my fate is, 'tis my fate to write' (l. 226). Pope, in his *Imitation* of Horace's Satire II.1, tells his friend:

> Whate'er my fate, or well or ill at Court, . . .
> In Durance, exile, Bedlam, or the Mint,
> Like Lee or Budgell, I will rhyme and print. (ll. 92, 99)

However, the most striking link with *The Dunciad* is not the element of 'personal experience' but Oldham's use of the metaphor of poetic 'creation'. Drawing on passages from Dryden[33] and Cowley, Oldham describes mock-heroically the process of his own creative imagination:

> 'Tis endless, Sir, to tell the many ways,
> Wherein my poor deluded self I please:

[30] See my *English Verse Satire 1590–1765* (London, 1978), pp. 108–10, 162.
[31] *The Restoration Mode from Milton to Dryden* (Princeton, New Jersey, 1974), p. 424.
[32] *The Honest Muse*, p. 102.
[33] Dedication to *The Rival Ladies*, cited by Brooks, 'Poems of Oldham', p. 197.

> How, when the Fancy lab'ring for a Birth,
> With unfelt Throws brings its rude issue forth:
> How after, when imperfect shapeless Thought
> Is by the Judgement into Fashion wrought.
> When at first search I traverse o'er my mind,
> Nought but a dark, and empty Void I find:
> Some little hints at length, like sparks, break thence,
> And glimm'ring Thoughts just dawning into sence:
> Confus'd a while the mixt Idea's lie,
> With nought of mark to be discover'd by.   (l. 162)

In the *Davideis*, Book I, Cowley presents the creation analogy in reversed form:

> As first a various unform'd *Hint* we find
> Rise in some god-like *Poets* fertile *Mind*, . . .
> Such was *Gods Poem*, this *Worlds* new *Essay*;
> So wild and rude in its first draught it lay.[34]

The Dunciad's note on the parody of Genesis in Book I acknowledges a direct debt to Garth's *Dispensary*, but the passages from Cowley and Oldham establish a topos which is equally important to Pope's conception.[35] One likes to think that Oldham's 'hints . . . like sparks' suggested Pope's 'hints, like spawn' (*Dunciad Variorum*, 1.59)

There are many other parallels and echoes of Oldham in Pope's satires which confirm the importance of his reading in Restoration 'rough' satire. Pope would have found a rich mine of Grub-street imagery in Oldham's 'Satyr upon a Bookseller' and his *Juvenal III*. These and other poems are full of that urban squalor and sordid description which Pope relished in *The Dunciad*.[36] In Oldham's *Spenser's Ghost* the person of Spenser is introduced 'Dissuading the Author from the Study of POETRY'. He is 'famish'd' in looks, sunken-eyed; 'like Morning-Gown about him hung his Skin' (l. 10). Pope's 'meagre, muse-rid mope, adust and thin' is similarly enveloped 'In a dun night-gown of his own loose skin' (*Dunciad*, II.37). Using Spenser as his spokesman, Oldham expresses indignation at the neglect of poetry and poets in his own day. Even though Pope had no experience of Grub Street life, he must have responded sympathetically to the Horatian élitism of Oldham's argument. Before lamenting the neglect of the great (Cowley, Waller, Butler), 'Spenser' notes how 'many now, and bad the Scriblers be', and 'The foul Disease is so prevailing grown' that a few sonnets

> Set up an Author, who forthwith is grown
> A man of Parts, of Rhiming, and Renown:

[34] *Poems*, edited by A. R. Waller (Cambridge, 1905), p. 253.
[35] For an analysis of this passage in *The Dunciad* in relation to Milton, see Martin C. Battestin, *The Providence of Wit: Aspects of Form in Augustan Literature and the Arts* (Oxford, 1974), pp. 105–07. See also J. Philip Brockbank, 'The Book of Genesis and the Genesis of Books: The Creation of Pope's *Dunciad*', in *The Art of Alexander Pope*, edited by H. Erskine-Hill and Anne Smith (London, 1979), especially pp. 193–95.
[36] See Emrys Jones, 'Pope and Dulness', *Proceedings of the British Academy*, 54, (1968), 231–63.

> Ev'n that vile *Wretch*, who in lewd Verse each year
> Describes the Pageants, and my good *Lord May'r*,
> Whose Works must serve the next Election-day
> For making Squibs, and under Pies to lay,
> Yet counts himself of the inspired Train.   (l. 61)

Again Oldham contributes something to the stock of satiric topoi passed on by Dryden to Pope: the satire on City poets and the reference to the fate of waste paper appear in all three poets' satires.[37] The second topos is developed by 'Spenser', who points out that Oldham's 'forefathers' (including Flecknoe, Quarles, Heywood, Withers, Wild, and Ogilby, all favourite dunces of Dryden's or Pope's) have grown 'contemptible', and are 'damn'd to wrapping Drugs, and Wares'. He continues:

> And so may'st thou perchance pass up and down,
> And please a while th'admiring Court, and Town, }
> Who after shalt in *Duck-Lane* Shops be thrown,
> To mould with *Silvester*, and *Shirley* there,
> And truck for pots of Ale next *Stourbridg*-Fair.
> Then who'l not laugh to see th'immortal Name
> To vile *Mundungus* made a Martyr Flame?
> And all thy deathless Monuments of Wit,
> Wipe Porters Tails, or mount in Paper-kite?   (l. 103)

When Cibber prepares to burn twelve volumes of his works as a sacrifice to Dulness, he gives thanks that they will not be condemned to the fate of their sister sheets, to be sent 'vagrant thro' the land' (compare Oldham's 'pass up and down') and to go 'Where vile Mundungus trucks for viler rhymes' *(Dunciad*, 1.234). Oldham's 'To vile *Mundungus* made a Martyr Flame' is directly used by Pope, and perhaps 'Martyr Flame' suggested Pope's metaphor, when Cibber tells his sacrificed volumes 'Go, purify'd by flames ascend the sky, | My better and more christian progeny!' (1.227). Oldham's 'truck for pots of Ale' may have influenced Pope's 'trucks for viler rhymes'. Pope's favourite topic of 'poverty and poetry' is also treated fully in the Spenser poem, although, unlike Pope, Oldham was uncomfortably close to the financial plight of the 'trading Scriblers' who 'write for Pence', and 'Must starve' if 'a thin House on the third day appear' (the third day of a play's performance was the author's benefit day). Pope's Cibber too suffered 'a thin Third day' *(Dunciad*, 1.114).[38] For Pope the scribbler's poverty was an emblem of his poetic degradation, while Oldham stressed the neglect which both scribblers and great poets have to endure. His indignant lines on Butler ('On *Butler* who can think without just Rage, | The Glory, and the Scandal of the Age?' (l. 175)) may have been in Pope's mind when he wrote of Erasmus, 'that *great, injur'd* Name, | (The *Glory* of the Priesthood, and the *Shame!*)' *(An Essay on Criticism*, l. 693).

---

[37] Oldham transcribed Dryden's *MacFlecknoe* in 1678 or 1679 (see Brooks, 'Poems of Oldham', p. 192). The 'waste-paper' topos is classical: see Persius, 1.43: Horace, *Epistles*, ii.1.269, and Catullus, xcv.7.
[38] Dryden refers to 'thin *Third-dayes*' in the 'Epilogue' to *The Unhappy Favourite* (1682). Compare Oldham's version of *Ars Poetica*, l. 320.

'A Satyr Address'd to a Friend' is probably Oldham's most Horatian poem, and one might suppose that it would have appealed to Pope as being more 'delicate'. The poet warns his friend of the disappointments in store when the poor graduate comes to town from the university looking for a place. Like the Spenser satire, it draws on several sources which reflect on the miseries of scholars and poets.[39] The fable of the wolf and the dog, with which the satire concludes, is classical. The general form of the poem resembles Horace's satire, 'The Town Mouse and the Country Mouse' (II.6), which Pope and Swift collaborated in imitating (as Cowley and Sprat had before). The first half of the poem includes Oldham's version of the 'Happy Man' topos, modelled on Horace and on Cowley's 'The Wish':

> 'T has ever been the top of my Desires,
> The utmost height to which my wish aspires,
> That Heav'n would bless me with a small Estate,
> Where I might find a close obscure retreat;
> There, free from Noise, and all ambitious ends,
> Enjoy a few choice Books, and fewer Friends,
> Lord of myself, accountable to none,
> But to my Conscience, and my God alone:
> There live unthought of, and unheard of, die.   (l. 115)

Oldham's expression of this familiar theme resembles Pope's in *An Epistle to Dr Arbuthnot*:

> Oh let me live my own! and die so too! . . .
> Maintain a Poet's Dignity and Ease,
> And see what friends, and read what books I please . . .
> I was not born for Courts or great Affairs,
> I pay my Debts, believe, and say my Pray'rs.   (ll. 261, 263, 267)

Oldham's poem not only has a Horatian form, but, in comparison with his other work, has a much less extravagant diction, a reduction in rhetorical vehemence, and even a tendency towards a neo-Classical antithetical balance ('Books . . . Friends'; 'my self . . . none'; 'my Conscience . . . my God'). Oldham warns his friend about the drudgery of school-teaching, and perhaps speaks from his own bitter experience at Croydon:

> For when you've toil'd, and labour'd all you can,
> To dung, and cultivate a barren Brain:
> A Dancing-Master shall be better paid,
> Tho' he instructs the Heels, and you the Head.   (l. 60)

This is good, but one should not overstate the significance of such passages or regard them as signs of a late-developing 'correct' Augustan poet. Oldham always possessed a strong sense of stylistic decorum, and was capable of modulating his usual manner according to his chosen 'kind'. Nevertheless, there remains a characteristic stylistic 'set', which includes a

---

[39] They include Juvenal VII, Burton's *Anatomy of Melancholy*, and L. Eachard's *Grounds . . . of the Contempt of the Clergy* (1670).

preference for dramatic utterance (dialogue or implied dialogue is very common), for a rhetoric shaped to crescendos, climaxes, and sustained rants, for a diction aimed at intensity (obscene and vulgar, or heroic and declamatory) rather than at antithetical wit, and for hyperbole rather than litotes.

Peter Dixon is surely right in his view that Pope 'assimilated the various and distinctive excellences' of his predecessors in satire. He versified Donne's satires and contemplated doing the same for Bishop Hall.[40] The Elizabethan satiric tradition was transmitted to Pope through various channels and emerges most strongly in *The Dunciad* and in the *Epilogue to the Satires*. In a note on the final line of 'Dialogue II' of the *Epilogue*, Pope declares that he felt the need to 'enter thus, in the most plain and solemn manner he could, a sort of PROTEST against the insuperable corruption and depravity of manners, which he had been so unhappy as to live to see'. While he considered Oldham to be 'a very undelicate writer' (Spence § 473), he was able to learn from Oldham's stance of indignant virtue. The satirist's first speech in 'Dialogue II' reminds one of Oldham's Juvenalian voice:

> Vice with such Giant-strides comes on amain,
> Invention strives to be before in vain;
> Feign what I will, and paint it e'er so strong,
> Some rising Genius sins up to my Song.   (l. 6)

Thomas Gilbert saw an affinity between Pope's satires of the early 1730s and Oldham's *Jesuits*:

> O *Pope*, thou scourge to a licentious age,
> Inspire these lines with thy severest rage;
> Arm me with satire keen as *Oldham* wrote
> Against the curst *Divan*, with poignant thought.[41]

Pope, it must be said, dignifies the indignant stance with moral and religious overtones. Oldham, in 'A Satyr Upon a Woman', is 'Arm'd with dire Satyr, and resentful Spite', while Pope, in his *Imitation* of Horace's Satire II.i., is 'arm'd for Virtue' when he brands 'the bold Front of shameless, guilty Men'. In 'Upon a Bookseller', Oldham adopts the Elizabethan style of self-righteousness:

> But I, whom spleen, and manly rage inspire,
> Brook no Affront, at each Offence take fire:
> Born to chastise the Vices of the Age,
> Which Pulpits dare not, nor the very Stage   (l. 11)

Oldham's indignation is often playful: he wears his pen like a sword and runs through 'each affronting Sot'. Pope too elevates the 'sacred Weapon' of satire above the pulpit, but his indignation has real moral intensity:

---

[40] *The World of Pope's Satires* (London, 1968), p. 8. Donne's Satire IV is related to Horace's *Satires*, 1.9, imitated by Oldham. Pope's versification contains one phrase, 'wild to get loose' (l. 116), which appears in Oldham's imitation (l. 16).
[41] *A View of the Town . . .* (1735), p. 18, cited by Weinbrot, p. 146.

> O sacred Weapon! left for Truth's defence,
> Sole Dread of Folly, Vice, and Insolence!
> To all but Heav'n-directed hands deny'd,
> The Muse may give thee, but the Gods must guide.
> Rev'rent I touch thee! but with honest zeal;
> To rowze the Watchmen of the Publick Weal,
> To Virtue's Work provoke the tardy Hall,
> And goad the Prelate slumb'ring in his Stall.   (l. 212)

While Pope's moral fervour differs markedly from Oldham's mock-serious rant, Oldham developed a version of the Elizabethan-Juvenalian satirist which Pope could adapt to his own purposes.

It is clear that Oldham is closer to Dryden than to Pope, and Pope closer to Dryden than to Oldham. It is tempting to say that Oldham might have developed a maturer Augustan style if he had lived longer. It is historically more valid, however, to recognize his actual achievement, which is distinctive, not merely derivative or anticipatory. He was responsive, as we have seen, to a considerable number of voices, traditional and contemporary, and his range includes Rochesterian intensity of feeling, metaphysical hyperbole, Ovidian passion, pastoral pathos, Elizabethan-Juvenalian vehemence, heroic rant, and poetry of irony and comic reversal. His later poems are less strident, but one should not exaggerate their departure from his favourite kinds of intensity. At the other end of the scale, the *Jesuits* were written at a time of peculiar public volatility and anxiety; they are not necessarily more typical than the later poems. He never again wrote with such declamatory fury. There is sufficient evidence to suggest that Pope read him carefully and assimilated several aspects of his work.[42] He dissolved the rough fibres of Oldham's wit in the powerful solvent of his allusive art, and in doing so he put the eighteenth century in touch with the rough 'masculine' wit of Restoration satire.

---

[42] Other parallels include *Boileau* VIII, ll. 94–95, 99–102 (compare Pope, *Imitations of Horace*, Epistle 1.6.112, and 69–72); *Juvenal* XIII, l. 137 (compare *Dunciad*, 1.48); *Letter from the Country*, ll. 224–27 (compare *Imitations of Horace*, Epistle 1.1.184); and *Horace his Art of Poetry*, ll. 704–05 (compare *Epistle to Arbuthnot*, ll. 159–60); ll. 813–14 (compare *The Dunciad*, III.289–90).

The Yahoo in the Doll's House:
Gulliver's Travels the Children's Classic

JOHN TRAUGOTT

University of California, Berkeley

Your spring and your day are wasted in play,
And your winter and night in disguise.
(Blake, 'Nurse's Song')

1 *Of Big and Little*

Boswell preens himself on his skill at making Ursa Major growl:

Johnson was in high spirits this evening at the club, and talked with great animation and success. He attacked Swift, as he used to do upon all occasions . . . I wondered to hear him say of *Gulliver's Travels*, 'When once you have thought of big men and little men, it is very easy to do all the rest'. I endeavoured to make a stand for Swift, and tried to rouse those who were much more able to defend him; but in vain. Johnson at last, of his own accord, allowed very great merit to the inventory of articles found in the pockets of the Man Mountain, particularly the description of his watch, which it was conjectured was his GOD, as he consulted it upon all occasions.[1]

It is another of Johnson's blunderbusses; potting greats was a recreation, but a more general animus was reserved for Swift — 'upon all occasions'. Swift is allowed a satiric device, big and little, by which things such as a pocket watch are made strange so as to yield up their significances as cultural peculiarities. Similar satiric devices were well known: simpleminded aliens, Persian, Chinese, Abyssinian, and so on, could be counted on to say the obvious about the moral and political problems with which Europeans liked to perplex themselves. Perhaps Johnson thought Swift's big and little only another attempt at this change of perspective, nothing new, and being a specialist in the vanity of human wishes he might well have found Swift's hateful impatience with men for not being perfect only another sketch of vanity: 'And Swift expires a driveller and a show.'

But what Swift was about with his big and little has almost nothing to do with this kind of shift in perspective, nor has it much to do with the grand pageant of the vanity of human wishes from China to Peru. From his superior altitude Gulliver is able to make precious few observations about men and manners and political principles. On the contrary, though his size

---

[1] *Life of Johnson*, edited by G. B. Hill, revised by L. F. Powell, 6 vols (Oxford, 1934–64), II (1934), 318–19.

is a constant danger to all, his stool a great embarrassment, and his sex a giant absurdity, he does his best to become a Lilliputian, proud as a Nardac. Politics aside, he seems like a child playing with dolls and other reduced models, and the imagery of such play is pervasive. As in Lilliput, so in Brobdingnag. It is his perspective not as a giant, but as a Platonic philosopher-king, that enables the King to analyse the skulduggery of English politics. For that, he could be Gulliver's size. Again the pervasive imagery is that of childhood play, this time with Gulliver the English chauvinist as the doll.

'Once you have thought of big men and little men, it is very easy to do all the rest.' The trick is to think of what big and little mean in the human economy. Only Swift between Rabelais and Carroll seems to have thought of big and little as fantasies of childhood play that live on in the adult.[2] So pervasive is the imagery of doll play in the first two voyages that often Swift seems to be indulging himself gratuitously without anything in mind beyond thinking up comic routines to put Gulliver through, including a good many that once were called 'the indecencies'.[3] Sometimes indeed he hardly seems to know whether he is giving vent to his famous 'savage indignation', or having a joke, or both. Commentators from his day to ours have strained to uncover references to the politics of the time or to political principles so as to rectify the irresolute and diffuse quality of the narrative.[4] But need it be rectified? Looked at not as a set of cryptograms but as a figurative relation between child play and the terrifying games of politics, a satiric device, the narrative is not at all diffused by stray or casual vignettes. The need to find a key to each one of them vanishes.

As for the 'indecencies', they have sometimes been termed 'coprology', to lend them dignity, and given a religious tincture by critics who want to do their best by Swift; they are said to remind us of original sin. That is uncertain. What is certain is that they make us laugh and that they resist allegorizing just by provoking laughter. These moments of bowel and bladder all come back to the device of big and little, the humour of admiration, exhibitionism, and embarrassment guaranteed by the absurd size-ratio.

But the 'indecencies' are venereal as well: the sly and admiring view of Gulliver's privates through the rent in his breeches, the reputed passion of the Treasurer's wife of his person, the masturbation joke at the very beginning, and the use of Gulliver as a sort of dildo by the maids of honour.

---

[2] Voltaire's *Micromégas*, though sometimes said to imitate *Gulliver's Travels*, does not in fact enter Swift's order of imagination because its use of the figure of big and little has nothing to do with childhood play. *Micromégas* is twenty-four kilometres high and cannot even see the creature called man.

[3] Aline Mackenzie Taylor has suggested that many of these comic routines are based on freak-shows that Swift could have seen in London. See 'Sights and Monsters and Gulliver's *Voyage to Brobdingnag*', *Tulane Studies in English*, 7 (1957), 29–82.

[4] For a review of interpretations of political allegory in *Gulliver's Travels*, see F. P. Lock, *The Politics of Gulliver's Travels* (Oxford, 1980).

None of these yields up any convincing allegories either of politics or of human nature. As Swift makes so much of his arithmetic of big and little, 12 to 1, 144 to 1, 1728 to 1, he must want us to play with these 'indecencies' for raucous laughs. If critics even looked at the provocative way the 'Master Bates' pun is teased out by playful incremental repetitions, they would find themselves facing the Swift who in trivial contexts obsessively juggles words, the more *double-entendres* the better, not Swift the priest shoring up Church and State. And this joke is apropos of nothing.[5] We shall come back to these matters, but a cursory look raises doubts about Swift's moral clarity. Knowing Johnson's moral seriousness and pudency, we can suppose that he was offended by these gratuitous images of play, 'indecencies' included, diffusing the satire; but so must be anyone bent on gleaning moral instruction from the Dean only to find himself faced with a dilly-dallying fellow who seems to enjoy fooling just for the sport.

II The Image of the Child

This perspective on material that cannot easily be translated into moral uplift, and which often enough seems irrelevant to any satiric point, perhaps allows us to take pleasure in the images of childlike doll play throughout the first two voyages without scurrying off to our moral bunkers. We can tarry and delectate the play, sharpening our nostalgia for freedoms long lost, abandoning attempts to translate each episode into a support for civilization and right reason, or into another abstraction equally respectable and vague. Let us record, first, the presence of this imagery, and then, putting away childish things, take up its satiric bearings.

Gingerly, gently he goes: mincing steps in the two great streets, utmost circumspection lest he trample someone. Happy thought to wear his short waistcoat; otherwise would not the skirts of his coat have tumbled roofs and eaves? There, on rooftops, masses of doll people admiring his progress. Two great streets, reticulating alleys and lanes, shops, markets, houses of three to five storeys, and in the centre of all a noble pile, the imperial palace. The Monarch, taller by a nail's breadth than the rest of his court, as befits his awesome presence among them, strong lip and chin of the Hapsburg, helmeted in bejewelled gold, has a great desire that the Man Mountain should see the magnificence of the palace and its royal apartments in the inmost court. By the clever contrivance of a footstool for himself, a scaffolding made from the tallest trees in the palace park, the delicate giant steps over the battlements and down into the court, where by lying on his side, his face applied to the windows of the middle storeys, his great eye (a foot and a

---

[5] Swift's teasing out of this gratuitous pun goes like this: 'Mr. *James Bates*'; 'When I left Mr. *Bates*, I went down'; 'my good Master Mr. *Bates* [recommended me as] Surgeon to the *Swallow*' (swift, swallow, and martin are often taken for the same bird); Mr. *Bates*, my Master'; 'my good Master *Bates* dying'; 'my Conscience would not suffer me to imitate the bad Practice of too many among my Brethren' (pp. 19–20). Being advised to alter his condition, Gulliver marries, and Master Bates dies. References are to *The Prose Works of Jonathan Swift*, edited by Herbert Davis and others, 16 vols (Oxford, 1939–74), XI (revised 1959).

half wide) can look in upon the most splendid apartments where the Empress and the young Princes of the realm, richly dressed, move about busy with their little lives.

It is the child's fantasy of dominion over the world, of absolute freedom to be a quick-change artist and perfect puppet master. The business of life is to go from big to little and back again at will, from gentle to fierce, demonic to angelic. Gulliver has just prostrated himself before the monarch who comes to his shoetops, and will soon stand as tall as any six-inch Lilliputian honoured as a Nardac. Sometimes the dolls are wicked, like Skyresh Bolgolam whose inveterate malice is without cause; sometimes good, like the lady of quality who comes to call and is shamelessly traduced for her decency.

Such scenes of child's play punctuate the narrative throughout. They are what they are. Insisting on drawing from them a moral allegory we become a species of the cryptographers of Laputa. Why the deployment of a troop of his Majesty's best horse, twenty-four in number, on Gulliver's handkerchief to perform mock skirmishes, discharge blunt arrows, flourish swords, and flee and pursue in the smartest military order? This charade of toy soldiers, a stock piece of children's shows, comes just after the radical satire of the court games and looks so much like them that we might skim the two together, remarking only that there is a lot of parade and prancing in this world. The court games, with which we shall deal at length, reminded contemporaries that Walpole had resuscitated a good many ribbon honours to bribe a good many biddable politicians, but that 'key' is only incidental to the satire, which is about the hateful connexions between perverse games and politics and whose affectiveness depends upon our memory of childhood games. The satire, therefore, begins just where the non-satiric or pointless tableaux of doll play, such as the handkerchief jousting, have their affectiveness, in the nostalgia for childhood play.

Similarly, a nearly identical image, of Gulliver's social receptions in which he draws up on his table the coaches-and-six of his callers, seems to defy translation, though the visits of the Treasurer's wife and the imputation of a sexual liaison, from which Gulliver so solemnly defends himself (without mentioning that the conjoining parts differ in volume in the ratio 1728 to 1), has been identified as a sneer at Walpole's wife, notoriously unfaithful to her notoriously unfaithful husband. The allusion is hopelessly off the mark, however, since it is comedy of absurd propriety, Gulliver's stock in trade, while the carryings-on of Walpole and his wife were neither absurdly proper nor innocent. But the vignette imitates, as a child imitates, the banal moral histrionics and stock postures seen anywhere, any time.

An even more problematic image is that of Gulliver supine, stretched out upon the landscape by a gossamer-web of threads, his body a sort of country swarming with mannikins who parade on the peninsulas of his legs and march over the plain of his belly. Later on, while he is sleeping, one more intrepid than the rest scales the crag of his chin to thrust his pike into the left nostril. The image has become a staple allegorical sketch in the repertoires of political cartoonists ever since. It is the giant-in-chains beset by little villains. The cartoon is so common that it must represent a universal political reality. But for Swift, what giant, what chains? Why does he not burst his bonds and scatter the little villains like so many bugs?

Gulliver never quite forgets that he might do just that: 'My left Hand being already loose, I could easily free myself: And as for the Inhabitants, I had Reason to believe I might be a Match for the greatest Armies they could bring against me'; 'I confess I was often tempted, while they were passing backwards and forwards on my Body, to seize Forty or Fifty of the first that came in my Reach, and dash them against the Ground . . . [but] I now considered myself as bound by the Laws of Hospitality' (pp. 22, 24). And this tentative, though obvious, opening to freedom remains a comic perplexity throughout. It is the indispensable illustration in every children's edition; it is never missing.

A little later on, Gulliver is playing mock-ogre, putting six of the little 'criminals' in his pocket, taking them out one by one, making a terrible face as if to eat the squalling rascal alive, and then setting him gently on the ground to run away. Next, they are playing hide-and-seek in his hair. And after all this playing at benign monster, Gulliver is on his knees beseeching the six-inch monarch for his freedom.

For the child reader these charades mime a familiar domestic game in which the adult plays victim to the child, letting him crawl over his supine and submissive body, pinning his arms and legs, and then, suddenly reversing roles, reasserting power, rises a monster, catching the child above his head, making as if to eat him. The child with his dolls can perform the same routine in three sizes at once, big and little, victim and master, friend and foe, and still always himself. And when the demands of ingestion and excretion are upon him, he may even incorporate that real time incongruously in play time — as does Gulliver. A gargantuan feast is hoisted to his giant maw by legions of servants each fetching his mite, shoulders and loins of mutton, two or three at a mouthful, endless loaves of bread, hogsheads of wine. And he urinates when he must, playing the cascade, admiring himself and the torrent through Lilliputian eyes. Multitudes wonder.

The questions that naturally arise as to the satiric meaning of these episodes that have made *Gulliver's Travels* a classic child's book are not easily answered. Coming as they do along with our literature's most virulent and relentless satire and irony, such episodes charm and disarm the reader who has to remind himself to be on the lookout for the victims and the moral uplift. There are a good many more such pleasures. The bathtub war is one near to everyone's recollection of childhood play, but others, such as the temple episode, are wholly baffling because they seem absolutely to require a key, though none has been found. Like a dog, Gulliver is tethered to a great temple, which having been 'polluted . . . by an unnatural Murder' is good for nothing but a kennel. In he creeps at night to sleep, out in the morning to defecate. A polluted temple?[6] And the excrements? Taking the average stool at six inches in length, a half-pound in weight, and calculating by Swift's ratios, that is a stool lying in Lilliputian eyes the equivalent of six feet long, weighing 864 pounds. How long would the Lilliputian workers who attend him require to cut it up and cart it away? No wonder Gulliver is embarrassed. But what does it all mean?

One answer that has not been tried out is that all this playing dog in his kennel and mucking about with excrements is regressive to childhood play which in turn sets off the perverse political games. If by attenuating his savage satire in these charades of child play Swift is playing games with our sensibilities, a lot of scholars are out of business. Finding him now joking, now raging, almost the two at once, play collapsing seriousness and seriousness forbidding play, the common reader, not being able to say what it all means and no nonsense, must resort to his imagination. It is the same case with Rabelais, another for play with big and little, who has suffered the scholar's reductions to allegories of history and religion, allowing precious little room for his play and its effects upon the reader.[7] Pantagruel drowns an entire army of encroaching miscreants, little people, our size, swarming about his ankles, by pissing on them. Without arcane learning, just at first blush, one might think this incident good comedy, a wish-fulfilment fantasy of power to distribute justice in a natural way without legalistic fretting, for Rabelais loves to reduce things to the truth of our bodies — and with a linguistic joke for good measure, for is not Pantagruel making literal a metaphor to be heard everyday in 'vulgar' conversation? He is good, the invading army a pack of rascals, and he has easily at hand the instrument to do what ought to be done to rascals according to this everyday metaphor. Such comedy founded in ordinary figures of speech does not require hierophantic interpretation.

When one comes to the same image in Swift, obviously borrowed, the commentators are again busy plumbing this mystery: why did Swift require Gulliver to piss on the palace fire? This is in fact the second time Gulliver urinates on little people. Swift would seem to have delighted in the Rabelaisian device of letting the giant work out this metaphor. But what of the allegory? Does the malevolence of the Queen towards Gulliver for saving her noble pile with such an instrument symbolize the inveterate prejudice of the 'royal prude', Queen Anne, for Swift after the indecencies of *A Tale of a Tub* by which he purposed to rescue her Church from sectarian fires? Or is it the Hanoverian resentment of the Tory peace of Utrecht,

---

[6] For a psychoanalytic interpretation of this passage, identifying the temple with Moor Park, see Phyllis Greenacre, *Swift and Caroll: A Psychoanalytic Study of Two Lives* (New York, 1955).

[7] See the discussion of this problem by Michel Beaujour, *Le Jeu de Rabelais: Essai sur Rabelais* (Paris, 1969).

consummated by Swift's friends, which put out the fire of the war of the Spanish succession in a way the Whigs did not approve? Or again, is it Oxford's final disgrace at the end of Queen Anne's reign when the 'prude' could no longer tolerate his licentious habits? But in this instance Swift himself has a word to say. Having heard that the maids of honour were sniffing at his indecencies, and more especially at Gulliver's engine for extinguishing the palace fire, he wrote as 'Lemuel Gulliver' to Mrs Howard, his friend and the Prince's mistress, to ask whether he could have used an 'improper Engine' to extinguish a fire kindled by the candle of a maid of honour who had carelessly fallen asleep while reading a romance.[8] When the vulgar metaphor is literalized in a representation of a common political situation about which Swift thought he knew a good deal, it is not surprising that it seems to fit several experiences of his own life in politics. It remains, however, a childlike fantasy of power setting off the impotence of political man before the capricious, irrational, and terrifying exercise of power. The ingratitude of the Queen and the nice 'reason' she gives for her pique do not admit of rational explanation; they are part of the game of power.

To the child's-book representation in Lilliput of play with reduced models of king and court, town and castle, politician and warrior, with quick changes of size and role, Brobdingnag returns the reverse image of the child's fears. Ineptitude of body and understanding, dependence on uncertain protectors, authority that may become capricious and dangerous: the stuff of nightmare is the main imagery of this voyage. And all this in the person of Gulliver, who is now a doll, toyed with by various protectors, housed in a doll's house, dressed and undressed by a girl, and, worst of all, encouraged to perform like a clockwork toy, first by threat and exploitation and then by his need to ingratiate himself with dubious protectors. To soften the withering gaze of some, to encourage the smiles of others, he does his cute routines of mimicry.

On the King's first conjecture, Gulliver must be a 'piece of Clock-work', which in his country (as well as in Swift's) had 'arrived to a very great Perfection' (p. 103). Gulliver, indeed, might be Descartes's automaton fashioned by artists in clockwork to resemble a man in every mechanical detail.[9] It could never think, and thinking act, because only God can make immaterial substance act on material, mind on body. Fixed phrases might be concocted for the automaton to utter but it could never speak of its own volition. Whether or not Swift was wryly exploiting the comedy implicit in the mockery of humankind by Descartes's automaton, Gulliver fills the bill, smartly acting the wind-up toy, speaking formulas as the puppet of his dear native land's political ventriloquists. In Lilliput he retains a residual humanity; here fear has turned him into this mechanism. He might have

[8] *The Correspondence of Jonathan Swift*, edited by Harold Williams, 5 vols (Oxford, 1963–65), III, 190 (28 November 1726).
[9] *Discourse on Method*, Discourse v.

been snuffed out by the oblivious reapers who are not looking out for weasels. He might have had his death through exploitation by the farmer who betrays his promise to his daughter that she should have him for a pet. He might have been dropped by a careless handler, eaten by a rat, loved to death by a monkey, murdered by a jealous dwarf, and, most pitiful, he might have perished a caged pet. All these dangers are obvious comic heightenings of typical childhood fears.

Gulliver's instinctual reaction is to act the doll, securing his safety by amusing his protectors with antics in imitation of the postures of man. He begins by bowing and scraping, drinking a little dram to the farmer's wife, stumbling against a crust of bread, and recovering to wave his hat and shout 'Huzza!' three times to show he is still going. That is dear. These ingratiating antics (he later calls them his 'Fopperies', p. 98) make of him a commercial property valuable to the farmer, to be shown off at fairs, and a pet of the nine-year-old mothering girl, Glumdalclitch, and of the Queen. As pet he develops a set of little routines, a sort of continual jig. The faster he goes the more people want to protect him in a world that could be fatal at any moment. He flourishes his minute sword, exercises a straw as a pike, parades on Glumdalclitch's leading strings, eats grandiosely 'in Miniature' from silver dishes of the kind seen in 'a *London* Toy-shop' (p. 106). Then there are his feats: swimming in a bowl of cream, sailing before the puffs of the court ladies in a trough fashioned for his yachting, running up and down the bench before a spinet keyboard to plunk out a little jig with his fists, showing his mettle by sticking a rat, defying the court dwarf's jealous malice by calling him 'brother', and so on. When not performing, he is packed away from harm in his little box with his little furnishings, hanging at Glumdalclitch's girdle.

With this olio of 'Fopperies' he becomes a bigger and bigger figure about the court (or so he believes) until he arrogates to himself the right to philosophize with his Majesty. Enfranchised by his knowledge of the ways European nations blow up one another's armies and navies for glory, he thinks to dilate on good government by telling England's story to the King. He is dummy to his culture's ventriloquism. What comes out of his mouth is what has been put in.

He is a living doll. By such stunts as Gulliver performs, children promise without words to grow into the required pattern. That earns smiles and indulgence. Louis XIII as an infant was given a doll got up as the perfect gentleman he was to become. Even a king will hear the formula: 'That's right, dear, be a doll.' It would seem that in the foregrounded imagery of the natural process of the child's fearful adaptation to approved social roles, Swift was figuring a political truth that obsessed him. His mouth stuffed with a pack of right-thinking clichés, and given a pompous little role to play, a man could be brought to do anything that a Yahoo could do — and with the best reasons in the world.

Again, as in *Lilliput*, we have two books: the child's book, here Gulliver doing his miming acts to ward off danger; and the satire, here Gulliver the political puppet, lately reduced from 'the greatest Prodigy that ever appeared in the World' (p. 86) to a weasel, trying to ingratiate himself with his betters by acting out doll roles and to aggrandize himself by prating chauvinist clichés to associate himself with power. The secret of power would seem to be, following Gulliver's career in Brobdingnag, to implicate the nice man, with all the glozing words he has learned to mouth, in blood. From the quick-changing role-playing of childhood, the reader's thought passes to the fixed roles of the political puppet.

III *The Pleasure of Being the Cause*

To die for the true faith that eggs should be opened at one end rather than the other — what does this parody parody? The political uses of religion, certainly, but what about the egg ends? Are the doctrines of religion only a game used by politicians to strike terror in the hearts of communicants? And how to separate religion from its doctrines? A six-inch doll, Reldresal the historian, standing in the palm of Gulliver's hand, exposes the long and terrible history of the egg religion. He has a solution for this game. It is certainly Swift's: believe what you like but keep your mouth shut, or believe what the magistrate tells you to believe. Religion would then be no theatre for martyrs, just a sort of piety towards the commonwealth, very Roman, or a transaction between a man and his god about which no one need be curious.

Having the freedom to dispose of time and space at will, to become or abolish the other, to concoct whatever rules he may please, the child might well get up this egg game to imitate what is said about religion and its wars. The egg game has everything one could need for religion: a primitive church, a reformation, a church established by law, a theology ('many hundred large Volumes', p. 49), holy wars, martyrs, an alliance of church and state with accompanying repression on both sides. But a religion of eggs makes no sense 'in the scheme of things', whatever that may be. But 'the scheme of things' being a creation, or at least a discovery, of religion, we have a tautology saying only that religion has its own internal coherence. But nonsense, even babble, has its internal coherence, too: the sense of nonsense, we may call it.[10] So this egg religion does not differ structurally from real religion.

Such are the speculations Swift's irony raises. We can do no more than speculate, but we must speculate. His irony, which is here as elsewhere incompletion, requires it. On the other hand there are several differences from a real game. Players in a game do not die. A game has no teleology; it has its end in itself. Not so the egg religion; players die; far from an end in

---

[10] The sense of nonsense is a leading idea of Elizabeth Sewell's *The Field of Nonsense* (London, 1952). Sewell shows that nonsense has its structure as well as what passes for sense.

itself, it is a device of power existing outside the rules. Inside the rules, the 'believers' (whether they believe or not) must play. It is a pseudo-game, though enough like a real one to serve nicely a child's fantasy, the sort of thing meant to amuse Alice Pleasance. The mind goes from that fantasy to the world's idiot business. The figurative nature of the transference is the important thing. Let us now consider the figure.

It is not the traditional metaphor, that man is a child and his business only a child's game. This metaphor, often heard in the wistful mutterings of world-weary moralists, is perhaps Pope's in his well-known passage, 'Behold the child', a sentiment that relieves the clanking of philosophical machinery in *An Essay on Man*:

> Behold the child, by Nature's kindly law,
> Pleas'd with a rattle, tickled with a straw;
> Some livelier play-thing gives his youth delight,
> A little louder, but as empty quite:
> Scarfs, garters, gold, amuse his riper stage;
> And beads and pray'r-books are the toys of age:
> Pleas'd with this bauble still, as that before;
> 'Till tir'd he sleeps, and Life's poor play is o'er![11]

Swift appears to have no use for either the *longueurs* or the sentiment that lie in this metaphor. Rope dancing is a device of tyranny fatal to the dancer, contests over the right end of an egg devastate nations, a monarch's play with the word 'clemency' signifies blinding and enslavement, a bathtub navy on strings is intended to subjugate a people for ever.

By this doll-house play of *Lilliput* that charms children, and adults who can remember childhood, the violent satirist calls up a nostalgia for the freedom of childhood games with reduced models in which the child gives himself 'the pleasure of being the cause', moving the puppet instead of being the puppet moved, mastering reality in fantasy, according to whim.[12] This charming play metamorphoses into the bitter charades of political power from which no player escapes, neither the right-thinking puppet of power called Gulliver nor its knowing functionaries who must play on within a system of rules controlled from outside the game. Swift's figure is in the order of metonymy, the relation of before and after, pristine and corrupt, good seed and evil flower, and in this relation would seem to lie the affective force of the satire. It is a horror of human life that Swift treats, whose only remedy is consciousness. The puppet shows of *Lilliput* and *Brobdingnag* are a manner of thinking, and it is now useful to think about the psychology of childhood games, so intimately bound up in the imagination of these voyages.

Let us go back to Piaget's summary proposition, that in doll play the child gives himself 'the pleasure of being the cause'. Cause of what? This remains

---

[11] Epistle II, l. 275, quoted from the one-volume Tickenham paperback edition of the poems, edited by John Butt (London, 1965), pp. 524–25.
[12] See Jean Piaget, *Play, Dreams, and Imitation in Childhood*, translated by C. Gattegno and F. M. Hodgson (New York, 1962), pp. 112, 151. Subsequent page references are given in the text.

unspecified, as the child's symbolic imagination opens to the universe, embracing, says Piaget, 'the whole life of the child', nothing less than a 'representational assimilation of the whole of reality to the ego'.[13] Even restricting the term 'doll' to a girl's toy, as is traditional, it has nothing to do with the 'maternal instinct'. The doll simply provides 'the opportunity to relieve symbolically her own life in order to assimilate more easily its various aspects as well as to resolve daily conflicts and realize unsatisfied desires' (p. 107). For Piaget then it is not the content of doll play that has significance but its part in the structure of the child's development. Doll play is the symbolic stage when assimilation, not accommodation, matters, when the child has a 'will to overcome', 'without rules or limitations', for the mere joy of mastering reality. He plays not because he has no conflicts; he has no conflicts because he plays. He does not know enough to accommodate himself to the world over his head (pp. 154, 89, 162). It is a precarious flight on the margins of existence.[14]

Play, says Johan Huizinga, becomes possible, thinkable, and understandable only when an influx of mind breaks down the absolute determinism of the cosmos.[15] The child works a kind of miracle: he abolishes the interior life of others, reducing them to roles which he too can play and yet be himself; he can bring to life a thing and be himself what he makes that thing; he can be himself outside himself.[16] This assimilation in play of the world without a feint towards accommodation to it, Erik Erikson calls evocatively the period of 'divine leeway'.[17] The child plays with causality, time and space, and all roles and rules he has met, to master all, turning passivity into activity, acquiring a virtuosity in role-playing and power over his own thought. For this single moment of life there is no barrier between the self and the other. Then the inroads of social accommodation require that the ludic instinct should find its expression in rule-bound games. The miracle of free passage between the self and the other vanishes and its absence is filled by a life-long nostalgia for this lovely state of narcissistic completion. The child is not deranged or idiotic. He knows when he is playing and he can stop whenever he wishes, he can throw his doll into a corner and forget it, change at will the roles in play, and by fiat create a new order of things. What he does not do is play according to prescription. This access of purity comes early, just at the point of mastery of motor control, speech, and representation by symbols.

---

[13] See Chapter 5, 'The Classification of Games'; Chapter 6, 'The Explanation of Play'.

[14] See Erik Erikson, *Childhood and Society* (New York, 1950), p. 212. Erikson, in Chapter 6, 'Toys and Reasons', discusses 'the world of manageable toys' in the child's psychological development.

[15] *Homo Ludens: A Study of the Play Element in Culture*, translated by R. F. C. Hull (London, 1949).

[16] Here and throughout this section I am much indebted to the work of Jeanne Danos, *La Poupée, mythe vivant* (Paris, 1967). Danos's study, both psychological and philosophical, treats the place of play with models in the development of the child's sense of self, and the importance of such play in the adult's appreciation of art.

[17] Chapter 6, 'Toys and Reasons'.

This brief genius for turning reality into a plaything must fade and lose its savour in a few short years. By eight the mind's eye is narrowing to social outlooks. Moral pronouncements and ukases from on high begin to sound like a more or less reasonable model for self rather than just arbitrary noises to be mimed as pleasurable nonsense in play. Perhaps one of the reasons *Gulliver's Travels* has made its way as a child's book is that, as in the *Alice* books, the representation of the child's life stands at the juncture between play assimilating the world to self and the advancing priggery of later childhood accommodating self to the world, well on the way to adult moral posturing. Returning from his bathtub naval war, a perfect child's game, Gulliver begins to do his characteristic worry-wart moralizing about the conflicting duties of a Nardac, who must enslave the Blefuscans for ever, and of the decent Englishman, who could never be party to such a scheme. Similarly he blandly reports Reldresal's story of the egg wars and their arbitrary rewards and punishments of a child's game, only saying primly that he must not take sides as a foreigner in party politics but if it is a question of invasion by Blefuscans he is ready to put his life at risk to defend the King's person and state.

This encroaching accommodation of self to the world freezes the child's keen sense of ritual by which he easily invents ceremonies and rules, invoking magical protection from harm, purifying by pain or by choosing out scapegoats, and appointing guardians of faithfulness and hope. The doll is an agent of passage between sacred and profane. And with these ritualistic rigmaroles the child repeats to dolls a helter-skelter version of the orders, rules, morals, and reasons raining down upon him.

At the ear of the supine and bound Gulliver a stage is erected for a communication to be delivered by the *Hurgo*, who 'acted every part of an Orator', enunciating periods of threatening, promises, pity, and kindness — all the figures and elocution of rhetoric. Gulliver understands him perfectly, knowing the forms of imperial oration. But given the orator's preposterously minute size and the total incomprehensibility of his language, the forms have been emptied of their supposed meanings: reason, purpose, authority, and other grand notions stored in the heads of politicians. And the giant makes his submissions in pantomime. Rhetoric, ritual, and personification remain, perfectly apprehended. It is a puppet theatre, miming the world's supposed seriousness, all form, no content. The passage is an exact representation of the meaningless forms that make up a child's game of imitation of adults.

To sustain this fantasy the child has free passage among three sizes, adult, child, and doll, playing the roles up and down, wilfully or willy-nilly, and all at once. Knowing nothing of philosophies and systems, he plays the role, goes through the ritual, with accompanying gestures, that he sees attached to various kinds of mumbo-jumbo going on in his space. Knowing nothing of the signified, he knows the signifier. The only imperative of the child at play is to imitate the form of things, making thereby a sort of sense of nonsense by laying down rules, procedures, postures, and sanctions, signifying nothing. He is a refined satirist unawares. Playing with the sense of nonsense, he discovers to the adult onlooker the nonsense of his sense. Thus the charm of *Lilliput*, an aesthetization of the life of Yahoos by miniaturization, transferring its terrible insanity to the nonsense of play.

The child Gargantua gone to Paris with his tutors urinates on the gawking mob about his shoetops and then tops off his prankishness by lifting the bells from Notre Dame. A learned sophist is sent by the Faculty to argue for their return. He has his doctor's hood and gown and five or six Masters of Arts behind him. He makes his harangue in a gibberish of Latin and the vulgar tongue with syllogisms, figures, and formal divisions of the oration: all the forms but no sense, for the learned sophist is drunk. Gargantua is big and little at once, tall as Notre Dame but easily carousing at table with people of ordinary size, and immediately following the prank he is only a child again playing through a three-page list of games. The game of big and little does not require sense, being a fantasy of childhood, but provides all the roles and gestures and rituals of what passes for sense in the world: a Rabelaisian lesson.

But did Swift 'laugh and shake in Rab'lais' easy chair', as Pope has it? The images of Gulliver urinating, his toying with the little people in his hair and pockets, his mock scare of eating them, are nearly direct borrowings and call up in us the sense of comic mastery of refractory life known for a moment by the child. But there is another indebtedness, this one turning Rabelais upside down. The giant can do anything his perversity or sense of justice may suggest, but Swift's dominant image in the first voyage is the giant-in-chains, essentially hopeless. We cheer him on to do what has to be done, but his essence lies in his name. If he can satisfyingly make water on the little martinets in the palace, why can he not do what Gargantua would easily do, make riot with the egg religion and the wars and all the other little enormities? Swift has invoked these allusions to pleasurable power in Rabelais to mock his giant-in-chains. Not for Swift, though he laughs enough, 'Rab'lais' easy chair'. He wants to make people better by killing them.

This theme of the giant-in-chains running through *Lilliput* (and its ironic reversal, the mechanical doll of *Brobdingnag*) was a new opportunity to express Swift's revolutionary (or perhaps only anarchistic) impulses under the guise of establishmentarianism during his bitter Irish exile. The theme, with all its revolutionary implications, boils up to nearly overt expression in *The Drapier's Letters*, almost contemporaneous with the writing of *Lilliput*. But it is implicit in the old theme, going back to *A Tale of a Tub*, of the fool among knaves. It is implicit as well in the ironic techniques by which the fool among knaves is given his wasting force, namely, by the echoing of every sort of received thought and social cliché until all attempt at rational life is deadened. With an uncanny ear for all the vagrant voices polluting the ambient airs, Swift was obsessed by the puppetry of his fellow creatures. This, rather than vice, hypocrisy, or even animality (so-called), was the central element of his consciousness, and it gave rise to playfulness and rage (often both at once), but above all to irony, which is essentially an echo of the fool among knaves. Our giant is hopeless, his hopelessness mocked by the Rabelaisian imagery, and by the end of *Brobdingnag* he is not only a silly puppet but a troublemaker of wicked possibilities. He has gone Yahoo.

In *Lilliput* there is something irretrievable in this corruption of childhood games: so the imagery of blinding and binding. We now turn to a close analysis of the way Swift imagines the foreclosure of the possibility of will and rationality by political games. Under the surface of these most innocuous of childhood games, by the aesthetic trick of miniaturization made charming and 'cute', the picture of political man is devastating and without relief.

IV *The Rules of the Game*

In the short section on the court games of *Lilliput* (Chapter 3), Swift has worked out the dynamics of political games. Here, too, the reader's mental journey from childhood doll play to deadly politics is most obvious. While the dancing and leaping and creeping of the games has often been identified with Walpole's notorious skills in manipulating factions, fiefdoms, and courtiers, the allegory is far more interesting than any putative hit at a contemporary figure could be. At the time of *The Drapier's Letters*, Swift's friend Carteret was caught in a death struggle with Walpole for the King's favour. Of the game Swift was a close student, hoping to appropriate it to his own game of the *Letters*. In the court games he has distilled the essence of political game as he sees it.

Gulliver plays the gentle simpleton with the little people (for he seeks admission of his great body to their minute circles): 'I would sometimes lie down, and let five or six of them dance on my Hand. And at last the Boys and Girls would venture to come and play at Hide and Seek in my Hair' (p. 38). All this makes such a good impression that it is decided not to kill him treacherously, for the time being. His deportment is worth an invitation from the Emperor to the 'Country Shows' at court. Without transition, the reader goes from this charming scene, not satiric at all, to the deadly satire of rope dancing, which is itself presented with such a look of dear play that we cannot know that this is a polity of slavery, degradation, and death worthy of a philosopher's wonder. The next thing, again without transition, we return to pure play in which Gulliver stretches his handkerchief upon sticks to make a field of honour for jousting horsemen. The way the mind goes in this transference, upon that and not upon allusions to persons and events, depends the force of satire.

'The Emperor had a mind one Day to entertain me with several of the Country Shows; wherein they exceed all Nations I have known, both for Dexterity and Magnificence. I was diverted with none so much as that of the

Rope-Dancers, performed upon a slender white Thread, extended about two Foot, and twelve Inches from the Ground' (p. 38). It is an excellent introduction to the scene by the ironist, being of a like naïveté, even insipidity, with the hide and seek game just before: little acrobatics by little people showing off with giddy tricks of mastery and muscle and nerve. But in fact the stakes in this game of equilibrists are a shaky tenure of power, or disgrace and death. What the players know is that it is not a game at all, for outside the 'game', not playing but playing off one 'player' against another, stands the master of revels, the Emperor. He requires the participants to play and he can change the rules when he wants. The real objects are to render the players impotent to act outside the confines of this pseudo-game and to control the outcome. The master has captured the players so that they can neither quit nor win. They are not even players, though they compete, for they have trained up from youth to do this work and no other, and they know that they compete for their own enslavement and at the risk of their lives. They are not necessarily of noble birth or liberal education (by Swift's lights the only proper requisites for great employment). They have been devoted to the power game by their progenitors whose own ambitions are in control. This pseudo-game is in fact a substitute for life. It provides chance or fortune, skills, rules, goals, illusions, gratification, and disappointment, but all under perfect control.

Now the first move: 'When a great Office is vacant, either by Death or Disgrace, (which often happens), five or six of those Candidates petition the Emperor to entertain his Majesty and the Court with a Dance on the Rope; and whoever jumps the highest without falling, succeeds in the office' (p. 38). Game being a stylization of life, style makes all the difference. Alliteration, 'death or disgrace', binds the two categories indifferently, for since the entire purpose of life is to gain the King's grace, disgrace is as good as death. Parenthesis, '(which often happens'), a casual consequence hardly worthy of notice, reduces life and death to incidental matters, another ingredient of the recipe for terror. In games 'dead' players return to play again; this 'game' having been made convertible with biological life, they will, sooner or later, not return. Note the circumlocution, 'petition . . . to entertain': petition for death or disgrace?, entertain with death or disgrace? (Court style, a part of the game. Under the bland surface terror, but unspeakable.)

Second move: 'Very often the chief Ministers themselves are commanded to shew their Skill, and to convince the Emperor that they have not lost their Faculty' (p. 38). 'Petition . . . to entertain' is replaced by 'commanded to shew' — and 'very often'. Once the entertainers at these 'Country Shows' (deadly sophisticates playing yokel) have been granted their request to perform, they are in it for good. No out, skill or no skill. As the Emperor must be convinced over and over, he is never convinced; as the game must be won over and over, it is never won. The officialese covers doom. And yet rewards may be won, perhaps they will not fail, maybe they will continue in power.

The game is the terror and the terror is the game. This tautology is not without meaning. Its meaning is that the qualities of game as a human activity — its assurance that it can be repeated endlessly, that the same players can play again with the same opportunities, that life's burden of teleology is lifted and replaced by an arbitrary goal having no relation to life, that time and space inside game are disjunctive from biological life, relieving it of life's irretrievable trials and troubles — all these have been invoked to mask the reality that the opposite conditions obtain. Pleasure, entertainment, inconsequentiality, these blandly innocuous promises of game, like the court style of *politesse* and deference, take away from the victims of terror the means to think about it or even express it. They are trapped, and politely go to their doom.

Third move: '*Flimnap*, the Treasurer, is allowed to cut a Caper on the strait Rope, at least an Inch higher than any other Lord in the whole Empire.' An 'Inch', a 'whole Empire': a little game, all of life. What does 'allowed' mean? (1) To acknowledge, admit, concede; (2) To permit (both senses of 'allow' were current). The first sense is the obvious one; it preserves the bland surface. Everyone knows that Flimnap goes higher: he is the Treasurer, the favourite, he must go higher, he must go higher again and again. Is this deference to Flimnap owing to his skill or to enforced flattery? The second sense of 'allowed' comes into play. Why is Flimnap 'allowed' to cut a caper an inch higher? Is the game one of skill? Are the rules really rules? Or can they be changed in the middle of the game? And to favour or hinder? Or both by turns of whim or policy?

There are three possibilities. First, as Flimnap is the most skilful, the other ministers required to compete must be protected against a dangerous and useless jump, all the while preserving the rules (a measure of solicitude; as long as the ministers keep up, do their frantic best, they will not be required to break their necks before their time has come). Secondly, as policy it is understood by all that no one must come within an inch of Flimnap as long as he continues the favourite. He must be praised and allowed to win (every minister is warned, as he values his life, to keep his place). Thirdly, Flimnap is being allowed to overplay his hand (a bit of induced hubris) with the expectation that he will show off and kill himself (Flimnap will never know). Of course the three cases may obtain at once, and this is the best condition, for then the King has absolute control of court politics: the ministers must play but the rules are his to keep or change.

Fourth move: 'These Diversions are often attended with fatal Accidents, whereof great Numbers are on Record. I myself have seen two or three Candidates break a Limb. But the Danger is much greater, when the Ministers themselves are commanded to shew their Dexterity: For, by contending to excel themselves and their Fellows, they strain so far, that there is hardly one of them who hath not received a Fall; and some of them two or three' (p. 39). 'Often' will in time become 'always'. Will Flimnap be proud and forget himself, or cautious and limit the risks? He cannot win in the end, but he will always be on his mettle, and circumspect: just the quality the Emperor desires.

Fifth and final move: 'I was assured, that a Year or two before my Arrival, *Flimnap* would have infallibly broke his Neck, if one of the *King's Cushions*, that accidentally lay on the Ground, had not weakened the Force of his Fall' (p. 39). Since the word 'accidentally', nicely sheltered in an appositive phrase to preserve the glacial surface, comes as the culmination of a deadly lexicon of court language, strategically put in the last move of the game, it must carry the greatest pressure. If the cushion can be 'accidentally' there, it can fail to be there. Did the King encourage Flimnap to a special vanity and then, anticipating a fall, have his cushion placed underneath to teach him a lesson in pride and remind him of his contingent benevolence? Or is it a message to Flimnap that he will always be taken care of? Or was it purely an accident? Flimnap will never know. He must keep capering, playing the game that is no game, as all must play, with terror.

This corruption of childhood games can be seen in a number of ways. In a game no player is outside the structure (the rules), and the structure controls itself; here the Emperor is outside and controls the structure. In a game, time and space are discontinuous with outside time and space. Here, there are two spaces (game space: Flimnap's jump, 'one inch higher' — and universal space: 'the whole empire'), and two times (game time: an afternoon's show — and biological time: life and death). Two spaces and two times are purposely confused to induce terror. In a game no one is compelled to play, else it is but social regimentation; in Lilliput, players are bred up to play. Volition is out of the picture. In a game there are no consequences beyond the game; here all consequences of the play are outside the game.

Having made such distinctions, one must add that all game, even that of childhood, tends to merge with the containing life and to blur distinctions, a natural process because the players occupy space in the real world and live biological lives.[18] The spillover from game to life and from life to game is continuous and the spills must be continually collected and put back in their proper place to preserve the mental construct of game. This mental construct reduces existential experience, which is always mysteriously subject to change, to a model which can be kept under control (space and time fixed, mystery removed by rules) and which provides a field for skills, competition, and role-playing, and all without consequences.

Alas, all teleologies, though absolutely alien to game, tend nevertheless to take on a game-like quality, introducing guile and ploy and strategy. Thus religion becomes religiosity, vision utopianism, education pedantry, military glory strategy, and so on. Conversely life invades game, making the

---

[18] See Jacques Ehrmann's argument in his essay 'Homo Ludens Revisited' (*Yale French Studies*, 41, *Game, Play, Literature* (1968), 31–57) that the usual opposition between play and work is illusory, and Roger Caillois's discussion of the corruption of games in *Les Jeux et les Hommes* (Paris, 1958).

playing fields of Eton into the battle of Waterloo. But it is only the infection, the perversion, the corruption that make game a useful concept for satirists. However perverted, game exerts its attraction to join in and it exerts its dominion once in. Perverse games are of the nature of a trap baited by the aesthetic need to play. Society will sooner forgive a cheat than a spoil-sport, says Huizinga (*Homo Ludens*, p. 11), for the spoil-sport shatters the necessary illusion. When game confuses its boundaries with life, cheating can even be admired if only one can preserve the look of playing the game, for the ways of outsmarting another player take on a ludic quality. Knowing the game to be poisoned by its confusion with life, men will yet prefer game to chaos; once in, they are part of the system and their roles become their egos. In Lilliput, as in any closed society, they can never quit the game. Nor would the good citizen think of quitting unless he should meet a Houyhnhnm to confirm Plato's view of things: that men are made by gods to be puppets until they be redeemed by reason (*Laws*, 1. 447).

v *The Rhetoric of Irony*

The figure of child play, for all its ingenuity, is only another of a group of fantastic figures (the mechanical operation of the spirit, religions of wind and clothes, a broomstick, an astrologer, a hardware dealer, and many others) which reduce political and moral postures to inanity or malignity in Swift's satiric art by echoing the formulas of pretended causes and coherences that are used to cover their mischief. Swift's masks are only collections of these formulas, not to be confused with either the types of comedy or the psychological figures of novelistic fiction. They are conventional fellows seeking to be in the swim. They hear what power or popularity says and they say it too, only with the grotesque caricature that turns conventional insipidity into the horror it masks.

Having put Gulliver through his doll tricks, finished off with a blathering recital of every cliché a good mannikin can mouth about English excellence in government, including the propriety of blowing up recalcitrants, Swift puts him to sleep in his doll's house for the last night in Brobdingnag. His fopperies now are ended and there is only one more use for him, to put him through a comic routine of adaptability to drive home the point of those fopperies. Swift sends a Brobdingnagian eagle to fly off with the doll's house (16 × 16 × 12 feet) and drop it down near an English merchantman. Floating in his house, the doll calls to the English sailor who is fishing him aboard to hook the box with his finger and put it in the captain's cabin. Once aboard, he is a Brobdingnagian fearing to step on his countrymen. But then chatting with the captain he is back to English size. Three sizes at once, inside and outside the box simultaneously. He begs off when the captain suggests he should write his story, saying that it 'could contain little besides common Events' (p. 147). He is so 'well-adjusted' (to borrow a delectable term from the future which Swift would have enjoyed putting in the mouth of one of his dummies) that he is mad.

This is Swift's grand subject. Here as in his other satires the formulaic voices he hears around him, lip service to every sort of uplift, authorize by their conventional emptiness the most inane or insane things human beings can do to one another. The relation of the figure of big and little in child-play to Swift's irony seems now clear, for the child's mimicry of adult formulas in play with models is a naïve version of the process of irony. Irony, too, is mimicry in which formulas are sounded, as in the childs game, as signifiers without signification. Only the adult formulas are dangerous; they authorize the Yahoo to exercise his desire to absorb the other in himself, a horrible travesty of the child's assimilation of the world to himself in play.

We naturally ask Swift to provide his remedies, and there are none. And so we provide them for him, supplying him putative morals and principles and positions by somehow drawing his 'real' meaning from his irony. But can irony provide a positive meaning from a hollow echo? The interminable debates about Swift's masks (who they are, what philosophical, religious, or political positions they represent, whether they are consistent, and so on) might seem largely futile if only we could reflect on the nature of the trope of irony, for the 'thought' of a radical ironist such as Swift must lie in his manipulations of the trope itself to create the consciousness of his reader. What follows is an attempt to assess the structure of the trope in relation to Swift's practice.[19]

(1) Irony is echo. The ironist hears the formulas of speech others cannot hear, and if they ring upon his ear as symbolic of a posture he does not like, he echoes them back at those who mouth them, but echoes them somehow inappropriately, off key, at the wrong place or time, with absurd exfoliations. The off-key echo will be picked up by the few and pass unheard by the many. Rhetorically then, irony has three persons, the few terrified by the echo of the many into joining the ironist lest they lose their being and become merely echo themselves. Irony is a trope for snobs or would-be snobs, but the ironist worth his attic salt turns the impulse of snobbery into a philosophical separation of being from non-being, consciousness from echo.

But if we began to take notice of all the formulaic echoes ricocheting in the void between ourselves and others, we would never get through the day. Speech is largely made up of formulas, and for good reason. The book of *politesse* is written not for its grammatical sense but for its gestures. The countless inanities people utter to one another to keep up the connexion, to show that they are there, to signal that they belong to the same crowd, are meant to relieve the pain of silence in the interstellar space and time between being and being. It is all part of the social contract. Formulas may signify

---

[19] In my discussion of the trope of irony, I am indebted to Dan Sperber and Deirdre Wilson, 'Irony and the Use-Mention Distinction', in *Radical Pragmatics*, edited by Peter Cole (New York, 1981), and to Søren Kierkegaard, *The Concept of Irony*.

nothing, and gratefully, reassuring a speaker that his opposite number is not dangerous.

To a man with a good ear for empty noises, formulas may even be a recreation, as in *Polite Conversation* where Swift gets up a miniature play composed of nothing but clichés from the town's smart talkers. On the other hand, all these expectations of accommodation by people who are just filling space and time open possibilities for social warfare if one's respondent deliberately uses formulas inappropriately to mock or menace. And it is warfare almost with impunity, since the betrayed will neither be certain of the speaker's intention nor wish to acknowledge an enemy in polite circles. His only recourse is to muster another polite formula to misappropriate even more deftly than his betrayer has done. The same sort of betrayal of the social contract that banality will be reciprocated with banality, but turned to symbolic representation, characterizes the irony of satire. The trick is to echo the formula inappropriately so as to make banality resonate its nothingness. Social warfare is declared.

The satiric ironist, however, hears a formula used not merely to fill the void with ordinary bromides but to dull consciousness to the ingenuities of human nastiness. Among the echoes that come out of Gulliver's mouth early on in Lilliput are a mess of niceties about his stool. Two days had gone by, he says in apology, since he 'last disburthened' himself, and as his gigantically obtrusive stool lies in our eye he utters a litany of nice bowel language: 'Necessities of Nature', 'under great Difficulties between Urgency and Shame', 'discharged my Body of that uneasy Load', 'only Time I was ever guilty of so uncleanly an Action', 'thought it necessary to justify my Character in Point of Cleanliness to the World' (p. 29). If a man is serious about anything he is serious about his bowels. But Gulliver is serious not about his bowels but his bowel-talk. How could such a nice globe-trotter end up 'so impotent and grovelling an Insect'? It is his author who has made this nice fool's bowel-language the figure of his soul. A set of moralistic and chauvinistic formulas packed up with the rest of his gear covers all nastiness, from the bowel's urgencies to the recommendation of gunpowder for better government and greater glory. 'A nice man is a man of nasty ideas' is one of Swift's odd thoughts. Gulliver speaks as though he were a man seeking to become a ventriloquist's dummy. Later on, meeting the Houyhnhnms (or perhaps understanding Plato, for the Hoyhnhnm Master 'agreed entirely with the sentiments of Socrates, as Plato delivers them'), he speaks as though he were a dummy seeking to become a man. Then he spills out the truth and, like the ironist his author, he is echoing the chauvinistic formulas of English imperialism. He has for this moment become his author, who was one of the few men of his age to hear these glozings of power for what they were, empty language concocted for the mouths of fools:

A Crew of Pyrates . . . go on Shore to rob and plunder; they see an harmless People, are entertained with Kindness, they give the Country a new Name, they take formal

Possession of it for the King, they set up a rotten Plank or a Stone for a Memorial, they murder two or three Dozen of the Natives, bring away a Couple more by Force for a Sample, return home, and get their Pardon. Here commences a new Dominion acquired with a Title by *Divine Right*. Ships are sent with the first Opportunity; the Natives driven out or destroyed, their Princes tortured to discover their Gold; a free Licence given to all Acts of Inhumanity and Lust; the Earth reeking with the Blood of its Inhabitants: And this execrable Crew of Butchers employed in so pious an Expedition, is a *modern Colony* sent to convert and civilize an idolatrous and barbarous People. (p 294)

(2) Irony says, 'Not this but something else'. Being only a mocking echo, irony obviously empties meaning, or empties pretended meaning (if the solecism of vacating what is already vacant can be permitted), and so whatever ought to be put in place of the ironic echo can come only from the person who hears the irony. Not inversion but incompletion is its character-istic. A negative cannot supply a positive unless the alternative is so clearly broadcast by the author, or the social situation so narrow, that only inversion is plausible. A good many of the one-line ironies put into Gulliver's mouth are of this sort. 'A STRANGE Effect of *narrow Principles* and *short Views!*', says Gulliver of the King of Brobdingnag's horror at the lovely mayhem made possible in England by gunpowder (p. 135). But here as always the implications are much wider and more problematic than the one-line inversion will allow. Eschewing force, how did the King establish his rule of the Good, maintain it? How is a lawyer kept to one interpretation of the law? Following Platonic utopias, the citizens presumably simply love the Good once they see it. But also following Platonic utopia, those who have not eyes to see are eliminated. Capital punishment is required, it seems, and once this utopia was as corrupt as Lilliput has become (and Lilliput was once as utopian as Brobdingnag has become). If the 'something else' does not provide the solution, as it cannot, the opening of irony must pass beyond negativity to the void. Much critical ink spilled to explain that Swift's irony yields a comforting orthodoxy might have been saved for more promising moral instruction.

(3) Irony asks to be saved from itself by an arbitarily imposed 'stop'. To begin with irony is to end with a chase after a will o' the wisp, there being no 'answer' to anything that does not echo hollowly its formulaic expediencies. That way lies 'nothingness', nothing occult, but the vanishing point after infinite retreats and reserves. But just as the true 'something else' can never be found, so 'nothingness' can never be reached, though the chase after the one always beckons, the fear of the other always threatens.

In practice, however, ironists fearing paralysis and loss of self, as the trope shears away positions of identity, impose an arbitrary 'stop' to the process. Beyond the stop, all is privileged, immune to encroachment. The peculiar quality of Swift's irony is that he does not impose a stop. He contrives a double bind, makes a joke of it, cuts the thread. Every reader to his own outcome, but whichever way he turns the bind tightens. One would say that

Swift manages to fulfil nothingness, complete the void, vanish himself, and abandon the reader in utter paralysis, except that against all logic the feeling of his end-games is one of vitality. It is by his humour that Swift rescues himself and his reader from the nothingness he gives us good reason to fear. Laughter has no future, no logic, no responsibility. When we laugh we express our grasp of the here and now; we have no sense of the other; we imply our distrust of modality in favour of the indicative, and of time past and future in favour of the present. The terminal thing for Swift is a joke to remind us that though our case is hopeless we are alive. The jokes about Gulliver's stable-pleasures put to rout all philosophical instabilities that have to do with hatred of the Yahoo and love of the Houyhnhnm. It is a characteristic end-game, a trick, a feat of aesthetic legerdemain, not a faith. We need not forget to be.

Now we are come full circle. Irony's echo is a very sophisticated game, very like the naïve games of childhood that recreate the forms of things without their sense. The ironist, too, plays the game of echo, but only to create our consciousness of the signifier signifying nothing, the language given us to chatter. If we chatter books of morality and theology and politics about Big-endianism and Little-endianism and then are cured of our chatter by the consciousness lent us by Swift, we are left with a hollowed out centre. We know what is not there but we haven't a clue from the ironist as to what could be there immune to irony.

Such strictures as to the trope of irony are particularly urgent in the case of Swift, whose idealism, the will o' the wisp of his irony, is 'Platonic', that is, ever seeking the idea of truth and justice and a society of collective identity in the idea, free of opinion, and of sect. As such things are unimaginable in actuality or, if imagined, soon wasted by irony, he preserves his idealism by enclosing it in the game 'utopia' in three of the four voyages. As for actuality, one thing is as good as another to provoke irony. Swift's offering is of consciousness, not programmes or positions.

The utopian games of *Gulliver's Travels* define the range of Swift's attitudes from playfulness to idealism, from an anarchic impulse figuring human 'purpose' in games of no purpose to a repressive impulse figuring human purpose in a rationalism that acknowledges the idea as obvious and sanctions a simple-minded collectivism. Not only is the land of the Houyhnhnms greatly beholden to More's *Utopia* and, at a greater distance, to Plato's *Republic*, but the original constitution of Lilliput as well as the philosopher-king's good government by fiat in Brobdingnag are earlier versions of the same Platonic dream, though adapted to differing rhetorics.[20] All three utopias are absolutist, all conceived to assure public virtue over private, and all severely restrictive of personal freedom. In each reigns the grand

[20] See my essay, 'A Voyage to Nowhere with Thomas More and Jonathan Swift: *Utopia* and *The Voyage to the Houyhnhnms*', *Sewanee Review*, 69 (1961), 534–65.

principle of simplicity: public affairs (including in Lilliput and Brobdingnag the judicial establishment) come back to acknowledged 'Truth, Justice, Temperance, and the like', assuring an easy collectivism and a predominant role of the state in personal affairs. None tolerates sect or faction and each separates opinion from truth. In Lilliput's original constitution (before the games of politics came in), thievery and murder, crimes of one man against another, are not counted so odious as ingratitude, fraud, and informing, crimes that injure the fabric of society. The young are brought up by the state, religion is established, dissenters disenfranchised. All this sounds like a rhetorical heightening of Dr Swift's everyday remedies.

Almost everything we can say about utopia is paradoxical. The game of somewhere is also the absolute idealism of nowhere. Game knows its goal to be defined by and to lie within the rules given and has no grasp beyond its reach. Idealism seeks, it hardly knows what or how, a teleology beyond conception. Utopia is a game played by rules and separated from the time and space of the real world. 'The irreversibility of history is stemmed, and outcomes determined by the contingency of actual experience, can, in utopia [writes Michael Holquist], be reversed in the freedom of the utopist's imagination. Another set of laws obtains in utopia, arbitrary but infinitely open to recombination. Utopia is play with ideas'.[21] The reader plays the game with the author, deciding who can win and who must lose, what is dubious and what indubitable. The end being both a game's goal and an ideal's figuration, utopia is open to infinite irony in More's as well as Swift's vision. If you do not like the chill and master-race eugenics of the Houyhnhnms or the genocide in store for the Yahoos, try your own hand at constructing a utopia that respects community and suppresses egotism. Probing the utopias of More and Swift, readers argue whether this or that is serious or a sly joke, but they can never be certain. This meeting ground between play and idealism is just Swift's province.

And yet these polar opposites do not come huddling together in a safe and liberal half-way house and so lose their qualities. When one longs to make men good and wise, free and reasonable (runs an adage), one is inevitably led to want to kill them all. Rage is the other face of idealism. The tension between Swift's impulse to kill to remake the world according to abstract conceptions of virtue, and his play, often close to anarchic, is fundamental to his work and reflected time and again in his life. The case is not so different from that of the child's play with reduced models. For the child, too, is assimilating the world to a game of mimicry that suits his own notions of a proper order. Indeed, Jeanne Danos argues that utopia is one of the imaginative remains of such play, representing in a rational idiom the same impulse to master the puzzling and incompatible forces in one's life.

---

[21] 'How to Play Utopia', *Yale French Studies*, 41 (1968), 106–23 (p. 119).

This is an essay of speculation, piecing together certain processes of thought that seem to have produced the child-play imagery of big and little. I have played down moral and religious positions thought to do us good, or at least to elevate Swift in our estimation, in favour of the play of the mind that makes for consciousness, which, I argue, is what the ironist, inviting us to make something of nothing, has to offer, and which, in the Platonic scheme to which Swift was attracted, is everything.

Paradise Gained by Horace, Lost by Gulliver

WILLIAM S. ANDERSON

University of California, Berkeley

The word 'paradise' occurs nowhere in Horace's poetry or in Swift's *Gulliver's Travels*. Nevertheless, critics quite legitimately use the word in the loose sense of 'a place of extreme beauty or delight' and 'a state of supreme felicity' to describe Horace's Sabine farm and his utter contentment there as well as Houyhnhnmland and Gulliver's sense of utter happiness there until he was sent away, much against his will. My title, therefore, will not have occasioned much surprise, for it is well known that Horace gained what he regarded as happiness or paradise in an idyllic spot of the Italian countryside, and it is equally well known (if not better known these days) that Gulliver lost his happiness or paradise when he was barred from the land and the companions he adored and went reluctantly back to his native England.

I do not wish to use the word 'paradise' loosely. The word possesses a complex history, and in its proper sense meant one thing for Horace and some rather different things for Swift. But I believe that Swift, an admirer of Horace and translator of several of his poems, was not uninfluenced by Horace's version of paradise. The word originates as a Persian noun denoting an enclosed park or garden. It became known to the Greeks in the fifth century B.C., as the Persians advanced to the coast of Asia Minor, occupying Greek terrain, and as the Greeks travelled eastward into the vast Persian kingdom.[1] What the Greeks viewed in these special Persian gardens stirred their admiration, and they felt impelled to borrow the Persian word, transliterating it as *parádeisos*, in order to convey the unique beauty and delight of these places. What struck the Greeks was the number and variety of trees, the many species of flowers, and the plentifulness of water — none of which was familiar in such lavish profusion in the Greek world; and sometimes the Persian king would stock his *parádeisoi* with wild animals for hunting, a custom which the Greeks did not employ. In the early fourth century the tyrant Dionysius of Syracuse, who controlled portions of Italy opposite Sicily, flaunted his power and culture at Rhegion by planting a park with imported plane trees and calling it *parádeisos*.[2]

Whereas the Greeks, after close contact with and admiration of those Persian parks, borrowed the exotic word and so made the exotic notion of paradise familiar to the Hellenic world, the Romans did not do the same. We

---

[1] On the Greek and Roman acquaintance with Persian Paradise, see Olck, s.v. 'Gartenbau', *Pauly-Wissowa Real Encyclopedie* (Stuttgart, 1912), cols 779–83.

[2] This detail about Dionysius is preserved by Theophrastus, *De Historia Plantarum*, 4.5.6.

may assume that they read the several references in Xenophon to Persian paradises and that the notorious park of Dionysius was known to them by reputation, but they made no effort to introduce a Latin transliteration until long after Horace. It may be that, in Italy, a stately park shaded by various trees and well watered by streams and/or springs seemed less exotic than in drier, deforested Greece. As we shall see, Horace regularly epitomizes the beauty of his friends' country estates in terms of trees, shade, and water. In the middle of the second century of our era, Aulus Gellius, who prided himself on his philology, referred in passing to the Greek word *parádeisoi* as equivalent to the Latin *vivaria*, which he glossed as 'enclosed places where wild animals are kept': 'saepta quaedam loca, in quibus ferae vivae pascuntur' (*Noctes Atticae*, 2.20). If Gellius correctly reported contemporary usage of *parádeisos*, then the concept had lost most of its meaning, unless we assume that the Greeks used the borrowed word to describe two types of park they considered exotic: a park of trees, flowers, and water, for easy walking, and a park stocked with wild animals, enclosed and used for hunting.

Near-contemporaries of Gellius who were Greek and wrote in Greek continued to use *parádeisos* primarily for the park without wild animals. Plutarch refers often to such Persian parks of the fifth and fourth centuries (*Alcibiades*, 24; *Artox*, 25). Longus invents a *parádeisos* at Mytilene on the island of Lesbos, where his hero Daphnis works for a while: it possesses the requisite trees, flowers, and water, but it also boasts a temple, no doubt to make it more appealing to his Greek readers (*Daphnis and Chloe*, 4.2–3). Thus, although Gellius in the first Roman usage surviving of *parádeisos* seems to restrict the meaning drastically, it is likely that the other sense of the Persian park remained common and indeed prevailed over that of the hunting-preserve. Confirmation comes from the second major development of the word in Greek, when the translators of the Septuagint rendered the Hebrew word for garden (*gan*) as *parádeisos* in Genesis 2 and 3, to denote the exotic eastern garden of Eden from which Adam and Eve were banished. Trees and water constitute the dominant features of Eden, but as a whole it symbolizes a place of perfection that stands in sharp antithesis to the world of our experience. In answer to the biblical myth of paradise lost, Jews and later Christians imagined a return to or escape to paradise. Paul writes to the Corinthians of a man he met who reported a spiritual experience of having been snatched up to the 'third heaven' or paradise, where he heard mysterious words (II Corinthians 12.1–4). Luke attributes to Jesus on the cross the now-famous words to his companion thief: 'To day shalt thou be with me in paradise' (Luke 23.43). And the writer of Revelations declares, as he is bidden, to the Church at Ephesus: 'To him that overcometh will I [the Spirit] give to eat of the tree of life which is in the midst of the paradise of God' (Revelations 2.7). It was this Jewish-Christian use of Greek *parádeisos* in connexion with the myth of Eden that eventually brought paradise into Latin when the Vulgate came into existence. Latin *paradisus* refers exclusively to Eden, but, through the first associations of the Septuagint translators, it retains some contact with the original Persian word.

Although in Horace's time the Greek usages of *parádeisos* were well established to describe both the exotic Persian park and the mythical garden of Eden, we may safely infer that Horace was familiar with the first from the normal literature of a well-educated Roman, but did not know of Eden because of the equally normal dislike of the Jews by Roman males of his era. In what he writes very rarely of Jews, Horace mocks their superstition and practice of circumcision, as others did, and he never hints that he has read or even knows of the Bible.[3] Nevertheless, I believe that Horace's own poetic genius responded to the political and spiritual crises of his age and his psyche in a way that parallels the Jewish-Christian longing for paradise. He took the Greco-Roman version of an actual garden or park-paradise and, reducing the physical description to stereotyped brief details about shade and water, transferred his attention to the symbolic meaning of retirement or withdrawal for the development of poetry, the mind, and the ethical consciousness.[4] At his modest Sabine farm he possesses little that resembles the true Persian paradise or its Roman imitators, the luxurious and spacious country villas. However, through his ironic stresses on the priority of human attitude over physical location, on the pleasures of the mind ever the material delights of Eden or the idyllic spot (*locus amoenus*) of Latin poetry, he creates a spiritual ideal that can easily fuse with the Jewish-Christian image of Eden-paradise. Jonathan Swift in the eighteenth century was a man who was peculiarly qualified to blend the long traditions of classical literature and biblical writings. When he invented the remarkable situation of Gulliver among the Houyhnhnms and traced the development of his foolish hero's sense of happiness there, his growing misanthropy, and finally his total dismay at being expelled, Swift combined, I believe, the satiric strategy and ironic vision of Horace together with the theological and homiletic methods for explicating paradise and fallen man, to contrive in the land of the Houyhnhnms a false or parodic paradise that is well lost.

1. *Paradise Gained by Horace*

As a young man, Horace believed in political goals and at twenty-one plunged into the confusion of the Civil War after Caesar's murder, on the side of Brutus and the so-called liberators. However, after fighting at Philippi and seeing his cause utterly crushed, escaping with his life but little more, Horace was obliged to revise his ideals. In the next seven years, as he developed his poetic techniques and themes while working on his first

---

[3] See the references to Jews in the early poems, *Satires*, 1.4.143, 5.100, and 9.70.

[4] On the themes of the ideal landscape, *locus amoenus*, and intelligent retirement in Horace, see G. H. J. Schönbeck, 'Der locus amoenus von Homer bis Horaz' (dissertation, University of Heidelberg, 1962); I. Troxler-Keller, *Die Dichterlandschaft des Horaz* (Heidelberg, 1964); and Michael O'Loughlin, *The Garlands of Repose* (Chicago, 1978), pp. 76–154.

Satires, he struggled free of ambition and was able to sketch out an early version of moral happiness in the process of rejecting political and economic preoccupations.

I find it significant that at this early stage happiness is not conditioned by or dependent on idyllic physical surroundings. Book I of the *Satires* represents Horace as a confirmed and contented inhabitant of Rome, where in fact we know he did live and work as a government clerk. Not that Rome signifies paradise for him, but he does not choose to regard it yet as a negative environment either. Only in Satire 5 does he venture forth from the city, in the retinue of his powerful patron Maecenas on the long journey to Brundisium. In his account, Horace concentrates on his own discomforts, inadaptability, and citified snobbery, all of which reinforces the impression that as yet retirement to the country holds no great attraction for him, and he is quite unfit for such a move. In the city, however, the satirist has been educated, and there he can assert his freedom and create a convincing type of happiness. Satires 6 and 9 illustrate important aspects of this urban freedom and contentment.[5]

In Satire 6, Horace manages his discourse in such a way that what at first seems a liability, his 'unfortunate' parentage (an ex-slave), emerges as an advantage that gave him the sense to recognize the merits of leisure outside politics. The technical term for the status of Horace's father was *libertinus*, freed man. Though legally free, his father and hence Horace faced social contempt, because for the average Roman 'freed man' connoted 'ex-slave', the ignominious former condition rather than the liberty to which the man was entitled. Horace demolishes that bias by demonstrating that his father was indeed a free man, legally and ethically, who had equipped his son for a special 'freedom'. The proud freeborn politician 'enslaves' himself to ambition, assumes crushing 'burdens', and leads a life of obligation, whereas Horace enjoys a life in Rome that epitomizes liberty. He goes where he pleases ('quacumque libido est', l. 111), whenever he wants, eats at odd times, reads and writes at will: his life consists of a series of pleasant options, for he is one of those who have been released, liberated from the painful burden of ambition: 'haec est | vita solutorum misera ambitione gravique' (l. 128).

In Satire 9, Horace dramatizes a threat to his contentment, in his encounter with an obnoxious social climber (often called a Bore). As he strolls idly through the Roman Forum, thinking about his poetry, his happy thoughts are rudely interrupted by a fellow who quickly establishes himself, in sharp antithesis to the poet, as crudely ambitious. Unable in any way to

---

[5] For recent discussions of *Satires*, 1.5, 6, and 9, see Niall Rudd, *The Satires of Horace* (Cambridge, 1966), pp. 36–64 and 74–85; C. J. Classen, 'Eine unsatirische Satire des Horaz? Zu Hor. *Sat.* 1 5', *Gymnasium*, 80 (1973), 235–50; K. Sallmann, 'Die seltsame Reise nach Brundisium: Aufbau und Deutung der Horaz *Satire* 1.5', in *Musa Iocosa: A. Thierfelder zum 70.ten Geburtstag* (Hildesheim 1974), 179–206; W. S. Anderson, 'Horace the Unwilling Warrior: Satire 1, 9', *American Journal of Philology*, 77 (1956), 148–66.

communicate with the man, failing even to frighten him off by mention of a sick relative and a long walk, Horace is helpless until divine intervention rescues him. As if he had been faced with an epic battle and preserved, he alludes to a heroic rescue in the *Iliad* in the final sentence: 'Thus Apollo saved me' (l. 78).[6] Normally when a god intrudes to help an endangered hero he transports his favourite away. Here, in an interesting inversion, the obnoxious climber is snatched away to face a lawsuit, and Horace remains at the scene, free to continue his leisurely poetic ruminations. Apollo, the god of poetry, makes the Roman Forum conducive for Horace. In later years and other works, Horace treats such antagonists no longer as isolated and removable but as a general epidemic, and it will follow that his 'rescue' must turn into an escape from Rome itself, the focus of anxiety. By then, however, he had a place of refuge in his Sabine farm.

The Sabine farm, which Maecenas presented to him shortly after Horace published Book I of the *Satires*, enabled the satirist to develop his idea of moral happiness and locate it in a particular place, outside Rome. He was just thirty years old, too young to make an absolute break with his friends in Rome, but quite capable of employing his poetic talents to sketch out a kind of ideal spot, a *locus amoenus* or paradise, in connexion with his country retreat. Today, when one drives to the ruined masonry that the archaeologists and tour guides have conspired to identify as the remains of Horace's Sabine farm, it is possible to see the layout among the hills, the still-fresh spring, the valley below, and to picture the small clump of shady trees once there, but those details merely add up to disappointment. We lack Horace, to transform those rather ordinary items into that rich fantasy which he first presents in Satire II.6 as the 'answer to his prayers'.[7]

In starting the Satire and his description of the spot with a prayer of thanksgiving, Horace encourages us in our assimilation of the Sabine farm with the biblical paradise. He clearly wishes to surround the spot with benevolent divine favour and to suggest that the place and he himself are fully attuned to the will of the gods. After a few scanty descriptive details of the setting, he addresses Mercury as his special benefactor, expresses his contentment with what he has received, and merely requests the continuing favour of the god.

After that opening, the satirist pauses to ask himself what he should take as his poetic topic, and automatically there occurs to him the contrast between his quiet creative contentment in the country and the frenzied upsetting life of Rome. A new image appears: the farm is a 'citadel', a place of refuge to which the poet has escaped from Rome (l. 16). It follows that Rome,

---

[6] The allusion is to the rescue of Hector in *Iliad*, xx.443.

[7] On Satire II.6, see Rudd, pp. 243–57; O'Loughlin, pp. 97–107; C. O. Brink, 'On Reading a Horatian Satire: An Interpretation of *Sermones* II.6', in *The Sixth Todd Memorial Lecture* (Sydney University, 1965); and David West, '"Of Mice and Men": Horace Satires 2.6.77–117', in *Quality and Pleasure in Latin Poetry*, edited by T. Woodman and D. West (Cambridge, 1974), pp. 67–80.

by contrast, seems harassing and hostile. When Horace is reluctantly pulled back to the city, he, too, becomes tainted by his belligerent environment. First, he gets involved in a lawsuit on behalf of a friend, undertaking to guarantee a risky loan which might ruin him, he says (l. 27). Then, when he tries to cross the city to visit his friend Maecenas, he must fight his way through the crowds and unintentionally inflict as much annoyance as he receives. *En route*, some people recognize him as the intimate of a powerful politician and they all try to load him with special requests: 'Hundreds of big deals from others', complains the poet, 'spring at my head and flanks' (ll. 33–34). The picture suggests the assault of a pack of lions or wolves. Utterly wretched in this unpleasant Rome, he prays again (ll. 59 ff.), invoking the country itself as a kind of friendly deity. There, reading or sleeping or idling away the hours (what he once could do as a mark of his freedom in Rome), he could achieve happy forgetfulness of this harried urban existence, what we call the 'rat race' and Horace himself will, in a few lines, turn into a comic 'mouse race'.

In the country, very ordinary food shared with the simple farmers at night stirs Horace into a lyrical apostrophe of its 'divine' qualities: 'o noctes cenaeque deum' (l. 65). And a rustic moralist, who draws on his store of animal folktales to 'prattle away' ('garrit', l. 77) about the anxiety of wealth, becomes, in an oblique way, the spokesman for Horace's sense of contentment in the country. The fable of the Country Mouse and City Mouse occupies the final section of the poem, and the Satire ends, not with a wise comment from Horace but with a rueful recognition from the diminutive Country Mouse, his amusing *alter ego*.

I hardly need to review the facts of the fable. Swift himself adapted Satire II. 6 to his own experiences, but quite deliberately omitted the mouse story (which Pope later supplied), relying on *his* audience's familiarity with the original. The rustic 'philosopher' manages to make his moral point, that riches are dangerous, but his dramatic flair gets the better of his theme, so that the impression firmly remains that pleasures, varied if precarious, are located in the rich city, whereas the country offers only security under rough conditions. The eloquent City Mouse, a plausible mouther of Epicurean tags, easily lures his dissatisfied country friend to the city in quest of pleasure, where in fact he thoroughly enjoys himself (l. 111) until the ferocious barking of the watchdog shatters his comfort. What Horace's audience must do, then, is reinterpret the fable with clues from earlier portions of the poem. We cannot identify Horace fully with the austere, abstemious, and secretly discontented Country Mouse, even though he ultimately realizes that his mousehole in the country protects him from 'ambushes' (l. 117), much as Horace's farm serves as a 'citadel' of refuge from the city. It is impossible not to recognize that the City Mouse parodies quite cleverly some of Horace's epicurean ideas, locates the life of true happiness in pleasurable things (l. 96), and possesses the gift of persuasion like Horace. So we must correct the fable's minuscule and unsatisfactory point by combining the two mice. What Horace has been doing by continuously changing the scene between country and city throughout the Satire, and now by dramatizing the 'human' sentiments of these amusing little mice, is to suggest that although the country provides certain advantages for him, *no* place in itself guarantees happiness: paradise ultimately depends on individual ethical maturity and can be found only by and in the human spirit and poetic imagination.

During the next decade, Horace pursues his inquiry into the relationship between physical conditions and spiritual contentment in the *Odes*. Thus, he continues to portray his Sabine farm as a refuge, but now he emphasizes its security from wolves and other wild beasts and its inspiring tranquility for the poet (*Odes*, I. 17 and 21). He also introduces as a significant antithesis the rich, ageing friend who possesses a splendid country estate but lacks the capacity to savour its delights. These estates exhibit ideal natural attractions with a splendour that makes the Sabine farm appear insignificant: shady trees, a cool spring or stream, and servants to bring on the plentiful quantities of expensive wine, flowers, and unguents that will make for an enjoyable symposium on the grass. Sometimes, Horace will add a compliant female to this predictable décor, to include erotic pleasure in the entertainment. In all these poems, which are especially common in Book II of the *Odes*, the luxurious physical circumstances of these millionaires fail to distract them from their nagging anxieties.[8] To deal with them, the lyric poet resorts to an epicurean protreptic that resembles the line used by the City Mouse: enjoy present pleasures while you have time. However, the deeper implication of these poems focuses on the priority of the mind and soul over physical surroundings: unless the mind is at ease, we cannot long relax *anywhere*. Thus, in the *Odes*, Horace concerns himself with the happiness not only of himself but of his friends, that is, anyone; and he carefully uses the scene of the millionaire's suburban estate, the Roman equivalent of the Persian paradise, to show that happiness depends not on place but on the state of mind.

A few years after publishing three books of odes, Horace, in his early forties, published a book of twenty epistles. There, the poet, writing in a colloquial manner, characterizes himself as one pursuing wisdom, seeking ethical *virtus*. In at least five of these letters he starts from a question about the place where he or his addressee is, but he soon abandons his concern with that actual geographical location in order to concentrate on the mind (*animus*) which alone determines whether one is good, wise, and thus happy (*beatus*). Personally, Horace declares that he prefers the country, and his feelings about it attribute to his Sabine home ideal qualities: it is lovely

---

[8] See *Odes*, II.3, 11, and 14. In Ode II.18 Horace, feeling 'sufficiently blessed on his unique Sabine property' ('satis beatus unicis Sabinis'), contrasts his bliss with the insatiable acquisitiveness and building crazes of contemporary millionaires.

(*amoenus*, 1.10,7, 14.20, 16.16) and *blissful* (*beatus*, 1.10.14). In two poems, Epistles 10 and 16, he writes from the farm to friends in Rome. In Epistle 10 his emphasis falls on his 'freedom' in the country: like a runaway slave, he has escaped his chains (the material traps of the city) and now, free at last, he feels alive, a veritable king: 'vivo et regno' (l. 8). Paradoxically, in his spiritual paradise he has achieved the happiness once assigned to the Persian king of the fifth and fourth centuries in his enclosed exotic park.

In Epistle 16 Horace begins with the fullest description of the farm that he ever committed to his poems. Though he adds little to the usual attractions of simple crops, shady trees, and a cool clear stream, he convinces us by his enthusiasm that he has found a delightful and lovely hideout ('hae latebrae dulces, etiam, si credis, amoenae', l. 15). It seems like an abrupt transition when he tells his addressee, Quinctius, that *he* lives right and is happy (there in Rome) if he sees to it that he *is* the kind of man that wellwishers and flatterers say he is. Without further reference to himself after line 16, he proceeds for over sixty lines to urge Quinctius to become a good and wise man ('vir bonus et sapiens', l. 73) in the basic ethical, not the vulgar, sense of the words. Once again, the point is that happiness is a spiritual and ethical condition and independent of location.[9] But Horace on his Sabine farm already comes close to being what he urges others in Rome and elsewhere to become, a truly good and happy person. He has earned that happiness by freeing himself from lesser things and searching out moral wisdom. Nevertheless, although the Sabine site helps Horace to achieve this paradise of the soul, it does nothing for fools like the fictional bailiff on the farm whom Horace addresses in Epistle 14: that man hates the country and wants nothing but the crude sensual pleasures available in Rome. For Horace, then, the lovely but modest Sabine farm offers a corrective to the material extravagance of the Persian paradise and its Roman version, the lavish rural estate, but it chiefly functions to symbolize the essential loveliness of a soul which locates paradise in the more profound ethical realities of our human existence.

II *Paradise Lost by Gulliver*

Students of Classical satire regularly view the differences between Horace and Juvenal as polar antitheses, and contrast the smiling indulgence of faults by the former with the vitriolic indignation against vice in Rome by the latter. Nevertheless, the two have much in common in social status, poetic training, intelligence, ethical seriousness, and personal integrity, and their attitudes towards Rome or the values of a country retreat differ in degree, not in substance. Swift creates a far sharper contrast to Horace in his Gulliver. Whereas Horace speaks from personal contentment and a

---

[9] That happiness is independent of location emerges clearly also from Epistle 1.7, where Horace, reversing the terms of his earlier Satire II.6, describes a happy auctioneer of Rome who found misery by leaving the city and attempting to become a farmer.

generally optimistic view of human beings, Swift makes Gulliver speak out from a profound sense of alienation, from self-hatred, and from hatred and actual disgust in relation to other human beings. Finding no person in England with whom he can tolerate association, no comfortable natural setting to which he can retire for creative meditation and at least self-improvement, Gulliver has withdrawn to the stable and the company of a pair of horses. Trapped in an England that stirs loathing, confident of his distorted view of human beings, Gulliver provides us with a vivid antithesis to the Horace we have seen so happy on his Sabine farm and in his spiritual paradise. But the antithesis becomes even more striking if we perceive that Gulliver's self-hatred and tragic pessimism arise from his despair over expulsion from Houyhnhnmland, a world which, as I shall argue, Swift presents as a distortion of Christian paradise. Losing this false paradise has permanently warped Gulliver's perceptions.

Scholars do not agree on the amount of theological doctrine which should inform the interpretation of *Gulliver's Travels*, and many shy away from a term like 'religious satire', quite rightly, I believe, because it limits the critic's viewpoint. Charles A. Beaumont, studying Swift's use of the Bible in 1965, claimed that no biblical allusions whatsoever occur in *Gulliver's Travels*; when that fact is combined with a second, the total absence of the word 'God' from the work, we should conclude, he wrote, 'that Gulliver has little or no religious sensibility'. It can be demonstrated that the first fact is incorrect, that Swift does refer to the Bible; and Gulliver's lack of religious sensibility, which may be granted, possesses far less significance than our rejection of Gulliver's insensibility, which Swift has engineered. Other scholars, there-fore, explore the significance of Gulliver's religious obtuseness and Swift's refusal to intrude an obvious religious corrective, of which he was manifestly capable. Martin Kallich suggested that there is a major current of religious satire in the work which Swift ultimately directs at the secular viewpoint of his era. Calhoun Winton proposed that Swift organizes Gulliver's experi-ence among the Houyhnhnms in the form of a parodic conversion, a comic inversion of the eye-opening experience of Paul on the road to Damascus.[10] Although we may agree that in a general way Gulliver is converted to some foolish beliefs, that his judgement is perverted among the Houyhnhnms, it remains highly doubtful that there are any allusions to 'conversion' or St Paul in Book IV. A more profitable track to follow, it seems to me, is marked by several allusions to the early chapters of Genesis.

I shall argue, therefore, that Swift created a significant thematic allusion to biblical paradise and the Genesis narrative connected with it, that Swift's eighteenth-century readers should have heard echoes from their familiar King James Bible and could have perceived a line of parody, thus realizing

[10] Beaumont, *Swift's Use of the Bible* (Athens, Georgia, 1965), p. 62; Kallich, *The Other End of the Egg: Religious Satire in Gulliver's Travels* (Bridgeport, Connecticut, 1970); Winton, 'Conversion on the Road to Houyhnhnmland', *Sewanee Review*, 68 (1960), 20–33.

how carefully Swift distanced them from the folly of Gulliver.[11] One important theme of *Gulliver's Travels* which still needs emphasis, then, depends on these several allusions to Genesis and on the clever fashion in which Swift portrays Gulliver as a foolish Adam in a false or fool's paradise, who falls from a distorted grace and is expelled from his beloved equine Eden and, never able to deal realistically with that experience, cannot adjust to the outside world, unlike Adam. Where Gulliver persists in his horse-loving misanthropy even after returning to England, Swift invites his audience by means of the biblical theme to ponder the hopeful Judaeo-Christian message for men that emerges from the Bible, traditional theology, innumerable sermons, and from Milton's epics. Because human beings are *not* Yahoos and are loved by God, not coolly dismissed by a Houyhnhnm, paradise, though deservedly lost, may be regained.

A good many scholars agree that Chapter 9 of Book IV contains a definite biblical allusion. That will be my starting point. Gulliver hears that the origin of the degenerate Yahoos goes back to the distant past when a pair of outsiders (like Adam and Eve) appeared in the ideal land of the Houyhnhnms. They and their many descendants have obviously failed to profit from this paradise. A connexion is occasionally detected between this account of the Yahoo's coming, like Adam and Eve, and Gulliver's incredible happiness among the Houyhnhnms as though in Eden, which he reports in Chapter 10. Two such allusions do not make a theme, and that is where I should like to add some evidence and identify Swift's theme.[12]

Chapter 9 contains a second allusion to Genesis, I think. Because of the pernicious corruption of these humanoid creatures, a serious question now preoccupies the Houyhnhnms: 'Whether the *Yahoos* should be exterminated from the Face of the Earth' (p. 271).[13] In much the same language, Genesis 6.7 lets God announce his decision to deal with corrupt mankind: 'I will destroy man whom I have created from the face of the earth.' The words and the context should make the reference unmistakable. Thus Swift in Chapter 9 touches summarily on the events of Genesis 2–6 to suggest that the Yahoos, like the generations of men in the Bible, have not only abused their paradise but also, utterly debased, now face the total destruction they have richly merited. He also suggests that, instead of the biblical God, the Houyhnhnms function, if not as creator, as almighty judge and destroyer:

---

[11] For some background on this matter, see Ernest Tuveson, 'Swift: The Dean as Satirist', *UTQ*, 22 (1952/3), 368–75, and R. M. Frye, 'Swift's Yahoo and the Christian Symbols for Sin', *JHI*, 15 (1954), 201–17. For a contrary view, see R. S. Crane, 'The Houyhnhnms, the Yahoos, and the History of Ideas', in *The Idea of the Humanities*, Volume II (Chicago, 1967), pp. 261–82, and 'The Rationale of the Fourth Voyage', in *Gulliver's Travels*, edited by Robert A. Greenberg, second edition (New York, 1970), pp. 331–38.

[12] Winton (pp. 28–29) identifies these two allusions from Genesis, as does Philip Pinkus in *Swift's Vision of Evil: A Comparative Study of 'A Tale of a Tub' and 'Gulliver's Travels'*, ELS Monograph series, 2 vols (Victoria, British Columbia, 1975), II, 89.

[13] Quotations are from Volume XI (revised 1959) of the *Prose Works*, edited by Herbert Davis and others, 16 vols (Oxford, 1939–74).

they, and in particular the significantly denominated Master of Gulliver, play the role of God.

After some debate, the wise Houyhnhnms settle upon a comically merciful variation on the Flood: they appropriate the fine practice of gelding or castration, which Gulliver had calmly described to his Master as the human method for controlling the population of their horses. Now the master-equines will apply the same method to the bestial Yahoos. Swift postpones until Chapter 10 the special decision taken in connexion with Gulliver, both to exploit suspense and to place the decision in the highly poignant context of Gulliver's deceptive bliss. Unaware of his imminent doom, then, Gulliver feels himself in utter happiness, in what we might view as a combination of Horace's relief at escaping the anxieties of urban civilization and of the Judaeo-Christian evocation of paradise. 'I enjoyed', he declares, 'perfect Health of Body, and Tranquility of Mind' (p. 276). That would accord closely with the classical ideal, but it also defines the fabled condition of Adam before he left Eden and became subject to disease and anxiety. In addition, Gulliver feels honoured by his special relationship with the admirable Houyhnhnms, towards whom he proclaims 'the highest Venera-tion', 'natural Awe', and 'a respectful Love and Gratitude' (p. 278). During his other trips Gulliver had shown deference to authority and exhibited proud vanity when rulers, especially the gigantic Brobdingnagian king, had deigned to show him some kindness. Here among the Houyhnhnms, however, pride yields to tones of what I would call religious adoration: he behaves as though he were associating with benevolent gods.

So fervently does he admire his Master and the other Houyhnhnms that he instinctively spurns his own kind (the Yahoos) and tries to imitate his 'gods'. Consequently, as Swift organizes the narrative in Chapter 10, Gulliver's bliss reaches a symbolic climax with his attempt to become like his idols, 'to imitate their Gait and Gesture' (p. 279). Lest we fail to let our imaginations develop this laughable picture, Gulliver projects us into the present and reveals that his loss of perspective has been permanent. In England still, as his friends bluntly note, '*I trot like a Horse*', and 'in speaking I am apt to fall into the Voice and manner of the *Houyhnms*'; that is, he whinnies. Though aware that others consider him ridiculous, as surely Swift planned for us to do, Gulliver expresses self-satisfaction and takes their (and our) response 'for a great Compliment' (p. 279).

'In the Midst of this Happiness', as the next paragraph begins, the Houyhnhnms' decision to banish him is suddenly announced. Gulliver reacts wildly: 'I was struck with the utmost Grief and Despair at my Master's Discourse; and being unable to support the Agonies I was under, I fell into a Swoon at his Feet' (p. 280). This sequence, namely, Gulliver's sense of bliss, the decision to expel him, and his agonized fainting, seems reminiscent of the Eden narrative as it originally appeared in Genesis 3 and, not long before Swift's birth, was superbly reinterpreted by Milton.

Although in Genesis, after God's irrevocable decision, we hear nothing of the reactions of Adam or Eve, later writers and artists easily conjectured and dramatized their state of despair. Thus in Milton's *Paradise Lost*, when Adam hears that God does not permit him 'longer in this Paradise to dwell' (XI.259), he is stunned and speechless for the span of thirty lines, during which Eve blurts out her misery. Only then, 'from the cold sudden damp | Recovering and his scattered spirits returned' (l. 293), does Adam speak.[14] Although he may not faint, his violent reaction might well have suggested to Swift the even more violent response of Gulliver, the would-be horse, to expulsion.

Why did the Houyhnhnms force Gulliver to leave? They objected to the way Gulliver's Master gave him special treatment, 'as if he [the Master] could receive some Advantage or Pleasure in my Company', and they feared what Gulliver might do with his 'Rudiments of Reason' to upset their good order (p. 279). From the Houyhnhnms' perspective (which Gulliver himself adoringly adopts as his own viewpoint), Gulliver's rudiments of reason consist in his loathing of his own kind (the Yahoos), his attempts to clothe his disgusting body, and his efforts to act like the venerated Houyhnhnms, efforts which, Swift insidiously notes, mainly involve trotting and whinnying like a horse. In other words Gulliver has become like them in certain limited respects, and they disapprove of the way his Master encourages him in that process.

The words of Genesis 3.22 bear closely on Swift's satiric situation: 'And the Lord God said, Behold, the man is become as one of us, to know Good and Evil: and now, lest he put forth his hand, and take also of the tree of life ... [God] sent him forth.' Adam had acquired the capacity to recognize the good in paradise and in the powers of God, especially immortality, and simultaneously his knowledge of evil is symbolized by that initial discovery of nakedness and shame which Milton has so marvellously expanded into a scene between Adam and Eve of sexual lust and mutual recrimination. The biblical God feared that Adam might seize the power of immortality and thus become godlike himself, to challenge the Lord God his Master. Gulliver, on the other hand, has acquired a distorted 'knowledge' of good and evil: he identifies evil with the Yahoos, with their human analogues back in Europe, and above all with himself (or at least with the Gulliver he was when he arrived); and he identifies good with everything about the rational Houyhnhnms. Much as the Yahoos resemble human beings in their more deplorable behaviour, much as the Houyhnhnms do in fact embody some aspects of a valid ideal, Swift does not let us agree with Gulliver's extremist reactions and half-baked 'knowledge'. The antipathy which drives him from the Yahoos to loathe himself and ape the Houyhnhnms is a faulty reaction.

[14] Quoted from the Oxford Standard Authors edition of *Poetical Works*, edited by Douglas Bush (London, 1966).

Living in his hand-made house, dressed in his carefully-made clothes, fed by his own efforts, Gulliver seems to resemble for a moment the wise man who has returned to basic simple existence. Then, as he launches into his tirade of hatred towards what he thinks he has escaped in England, he loses his sage's status: he lacks the discrimination of Horace and the Horatian ability to convert simple Sabine retirement into a creative experience of the mind and soul, to be open, not myopically closed, to others, and to be ironically indulgent rather than hostile. To the extent that he has worked out this pattern of life, which is not horse-like, he earns our respect. But when we also see him trotting adoringly after the Houyhnhnms, whinnying to the best of his ability, he earns our ridicule. He has obviously failed to distinguish the relatively praiseworthy rationality of the Houyhnhnms, which he can and should imitate within human limits, from the equine form in which it here exists, a form that he cannot, and yet foolishly tries to, imitate. If Gulliver appears defective in relation to Horace and manifests a ridiculously shallow grasp of good and evil as the classical world defined them, he appears even more defective in Christian terms. We might compare him, in his blissful freedom from other human beings, to a monk alone in a cave or monastery, a St Anthony or Jerome. The monk subsists on little, like Gulliver, but his primary actions are reading the Bible and praying on his knees, praying to the *true* God for his own spiritual improvement and for the welfare of the world which, he knows, God has made and loves. Gulliver, on the other hand, has no Bible, no profound religious perspective to understand the error in his idolatry of the Houyhnhnms and in his hatred of God's world and people. Denying his own humanity by his self-disgust, his pathetic longing for utterly passionless rationality, and his absurd imitation of the horse's gait and whinnying, Gulliver emerges less a horse than an ass, an uncritical resident in a fool's paradise.

Swift, I believe, uses the paradise motif in two separate ways in Chapters 9 and 10. On the one hand, in Chapter 9 he concentrates on the Yahoos, who resemble descendants of Adam and Eve, who left paradise, degenerated, and now deserve to be exterminated from the face of the earth, as all but Noah's family were wiped out in the biblical flood. The picture of the Yahoos which we progressively form amply justifies this bleak conclusion. On the other hand, Swift creates a separate development for Gulliver, which he emphasizes by his deliberate postponement of the decision reached by the Houyhnhnms on his account. Gulliver, a recent arrival in paradise, feels himself in bliss and yet, because of the menace perceived in his rudiments of rationality, is treated by the Houyhnhnms with a severity analogous to that visited by God on disobedient Adam: he is banished from paradise. Swift's division of the paradise motif invites us to consider whether Gulliver really is a Yahoo, an extreme and unforgivable version of fallen man.

The evidence of Swift's text suggests that if Gulliver has 'fallen' it is a special kind of fall, and neither naïve non-religious Gulliver nor super-rational, non-human, non-religious Houyhnhnms are capable of grasping the nature of this fall. Only Swift and his better-informed eighteenth-century readers could do so. For Swift, Gulliver's fall consists in his faulty reactions to the fool's paradise of Houyhnhnmland and to the erroneous 'knowledge of good and evil' which he has achieved by Chapter 10. Let us go back to the moment of his arrival. Upon being put ashore, Gulliver assumes that he is a civilized Westerner among savages, and he prepares to use cheap trinkets to establish his mastery. However, when he moves inland, his expectations require major revision. The land turns out to be well cared for, by no means wild. Attacked by what he regards as animals, not human savages (these prove to be Yahoos), he is rescued by another animal, what he then regards as only a horse — obviously a Houyhnhnm. These initial perceptions are important. Essentially, Gulliver has correctly interpreted the Yahoos on first meeting: they are bestial creatures, below the level of savages, far below that of himself. However, because they do possess physical characteristics that seem recognizably human and their behaviour exaggerates the worst human faults, Gulliver can be and is eventually trapped into seeing them as human and consequently himself as a Yahoo. This error in self-perception receives full encouragement from the Houyhnhnms, about whom Gulliver must simultaneously revise his first impresions. Horse-like in physique, they possess more than equine dexterity and domesticity, and their rationality evokes Gulliver's adoration. It is they who first identify Gulliver as a Yahoo, an error which is or should be as manifest to us as is Gulliver's first inference that they are horses. But Swift obscures that error by the dramatic force with which he describes Gulliver's growing horror as he, who is neither Yahoo nor Houyhnhnm, accepts their judgement and torments himself with self-disgust and ridiculous horse-imitations.

Gulliver's first contact with the Yahoos fills him with disgust and fear. Interpreting their gestures and facial expressions as frightening, he draws his sword and initiates hostilities against these animals, who then proceed to attack him in a herd. When some of the beasts climb into the tree above him and discharge their excrement on his head, his alienation from them is disgustingly and laughably symbolized. Saved by the approach of a Houyhnhnm, Gulliver encounters this creature with a surprise which the creature curiously reflects. No doubt we are to picture him in all his ignominy as he emerges from under the tree branches covered with dung. But Swift adds other unsettling details. What Gulliver regards as a horse does not act like a horse, shows no fear or respect towards man, definitely no inferiority, but instead reveals authority, rationality, and a strange puzzlement about Gulliver. I suspect that Swift may allude to Genesis and initiate his paradise theme in this first encounter with the Houyhnhnm. 'In the Midst of this Distress' (from the Yahoo attack), reports Gulliver, 'I saw a Horse walking softly in the Field' (p. 224). The adverb 'softly', which clashes with customary literary descriptions of horse movement and yet somehow accounts for the sudden terrified flight of the bestial Yahoos, emphasizes a special quality in this horse. Recognizing their master, like guilty Adam and Eve in Genesis 3.8, who 'heard the voice of the Lord God walking in the garden', the Yahoos fled and hid. But what for me confirms the allusion is the reaction of the Houyhnhnm to Gulliver. He has no doubt of his dominance over the Yahoos, but something about Gulliver puzzles him. As Gulliver moves away from the tree, covered with that symbolically significant dung, it is not so much his human assumption of superiority that amazes the Houyhnhnm, as it is his clothing, which the Houyhnhnm, accustomed only to unclothed Yahoos and unfamiliar with the very concept of clothing, treats as some odd form of skin. For the Houyhnhnms, clothing, once Gulliver explains it to them, will constitute a disturbing sign of rationality, ultimately a threat to their domination. Thus, had this first Houyhnhnm been able to communicate his question to Gulliver, as God does to Adam, he might have asked with a similarly accusing voice: 'Who told thee that thou wast naked?' The tree in the background thus forms part of the allusion.

If, as I suspect, Swift uses this opening encounter to introduce the paradise allusion, it is important to realize that, whereas Gulliver in his clothes impresses his first Houyhnhnm as a fallen Yahoo, for Gulliver that conclusion is only gradually and mistakenly reached. In Chapter 3 he reveals to his Master the secret of clothes, stripping himself almost bare except for a kind of girdle 'to hide my Nakedness'; and he expresses great distress and uneasiness when the admired Houyhnhnm keeps calling him 'a perfect *Yahoo*' (p. 237). It had not occurred to him, at the time of his first hostile meeting with the Yahoos, that their gestures and grimaces indicated that they, like the Houyhnhnms, viewed him as an odd Yahoo. But by Chapter 8 he reveals with disgust: 'I have Reason to believe, they had some Imagination that I was of their own Species (p. 265); and he admits that he unintentionally fostered this feeling by rolling up his sleeves, opening his shirt, and exposing Yahoo-like skin. However, a terrible incident, a gross parody of Adam's Fall, brings home to him the hateful conclusion that he is indeed a Yahoo. Pausing one warm day by a river, he stripped naked and plunged in. At sight of his male body, a young female Yahoo leapt into the water, too, and started embracing him. Gulliver comically resisted, roared out his protest, and eventually was saved from the reluctant howling female by his so-called Protector. All this merely confirms the prejudice of the Houyhnhnms, who accordingly treat it as 'Matter of Diversion', but Gulliver is appalled. 'Now I could no longer deny', he says, 'that I was a real *Yahoo*, in every Limb and Feature, since the Females had a natural Propensity to me as one of their own Species' (p. 267). But if Gulliver could not deny it, Swift ensures that we can. We share the amusement of the Houyhnhnms without their prejudice. And we can perceive that the abortive sexual encounter, which differs so strikingly from the carnal desire that inflames both Adam and Eve and leads to mutual sexual satisfaction in *Paradise Lost*, proves what Gulliver's human instincts have all along protested: he *is* different from the Yahoos. Gullible Gulliver has caved in at last to the combined ignorance of Houyhnhnms and Yahoos, who both perceive him as a Yahoo because of his physical characteristics.

Gulliver, then, has lived in a fool's paradise, and Swift has proposed these allusions to the Eden-story of Genesis and of later Christian interpreters, notably Milton, primarily to inform the reader's perspective. Deficient in religious background, Gulliver does not use the word 'paradise' or grasp the important distinctions between the false Eden among the Houyhnhnms and the true Eden. When confronted with an opportunity to discover, as Horace does on his Sabine farm, some essential realities about human nature and hence about the ethical goals to pursue; or, to state it in biblical terms, when brought to that awful moment when, at the price of losing paradise, he might achieve Adam's special knowledge of good and evil, poor, foolish, impressionable Gulliver settles, ridiculous in his self-disgust, ridiculous in his veneration of rational equines, for others' denial of his humanity. As Ricardo Quintana has stated it, we have been watching in Book IV 'a comic debate taking place in the psyche of the absurd anti-hero'.[15] Gulliver reluctantly leaves his false paradise, to the end so pathetically venerating the Houyhnhnms and accepting their view of him that he is proudly grateful to be permitted to kiss the hoof of his Master. Off he goes, accompanied and consoled by no Eve, so twisted in judgement that he will be unable even to view his wife without disgust. Although Gulliver fails to resolve properly his 'comic debate', Swift has made amply clear that humanity does not deserve total condemnation for its partial resemblance to the disgusting Yahoos, that Houyhnhnms and horses do not alone possess rationality. Both the classical and Christian visions define humans beings as hopeful compounds of reason and emotion. As he leaves his fool's paradise to return to the human world, Gulliver's wretchedness and blind prejudice reveal to us how far he is from the equanimity of Horace, how very far from the resolute fortitude of Milton's fallen Adam and Eve.

[15] '*Gulliver's Travels*: the Satiric Intent and Execution', in *Jonathan Swift 1667–1967: A Dublin Tercentenary Tribute* (Dublin, 1967), pp. 78–93 (p. 92). See also Edward Stone, 'Swift and the Horses: Misanthropy or Comedy', *MLQ*, 10 (1949), 367–76.

Pope and Horace on
Not Writing Poetry:
A Study of *Epistles*, II.2

NIALL RUDD

University of Bristol

We are all familiar with Dr Johnson's definition of imitation as 'a kind of middle composition between translation and original design, which pleases when the thoughts are unexpectedly applicable and the parallels lucky'. The present paper examines how this convention operates in one of Pope's major poems. I am aware that by going through the texts section by section I may seem to have offered a series of notes rather than a continuous exposition; but I end by summarizing Pope's alterations and additions in terms of a few general procedures; and these procedures will indicate, I hope, that imitation, as practised by Pope, allowed more freedom and more scope for resourcefulness than might be inferred from Dr Johnson's description.[1]

Horace, ll. 1–25. (Excuse 1: 'I told you I was a wretched correspondent.') Addressing Julius Florus, who is abroad with Tiberius the future emperor, Horace puts a hypothetical case: 'If a man sold you a slave, *admitting* the boy's defect, you would not try to sue him, would you?' The point would have been readily acknowledged, for the principle *caveat emptor* did not apply to transactions of this kind.[2] But what is Horace driving at? We must wait nearly twenty lines to find out. 'I told you I was a wretched correspondent, yet you still make accusations; you also complain that I have failed to send the lyrics I promised.' So the opening verses, with their lively sales-talk and legal terminology, turn out to be part of an excuse for not writing poetry. The tactics are ingenious. Horace presents Florus with a kind of parable, in function rather like that offered by Nathan to David in II Samuel 12. As a result, by the time he has reached line 25, the aggrieved Florus has been put in the wrong. And yet, although Horace speaks firmly to

---

[1] *Lives of the English Poets*, edited by George Birkbeck Hill, 3 vols (Oxford, 1905), III, 176. Epistle II.2 is quoted from Volume IV of *The Twickenham Edition of the Poems of Alexander Pope*, edited by John Butt and others, 11 vols (1939–69). In this edition the reader may wish to note the following misprints: l. 17 read *poenae* for *poena*, l. 168 read *Emtum* for *Emtor*, l. 215 read *aequo* for *aeque*. Two studies directly concerned with Pope's imitation of *Epistles*, II.2 are A. L. Williams, 'Pope and Horace', in *Restoration and Eighteenth-Century Literature*, edited by C. Camden (Chicago and London, 1963), pp. 309–21, and T. E. Maresca, *Pope's Horatian Poems* (Columbus, Ohio, 1966), Chapter 4. On the structure of Horace's poem, see M. J. McGann, 'Horace's Epistle to Florus', *Rheinisches Museum*, 97 (1954), 343–58.

[2] See J. Crook, *Law and Life of Rome* (London, 1967), pp. 181–82.

his friend, providing neither a letter nor a collection of lyrics, he does present him with something of each: a verse epistle.

Pope, ll. 1–33. 'Dear Col'nel!' According to Warton, this was Colonel Cotterell of Rousham near Oxford. John Butt (Twickenham edition) demurs, pointing out that in lines 232–33 the addressee is the tenant of Abscourt, near Walton-on-Thames, a man whom he identifies as Anthony Browne. But we have no evidence that Browne was a colonel; nor is it certain that he was at Abscourt in 1737. George Paston gives reasons for thinking that the man in question was James Dormer, a colonel in the Grenadier Guards.[3] On this view three different men are addressed in the poem: the Colonel, the tenant of Abscourt, and Bathurst (l. 256). So it seems that for Pope the epistolary form was of secondary importance. The same is true of the rhetorical structure. Like Horace, Pope is supposed to be excusing his failure to write verses (see, for example, ll. 31–32, 71). Yet in the second line he presents the poem to the recipient with a bow: 'You love a Verse, take such as I can send', thus destroying the ironical situation exploited by Horace. Finally there is a question of relevance. The Roman slave, we are told, has a little Greek, is something of a singer, and has been known to evade his obligations. In these respects does he not resemble Horace himself? The correspondence between the French boy and Pope is much less clear. Even if one grants that the boy's stealing is a joking parallel to Pope's literary borrowings (which seems rather unlikely), there is still no connexion between Pope's thievery and his failure as a correspondent and as a composer. It can, of course, be argued that Pope had never undertaken to send poems to his friend; certainly the Colonel makes no complaint about broken promises. And so there was less need of a systematic defence.

Horace, ll. 26–54. (Excuse 2: 'When I was poor I was energetic, but why should I exert myself now?') In the war against Mithridates one of Lucullus's soldiers was robbed of his hard-earned savings. In his anger he stormed an enemy position and was handsomely rewarded. Shortly after, the General called on him to lead the attack on another fort: 'Go, my good fellow, go where your courage calls; and the best of luck to you! You'll win a rich reward for your services. What's keeping you?' The man, though a country bumpkin, was no fool. 'If you want someone to "go go" to the place you have in mind', he replied, 'find a man who has lost his wallet!' There follows a famous passage of autobiography in which serious, and at times tragic, recollections are summarized in a throwaway, almost flippant, style. For twenty-five years Horace was apparently the passive victim of circumstances: it happened that he was reared in Rome; Athens added a little higher education; the times uprooted him; the surge carried him into battle;

---

[3] *Mr Pope: His Life and Times*, 2 vols (London, 1909), II, 563 n. 1. One may also ask whether Browne was a friend of Cobham (l. 1); Dormer certainly was.

Philippi discharged him; finally Poverty forced him to write. So Horace's career as a poet is explained by the fact that he needed the money. The self-depreciatory tone is typical. For example, in the student's search for truth ('atque inter silvas Academi quaerere verum') the familiar translation ('the groves of Academe') tends to obscure the fact that a *silva* is not a place where one expects to find anything very easily. Nor does he make capital out of his military career. He had, after all, been on the wrong side: hence the tactful reference to 'the strong arm of Caesar Augustus'. The compliment, however, contains reserves of irony which protect the poet's self-respect. For it was, of course, Antony who won the battle of Philippi: the strong-armed Caesar Augustus was indisposed.

Pope, ll. 33–71. Pope transfers the scene to 'Anna's wars' and enlarges the scale of operations. Incensed at being robbed, the soldier

> leapt the Trenches, scal'd a Castle-Wall,
> Tore down a standard, took the Fort and all.

But Pope now found himself in a quandary. The story required that the man be given a substantial reward. Horace mentions a sum of 20,000 sesterces.[4] But Pope could not bring himself to ascribe such generosity to Marlborough. So instead of a climax we get a satirical innuendo:

> 'Prodigious well!' his great Commander cry'd,
> Gave him much Praise and some Reward beside.

Similar reservations about 'the great Commander' are implied in the next couplet:

> Next pleas'd his Excellence a Town to batter;
> (Its name I know not, and it's no great matter).

As a result we derive extra pleasure from Marlborough's rebuff:

> D'ye think me, noble Gen'ral, such a Sot?
> Let him take Castles who has ne'er a Groat.

Elwin and Courthope comment disapprovingly that 'such a reply from an English soldier to his General would have been impossible' — as if rudeness and insubordination were normal in the Roman legions.[5]

The autobiographical passage is brilliantly adapted to Pope's own life:

> Bred up at home, full early I begun
> To read in Greek the Wrath of Peleus' Son.

Horace's phrasing is rather different. He was taught 'how much harm the wrathful Achilles had done to the Greeks'. In other words the teaching had a Stoic slant: anger is wrong — look at what happened to the Greeks when

---

[4] Caesar paid his soldiers about 900 sesterces a year. Poorish land could be bought for about 2,000 sesterces an acre.

[5] *Works*, edited by J. W. Croker, W. Elwin, and W. J. Courthope, 10 vols (London, 1871), IV, 381n.

Achilles was sulking in his tent. In Pope's case the moral element was
provided by his father (ll. 54–55); so there was little point, he says, in going to
Oxford. But their moral concerns did not save them from being evicted. The
sardonic tone continues:

> And certain Laws, by Suff'rers thought unjust,
> Deny'd all Posts of Profit or of Trust:
> Hopes after Hopes of pious Papists fail'd,
> While mighty WILLIAM's thundring Arm prevail'd.

The last couplet is especially sonorous, with its opening trochee, its succession of plosives, and its apt Homeric parody.[6] We may guess that Pope was
directed to the Iliadic line by the presence of *lacertis* (arms) on the opposite
page. He then returned to the subject of his father, who had suffered for
supporting James II:

> For Right Hereditary tax'd and fin'd,
> He stuck to Poverty with Peace of Mind.

The word 'Right' is cunningly chosen, for it lends an air of martyrdom to the
father's sufferings. Such a protest was not possible for Horace. The loss of his
property had been a penalty for siding with Brutus against Octavian, who
was now the all-powerful Augustus. So all he can say is that he was 'left
without' his home ('inopem . . . laris et fundi'), adding ruefully that the
former high flyer has been brought down to earth with a bump ('decisis
humilem pennis'). Thanks to his translation of the *Iliad* Pope was able to
assert his independence with a defiant flourish: 'Indebted to no Prince or
Peer alive'. That, too, was impossible for Horace; for although he was now
fairly well off, he owed his financial security to Maecenas and Augustus. In
Rome no profits could be had from the book trade.

Looking at the two autobiographies, we are struck at once by the common
pattern of attentive father, classical education, civil war, defeat, eviction,
poverty, and eventual literary success. Yet the differences are no less
instructive. Horace moved easily among people and took part in major
events. For physical and religious reasons Pope's experience was far more
restricted. He knew little of school, university, or court life, and nothing of
war. He grew up in the *aftermath* of civil war. Horace had been at Philippi,
that calamitous battle in which the Roman nobility was almost wiped out.
The disabilities Pope suffered as a Catholic, though extremely vexatious,
could not be compared to the vast convulsion in which Horace was caught
and which provided such a sombre background to the sketch of his early life.
This, paradoxically, may have given Pope a sharper sense of private
resentment; for he no doubt believed that, were it not for prejudice in high
places, the anti-Catholic legislation could be repealed. But Horace, apart
from his delicate position as a former republican officer, could not readily

---

[6] Pope's *Iliad*, IX.666.

attribute his misfortunes to the malice of a group. Like the students of 1914 and 1939, his generation had been through a tempest.

Finally, we come back again to the sequence of the epistle's argument. Horace alleges that he took up poetry only because he was destitute; now that he is comfortably off, why should he write any more? Pope was unable, or unwilling, to take that line. Instead he made a different point, namely that while he and his father were poor the pleasure of composition eased his misery. This, however, weakens his fictitious case; for if he enjoyed writing *before* the *Iliad* made his fortune, why should he not continue now?

Horace, ll. 55–57. (Excuse 3: 'I'm getting old.')   'As the years go by, they rob us of one thing after another. They have already made off with fun, sex, parties and sport; now they are straining to pull away my poems. What do you expect me to do?' ('Quid faciam vis?') The desired answer, of course, is 'nothing'.

Pope, ll. 72–79.   Pope felt with good reason that Horace's passage was disproportionately short. So he increased it from three lines to eight, producing a beautiful piece of elegiac reflection. Scholars have heard echoes of Shakespeare, Milton, and Dryden; but Horace's voice is there too. In *Odes*, IV.13.17–22 he wonders sadly what has happened to the girl whose very breath was love and who stole him from himself away ('quae me surpuerat mihi'). Again, when Pope speaks of the passing years and says, 'In one a mistress drops, in one a friend', he lightly evokes an image of falling leaves. This must surely have been prompted by another Horatian passage about the years: 'The forest's leaves change as the years roll on; the earliest drop' (*Ars Poetica*, ll. 60–61). Johnson saw the connexion when, in *The Vanity of Human Wishes*, he wrote

> Year chases Year, Decay pursues Decay,
> Still drops some joy from withering life away.   (l. 305)

The last two lines of Pope's section are also very fine; but once again Pope shows his indifference to the argument. Instead of making advancing age an excuse for not writing, he merely says 'What shall I do when my Muse falls silent?', which is a moving reflection, but not really germane.

Horace, ll. 58–64. (Excuse 4: 'It's impossible to please everyone.')   One might conjecture that on reading over the previous section Horace fastened on the final question ('Quid faciam vis?'). By interpreting this in a different sense, namely 'What do you want me to produce?', he was led on to his next idea: 'Different people ask for different things.' This is illustrated by three guests with various preferences in food.

Pope, ll. 80–87.   Starting from 'Quid faciam vis?', Pope fixes on specific dishes where Horace had been wholly general; and he adds two proper names to give the lines a sharper focus.

Horace, (a) ll. 65–76, (b) ll. 77–86. (Excuse 5 (a): 'How do you expect me to write poetry in Rome where I am subjected to so many physical and mental strains?')   After reading the vivid lines that follow, it is churlish to recall that we are listening to a piece of exculpatory blarney. Was Rome so totally chaotic? If so, how are we to account for the beginning of *Satires*, 1.9: 'I was wandering along the Sacred Way, composing some trifle as usual'? And if Horace never has a free moment, what becomes of his later excuse that he is devoting himself to philosophy? But Florus, of course, is not supposed to think of such tiresome questions.

(b) 'Poets, obeying Bacchus, make for the countryside. How can I sing amidst the din of Rome and follow the bards' path? Here we have a combination of two ideas from very different periods. The first (poets as the attendants of Bacchus/Dionysus) comes from the farthest reaches of the Greek memory. The second (the poets' path) only goes back to Callimachus, the third century Alexandrian who urged poets to avoid the broad well-trodden highway of epic.[7] A further argument is added: even in Athens, with its favourable conditions, dedicated men fail to get anything written, and make themselves ridiculous; so why should I try to compose in Rome?

Pope, (a) ll. 88–109, (b) ll. 110–26.   The account of London's distractions illustrates very well how Pope elaborates on his original. First, instead of Horace's general introductory phrase, 'tot curas totque labores', he gives us a line packed full of busy detail: 'In Crouds and Courts, Law, Business, Feasts and Friends'. Then, taking up the requests mentioned by Horace, 'My Counsel sends to execute a Deed: | A Poet begs me, I will hear him read' (l. 67), he brings in the voices of other people, each one clamouring for an appointment: 'In Palace-Yard at Nine you'll find me there', and so on. This is not in the original, but it was influenced, we may be sure, by a similar passage in *Satires*, II.6: 'Roscius wanted you to meet him at the Exchange before eight tomorrow'; 'The Department said to be sure to come in today, Quintus; an important matter of common concern has just cropped up'; 'Get Maecenas' signature on these documents' (ll. 34–38).

Then something more adventurous takes place. The first hint comes in line 99:

> 'Oh but a Wit can study in the Streets,
> 'And raise his Mind above the Mob he meets.'

The second line is not in Horace, but it sounds like a transformation of another passage: 'As the *mob* gives way, the rich man will speed above their faces in a huge Liburnian.' That, as I say, is only a hint. One does not yet realize what is happening, and one reads on: 'A Hackney-Coach may chance to spoil a Thought.' The ancient hackney was a litter, which, although it had

---

[7] See Callimachus (*Aetia*, 1.1), edited by C. A. Trypanis, Loeb Classical Library (London and Cambridge, Massachusetts, 1958), pp. 6–9.

no wheels, could do a lot of damage with its poles: 'Another fellow bangs you with a hard litter-pole.' Worse still: 'Another *hurts* your *head* with a *beam*.' By now we are getting our bearings. This is not Horace's Rome, but Juvenal's (*Satires*, 3.239–56). Another hazard, one recalls, was caused by tree-trunks being carried to building-sites: 'They *nod* overhead.' Let us now step back and look at the three lines of Pope:

> A Hackney-Coach may chance to spoil a Thought,
> And then a nodding Beam, or Pig of Lead,
> God knows, may hurt the very ablest Head.

The pig of lead is, of course, a witty metamorphosis of Horace's muddy pig.

But Pope has not finished his Juvenalian excursion. Juvenal had described waggons passing in the *narrow* winding streets and the drovers hurling abuse when their cattle were brought to a standstill. This reappears in Pope as

> Have you not seen at Guild-hall's narrow Pass,
> Two Aldermen dispute it with an Ass?

Juvenal's waggons are then combined with the earlier couplet (*gives way* . . . above . . . in a . . . Liburnian) so as to provide an ordurous climax:

> And Peers give way, exalted as they are,
> Ev'n to their own [Sir-reverence] in a Carr?[8]

This is all so deft that we almost overlook the weakness of the rhetorical point at the end of the next couplet. Horace had said 'Go now (in view of all I've described) and try to compose melodious verses' (l. 76). Pope says:

> Go lofty Poet! and in such a Croud,
> Sing thy sonorous Verse — but not aloud.

This shifts the thought from composition to utterance: to recite one's verses in such an uproar is futile. No doubt it is; but what does that do to reinforce lines 88–91?

(b) The chief innovation here is the ironical reference to Sir Richard Blackmore, as if he were the exemplar of all true poets. The great god of inspiration is not mentioned; his presence is deducible only from the rather drunken condition of the old knight. At the same time, by printing Horace's 'rite cliens Bacchi' on the opposite page, Pope obtains a piquant effect.

The next point is textual. Horace (l. 80) said, 'How do you expect me to follow the bards' narrow path?' ('contracta sequi vestigia vatum'). Pope's text read, with several MSS, *contacta*, which would have to mean 'to reach and follow the bards' path'. Pope sensed the weakness of this and turned to Bentley. There he found the conjecture *non tacta*, that is, 'to follow the path of the [Greek lyric] poets not trodden [by any Latin writer] before'. This appealed to him and he translated it as, 'How match the Bards whom none

---

[8] Pope may have recalled that the only waggons allowed in Rome in daylight were those carrying building materials and carrying out excrement.

e'er match'd before?'. But he could not bring himself to put 'slashing Bentley's' conjecture in his text. In lines 116–22 Pope develops the comical element in Horace's picture. The scholar poet is covered with dust, wears his nightcap in the street, and in general gives the impression of being a kind of cosmic freak. So too, for Horace's rather stately lines, 'amid the waves and tempests of the capital', Pope substitutes a Hogarthian scene of mobs, duns, soldiers, and fools.

Horace, ll. 87–105. (Excuse 6: 'By ceasing to write I am absolved from attending recitations.')   In lines 99–101 there is some reason to think that Horace is glancing at Propertius, who called himself the Roman Callimachus (IV.1.64) and declared that in matters of love a line of Mimnermus was worth more than the whole of Homer (1.9.11). But one cannot gauge the degree of malice intended. In the section as a whole one notes the balanced arrangement of line 89, which represents a polite version of 'you scratch my back and I'll scratch yours'; the metrical licence of lines 93–94, where the compound verb slowly lurches over into the next line; the presentation of an exchange of compliments as a mock duel (ll. 97–99); the playful allusion in line 105 to the poet's own name, Flaccus ('Floppy-ears'); and the trick whereby Horace includes himself in the poetic set, so that he can pillory its vanities, and then withdraws from it. Above all there is the subtle control of direction. In line 87 we enter a new section which culminates in a further excuse, but we are unaware of doing so: indeed the word *Romae* (l. 87) might suggest we were still dealing with the hectic life of the city (*urbis* in line 85). The thread to hold on to is that of mutual congratulation, which leads from the two lawyers to the two poets. Then comes the excuse: Horace played the game (that is, he attended other poets' recitals) as long as he was writing himself: now such tedium is unnecessary — a great relief. Finally, the idea of second-rate poets reciting their work carries us smoothly to the *next* section, which has to do with poetic quality.

Pope, ll. 127–52.   Pope realizes the situation more fully by *quoting* the two lawyers (ll. 133–34); again, after reporting the mutual flattery of poets (ll. 135–38), he *quotes* the interchange which takes place in the library of Merlin's cave, and in doing so gives two versions of Horace's joke. Secondly, whereas Horace names only three poetic models, Pope gives seven English, three Roman, and one Greek. At the end of the section one line stands out. Speaking of his fellow poets (Horace's 'genus irritabile vatum'), Pope packs an extraordinary amount of exasperation into ten snarling syllables: 'This jealous, waspish, wrong-head, rhiming Race'. With all this abundance there is a loss of clarity. Horace reserves the second person singular for the reader. In Pope we are not always quite sure who is being addressed. In line 136, for instance, 'yours' seems to refer to an unspecified poet who happens to be reading the epistle; Cibber is apostrophized in line 138, and perhaps he is 'you' in line 140; but then in line 141 it is the ordinary reader who is invited to 'walk with respect behind'. At the same time, so many names are tossed about that the two central figures tend to slip out of focus. Not surprisingly, the metaphor of the duel is abandoned.

Horace, (a) ll. 106–25, (b) ll. 126–40 (Excuse 7).

(a) ll. 106–25. 'While complacent illusions may be agreeable, to produce something entitled to be called a poem [that is, a 'legitimum poema'] is hard work.' This section is dominated by the figure of the Censor, the magistrate who, along with his colleague, regularly revised the lists of the senate, removing those who had shown themselves unworthy. The Censor-poet, says Horace, should investigate his own poetry, expelling those words which are deficient in lustre and solidity.[9] Conversely he will bring other words out of obscurity and admit to service new expressions which have been brought up by father Usage. Now the metaphor changes, first to a river, then to a man working with vines or olives, and finally to a dancer.

Pope, (a) ll. 153–79.   Since the Censor-poet could not be transferred, Pope did what he could with the Judge-poet: hence 'proceed' (l. 157), 'Judges' and 'spare' (l. 159). But since a judge's powers did not include *admission*, the analogy with the poet's activity could not be sustained. Thus 'revive', 'command to wake', and 'bid be English' are not really part of the metaphor. Likewise Horace's cultivator, who will prune, strip, and uproot, is not fully matched by Pope's, who will prune, refine, and show no mercy (ll. 174–75).[10] On the other hand Pope has made some interesting additions. In line 164 he says the true poet will sometimes 'In downright Charity revive the dead'. This is based, not on the epistle, but on a similar passage in the *Ars Poetica*: 'Many words will be born again which now lie dead' (l. 70). But Pope has made this rebirth the act of the creative poet, and his phrasing would have recalled for many the restoration of Lazarus and of Jairus's daughter. In lines 176–79 we read:

> Then polish all, with so much life and ease,
> You think 'tis Nature, and a knack to please:
> 'But Ease in writing flows from Art, not Chance,
> 'As those move easiest who have learn'd to dance.

'Polish', 'life', 'ease', 'Nature', 'Art', and 'Chance' are not in Horace, but most of them, it turns out, are in the notes of the Delphin commentary by Desprez (1691): 'duriora scite expoliet' ('he will deftly *polish* the rougher bits'); 'adeo res quaeque . . . facile scriptae apparebunt' ('each thing will seem to have been written with *so much ease*' that anyone would think himself capable of doing the same); 'velut eximius pantomimus . . . tanta arte ut ipsa Satyri vel Cyclopi natura et persona agere credatur' ('like an outstanding

---

[9] The reference to the temple of Vesta in Horace (l. 114) is explained by the ancient commentator (Pseudo-Acron) as meaning 'although the words may seem, as it were, sacrosanct to the writer'.
[10] See Cato, *De Agricultura*, 44 (olives) 'make the stems smooth', and Columella, *De Re Rustica*, IV.10.2 (vines) 'the vine should be trimmed . . . the smooth straight vine without a scar is the best'.

dancer' he will perform 'with so much *art* that the very *nature* and character of the Satyr and Cyclops are *thought* to be acting'). One cannot say, of course, in what order the ideas came to Pope. He may have thought first of lines 178–79, which are a close repetition of two lines from the *Essay on Criticism* (362–63). But this hardly affects our present argument; for those lines are clearly modelled on the same passage of Horace.

Horace, (b) ll. 126–40. 'Happy illusions are pleasant' (compare ll. 106–108). 'I should prefer to be a crazy scribbler than to be sane [*sapere*] and bare my teeth in frustration — provided I was unaware of my incompetence, like the lunatic of Argos.'

Pope, (b) ll. 180–97.   There is perhaps a slight lack of clarity at line 190; for the meaning has to be confirmed by referring to Horace's text, where 'non insanire' has been printed in capitals. But it is hard to agree with Elwin and Courthope that the picture of the lunatic peer is 'very inferior to the original'. By altering the sense of Horace's 'haud ignobilis' (capitalized in the text) from 'famous' to 'aristocratic' and hence 'a member of the House of Lords', Pope has injected an element of *political* satire. Many would regard the result as superior to the original; certainly the final stroke of wit (ll. 195–97) has no counterpart in Horace.

Horace, ll. 141–216. (Excuse 8: 'I ought to be concentrating on philosophy instead of poetry.')   It will be best to consider this long closing section in a series of subdivisions.

Horace, (a) ll. 141–44. 'One should grow up, have sense [*sapere*], and not hunt for words to be set to the music of [*modulanda*] the Latin lyre, but rather master the rhythms and modes [*modos*] of true living.'

   In view of the earlier *sapere* (l. 128) and the story of the lunatic, we are tempted to take *sapere* (l. 141) in its medical sense, but we soon realize that it now has an ethical meaning; it thus indicates the new direction which the poem is going to take. Another feature of this hinge passage is the play on *modos*. From now on Horace will be concerned, not with musical and poetical *modi*, but with moral *modi* (forms of behaviour).

Pope, (a) ll. 198–205.   Pope contrives a clever link with the previous passage. As the lord was dismayed at being restored to his senses, so Pope implies that the onset of wisdom will be distinctly unwelcome: 'Wisdom (curse on it) will come soon or late'. When we reach 'I learn' (l. 203) we infer that he is already adjusting himself to the new spiritual life.

> To Rules of Poetry no more confin'd,
> I learn to smooth and harmonize my Mind,
> Teach ev'ry Thought within its bounds to roll,
> And keep the equal Measure of the Soul.

As well as reproducing the play on *modulanda* and *modos*, this adds a further touch of wit; for 'bounds' (echoing 'confined') plays on yet a third meaning of *modi.* One also notes how the whole idea has been turned inwards. Horace's attention is focused on behaviour; Pope's on the inner life.[11]

Horace, (b) ll. 145–57. 'Acquisitiveness is not cured by making money.'

Pope, (b) ll. 206–29.   Pope now goes on to speak of the place which not only provides a setting for introspection but also promotes it. By taking us out to Twickenham these lines move away from the situation envisaged at the start. To a lesser extent the same is true of the original: from now on we hear no more of Florus. Yet the closing section in each poem is not just a loose appendage. Its function is to *demonstrate* (not merely talk about) the poet's new preoccupation.

Lines 212–15 are, for Pope, rather clumsy; and in the next two lines he is betrayed into answering his own rhetorical question. But the transition from 'sober' (l. 211) to 'drink' (l. 212) is cleverly managed, and in the 'golden Angels' Pope hits on something which was not only medically useless but also pointed directly to money, which was morally useless: a brilliant stroke. Then, with Horace's deceptive advisers in mind (*monitoribus*), Pope switches to Bishop Kennet, who in turn prepares the way for an attack on the Duke of Devonshire and on the wealthy Vanneck. As often, a general reflection in Horace has been conjured into something stingingly topical.

Horace, (c) ll. 158–79. 'In law there are two ways of acquiring ownership — purchase and *usus.* The land which supports you by its produce is yours, and the steward regards you as the owner (though actually you are renting it from Orbius). The man who has purchased a property speaks of its produce as "his own"; but in fact he is eating bought produce, because he bought it with the original purchase price. Anyhow ownership is never more than temporary; so what good are large estates? Orcus reaps us all, large and small, and he cannot be moved by gold.'

Such is the pattern of Horace's argument; the actual thread is taken from Roman law: *proprium, mancipare, usus,* etc. How, then, does Horace prevent the passage from becoming dry and prosaic? First, he puts himself on the layman's side at the outset by slipping in the parenthesis, 'so the lawyers tell us' (l. 159): this is not going to be a technical disquisition. More important, instead of dwelling on the tedious litigation of the city, he takes us out into the countryside, where the old conditions still exist. We hear of corn, grapes, and chickens; a kettle boiling on a log fire in the chilly evening; a line of poplar trees. As in the opening of Gray's *Elegy,* the antiquity of the scene leads us back over earlier generations; and from that we move naturally to thoughts of transience.

Pope, (c) ll. 230–63.   At the very beginning we have a hint of Horatian ambiguity, for 'on which' (l. 231) can mean 'on the produce of which' as well

[11] See G. K. Hunter, 'The "Romanticism" of Pope's Horace', *Essays in Criticism,* 10 (1960), 390–404.

as 'on the site of which'. After addressing the tenant of Abscourt, Pope introduces another character:

> All Worldly's Hens, nay Partridge, sold to town,
> His Ven'son too, a Guinea makes your own.

This must mean: 'You obtain cheaply from Abscourt as many hens as Worldly [that is, Wortley Montagu] sells in his local market town in Yorkshire.' Pope then goes on to point a double contrast: Worldly paid a huge sum for his estate and now sells the produce to make money; the tenant of Abscourt pays a modest rent and enjoys the produce himself. Why, one wonders, should Worldly be mentioned here? There is nothing about selling goods in Horace. The answer probably lies in the name of Horace's landowner, Orbius. To a lively imagination that was almost bound to suggest 'Worldly'. The rest followed by association.

Heathcote and the other 'large-acred men' (l. 240) have to pay (through the original purchase price of their estates) for everything they consume. Yet the poor creatures think they *own* half the county: 'Half that the Dev'l o'erlooks from Lincoln Town'. This is odd. The sense requires that the Devil should be looking over the surrounding countryside from a vantage point in Lincoln (most naturally the cathedral). Pope has therefore altered the proverb, which (as far as I know) invariably has the Devil looking at Lincoln from a position overhead. If the change was intentional, its point is not obvious.

In the following lines (246–49) the mention of God and the biblical flavour of the language remind us that Pope's argument is based not only on traditional wisdom but on Christian theology.[12] Line 249, however, is not easy. The general sense must be 'liable to take off at any moment', but how this can be extracted from the text is far from clear. There is no problem with Horace, for 'puncto . . . mobilis horae' means 'at a moment in the moving course of time'. The next couplet reads:

> Ready, by force, or of your own accord,
> By sale, at least by death, to change their Lord.

There are only three possibilities: force, sale (that is, with your own consent), and death. Pope read, with Desprez, *sorte suprema*. Modern editors, since Bentley, prefer *morte suprema*. The general sense is much the same, but Pope's imitation is closer to Bentley's reading. It is also, perhaps, worth observing that in view of *suprema* Pope must have considered 'at last'. It is not easy to guess what tipped the balance in favour 'at least'. In lines 252–63 Pope gains in power. When read aloud the lines have an exceptional sonority, which comes not only from the open vowels but also from the series of internal correspondences (Heir . . . Heir, Wave . . . Wave, Hills . . . Dale, Towns . . .

---

[12] Compare Proverbs 23.5: 'Wilt thou set thine eyes on that which is not? for riches certainly make themselves wings; they fly away as an eagle toward heaven', quoted by P. Dixon, *The World of Pope's Satires* (London, 1968), p. 145.

Towns . . . Downs), which produce an incantatory effect. The etymology of 'inexorable' still works (especially with the Latin opposite). Death 'cannot be moved by entreaty'. He is also 'Death the leveller', and he will justify his title in an unexpectedly literal way. In the last line the succession of collapses is conveyed by the series of 'and's, each forming part of a self-contained iambic foot: 'and Trees, and Stones, and Farms'; then the three syllables of 'and Farmer' draw in the short element of the fifth iamb, allowing a momentary pause before the final monosyllable, 'fall'. The spirit is satirical in that it mocks human pretensions, yet it has a sombre gravity which looks forward to *The Vanity of Human Wishes*.

Horace, (d) ll. 180–204. ('People differ widely in temperament; I aim at the mean.')

Horace has concealed the transition by ending the last section with 'gold' and beginning this with 'jewels, marble, ivory', etc. The guardian spirit (*genius*) is invoked as a way of acknowledging temperamental differences. It is not meant, however, to open the way to ethical relativism. For when all allowance has been made for character and circumstance there is still a valid Aristotelian system of praise and blame; both the industrious miser and the idle spendthrift are reprehensible.

Pope, (d) ll. 264–303. Etruscan bronzes give way to vases, and African purple is replaced by Persian dye. With these minor adjustments the luxurious contents of a Roman villa are transported to an English country house. In the picture of the two brothers, Horace's oil massage (*ungui*) is discarded as un-English, and Herod's palmgroves disappear in favour of Townshend's turnips and Grosvenor's mines. The setting is now unmistakably that of England on the eve of the agrarian and industrial revolutions. Another sign of modern times is the complimentary reference to Oglethorpe. Founding colonies was a familiar enterprise in Roman times too, but the pioneers, however worthy, would never have been praised for their 'strong benevolence of soul'. Now we come to a theological point. In Horace a man's temperament was said to depend on his *genius*. For Pope this was impossible. There could be only one divine being who presided over human variability, namely the Christian god, the *naturae deus humanae*, and he was certainly not *mortalis*. As a result, Pope's statement is one of serious religious belief, and so carries much more weight than the original. The links with Horace are only superficial. Pope's 'genius' is not a man's guardian spirit, but rather his disposition. Likewise 'the natal Hour' has lost its ancient connexion with astrology. In spite of such changes, Pope's reference to 'that Directing Pow'r, | Who forms the Genius in the natal Hour' could have left him open to attack (he had already been criticized for his *Essay on Man*). So he added an explicit affirmation of free will (ll. 280–81):

> That God of Nature, who, within us still,
> Inclines our Action, not constrains our Will.

All this safeguarded Pope's orthodoxy, but it also redistributed the emphasis of the argument. In Horace the two brothers and the *genius* take up only seven lines; their main function is to lead us smoothly to the poet's statement of his own outlook in lines 190–204. Pope has given us a piece of Christian theology which stands on its own feet.

We have now noticed most of the ways in which Horace's passage has been modified. But if it is to become Pope's own it must also in some way project the poet's self. This projection begins in line 284. Unlike Horace, who inserts a purely general statement (ll. 195–98) into his personal reflections, Pope keeps the first person throughout. He begins by referring to his independence:

> My Heir may sigh, and think it want of Grace
> A man so poor wou'd live without a *Place*.

Pope was, of course, unplaced because he was a Roman Catholic. His religion also affected his will. By an act of 1700 Catholics were debarred from inheriting land, and so Pope's heir (we are told) can have no say in how he disposes of his property (ll. 288–89). But did Pope in fact have an heir? Certainly not of his blood. Neither did Horace. The grasping heir was, rather, a conventional figure of comedy and satire, whom it was desirable to cheat. Finally, Horace claims to be a living embodiment of the mean: 'In strength, talent [*ingenium*], appearance, valour, status, and wealth I am last among the first, but always ahead of the last.' The claim should not be inspected too closely. Elsewhere Horace himself tells us that he was below average in size;[13] on the other hand the man who wrote *exegi monumentum* (*Odes*, III.30) was fully aware of his exceptional talent. Pope's lines also discourage a literal approach:

> In Pow'r, Wit, Figure, Virtue, Fortune, plac'd
> Behind the foremost, and before the last.

Pope's 'Wit' is Horace's *ingenium*. In the context of English poetry the assertion cannot be taken seriously, unless we interpret 'the foremost' as including only Chaucer, Shakespeare, Milton, and perhaps Dryden. The claim to virtue is not excessive, and so we concede it without bringing in awkward questions from the letters. But what of 'Pow'r'? The word was designed, no doubt, to blur precision (Horace's *viribus* meant physical strength). But really there was no sense in which Pope's power was average. And any comment on 'Figure' would be unkind. What the whole section offers us, then, is partly the historical individual (Pope the penalized Catholic), partly a figure projected by the topos of present enjoyment (Pope the testator), and partly a literary persona (Pope as Horace *redivivus*).

Horace, (e) ll. 205–13. 'You say you aren't a miser; well, have you got rid of other vices too? If you can't live properly, make way for those who can.'

---

[13] *Epistles*, I.20.24 (*corporis exigui*).

Ambition, fear of death, superstitious fantasies: these were the great bogies attacked by Lucretius. Horace's closing lines about the banquet were also inspired by the *De Rerum Natura*. In Book III, lines 955–62, Nature addresses a querulous old man. 'Because you have always been discontented', she says, 'your life has slipped by, unfulfilled and unenjoyed. Now suddenly death is standing at your head; it is too late to eat and fill yourself with good things before you depart. Now you must resign all those pleasures which are out of keeping with your age. Come, give way cheerfully to those who are fit to enjoy them.[14] There is no choice.'

Pope, (e) ll. 304–27.   Pope is aware of the passage's Lucretian flavour, and so he expands on Horace by going directly to his source. Lucretius had linked avarice with 'the blind craving for office', 'avarities et honorum caeca cupido' (III.59). This could well have suggested 'the Avarice of Pow'r'. But we can be quite certain about 'the black fear of Death, that saddens all' (l. 309). This comes from *De Rerum Natura*, III.39, where the fear of Acheron is said to ruin men's lives: 'clouding all with the blackness of death', 'omnia suffundens mortis nigrore'. Unlike Horace, Pope apparently concedes the existence of Witches, Devils, and Hell Fire, and he does not invite his readers to treat them with ridicule. He also believed, of course, that life on earth, with all its ugliness and suffering, was merely a preparation for the hereafter; and so he could 'despise the known', as Horace could not. Yet the similarity of spirit is still remarkable. As apostles of good sense, both hoped that Reason could hold her throne; yet both had seen enough of life to know that her reign would always be precarious.

In his concluding lines Pope has rightly acknowledged the erotic element in *lusisti* by rendering it as 'play'd, and lov'd'. But after using Horace's metaphor of a banquet, he switches to life as a stage. The new idea (which may have been imposed by rhyme) is somewhat awkwardly managed, for Pope implies that the banquet has been taking place on the stage. The final couplet, too, is not as neat as the original.

At times, then, the imitation falls short of its model. Just occasionally the rendering is a little flat, and the thought obscure. Sometimes a Latin metaphor (for example, that of the Censor) cannot be fully transferred. The epistolary convention is not consistently observed, and the rhetorical fiction of an apology, which gave Horace his structure, is often ignored. All this was to be expected. No one could take on Horace in a game of this kind and hope to win *all* the points. Pope knew that very well. Nevertheless, the imitation is surely a magnificent performance, and it is worth trying to summarize the main procedures which it entailed.

First, Pope had not only to follow the situation and argument of the original but also to achieve a comparable range of tone. This could only be done by listening carefully to the text. But he did not feel confined to the text.

[14] Reading Lachmann's *dignis*.

He would use the Latin as a point of departure, drawing by free association on lines from the *Satires*, *Odes*, and *Ars Poetica*, moving backwards to Lucretius and forwards to Juvenal, incorporating ideas from Bentley's text or the Delphin's paraphrase. At the same time he had to build a new artefact, capable of standing on its own feet: an English, eighteenth-century, Christian poem, inhabited by real people. That this double task could be attempted was due to the strange combination of circumstances which produced the English Augustan age. For it to be done with style and conviction there was need of a poet so akin to Horace that he could use the Latin epistle as a means of realizing himself. That such a poet should actually have emerged seems little short of a miracle.

The Satirical Game at Cards in Pope and Wordsworth

HOWARD ERSKINE-HILL

Pembroke College, Cambridge

'Taken as a whole', remark the editors of *The Prelude, 1799, 1805 and 1850*, 'Wordsworth's card game is a playful imitation of Pope's mock-heroic game of ombre, *Rape of the Lock*, III, 37–100, but 221–22 echo "The Winter Evening" (1785) of William Cowper'. This is said of lines 213–33 of the two-part *Prelude* of 1799; of the 1805 and 1850 versions they say: 'In Wordsworth's extension here of the description of the card game in *1799* . . . the influence of Cowper is less apparent, and that of Pope is more obvious.'[1] Already a poetic topos is apparent, but both Pope and Wordsworth are writing in a longer tradition than their editors recognize. The regular content of this tradition is political: not only are the cards in games such as Ombre, Whist, and Lu given political form from the beginning (King, Queen, Knave, etc.), but the conventions of card-playing, certainly by the seventeenth century, had become a well-understood way of alluding to contemporary affairs of state. In his *I Ragguagli di Parnasso*, translated into English as *The New-Found Politicke* (London, 1626), Trajano Boccalini notes (p. 207) that Trump (Ombre) is a game with republican implications, for in Ombre the Trump can be given a greater power than any of the court (or 'coat') cards in the pack. Pope, who had a translation of Boccalini in his library, probably knew of this remark when he devised the Game of Ombre for the expanded version of *The Rape of the Lock* (1714).[2] The bond between card- games and political affairs would, of course, have been vividly fixed in the mind by the existence of packs of cards which represented particular historical events. One such was recorded by Edmund Goldsmid in 1886: *A Pack of Cavalier Playing Cards, Temp. Charles II. Forming a Complete Political Satire of the Commonwealth.*

---

[1] *The Prelude 1799, 1805, 1850*, edited by Jonathan Wordsworth, M. H. Abrams, and Stephen Gill (London, 1979), pp. 7, 58. De Selincourt too thought the echo of Pope quite clear.
[2] See Maynard Mack, 'Pope's Books: A Bibliographical Survey With a Finding List', in *English Literature in the Age of Disguise*, edited by Maximillian E. Novak (London, 1977), p. 239. The passage, which is prominently placed in the translation, describes how an arrested poetaster demonstrates the game of Trump to Apollo:

Apollo penetrating into the deep mysteries thereof, cried out, That the Game of Trump was the true Court-Philosophy; a science necessary for all men to learn, who would not live blockishly. . . . when the Learned found out the deep Mysteries, the hidden secrets, and the admirable Cunning of the excellent Game of *Trump*, they extolled his Majesties Judgement, even to the eighth Heaven, celebrating and Magnifying every where, That neither Philosophy, nor Poetry, nor Astrology, nor any other of the most esteemed Sciences, but only the miraculous Game of *Trump*, did teach (and more particularly, such as had business in Court) the most important Secret, *That every the least Trump did take all the best Coat-Cards.*

Poems using the conventions and terminology of card-games to allude to current affairs of state were to be found in seventeenth-century and early eighteenth century England. Here is part of a Civil War card-game of the seventeenth century:

> The Stake's three Crowns, four Nations Gamesters are;
> There's Three to One, and yet no Man that dare
> Take these great Odds? The Cause is as they say,
> The Fourth knows both our Stock, and Cards we play . . .
> My Masters, you that Undertake the Game,
> Look to't, your Country's Safety, and her Fame
> Are now at Stake; be careful how you cut,
> And deal as known occasions put you to't.
> The Cards are strangely shuffl'd, for your Parts,
> The Odds you never get the Ace of Hearts.[3]

This poem seems unsophisticated, and its political reference specific. Its wit is rudimentary, and lies in the simple application of the terms of gaming to a war just breaking, or seeming to be just breaking out. Another poem from the *Harleian Miscellany*, *The Royal Gamesters: Or, the Old Cards new shuffled for a Conquering Game*, alluding to the European wars of 1702–1706, brings us to the era of *The Rape of the Lock*. It is a game of Trump, the same or similar to Ombre, and is directed against 'the ambitious and treacherous Views and Attempts of *France* and *Spain*'. A preamble shows the nations in dialogue with one another:

Germany	Er'e we to play this Match prepare,
	Let's know first, who together are.
Holland	Let *England* deal the Cards about,
	The four Knaves play, the rest stand out.
Prussia	*France* is a Gamester, and must fall,
	Else Odds will beat the Devil and all.
France	What I have won, I'll venture still,
	I'll give you nothing but the Deal.
England	Play fair then, and it is agreed,
	The two black Knaves, against the red.
	The Kings shall hold another Set,
	And the four Queens shall sit and bet.
	The Knaves of *France* and *Spain* are black,
	'Tis *Germany* must hold the Pack.
Germ.	Give me the Cards, the Deal is mine;
	Diamonds are Trumps, who bets this Time?
Holland	I'll hold ten-thousand Livres by,
	'Gainst *France* and *Spain*, the Reason why;
	Because the Odds is Ten to One,
	They'll certainly be both undone.
Savoy	I'll take you up, with you I'll lay,
	That *France* and *Spain* will hold you Play.
Denmark	I'll nothing bet on either Side;
Portugal	Nor I, until I see them try'd.

---

[3] *The Harleian Miscellany* . . ., 8 vols (London, 1744–46), VII, 211. This is certainly a poem for 'Laws and Liberty' and against '*Rome*, and all her Train'.

Bavaria	I know on which Side I would bet,
	But will not tell my Mind as yet;
Sweden	Nor I, but still will Neuter stand,
	And do them Service under-hand.
Poland	One single Game with *Swedes* I'll try,
	I'll make the smooth-fac'd Youth comply.
Venice	Go on and prosper all, say I.

The poem is divided into five games, one for each of the years 1702–1706, the last and longest of which is designated *The Conquering Game*. The game is clearly made to fit a political narrative, and, as in reality no doubt, keeps looking as if it is about to come to a climax, but never does until the expectation, or *hope* of victory at the end. This game is, however, a good example of the card-game as political commentary.

> *England* deals next, and *France* is fain,
> To lend a losing Stake to *Spain*.
> *Savoy* bets all; *France* threatens hard,
> To take from him his leading Card;
> But *England* all the rest restore,
> And tell him, they will lend him more.
> Now on all Sides the Stakes are down,
> And *Spain* plays briskly for the Crown:
> And *Portugal* some Bets doth lay,
> Which *England* does, and *Holland* pay . . .
>
> *France* with his best Court-Cards begins,
> While *Spain* lose faster than he wins.
> The Set grows warm; brisk Play is shewn,
> And *Savoy* lays his last Stake down.
> But *Germany*, with Trumps supply'd,
> Soon turns the Game o'th' t'other Side.
> *France* with his Ace of Hearts doth join,
> But *England* plays the King and Queen.
> Old *Lewis* vex'd, yet looking grave,
> With Speed throws down another Knave,
> And questions not the Game to save . . .
>
> *France* offers now to part the Stakes,
> And *Spain* the self-same Proffer makes:
> But *England* will to neither stand,
> For all the Honour's in their Hands.
> *France* plays a Trump about to try,
> In whose Hand, all the rest did lie:
> Which he soon finds unto his Cost,
> When *Spain*, perceiving all was lost,
> Throws down his Cards, and gives the Set for gone,
> *Bavaria* takes it up, and plays it on.
> But *England* trumps about, and so the Game is won.
> *France* seizes on those Stakes he'd made from *Spain*,
> But *Germany* recovers all again.
> Thus ends the Game which *Europe* has in View.
> Which by the Stars may happen to be true.[4]

---

[4] *The Harleian Miscellany*, I, 173–76.

It is to be noted that in this poem the cards of the pack are generally subordinated to the players, who are named states, and even, as in the case of 'Old *Lewis*', named monarchs. '*England* plays the King and Queen' might possibly allude to Queen Anne and her Consort, George of Denmark (though he never shared the throne), but seems more likely to refer to the level of military activity at that juncture of the Wars of the Spanish Succession.

The Wars of the Spanish Succession prompted at least one other political Game of Ombre, though not in this case a poem. '*Le nouveau jeu de l'ombre*, 1707', belonging to Basil Kennett, is a series of MS notes for a longer work.[5] What survives corresponds, in part, to the preliminary dialogue in *The Royal Gamesters*, for here the actors in the war speak rather than play. Among the named players are rulers: *La Reyne Anne*, *Le Prince Duc de Marlborough*, and *Le Roy Stanislas*; and also nations: *L'Angleterre*, *L'Ecosse*, and *L'Espagne*. Each of these has something to say, and in one or two cases something interesting:

La Reyne Anne
    Jouons jusque a la premier [?] Volte.[6]

L'Angleterre
    . J'aime mieux fair gagner le codille que l'ombre.

Le Prince Duc de Marlborough
    Depuis que je joue, j'ay bien fait faire des Bestes.

Le Roy Stanislas
    Spadille ne m'abandonne pas.

L'Ecosse
    J'ay perdu, s'il ne m'entre un Roy.

L'Espagne
    Le jeu ne vaut rien, j'ay deux Roys de même couleur.

Some of these remarks may seem as dark to interpret as, in one or two cases, the hand is hard to decipher. The remarks of Scotland and Spain are, however, of particular interest. In Scotland's statement, 'Roy' is not just a reference to a level of military activity: its aptness lies obviously in its literal significance. Scotland could save herself only if she had her own candidate for the throne: the Pretender. The Act of Union was passed in the Scottish Parliament in January of this year. Spain's statement is also of great interest. The two warring candidates for the Spanish throne, the Bourbon Philip V and the Habsburg Charles III, were 'de même couleur'; presumably, of the same religion. In each of these instances there is a kind of wit in the way the potentiality of the playing-cards has been exploited to say something specific about the contemporary political world. As in pieces of successful word-play, which in a way these are, there is a small shock of recognition: a special aptness.

---

[5] B. L. Landsdowne 927, ff.82–84, 86–87. (I owe this reference to Dr Ian MacKillop.)
[6] A conjectural reading which I owe to Dr Jonathan Mallinson of Pembroke College.

Warburton stated that the card-game in *The Rape of the Lock* was imitated from Vida's *Sacchia Ludus*. Joseph Warton concurred, affirming that it was 'certainly imitated from the Sacchia of Vida, and certainly equal to it, if not superior'. He added that, 'as Chess is a play of a far higher order than Ombre, Pope had a more difficult task than Vida, to raise this his inferior subject, into equal dignity and gracefulness'.[7] There need be no doubt that in a general way Pope sought to emulate 'immortal *Vida*' whom he had praised in his *Essay on Criticism* (ll. 704–08). But the game of Ombre was more appropriate to the milieu of Belinda, and given Pope's choice of Ombre it seems worth looking at his game in relation to the Ombre satires so much closer to Pope's time and audience than Vida. One thing is clear. In choosing to add to his poem a mock-heroic game of Ombre, Pope must have known that he was, at least at first sight, likely to arouse expectation of political satire.

The question is what Pope meant to do with his readers' expectation. If they expected political satire it did not necessarily mean that he would offer it. It might be argued that he chose Ombre because such a card-game was a social ritual of Belinda's world, and that he handles it in such a way as to focus solely on the social and sexual awareness of Belinda, the Baron, and the other gentlemen and ladies present. One modern editor of Pope's poem has stated that the game is 'an allegory of the sex war':[8] whether it be an allegory or no, it certainly does dramatize the sexual awareness of Belinda and her antagonist; she wanting to overcome him with her beauty without becoming his prey, he designing to make her his own by a symbolic theft. Each seeks to make a conquest. If Pope intended this and this alone he will have taken care not to activate any of the political signals which lie latent in the card-game.

Of course the game is introduced as a kind of sexual war:

> *Belinda* now, whom Thirst of Fame invites,
> Burns to encounter two adventrous Knights,
> At *Ombre* singly to decide their Doom;
> And swells her Breast with Conquests yet to come.   (III.25)[9]

Similar terms are adopted when, after the game, Clarissa draws forth the fatal scissors:

> Just then, *Clarissa* drew with tempting Grace
> A two-edg'd Weapon from her shining Case;
> So Ladies in Romance assist their Knight,
> Present the Spear, and arm him for the Fight.   (III.127)

But these lines depict the situation of the game, rather than the game itself. The game too has moments which may have been meant to suggest a war of

[7] *An Essay on the Genius and Writings of Pope*, third edition, corrected, 2 vols (London, 1772), I, 238.
[8] *The Rape of the Lock*, edited by J. S. Cunningham (Oxford, 1966), p. 68.
[9] Quotations are from the Twickenham Edition of *The Poems of Alexander Pope*, edited by John Butt and others, 11 vols (London, 1939–69), II, *The Rape of the Lock*, edited by Geoffrey Tillotson (1940).

the sexes: the King of Spades 'Puts forth one manly Leg, to sight reveal'd', while the Queen of Spades is made a 'warlike *Amazon*'. Nothing so consistent as an allegory can be made of this, however, since the Amazon fights for the Baron and the King of Spades for Belinda.

On the other hand it does seem that Pope was at pains to emphasize political ideas in his card-game. Look again at the sequence dominated by one of Belinda's champions, the King of Spades:

> With his broad Sabre next, a Chief in Years,
> The hoary Majesty of *Spades* appears;
> Puts forth one manly Leg, to sight reveal'd;
> The rest his many-colour'd Robe conceal'd.
> The Rebel-*Knave*, who dares his Prince engage,
> Proves the just Victim of his Royal Rage.
> Ev'n mighty *Pam* that Kings and Queens o'erthrew,
> And mow'd down Armies in the Fights of *Lu*,
> Sad Chance of War! now, destitute of Aid,
> Falls undistinguish'd by the Victor *Spade*!   (III.55)

The notions of a rebel in defeat, and of a leader that (in a different game) overthrew kings and queens, are certainly political. The same might be said of Belinda's other king, 'The *Club*'s black Tyrant', where the emphasis is upon the political phenomenon of unwieldy power and (perhaps) of world-empire: '[He] of all Monarchs, only grasps the Globe' (l. 74). Similar responses are actuated by 'Th' embroidered *King* who shows but half his Face, | And his refulgent *Queen*' (l. 76), and by the '*King* unseen' (l. 95) whose sudden appearance on the field of battle is the occasion of Belinda's triumph over the Baron at the game of Ombre. Kings who conceal half their motives, and hidden kings who emerge from exile to take up arms, are again recognizable political phenomena. Pope, therefore, is not taking over a convention of political allusion for purposes of social and sexual motive alone, but is exploiting that potential for political allusiveness in the card-game of which his contemporary reader would be aware.

This conclusion is not really surprising when one considers the poem as a whole.[10] If it is conceded that *The Rape of the Lock* is mock-heroic or heroi-comical, then there must always be larger matters than the affairs of Belinda's world by which her affairs may be mock-heroically dignified. If these larger matters are epic matters, then the world of war and battle, armies and leaders, victory and defeat, is in the reader's mind throughout the poem. The card-game simply adds a seventeenth-century, Boccalinian aspect to the world of epic: Royal Gamesters as well as ancient heroes. Furthermore, it is worth remembering that it is the duty of the sylphs not

---

[10] I have discussed political affairs in *The Rape of the Lock* in my essay, 'Literature and the Jacobite Cause: Was There a Rhetoric of Jacobitism?', in *Ideology and Conspiracy: Aspects of Jacobitism, 1689–1759*, edited by Eveline Cruickshanks (Edinburgh, 1982), pp. 49–69. There, and in a shorter and earlier piece ('Literature and the Jacobite Cause', *Modern Language Studies*, 9, 3 (Fall, 1979), 15–28), I referred to material which the present essay gives me the opportunity to quote and discuss.

only to protect Belinda's honour, but to 'guard with Arms Divine the *British Throne*' (II.90). The central action of the poem, in the absence of any warrant from biographical evidence, takes place in a royal palace, Hampton Court, once much favoured by King William III, now where Queen Anne takes tea and counsel, and where

> *Britain*'s Statesmen oft the Fall foredoom
> Of Foreign Tyrants, and of Nymphs at home.   (III.5)

Indeed the central canto of the poem, in which the rape takes place, is not only set in a palace but begins and ends with allusions to affairs of state: lines 1–8 open the play, lives 171–78 close it with a good example of how the world of ancient epic blends with that of more modern sovereignty (triumphal arches linking ancient Rome with Renaissance Europe):

> What Time wou'd spare, from Steel receives its date,
> And Monuments, like Men, submit to Fate!
> Steel cou'd the Labour of the Gods destroy,
> And strike to Dust th'Imperial Tow'rs of *Troy*;
> Steel cou'd the Works of mortal Pride confound,
> And hew Triumphal Arches to the Ground.
> What Wonder then, fair Nymph! thy Hairs shou'd feel
> The conqu'ring Force of unresisted Steel?   (III.171)

If Pope's Game of Ombre is in part political, so (though to a lesser degree) is the whole poem.

Here, however, we must distinguish between different kinds of political allusion. The political allusions we have seen in Pope's game have so far appeared to be of a general kind: not (like those in *The Royal Gamesters* or 'Le nouveau jeu de l'ombre') to particular political events, but to general political phenomena: aged kings, defeated rebels, warlike queens, mighty generals, politic princes, and dangerous exiles. This much, probability permits us to recognize, and it may be thought that this fits in well with a poem the mock-heroic logic of which is to allude not to specific moments in particular ancient epics, but rather to what is typical in the world of the ancient epic. To press the argument for political allusion further may well be to over-interpret. Indeed, no more specific interpretation of the Game of Ombre is at all obvious.

Yet it is worth thinking about the interpretation of the two card-game poems quoted earlier in this essay. Their allusions appear to be of a quite specific kind, but it is not easy for the modern reader to, say, date the first poem (is it 1642, or 1689? what is the fourth nation?) or to specify the military and political events which constitute the four games of *The Royal Gamesters*. If we cannot interpret these poems, the chief point of which looks as if it were specific political allusion, is it safe to assume that Pope's game, so much more witty and exciting, contains no specific allusions awaiting recognition? Have wit and excitement, the amusing and dramatic shaping of the game, supplanted particular political reference? Perhaps so. But on this occasion I want to explore the alternative possibility.

In an earlier essay I have argued, from a considerable though probably not definitive body of contextual evidence, that the rape in Pope's poem alludes in part to the events of 1688; so vociferously trumpeted by Jacobites and Non-Jurors as the rape (or wrongful conquest) of their kingdom, so vehemently acclaimed by the more extreme Whigs as the deliverance from a rape of political liberties by a papist prince.[11] These political arguments and the sensational image of rape which so often conveyed them had been re-impressed upon the public mind before the publication of Pope's poem, by the Sacheverell Crisis and trial of 1710. I argued in that essay that one of the traditions to which *The Rape of the Lock* belongs is that of the Poems on Affairs of State, and that in the longer version of his poem Pope placed the card-game immediately before the rape of the lock in order to put political affairs into our minds. This last point can, I think, hardly be denied. What now follows, on the other hand, is proposed as an hypothesis of the most provisional kind only. My aim is merely to investigate possibilities. The hypothesis may be on the right lines but come up with the wrong answers. Or it may be an entirely misconceived approach to Pope's poem. It is offered as an incentive to further thought, and as an example of its hazards and rewards.

There are, in Pope's poem, I have argued, two particular indentifications hard to resist. 'Mighty *Pam* that Kings and Queens o'erthrew, | And mow'd down Armies in the Fights of *Lu*' (III.61) is a commander (probably Marlborough) strikingly victorious in the wars initiated by William III; read against the background of poems on affairs of state, '*Lu*' is a reference to William III's Dutch palace, as well as to a different card-game. Again and again, Anti-Williamite poems refer contemptuously or jealously to Loo, as in *The Mourners*, ascribed to Bevil Higgons in Pope's copy of *Poems Relating to State Affairs* (1705), which evokes '*Windsor*, gutted to aggrandise *Loo*' (l. 8).[12] Marlborough helped overthrow King James and Queen Mary by his defection to William of Orange in 1688, and subsequently, in a different game, that is, a different war, mowed down armies in the prolongation of William's wars under Anne.[13] The '*Queen* of *Hearts*' is likely to be an allusion to Queen Anne. 'Hail Queen of Hearts! to whose true English praise | The faithfull Commons vote new holy-days', began the poem 'On the 8th March 1703/4', another recent poem on state affairs.[14] The allusion is probably to Anne's words from the throne at her accession ('I know my own Heart to be entirely English'), and it is notable that 'King (or Queen) of Hearts' seems to

---

[11] *Ideology and Conspiracy*, pp. 49–54, 66.

[12] *Poems on Affairs of State: Augustan Satirical Verse 1660–1714*, edited by G. de F. Lord and others, 7 vols (New Haven, Connecticut, 1963–75), VI, 362. See, too, *Ideology and Conspiracy*, p. 66.

[13] In *A Key to the Lock* (1715), Pope makes Esdras Barnivelt say that 'mighty *Pam*' is Marlborough (*Prose Works of Alexander Pope*, edited by Norman Ault (Oxford, 1930), p. 193). This may be read as evidence against any such identification, but for the case that Pope designed *A Key to the Lock* as a blind or 'ward', designed to fend off embarrassing political interpretation after 1715, see *Ideology and Conspiracy*, pp. 54, 67.

[14] *Poems on Affairs of State*, VI, 614; *Ideology and Conspiracy*, p. 66.

have been a title bestowed on rulers who owed their position to popular choice rather than legal and/or divine right. From a Jacobite viewpoint Anne was a 'Queen of Hearts' in this sense: a loved but not legitimate sovereign.

These identifications, if accepted, suggest a scheme of interpretation. This scheme analyses Pope's game as a conflict between two specific sides in recent affairs of state. The King of Spades and the King of Clubs are of Belinda's party, are of the same colour (which may mean the same religion, as in 'Le nouveau jeu de l'ombre'), and express the Stuart, French, and Spanish interest in Europe. *'Spadillo'* suggests 'Old *Lewis*' (which he appears to be in Kennet's game). The King of Spades's victory over the 'Rebel-*Knave*, who dares his Prince engage' (III.59) suggests James II, and his victim (the Knave of Spades) the Duke of Monmouth: the best candidate in recent history for an unsuccessful rebel of the same family as the King he challenges. The King of Clubs, a tyrant whose unwieldy power 'grasps the Globe', suggests the King of Spain. On the other side, the King and Queen of Diamonds are the strong suit of the Baron: they act together and seem to suggest William and Mary in 1688, William not disclosing his full intentions in invading England, Mary lending attraction to their cause. They 'with Pow'rs combin'd, | Of broken Troops an easie Conquest find' (III.77). The rebel Knave of Spades is also of the Baron's party, but meets early defeat in the conflict, as Monmouth had done in 1685. In this game of love and war both Belinda and the Baron strive to win and hold the Hearts. The Queen of Hearts is actually won over by a court card from the Baron's suit.

> The *Knave* of *Diamonds* tries his wily Arts,
> And wins (oh shameful Chance!) the *Queen* of *Hearts*.
> At this, the Blood the Virgin's Cheek forsook.   (III.87)

If the Queen of Hearts indeed refers to Anne, this must allude to her early defection from James II in 1688. The Knave of Diamonds is the adviser who persuaded her to keep clear of her father's court and cause at the moment of crisis (there are one or two candidates, including Compton, Bishop of London). If Belinda loses the Queen of Hearts, however, she secretly holds to the King of Hearts, 'The *King* unseen'. In 1689 Dryden wrote his *Don Sebastian*, about the mysteriously lost King, Sebastian of Portugal: the hidden King. Contemporaries saw here signs of Dryden's Jacobite sympathy, and spoke of the play

> Which Abdicated Laureat brings
> In praise of Abdicated Kings.[15]

When Dryden wrote *Don Sebastian* it was clear only that James II had withdrawn, had become, in effect, the lost or hidden king. But soon that

---

[15] John Dryden, *Four Tragedies*, edited by L. Beaurline and Fredson Bowers, Curtain Playwrights (London, 1967), p. 281.

unfortunate monarch, supported by Louis XIV, reasserted himself in one of his native kingdoms, and seized Ireland. This, it may be thought, is the allusion of the final phase of Pope's game of Ombre, when Belinda, all too briefly and foolishly, sees herself triumphant. The King of Hearts is here James II, therefore the 'captive *Queen*' is the princess who was to become the '*Queen* of *Hearts*' and the '*Ace* of Hearts' is Ireland (in Pope's game it is played not by the Baron, but by the third player). This builds up with fine dramatic irony to the rape itself, after coffee 'which makes the Politician wise' (III.117), when the Baron will wrest all 'three Realms' away from Belinda's side: will ravish her lock from her.

At this point the considerable problems of such an analysis must be conceded. No tidy political allegory is revealed. It is not like Middleton's *A Game at Chess*. If religion is supposed to divide the conflicting parties, there is the problem, first, that in real life the originals of Belinda and the Baron were both papists, secondly that each of them holds some cards of both colours. Of course the political sides in the European wars were mixed in religious commitment, if predominantly Protestant versus Catholic, and the 'many-colour'd Robe' of the King of Spades may be a notable feature if this card is indeed linked with the convert, James II, who sought toleration for both dissenters and papists. A still graver objection is the reliance of the analysis on dual identification: James II is expressed by both the King of Spades and the King of Hearts; and if this is entertained it may be followed up by the argument that Anne is expressed not only by the Queen of Hearts but by the 'warlike *Amazon*' who fights on the Baron's side. What other queen of that era won such military success? But if this is another dual identification it disrupts the sequence, for Anne changed sides before, not after, she became a warrior queen.

What then are the possibilities? They are four. First, that Pope's game is not in the least political. That view is on the present showing scarcely tenable. Secondly, that the game makes general political allusion only. That view is in the main soundly based, and is perhaps the most cogent and prudent interpretation. But it does not account for the several moments where particular allusions are found, such as the 'Fights of *Lu*' and 'the *Queen* of *Hearts*'. Is Pope's game then an allusion to affairs of state with specific allusions included to beguile the over-curious reader into the hunt for a parallel? This third view is one which must seem quite consistent with Pope's general poetic practice, and has the merit of bringing all the evidence so far presented into a formula. But the unwelcome possibility remains that there is indeed a political parallel, that the scheme suggested above is not it, and that it will not yield itself up without more detailed examination of analogous literary works, and fuller recall of the diplomatic and military revolutions of the times as they would have revealed themselves in the year-to-year experience of a person of Pope's age and circle. For if the fourth view is correct, we are almost certainly in the realm of coterie interpretation.

The changes which Wordsworth introduced into his account of his boyhood card-games, between the 1799 and 1805 *Prelude*, show the level at which he responded to Pope's game. The latest editors compare Pope's 'Gain'd but one Trump and one *Plebeian* Card' with lines added by Wordsworth in 1805:

> Uncouth assemblage was it, where no few
> Had changed their functions — some, plebeian cards
> Which fate beyond the promise of their birth
> Had glorified, and called to represent
> The persons of departed potentates.   (1.548)

The echo of the plebeian card shows each poet exploiting the character of the card-game to make general political allusion. And this, at least, can be said of the main features of the 1799 description:

> And to the combat — lu or whist — led on
> A thick-ribbed army, not as in the world
> Discarded and ungratefully thrown by
> Even for the very service they had wrought,
> But husbanded through many a long campaign.
> Oh, with what echoes on the board they fell —
> Ironic diamonds, hearts of sable hue,
> Queens gleaming through their splendour's last decay,
> Knaves wrapt in one assimilating gloom,
> And kings indignant at the shame incurred
> By royal visages.   (1.216)

Here are the ordinary soldier 'discarded' and neglected after his service, queens still royal despite decay of state, knaves whose dark deeds are aptly enshrouded in grime, and kings resentful at the world's loss of reverence for them. As in Pope, a mock-heroic mode works in two directions: the 'high' language ('kings indignant' and 'splendour's last decay') does reflect humorously on the boys' grimy, dog-eared, and patched-up pack, but it also reminds us of a real world of affairs of state. This world, it is to be noted, is decisively different from that painted by Pope. The pack used by Pope's polite assembly was crisp and gleaming: all the detail of the court cards ('one manly Leg, to sight reveal'd', 'of all Monarchs only grasps the Globe', 'Th' embroider'd *King* who shows but half his Face') is visible for satiric exploitation, and while in this world kings and queens can be overthrown, the pomp and power of regality is unquestioned: it is the late Stuart era exactly.

How changed is Wordsworth's world! Pope's game was played in a palace, Wordsworth's in a cottage. Pope's game was played by adults, Wordsworth's by children. Pope's pack is pristine, hierarchically distinguished, Wordsworth's 'a congregation piteously akin' (1805, 1.555). Outside Hampton Court the sun is setting after a bright day; outside the cottage 'heavy rain was falling, or the frost | Raged bitterly', while further off the ice on the lake split and cried (1799, 1.226–33; 1805, 1.536–43). The political world has changed: kings are insulted, the splendour of queens is fading, and (a detail so pointed as to suggest a specific allusion) plebeian cards achieve glory and replace potentates. The boys' makeshift substitute for lost court cards teaches a lesson that the world will display. Between 1799 and 1805 (on 2 December 1804), the plebeian Buonaparte had shown this by having himself crowned Emperor.

Even when it is granted that this allusion refers chiefly to a process within revolutionary events (it must suggest Napoleon but might also recall Cromwell), this telling addition of 1805 brings some of the 1799 allusions into sharper focus. The first of these is attested to by Wordsworth's editors themselves. The card army,

> not as in the world
> Discarded and ungratefully thrown by
> Even for the very service they had wrought,
> But husbanded throughout many a long campaign,   (1799, 1.216)

was linked, in the poet's mind at least, with the discharged soldier of his own poem, written very early in 1798 and in due course to take its place in Book IV of the 1805 *Prelude*. Behind the 1799 lines, with their plain humour and open Cowperian morality, already stood that figure of desolation and simplicity who

> told in simple words a soldier's tale:
> That in the tropic islands he had served,
> Where he had landed scarcely ten days past —
> That on his landing he had been dismissed,
> And now was travelling to his native home.   (1805, IV.445)

If the 'plebeian cards' in Wordsworth's account have these specific allusions, so, it may be thought, have the court cards. 'Queens gleaming through their splendour's last decay' (1799, 1.232) is surely an ironic rejoinder to Burke's presentation of Queen Marie Antoinette in the celebrated passage of his *Reflections on the Revolution in France* (1790). Burke lamented the situation of the Queen, once 'glittering like the morning star, full of life, and splendour, and joy', now 'obliged to carry the sharp antidote against disgrace' concealed in her bosom, now with 'disasters fallen upon her'. Wordsworth's first response had been to describe the passage, with some sarcasm, as a 'philosophic lamentation over the extinction of chivalry' — that was in the unpublished 'Letter to the Bishop of Llandaff' (1793).[16] Now he gives the humble card-game of the lakeland children a truly pastoral role in prefiguring the downfall of regal splendour. The same is true of the final detail of Wordsworth's account: 'kings indignant at the shame incurred | By royal visages' (1799, 1.224).

In so far as *The Prelude* is taken as a biographical record, Wordsworth, in Paris just after the deposition of Louis XVI and the September Massacres had

---

[16] *The Works of the Right Honorable Edmund Burke*, new edition, 14 vols (London, 1815–22), V, 149; *The Prose Works of William Wordsworth*, edited by W. J. B. Owen and J. W. Smyser, 2 vols (Oxford, 1974), I, 35.

> passed
> The prison where the unhappy monarch lay,
> Associate with his children and his wife
> In bondage, and the palace lately stormed
> With roar of cannon and a numerous host.   (1805, x.42)

But of course the lines on the kings, like the lines on the soldiers, not only reach back into the poet's past but are proleptic within the reading experience of *The Prelude*. The discharged soldier and the imprisoned king, in turn, measure a distance from the boyhood game in an accession of experience and understanding which are far from wholly happy. In the intricate turning and returning of *The Prelude*'s narrative (compare 1850, IX.1–23), the card-game is one of the clearest examples of how childhood and boyhood experiences are the seeds which germinate in the later life of the poem, how ideals early implanted are tested out in a world dominated by high politics and the great revolutionary crises of the age. If Pope's card-game must refer back to the continental wars, the revolutions of the later seventeenth century, and the realm of ancient epic, Wordsworth's poem carries within itself, in its later books, the greater and more destructive world to which games at cards, simply and generally, or with deliberate detail, always allude.

Play, one may think, is often a kind of mockery and often a kind of learning. The rapt attention with which Pope recounts his game never admits that anything is absurd, Ombre or affairs of state. It is indeed hard to think of a more exciting and dramatically-shaped narrative of a game in literature, though the game of cricket in L. P. Hartley's *The Go-Between* must run it a close second. It is the very peak of Pope's mock-heroic humour not, as it were, to laugh out. The ridicule is held, a pure vitality of wit at the centre of the game, as the concept of play, of royal gamesters, circles outward wide and more wide to encompass card kings and all kings. Yet Belinda, involved as she is in the ridicule, has a real lesson to learn from the game of state affairs at cards, as from the Baron's play at rape. She must learn how 'Time conquers All' and life itself will come to despoil. Wordsworth's stance is more lofty than Pope's, for he only describes the playing in general, and does not enter into a particular game. Influenced in part by Cowper, his mockery and morality are more open, yet, despite his almost overblown mock-heroic style, there is a levelling wit in the very application of the children's grimy patched-up pack to the Bourbons and Buonapartes of the world. This is genuine satire, but satire well adapted to the different character of Wordsworth's poem, a poem on the growth of a mind. His stress is more strongly on the sub-conscious learning in play, and as we read these lines we are not, perhaps, far from the lines on the child in the 'Intimations' Ode:

> See, at his feet, some little plan or chart,
> Some fragment from his dream of human life.

Hogarth's
'Country Inn Yard at Election Time':
A Problem in Interpretation

RONALD PAULSON

Yale University

The print usually called *The Stage Coach or Country Inn Yard* (see cover) has never been seriously dealt with by Hogarth scholars.[1] A relatively slight piece, it has been overshadowed by the immensely popular *Simon Lord Lovat* that preceded it in 1746 and by the twelve plates of *Industry and Idleness* that followed later in the same summer of 1747. It has, however, its mysteries; its transparency is clouded in certain particulars. Moreover, it stands at a pivotal point in Hogarth's career, between the complex reading structures of his earlier 'Progresses' and the simple contrasts employed in his popular prints of 1747–51 and later formulated in the aesthetic theory of *The Analysis of Beauty* (1753).

The print was announced in both the *Daily Advertiser* and the *General Advertiser* on 26 June 1747: 'This Day is publish'd (Price 1s.)', a print 'representing A Country Inn Yard at Election Time'. This title, however, never appeared on the print itself, which was accompanied only by a publication line. In Hogarth's price-lists for his prints it was called simply *Country Inn-Yard*.

The advertised title may have introduced a topical dimension with which Hogarth did not wish permanently to encumber his print. We know that on 17 June, at the end of the current session, Parliament was prorogued and the next day dissolved. On 18 June the King's chief minister, Henry Pelham, unexpectedly announced a General Election to be held at the end of the month. In terms of the Septennial Act a new General Election was not called for until the summer of 1748. Pelham's reason was ostensibly that England's allies in the peace negotiations to end the War of the Austrian Succession might be unwilling or unable to negotiate with a lame-duck parliament. A less idealistic motive may have been the desire to forestall the Prince of Wales's Opposition party, which, having got under way that spring, was not yet a threat to the Pelham ministry but might well become one by the time of the mandatory election.

---

[1] See Paulson, *Hogarth's Graphic Works* (New Haven, Connecticut, 1965; second edition 1970), cat. no. 167, pl. 179.

By 26 June Hogarth had finished and published his shilling etching. At first glance, given the speed with which it was produced following the announcement of the General Election, and given our knowledge of Hogarth's eagerness to exploit topicality, it appears that he may have been working on a picture of the humours of a country inn and then inserted an allusion to the election. Besides the title (appearing only in the advertisements) the allusion consisted of a crowd of election campaigners at the far end of the inn yard and, in particular, the image of a baby they are carrying aloft and a sign (added after the first state of the print and removed in a later post-election state), 'No Old Baby'. There is also a paper protruding from the pocket of the man who grudgingly pays his inn-reckoning, which says 'An Act . . .' — probably for preventing election bribery, an act that was much discussed in the newspapers that spring.

If we may for the moment suspend the political dimension, it will be possible to discern the essential, perhaps the originary, elements of Hogarth's design. The most prominent feature is the central shape of a coach and its door, and the backside of a large woman who is being crammed into the coach. Another largish woman is visible inside. A fat man standing in profile beside the coach door is next in line, and the man settling his inn-reckoning is presumably the other prospective occupant of the coach: we can estimate how little space there is to hold them all. The coach itself fills the gateway of the inn yard, a space which though outdoors is completely enclosed, no trace of sky showing. Within the inn yard there are many more doorway-like apertures. A dog is in its kennel, only its head and shoulders protruding; a pair of lovers embrace inside a doorway, and another between two columns of the balcony at the right of the scene; a couple of inebriated revellers lean out of a window-space on the second floor of the inn, one smoking a pipe and the other blowing a horn; and a fat refreshment-seller stands enclosed within her booth, the counter protruding to accommodate her girth.

All of these details tell a story of space, juxtaposing rectangular openings and the people who fill them. If we tilt the emphasis in the direction of satire the message is the incompatibility of human bodies and man-made structures such as coaches, doorways, or windows, even dog kennels — or the threat of human containment within these containers. The scene may recall the first plate of *A Harlot's Progress* (1732), in which the inn yard had only one small area of sky, silhouetting a single woman, hanging out washing on a balcony, to indicate the sort of life the Harlot is turning her back on. In that series the closure was only complete when the Harlot's body lay in its coffin. This inn yard is far less threatening and claustrophobic, but everyone in it is nevertheless related to the central relationship of container to contained. Between *Harlot's Progress* and *Stage Coach* Hogarth produced *The Enraged Musician* (1741) with its fussy musician inside a window frame showing outrage at the burgeoning and uncontained disorder of plebeian music-makers outside in a city street. Totally within his window, he was withdrawing from the disorder; here the horn-blower, quite obviously uncontained by his window, extends the disorder.

The motif looks forward to William Blake's use of similar relationships in the darker satire of *Urizen* (1794). In these prints Hogarth's musician has become the Reason that forces rounded human (and animal) shapes into Procrustean squares, rectangles, and other geometric patterns. People are bent into the right-angles of man-made doorways and other enclosures. Hogarth's rectangles do *not* contain his exuberant humanity. His *Stage Coach* looks more directly towards Thomas Rowlandson's bulging coaches that are never able to hold the enormous people who are stuffed (or try to stuff themselves) into them: a situation for which nobody is to blame. In one sense, then, Hogarth's print opens up a new line of development of his art away from the satiric towards sheer comic incongruity. It shows the emergence of a comic mode in which the artist does not take sides, in which contrast and formal play matter more than the referential details and allusions to particular literary or graphic texts, particular events or people, that he had developed so thoroughly in the *Harlot's Progress* and *Rake's Progress*.

For example, the puns that illuminated the satiric meaning of every scene in the *Harlot's Progress* are now disinterested visual comedy. The central shape of the woman's backside is geometrized, or emphasized, or rhymed, by the coach's wheel to the right of her. The two figures to the right of the coach door can also be said to rhyme: the round stomach of the one is repeated in the circular hat held out for a tip by the other; the one's round shoulders become the other's humpback (or an inversion of the fat man's stomach), and these are echoed again in the wheels of the coach. In the same way the refreshment-seller and her stall seem in terms of shape made for each other. There is comic appropriateness or decorum between these round shapes, as there is a comic incongruity between them and the rectangular enclosing shapes of the coach doors, inn doors, windows, and gate through which the coach is departing for London.

We might compare the situation of the Frenchman seated atop the coach with the coachman in the signboard of the second *Election* print (1757), who loses his head by driving the English State Coach through the archway of William Kent's Admiralty Building. The coachman is being beheaded by the arrogance of an architect who designs according to formal rather than human requirements. Both the Urizenic architect and the establishment he represents are summed up in the too-low lintel. In *The Stage Coach*, on the other hand, the sober Frenchman's hat, which may also be in danger of being knocked off by the low lintel of the inn yard gate, is playfully tipped off by his laughing companion. The plainly English joy of the one is contrasted with the solemn French torpor of the other, as are their swords, one tilted upward to do mischief and the other sagging inert between the Frenchman's legs.

Another contrast is in terms of noise. The silent centre of the woman's backside being helped into the coach is flanked by noise that again recalls *The Enraged Musician*. The victualler is bawling out her wares and ringing a bell (parallel to her mouth), the horn-player is blowing, and the smoker is opening his mouth either to yell or to vomit. All of this noise at the left is balanced by the noise from the open mouths of the election mob at the right; while on top of the coach noise is potential in the Frenchman who, we know, is about to cry out.

These are the 'incompatible excesses' that meet in comedy as Hogarth describes it six years later in *The Analysis of Beauty*. Not only designs composed of only 'straight or only round' lines are comic, 'especially when the forms of those excesses are inelegant, that is, when they are composed of unvaried lines' (as opposed to serpentine Lines of Beauty), but in particular those formal contrasts that also join 'opposite ideas' as when we 'laugh at the owl and the ass, for under their aukward forms, they seem to be gravely musing and meditating, as if they had the sense of human beings'.[2] One of Hogarth's examples of such 'an improper person', visually reproduced in Plate 1, number 17, of the *Analysis of Beauty* is the 'No Old Baby' of *The Stage Coach*. This figure, he writes, 'represents a fat grown face of a man, with an infant's cap on, and the rest of the child's dress stuff'd, and so well placed under his chin, as to seem to belong to that face. This is a contrivance I have seen at Bartholomew-fair, and always occasion'd a roar of laughter' (p. 48). In other words, even without its political reference, 'No Old Baby' serves this essentially comic role. It fits in with the general comedy of incompatibles including the round woman who will not fit into the rectangular door of the small coach and the round victualler whose counter miraculously swells out to accommodate her belly. The incongruity of the child's shape and the old face epitomizes the whole scene, in which (according to *The Analysis*) 'the ideas of youth and age [are] jumbled together, in forms without beauty'.

Hogarth calls his inn the Old Angel. The sign of the Old Angel hangs directly above the head of an old crone, on the other side of whom is the 'Old Baby'; and directly above the baby, as in a genealogical table, a pair of lovers embrace on the balcony. On the other side of the scene another pair of embracing lovers are not far from another baby being held up for a thin spinsterish old woman to view. These figures project a Four Ages of Man that juxtaposes childhood with young lovers, middle age, and old age. The angel gesturing towards the inn-yard door may be pointing to the final exit for all of these people. At any rate, the crone offers the perspective of old age on life, lovers, infancy, and the milling crowd. She is lodged in the large basket kept on every coach for 'excess baggage'. Her smoking pipe has an iconographical reference. In Dutch still-life paintings pipes were symbols equivalent to skulls, and a smoking pipe was a sign of near mortality: 'For my

---

[2] *Analysis of Beauty*, edited by Joseph Burke (Oxford, 1955), pp. 48–49.

days are consumed like smoke' (Psalms 102. 4). In his *Tailpiece* (1764) Hogarth showed Time himself holding a broken pipe and his last breath emerging in a billow of smoke labelled 'Finis'.

Hogarth's coach stands within the yard of the Old Angel Inn, in fact preparing to leave it, thus reflecting two of the basic metaphors of eighteenth-century fiction: life as a journey and as an inn.[3] The inn projected a milieu through which a traveller passes, encountering strangers (not his family or established friends) and new configurations out of which he tries to make some order. The most obvious eighteenth-century novel informed by the principle of an inn was Fielding's *Joseph Andrews* (1742), which preceded Hogarth's print by four years but invoked earlier Hogarth prints in its preface; its ultimate model was *Don Quixote*, the novel *par excellence* where characters and actions converge in inns. As *Joseph Andrews* shows, the inn was a nexus for the gathering of rural society mingled with city visitors, and so involved a country-city theme with both rustic humours and reverberations of the popular contemporary topos of retirement. The inn was also a place where inhibitions could be left behind or stripped away, true or new identities revealed, as in the famous adventures of a night in which Parson Adams and other characters get into the wrong beds — as also in the implications of Hogarth's drunken revellers, passionate lovers, and newborn babies.

Both Fielding and Hogarth were concerned with the inn less as a prevalent metaphor than as a way-station on the journey of life which is a pilgrimage. An Angel Inn was on the New Road, Clerkenwell, and the Angel (taken from the Angel of the Annunciation, a derivation which may also help to explain the babies) was one of the most popular of inn signs, especially on the roads used by pilgrims.[4] Hogarth joins the ideas of inn and pilgrimage by showing the coach, with a symbolic cross-section of passengers preparing to leave, projected out of the inn yard into another, unindicated world. The sign of the inn, in short, suggests that in larger terms the formal comic play we have observed may embody an allegory of life. Youth and age, the fat body and the thin door, can be either juxtaposed or seen consecutively as stages in a progression leading to exits of various sorts.

It is also possible to see this print as a departure in the direction of Hogarth's nightmare allegory of 1762, *The Times, Plate 1*, which opened his final phase of political satire (ushered in by his modification of the Muse of Comedy in *Hogarth Painting the Comic Muse* to the Muse of Satire). We can hardly fail to notice, for example, that the inn sign is in fact spelled 'Old Angle In', a mis-spelling which produces a verbal pun: 'Old England'. A reader would have recalled lines like the ones spoken by Morocco in *The*

---

[3] Addison, *Spectator* no. 219 (10 November 1711), discusses these metaphors; see Paulson, *Popular and Polite Art in the Age of Hogarth and Fielding* (South Bend, Indiana, 1979), pp. 115–33.
[4] W. J. Pinks, *History of Clerkenwell* (London, 1881), p. 550; Bryan Lillywhite, *London Signs: A Reference Book of London Signs from Earliest Times to about the Mid-Nineteenth Century* (London, 1972), pp. 8–13 (and addenda, p. 670).

Merchant of Venice: 'They have in England | A coin that bears the figure of an angel stamped in gold' (II. 7. 55). The signboard turns the inn yard into a scene very like the street in *The Times*, which is Europe afire in the Seven Years' War. In the present situation, the War of the Austrian Succession is reduced to a comic squabble on a coach roof between an English sailor off the Centurian Man-of-War and a Frenchman (perhaps a sailor, perhaps only a valet) with the Englishman tipping off the Frenchman's hat. In terms of *The Times*, the scene offers a travesty of the war in a petty private skirmish; and in this context the watchdog, England's watchdog, is significantly asleep while everyone in sight is either drunk, amorous, cheating, rioting, or departing.

The presence of the electioneering itself raises particular issues that complement the formal play of container-contained. The crowd, as the ultimate human force that cannot be contained, already points towards the theme of uncontrolled mob violence in the *Election* prints of a decade later (1754–58), which relate the squabbles of domestic politics to the Seven Years' War. A new subject that begins to emerge here, and was not present in *The Enraged Musician*, is the plebeians who influence electors by their sheer mass, not themselves having a vote. A forty-shilling freehold was the qualification for admission to the franchise. In the first two scenes of *The Election* the electors are being terrorized by the voteless mob into voting for the more 'popular' candidate and bribed by the party canvassers into voting for the richer candidate. In the third plate the halt, lame, blind, and moribund electors are being conveyed to the poll to register their votes. Meanwhile, in the background, another allegorical vehicle, Britannia's coach of state, is collapsing. Then in *The Times* the street filled with the lower-class noise-makers of *The Enraged Musician* and the encroaching election crowd of *The Stage Coach* have become the inchoate forces that, led by demagogues, are now overrunning England (which in a still later allegorical stage, in the revision of *Rake 6*, becomes Bedlam).

These considerations may give us a context with which to return to *The Stage Coach or Country Inn Yard* — and to the 'No Old Baby'. For the 'No Old Baby' has always been the crux of puzzlement in the print, the stumbling block for interpretation. This baby carried by the parading election crowd, with its sign 'No Old Baby', was connected by Hogarth's early commentator John Nichols with an election anecdote. 'No Old Baby', he recalls, was

the cry used by the opponents of the honourable John Child Tylney (then Viscount Castlemain and now Earl Tylney) when he stood member for the county of Essex, against Sir Robert Abdy and Mr Bramston [in 1734] . . . a man was placed on a bulk with an infant in his arms, and exclaimed, as he whipt the child, 'What, you little Child, must you be a member?' The family name was changed from Child to Tylney by an act of parliament in 1735. In this disputed election, it appeared from the register-book of the parish where Lord Castlemain was born, that he was about 20 years of age.[5]

[5] *Biographical Anecdotes of William Hogarth* (1782 edition), p. 230.

The story has come down unchallenged in Hogarth commentaries; Sean Shesgreen, for example, merely asserts that 'the protest is an expression of opposition to the candidacy of John Child Tylney, only twenty years of age when he ran for election in Essex'.[6] Surely, however, this slight story of 1734 was not one Hogarth could rely on to amuse his audience fifteen years after the event in 1747.

I can now add a little more about the 'No Old Baby' sign. Child Tylney, besides being very young, was a Tory and an alleged supporter of the Stuart pretender. The label 'Old Baby' attached to him was derived from earlier elections and employed in later ones. *The Election, a Poem*, printed in 1701, during a London parliamentary election in the reign of William III, also included a candidate named Child, who was a supporter of the 'prince over the water'. As a 'Babe of Grace' he steps forward and speaks to the crowd:

> Tho' I'm a Child, my parts are come to age,
> And for my sense the monied men engage:
> Both kings and people have esteemed it fit,
> That those who have most money have most wit.
> Men they are pleas'd with great and manly toys,
> But baubles are the true delight of boys.
> I hate of Barons the renownèd Tales
> And recommend you to the Prince of Wales [the 'prince across the water']
> Who in the Senate I will move to come
> Into our Church from the curst See of Rome;
> Where he shall hector like the son of Priam,
> And be as wise a Protestant as I am.[7]

The basic reference here, for which Child Tylney may have stood, is to the 'Babe of Grace', also known as the 'Warming Pan Babe', who was claimed by James III to be the crucial son he needed as heir to his throne and perpetuator of Catholicism in England. By the Protestants the baby was scoffed at as an imposter brought into the bedchamber in a warming pan to substitute for the non-existent heir. If with much fanfare James II's wife thus produced James III, the so-called 'Old Pretender', the latter's wife in 1720, with even more fanfare and documentation, gave birth to Prince Charles Edward, the 'Young Pretender'. And so in 1747 the pretender to the throne at the moment was still the 'Old Baby' of the warming-pan episode, although there was also a 'young Baby' who actually conducted the invasion of 1745 in the name of his father. Fielding and the Whigs continued throughout these years to perpetuate the fiction that Charles Edward was in fact a bastard.[8]

[6] *Engravings of Hogarth* (New York, 1973), note to Plate 59.

[7] The situation at the time of the election of January 1701 was in some ways similar to the situation in 1747: it was the first General Election since William III began to rule alone; he was unpopular and at the same time wanted to secure a Protestant succession. Thus the attack on James II's twelve-year-old son, James Edward, the hope of the Jacobites. The election in December 1701 was even more tense: in September James II died and Louis XIV recognized his son as James III of England (a violation of the Treaty of Ryswick) and William III withdrew his ambassador from Paris. For the poem cited, see Joseph Grego, *A History of Parliamentary Elections and Electioneering from the Stuarts to Victoria* (London, 1892), p. 62; see also pp. 123 and 61–62; on the General Election of 1747, pp. 107–24.

[8] See Hugh Amory, 'Law and the Structure of Fielding's Novels' (Columbia University doctoral dissertation, 1964), p. 299.

Babies figure in some of the prints published in England during the 1747 campaign. For example, in *Great Britain's Union or the Litchfield Races Transposed* (September 1747) a child appears in a cradle under a coverlet of divided Scotland–England, immediately adjacent to a tent of Jacobites toasting the Pretender. The baby represents either the warming-pan baby or the Young Pretender. Another print, *The Cradle: or No Crazy Baby*, gives the baby what looks like the face of James III, the Old Pretender.[9] Moreover, one of the potential candidates on the Tory side for Middlesex in 1747 was a fifty-four-year-old named Samuel Child. It is possible that Hogarth inserted 'No Old Baby' as a mistake on the assumption that it was the same Child as the earlier one; but more likely he reapplied the old slogan which supported the Jacobite label. It is certain that Middlesex was one of the constituencies where the Jacobite slur operated with effect in this election.[10]

'Jacobite' at this time, as Fielding was to show a few months later with his ironic publication *The Jacobite's Journal*, was a term that was applied by the Pelham Ministry to the Opposition: to those who wanted to end the war with France, were thoroughly disillusioned with the Hanoverian royal family, and were distrustful of Pelhamite policies. But in a more particular way the term carried an allusion to the reports in May that the Prince of Wales's Opposition party (which he had made public at the beginning of the year, and which may have occasioned the call for a General Election) was basing its strategy on attracting Tories and Scottish MPs to its banner.[11] The emerging polarization pitted the Duke of Cumberland (the 'Butcher of Culloden') and the monarch against the Prince of Wales, the Scots injured by the repression following the Forty-five rebellion, and by implication the Jacobites themselves. Though a screen for other Scottish problems, the Jacobite issue was still present in the memory of the trials of the Scottish rebel lords in 1746, and was revived in March–April 1747 by the trial and execution of Simon Lord Lovat, the prototypical Scottish Jacobite.[12] Hogarth's print of Lovat (of 25 August 1746), first published at the time of his capture, was reissued and sold in quantities at the time of the trial a year later.[13] And, as Linda Colley has shown in her history of the Tory party, in

[9] *British Museum Catalogue of . . . Political and Personal Satires* (London, 1873–83), no. 2864. *The Cradle: or No Crazy Baby* is in the Lewis–Walpole Collection.
[10] See Nicholas Rogers, 'Resistance to Oligarchy: The City Opposition to Walpole and his Successors, 1725–47', in *London in the Age of Reform*, edited by John Stevenson (Oxford, 1977), pp. 21–23; and Romney Sedgewick, *The History of Parliament: The House of Commons 1715–1754*, 2 vols (London, 1971), I, 550.
[11] See Linda Colley, *In Defiance of Oligarchy: The Tory Party, 1714–60* (Cambridge, 1982), p. 254: 'On 4 June 1747, fourteen days before Parliament was dissolved, Frederick [Prince of Wales] sanctioned the Carlton House declaration. This document [which rapidly passed into the hands of prominent Whigs] promised the tories moderate constitutional reform: Place and Militia Bills, restrictions on the Civil List, and a £300 *per annum* landed qualification for J.P.s. It also urged them to "coalise and unite" with the Prince, and made clear their incentive: "His R.H. promises . . . totally to abolish for the future all Distinctions of Party . . . to take away all Proscription from any Set of men whatever, who are Friends to the Constitution."'
[12] See W. B. Coley, introduction to Henry Fielding, *The Jacobite's Journal and Related Writings* (Oxford, 1974), pp. xxv–xxvii. I use Coley's text for my quotations from Fielding's *A Dialogue between a Country Gentleman . . . and an Honest Alderman . . .*
[13] Joseph Spence wrote to his friend Burrell Massingberd on 23 March 1746/7 that 'all the world here has been taken up with my Ld Lovat's Tryal. There is a print of him, from a drawing of Hogarth, which is not unlike him' (quoted in Austin Wright, *Joseph Spence: A Critical Biography* (Chicago, 1950), p. 221).

the metropolitan contests of Middlesex, Westminster, and London the Tory defeats 'owed something to their opponents' exploitation of those Jacobite trials which had been held in the capital' (p. 253).

The chief anti-Ministerial journal (also strongly anti-Fielding) was called *Old England; or, the Broadbottom Journal, by Argus Centoculi, Inspector General of Great Britain*. In the context of the General Election, the 'Old England' of Hogarth's inn is not just ancient England but the sign of the Country Party, and the central figure in his design, climbing into the stage coach, may recall the sub-title 'Broadbottom Journal' with its allusion to the broad-based Coalition government advocated by the Country Party.

Perhaps the most local context of all for Hogarth's print is Fielding's pamphlet, *A Dialogue between a Gentleman of London, Agent for two Court Candidates, and an Honest Alderman of the Country Party*, which was announced in the *General Advertiser* of 23 June, three days before Hogarth's print was advertised in the same periodical. We may sense an anticipation of the Hogarth–Fielding collaboration of February 1751 when they co-ordinated the publication of Hogarth's engravings, *The Stages of Cruelty* and *Beer Street* and *Gin Lane*, with Fielding's pamphlet, *An Enquiry into the Late Increase of Robbers*.

In the *Dialogue* Fielding's spokesman is the Gentleman, 'Agent for two Court Candidates', and his adversarius, the Alderman, is a spokesman for the 'Country Party', the Prince of Wales's Opposition to the King's Ministry: we notice that, as his advertisement states, Hogarth's print is laid in a 'Country Inn Yard at Election Time' (the inn sign tells us that the coach comes 'From Lundun', the 'country' spelling for London). Concerning 'Old England', we read in Fielding's *Dialogue* that the Alderman says he wishes to 'consult the Good of Old England only' (p. 8), by which he means the journal that expresses his and the Jacobites' point of view. The emphasis is on *Old* England, the England of the Stuarts and the Old Pretender as opposed to contemporary England.

And so, interpreted in the context of contemporary election polemics and Fielding's *Dialogue*, the scene may be 'Old England' specifically in the journal's sense and not (or only secondarily) in any larger allegorical sense. This 'Old England' is where we find the lovemaking and boozing that Fielding associates with the Jacobites (even more forcibly stated in his *Jacobites' Journal*). Fielding's Gentleman in the *Dialogue* notes that 'it is well known how gloriously and openly they draw their Corks [versus their swords] in the Pretender's Favour' (p. 7). The tipsy men at the inn window and the 'broadbottomed' woman whose flask is handed up after her are those Jacobites whose 'arguments and their Weapons are indeed one and the same; Songs and Toasts, Curses and Huzzas' (p. 23). Or they represent the more general 'Reign of Drunkenness, Idleness, and other Enormities attending Elections', which the present shortness of time between announcement and election (according to the Pelhamites, p. 56) was intended to prevent.

The three election issues stressed by Fielding in his *Dialogue* were Jacobitism, the continuing war, and the supposed 'corruption' of the incumbent ministry. Hogarth picks up only one aspect of the war theme, summed up in the Gentleman's remark: 'At Sea we have a most powerful and victorious Fleet, under two Admirals [Anson and Warren], who have retrieved the Glory of the Navy of England, and to whom we owe the greatest Advantages gain'd in this War', which 'must naturally incline the French and Spaniards to think of Peace' (p. 45).[14]

The reference to 'The Centurion' on the duffle bag of the British sailor atop the coach indicates a patriotic position, or (more particularly, given the pro-war and anti-war issues of the General Election) a pro-Ministry position. The Opposition was against continental entanglements and in favour of getting out of the war that had dragged on since the early 1740s. The sign of English seapower, the Centurion was the ship of George (later Lord) Anson which had distinguished itself first in May 1742 by capturing the great Spanish Acapulco galleon. More recently, it had become known for its anti-French exploits, passing in June 1744 through the whole French fleet in a fog-shrouded Channel and returning safely to England. In May of the year in question, 1747, under the command of Captain Dennis, the Centurion's main-topmast had been shot away in battle with the French fleet off Cape Finisterre, but it had nevertheless returned to participate in the victorious battle. At the time Hogarth made his print it was again in the news for a case before the Privy Council that was decided in May in favour of its crew against the crew of the 'Gloucester' and the 'Trial'.[15]

It also seems that Sir Peter Warren, a Vice-Admiral and Commander of the Fleet in June 1747, was one of the court candidates who stood for Westminster. In his campaigning he was (in Joseph Grego's words) 'as usual . . . supported by a mob of Jack Tars, or of ruffians dressed in sailors' clothes for the occasion'.[16] So the sailor tilting the Frenchman's hat could also allude to Warren and the court party discomfiting the supposedly-Jacobite, therefore French, 'Independent Electors', the Country party, of Westminster (who indeed lost the election).

The final fact to note about the Centurion's sailor, however, is that he is lodged *atop* Old England's coach, his duffle bag tied to his arm so that it will not fly away in the wind. The 'broadbottom' woman and the other bulky passengers can afford to ride comfortably inside the coach (meanwhile the French valet riding on top may mean that his French, or at least Jacobite,

[14] The anti-Jacobite strain appears in the contrast Fielding makes between 'a King respected all over Europe, whom, if his whole People personally knew, they would all personally love' (that is, a reference to the German-speaking, reclusive, unpopular George II) and 'a tyrannical Papist to be introduced here by the Cabals of Rome, and by the Arms of France, and who hath dared to affect absolute Power even in his Declaration [proclaiming his legitimacy]' (p. 57). The Opposition candidate is one who 'would destroy the Government, to introduce the Pretender' (p. 60).
[15] See the *London Magazine*, 16 (19 May 1747), 243; and *Hogarth's Graphic Works*, cat. no. 167.
[16] Grego, p. 110.

master rides within). If this coach with its 'respectable' folk inside and its poor-but-heroic sailor outside (and indeed its pathetic little postilion to one side) recalls the famous coach that mistreats Joseph Andrews on the road in Fielding's novel, it must also be taken, in the context of the comic play of container-contained, as a symbol of all elections that ask the question 'Who's out and who's in?'

The third issue raised in Fielding's *Dialogue* was corruption, alluded to by the 'Act' in the traveller's pocket. The 'Act' finds echoes in various parliamentary bills all associated with the corruption attached by the Country Alderman to the Pelham ministry, and defended by the Court Gentleman. It could be the Place-Bill or the Bill for annual or triennial parliaments, but more likely it is 'An act for the more effectual preventing bribery and corruption in the election of members to serve in Parliament', which required an oath of every voter if demanded by a candidate or by two electors. 'The bare mention of it is enough to fill any honest Man with Horror' writes Fielding (pp. 22–23). All of these, from Fielding's point of view, are ridiculous and impractical expedients urged by the Opposition, who are proposing to combine Jacobitism with republicanism in their 'Broadbottom' ministry. Corruption is the issue the Alderman makes most of, and which Fielding's Gentleman spends most time defending. He sums up with the words: 'As to the Corruption practised at Elections, it is so known and certain, that I should think no Man deserved the lest Credit who denied it; but as to the Corruption of the Elected, I can lay my Hand on my Heart and Declare, I believe it to be infinitely less than it hath been represented' (p. 28). Hogarth in his print makes the point clear: the bribery is at election time; but he leaves ambiguous the question of whether the man with the paper in his pocket is an elector, an election agent, or merely someone who is ignoring the election, turning the Act against Bribery into an objection to an excessive inn-reckoning. On such a point the general and particular references of Hogarth's print hinge. 'An Act' catches the moment of corruption far from London and the Pelham ministry in a country inn yard; but after the election 'An Act' remains a metaphor for the failure of controls over human actions, a verbal analogue to the window and door frames.

So far we have interpreted 'Old England' in the context of contemporary election polemics and Fielding's *Dialogue*. But what of the election parade at the distant end of the inn yard? Our interpretation depends on how we read the 'No Old Baby' sign: Is the election crowd that carries it pro-Ministerial or Tory–Jacobite? If the 'No' is to be believed, the crowd, rejecting the 'Old Baby', is anti-Jacobite.

We must not forget, however, that in *The March to Finchley* (1750) Hogarth labelled a Jacobite by having her hold a copy of *The Jacobite's Journal* despite the fact that both he and his audience would have known that this was Fielding's parody of a Jacobite's periodical and in fact an attack on

Jacobitism.[17] The point is an important one, for if the sign is read as an emblem indicating Jacobites (and indeed if we presume that Hogarth later burnished it out because he found that it obscured his meaning) then we see the Jacobite cause as dominant in this 'country' inn yard. The process then is a triumphal 'chairing' of the winner of the election pole: the election pole that all of the people in the foreground are now preparing to leave behind, presumably having cast their votes. The whole scene is one of darkening chaos in which the forces of disruption are being left by deserting citizens and sleeping dogs to follow their natural course.

But one historical fact is that in distant counties like Lancashire and Yorkshire that had been affected by the Jacobite rebellion of 1745 (in Linda Colley's words), 'some tory candidates received the attentions of anti-Jacobite mobs' (p. 253). These people, unlike Londoners, had felt the bite of the Jacobite troops and knew what 'country' really meant. This fact leaves us with the more plausible interpretation that Hogarth is showing not an allegorical 'Country Party' but an actual 'country' inn yard with a 'country' crowd that is repudiating the position of the so-called 'Country Party', perhaps including the Old England, Broadbottoms, and tipplers in the foreground.

If this is the case, then the election crowd (and the election itself) is shown to be as peripheral as the figure of the falling Icarus in Brueghel's painting, and the Old Angel (Old England) with her outstretched arms is all that attempts to draw together the election and the unconcerned people who are in the process of departing the 'country' for London. Then the lovers on the balcony above the crowd show, by their juxtaposition with the double sense of 'Baby', how life goes on despite elections, despite Old Pretenders. Then, though anticipating the crowd of the *Election* and *The Times, Plate 1*, the election crowd here is manifestly not dangerous or central to the concerns of the prosperous 'respectable' folk (the citizens with the franchise) entering the coach either to avoid voting or to return unfazed by their country experience to vote 'country' in one of the London contests.

Then in terms of the General Election, Hogarth's comedy of containment, or of 'Who's out and who's in?', becomes merely a satire of concealment and withdrawal. Nor is it partial concealment (of the hiding lovers in the doorway, the two revellers *un*concealed by their window, the dog too long for his kennel, or the woman trying to get into the coach) but rather withdrawal of people into private concerns at the time of a public crisis: private concerns that happen to be equated with the 'Country Party's' concerns as outlined in Fielding's *Dialogue*. Apathy or distraction amounts to the same theme here, summed up in the fat woman at the centre, the man for whom 'An Act' refers only to an inn-reckoning, and the dog off to the side like a mute chorus.

We are aware of the woman's back as the central fact of the picture. Whether we think of her as 'Broadbottom' or as backside, she embodies

---

[17] See Paulson, review of Coley's *Jacobite's Journal, MLR*, 71 (1976), 890–91.

self-absorption and unawareness of what is going on around her as she prepares to disappear inside the coach. The composition focuses on her back, and creates another verbal pun: she is literally 'turning her back' on the urgency of the election issues here in the country where it is most deeply felt because most deeply remembered. And the dog then becomes verbalized as the proverb about 'letting sleeping dogs lie', which is the sentiment of the Englishmen who are ignoring the General Election, or the threats posed to England by Jacobitism (indeed the secreting of Frenchmen without and Jacobites within the coach), and the message of the parading of 'No Old Baby' they are leaving behind them.

There is finally no way of avoiding the fact that the composition renders the Election marginal, 'in the background' so to speak, suggesting that the English are too preoccupied with their own petty day-to-day doings to take an interest in politics at a moment of actual crisis. The sleeping dog, however we may proverbialize him, is a motto for these people who are unconcerned with the Election or, by implication, with their Old England.

From the beginning of this essay I have suggested that in interesting ways Hogarth's *Stage Coach or Country Inn Yard* illustrates the interaction of general and particular satire, of the universal and the local, even of the polarities comedy and satire. The crucial words that are summed up by the images ('country', 'Old England', 'Broadbottom' or 'back', and 'sleeping dog') are all interpretable in both a general and a particular way. I hope I have shown that they are not mutually exclusive. The superimposition of the title and the marginality of the crowd, and especially the hesitant presence/absence of 'No Old Baby', not only underline a theme of overly-detached Englishmen at a time of crisis; they also offer the spectator a more general interpretation that ignores the General Election altogether, once it is history and once the print goes into Hogarth's folio as simply 'Country Inn Yard'.

Satire and the Images of Self in the Romantic Period: The Long Tradition of Hazlitt's *Liber Amoris*

MARILYN BUTLER

St Hugh's College, Oxford

Satire is a mode with which we do not as a rule associate the Romantic period. Among the trees of the literary forest a few scrubs can still be picked out: minor satirical verse like Mathias's *Pursuits of Literature*, Gifford's *Baviad* and *Maeviad*, the contributions of Canning and Frere to *The Anti-Jacobin*, and the Smith brothers' *Rejected Addresses*. These sold well at the time but have not worn well since, for future generations have become convinced that the Spirit of the Age was very different. Symptomatically, the two substantial writers whose bent was unequivocally satirical, Byron and Peacock, are generally represented in the twentieth century as, one way or another, marginal (though some unease is often expressed, very reasonably, at the demotion of Byron that this entails). As satirists, Byron and Peacock attract similar criticisms. They are irresponsible jesters, without clear satirical aims in view, even to themselves, and anachronisms, lacking a proper understanding of the age they were born into.

But an age's self-image may not be as distinct as posterity's view of it. The so-called Romantics did not know at the time that they were supposed to do without satire. Obvious if sometimes superficial changes in fashion had come about with the passing of time and with the marked growth of the educated reading public. Pope's closed couplet had been under attack since the late eighteenth century, and in the early nineteenth century sophisticated writers could no longer appeal with confidence to a social norm and a moral consensus. But it is easy to exaggerate the break with the recent literary past, or with that portion of it we now designate Augustanism. Swift remained a much-admired writer. Byron's well-known tribute to Pope may have been controversial; Scott's even better-advertised tribute to Dryden was less so. Though the writers of the period are often linked with Shakespeare, partly because it is the era of the brilliant Shakespeare criticism of Coleridge and Hazlitt, in their poetry they are more inclined to draw on Milton, who was probably the most admired classic English writer precisely on account of his intellectuality and his public role. If Peacock is to be dismissed as an eccentric, it may not count for much that in a list of favourite great writers he named Rabelais, Burton, Swift, Fielding, and Sterne. It *is* significant, and typical (but not stereotypical), that Lamb and Hazlitt both defended Restoration comedy against those who wanted comedy without 'disagreeables'.

Admittedly it became fashionable to announce, as Shelley and Keats did in very similar terms, 'didactic poetry is my abhorrence'. Satire is not merely didactic, but has to be specifically and pellucidly so, or it cannot be effective. Shelley's poetry remains essentially didactic, and even Keats's seems far more so than he allows; all that these two poets can really be claiming is that their means are generally allusive, fanciful, pictorial, and narrative rather than directly argumentative. Yet even if it is relatively rare for either Shelley or Keats to write formal satires, their sense of the scope and social function of poetry remains in large part traditional. The old questions asked by Jonson in 'To Penshurst', by Dryden in *Absalom and Achitophel*, and by Pope in *The Dunciad* — how to judge a good way of life or a good man or a good poet — are also asked by Byron in *Childe Harold* III and IV, by Shelley in *Prometheus Unbound* and *The Triumph of Life*, and by Keats in *The Fall of Hyperion*.

Nineteenth-century readers gradually came to expect good creative writing to be self-referential, and did not cavil if writers took themselves and their problems very seriously. Readers also became less inclined to want, and less inclined to notice, satire, intellectual analysis, debate, and controversy. But in what we now call the Romantic period, writing directly about the self was still problematical. On the one hand, the reader seems to demand, and the writer to strive for, a new fullness of self-expression: the qualities prized include sincerity, emotional intensity, and particularity in rendering place, especially the haunts of childhood. On the other hand, as this paper will demonstrate, any work which appears to have self-expression or self-validation as its goal is liable to set up an ethical backlash, a complaint that the individual is not autonomous, that society has claims, and that artists are as much bound by moral law as anyone else. This hostile response is not confined to the reviews, where it would be predictable, since many were written for sections of the public suspicious of the arts and of the increasingly self-important claims of artists. The critique of Romantic autobiography, which is also a critique of a growing aestheticism, seems interesting precisely because it occurs within the major poetry and prose of the first three decades of the century. It is the proposition of this paper that some well-known Romantic self-portraits are satirical portraits, and even the rest frequently a source of satire in others.

For modern critics, Wordsworth's *Prelude* has a central position in English Romanticism. Its innovation is to adapt epic, a genre concerned with society, to the topic of a single private life: an epic about the growth of a poet's mind is, properly, a contradiction in terms. Where Milton's *Paradise Lost* was ornamented with similes which spanned the story of mankind in time and space, in fact and fiction, Wordsworth derives his illusion of depth from 'spots of time' which throw out their unexpected lines of sight into the poet's own private experience. Classic antecedents for *The Prelude* are identifiable, not only by Milton but by autobiographers like St Augustine and Rousseau. Citing them normally operates to stress that Wordsworth's treatment is revolutionary not only in his 'naturalness' but in his self-absorption, raised to the level of a new metaphysical system.

As it happened, Wordsworth's contemporaries outside the circle of his friends did not know *The Prelude*, but they did know 'Tintern Abbey' (1798), that intense exploration of private memory and of the poet's relationship with his sister, and *The Excursion* (1814), in which the poet seems to present himself in the guise of two personae, the Wanderer and the Solitary. The preface and first book of *The Excursion* (1814), firmly declaring its subject to be the inner life, functioned for younger contemporaries as *The Prelude* does for us. The verse preface speaks of 'ill sights' among 'the tribes | And fellowships of men . . . the fierce confederate storm | Of sorrow, barricadoed evermore | Within the walls of cities' (ll. 73, 78), and in these circumstances it declares that it is better to muse in solitude:

> Of the individual Mind that keeps her own
> Inviolate retirement, subject there
> To conscience only, and the law supreme
> Of that Intelligence which governs all —
> I sing — 'fit audience let me find though few'.   (l. 19)

The quotation from Milton, with his public and universal subject, must have struck alert readers as paradoxical. It was on this kind of evidence that Keats, following Hazlitt's lead, thought of Wordsworth as the Egotistical Sublime.

And yet, other poems by Wordsworth, also well known at the time, themselves ridiculed the notion of the self-satisfied and self-absorbed poet. An unmistakably detached and even satirical attitude to the poet's persona emerges in 'Anecdote for Fathers' and 'We Are Seven', both of which appeared in *Lyrical Ballads* in 1798, and above all in 'Resolution and Independence', first published in 1807, which humblingly contrasts the conceited, absorbed literary man with the leech-gatherer, representative of humanity at one with nature. The curious fact is, then, that Wordsworth himself was a pioneer critic of that notion of the solipsistic poet with which readers of his own day and ours have identified him. And not uninstructed readers alone: Wordsworth's supposedly uncritical image of himself became an important negative inspiration to Shelley and Keats.

Shelley's poem *Alastor* (1816), written the year after *The Excursion* appeared, features a Narrator who tells the story of another idealistic young poet. The latter figure, whom we can distinguish from the Narrator by calling him the Visionary, tries to live by the light of Nature and by an altruism fostered narcissistically within his own mind and imagination; he cuts himself off from sympathy with his own species, and dies. Victorian readers were evidently quick to take the Visionary for Shelley himself, and Mary Shelley in her editorial note on the poem in 1839 contributes to that identification by writing of the bleak autobiographical circumstances in which the poem emerged. But the immediate model for the visionary Poet in *Alastor* is, surely, the Wanderer as a young man, described approvingly by Wordsworth in *The Excursion*, Book 1. The Wanderer's life has been devoted to virtue and to religious idealism, and has apparently been entirely solitary, which means, among other things, celibate:

> There he kept
> In solitude and solitary thought
> His mind in a just equipoise of love.
> Serene it was, unclouded by the cares
> Of ordinary life; unvexed, unwarped
> By partial bondage.   (l. 353)

In short, Wordsworth seems to redefine 'love' so that it needs no second party, just as he redefines religion so that it needs neither a church nor an independent deity:

> sometimes his religion seemed to me
> Self-taught, as of a dreamer in the woods;
> Who to the model of his own pure heart
> Shaped his belief.   (l. 409)

Shelley's poem guys such a creed when the Visionary fails to notice an Arab maiden who offers him 'sweet human love'. The only sexual experience he proves capable of is a perverse and onanistic one, with a fantasy-woman projected in his dreams; and this figure is, significantly, equated with his own thoughts and his words when making poetry:

> Her voice was like the voice of his own soul
> Heard in the calm of thought . . .
> Knowledge and truth and virtue were her theme,
> And lofty hopes of divine liberty,
> Thoughts the most dear to him, and poesy,
> Himself a poet.   (ll. 153, 158)

In the Narrator's introduction to the Visionary's story, and in his summing up afterwards, there are specific quotations from Wordsworth, especially from the 'Intimations' Ode: 'natural piety' (*Alastor*, l. 3), 'obstinate questionings' (l. 26), and 'too deep for tears' (l. 713). It has thus become almost standard to identify the Narrator with Wordsworth; what should follow, and generally does not, is the equally Wordsworthian derivation of the other principal figure, the Visionary. By evoking the lifestyle of the Wanderer, but interpreting his solitariness as narcissistic and doom-laden, Shelley turns the idealization into a critique. The attack is brought home to Wordsworth personally, since Shelley reads the Wanderer as Wordsworth's complacent representation of his decision as a young man to forsake progressivism for a visionary, private, self-nurtured religion. On the contrary, Shelley believes that withdrawal led to Wordsworth's death as a poet, a point he reiterates in the sonnet, 'To Wordsworth', which appeared in the *Alastor* volume:

> In honoured poverty thy voice did weave
> Songs consecrate to truth and liberty —
> Deserting these, thou leavest me to grieve,
> Thus having been, that thou shouldst cease to be.

In his 'Preface' to *Alastor*, Shelley hints hard that he means us to associate *both* poet-characters with the single figure of Wordsworth. The 'Preface' ends with Shelley quoting ironically those lines from *The Excursion*, Book I, in which the Wanderer really does speak of human love, his own for his 'daughter' Margaret: 'the good die first | And they whose hearts are dry as summer dust | Burn to the socket' (l. 500).[1] The 'Preface', like the poem, has apparently been about two types of men: the failed imaginative youths, and the delinquents who keep aloof from sympathies with their kind. Wordsworth has been both, which is why his portrait in *Alastor* is a complex one.

Shelley's poem mars its own critical case by conveying a confusing element of sympathy with doomed idealists (even Wordsworth), so that it is perhaps not surprising that it has generally been taken for a classic instance of that poetic indulgence it sets out to satirize. The same fate has met another immature exercise in the same kind, Keats's *Endymion*. The models for Endymion's behaviour are, presumably, both the youthful Wanderer and the Visionary in *Alastor*. The clues that Keats is thinking of Shelley's Visionary are that he gives his own hero some of the same adventures, including sexual encounters with two girls, one belonging to the human world (Keats has an Indian maiden where Shelley had an Arab), the other a dream-figure, who in the Keats poem is the moon-goddess Cynthia. True, Keats does not set out with quite the same overtly critical and intellectual intentions as Shelley. He identifies more naïvely and heartily with his hero, who is allowed to choose the right option at each juncture. Endymion goes ahead and makes love to his Indian girl, as it happens a wise move which earns him his moon goddess after all. This does not alter the fact that Keats in *Endymion* makes the same general point as Shelley in *Alastor*: solitary idealists do no good to themselves or to anyone else, and love as an ideal, though universally professed by literary altruists, can be put into practice only in relationships with others.

What is surprising about Keats's poem is not that it accuses Wordsworth of narcissism and asexuality — these were the commonplaces of the day in critics hostile to Wordsworth — but that it goes out of its way to implicate Shelley too. Keats cannot, it is clear, read the Poet in *Alastor* as a critical

---

[1] Shelley's version of line 501 in the 'Preface' to *Alastor* reads: 'And those whose hearts are dry as summer's dust'.

portrait. He must think he is setting Shelley straight when he has Endymion make love to the Indian; though the failure of Shelley's hero to make love to his Arab looks now like a distanced ironic way of making the very same point. Here is evidence of a pattern that is to be repeated many times, more frequently with reference to Byron's Childe Harold of Canto III than even to the Wanderer. Writers put forward an unromantic anti-type to correct what they see as a too-romantic prototype, each time overlooking an element suspicious of egotism in the first writer. This cannot be thought of as an example of unconscious Bloomian 'misreading' by the second author, since it occurs in conscious and virtually satirical locations. The cumulative effect of the practice is to lead us to underestimate the element of scepticism actually present in Romantic portraiture of poets.

Given the pattern, one begins to wonder where, if anywhere, a 'pure' Romantic autobiography is to be had. Byron wrote a number, if he is to be identified with the heroes of a number of his early and middle poems (the Giaour, the Corsair, Lara, Manfred), though for late twentieth-century readers the debunking tone of Byron's journals and letters also makes him an arch-critic of romanticizing. Otherwise, Wordsworth's Wanderer is surely too dramatized and fictionalized a figure to stand in for his creator. Coleridge gives a fillip to the writer's status with his demon-poet in 'Kubla Khan', and he supplies copious if abstruse further documentation in *The Lay Sermons* and the *Biographia Literaria*; but the very difficulty and eclecticism of that material is off-putting, and anyone attempting to track Coleridge as an autobiographer (let alone approach him as a biographer) has been inclined to lose heart.

According to some readings, another contender for a 'straight' Romantic autobiography might be Hazlitt's eccentric 'novel', the *Liber Amoris* of 1823, which, as the agonized record of a man in the grip of a sexual obsession, has been commonly regarded as an uncomfortably artless example of the Romantic compulsion towards self-expression. But is the hero of the *Liber Amoris* Hazlitt? Is he an emanation of Hazlitt's persona as a writer, being subjected to criticism and mockery? Is he a yet more detached figure, a composite of other characters in life and in books? The divergent possibilities make it a classic instance of the period's sceptical and divided approach to the self.

Hazlitt in February 1822 was forty-four, and in the grip of a mid-life crisis. His first marriage, to Sarah Stoddart in 1808, had broken down by mutual agreement, and Hazlitt now set off to Scotland to obtain a divorce. At Stamford on the way north he began writing first recollections and then a series of letters, some direct to the daughter of his London landlord, Sarah Walker, most to his friend P. G. Patmore, a few to another friend, J. S. Knowles. Hazlitt was attempting to memorialize, perhaps to exorcize, perhaps even yet to consummate, his passion for the nineteen-year-old Sarah. He agonized to Patmore over the details of her past behaviour to him, the conversations they had had, the wording of her brief inarticulate replies. Was she a goddess? was she a slut? was she just a coarse, dull teenager? To conform with Scottish divorce law, Hazlitt had to put in three months' residence in Scotland, and he spent the spring, from February to May 1822, at an inn at Renton, Berwickshire, thirty miles from Edinburgh, composing his increasingly steamy series of letters and, in the act of writing, further intensifying his emotions.

The correspondence as Hazlitt actually penned it has long been known. Indeed one letter from Hazlitt to Patmore was published by a journal hostile to Hazlitt, the Tory *John Bull*, in July 1823, only two months after the publication of an edited 'formal' version of the same letter in the *Liber Amoris*. But the real-life series appeared in its entirety only in 1978, in the Sikes, Bonner, and Lahey edition of the *Letters of William Hazlitt*. The publishers of that edition, faced with the unenviable task of advertising the coldest and most impassive of Romantic letter-writers, understandably dwell on the merits of the torrid letters of 1822:

In an age of self-revealing, 'confessional' autobiography, such as that of Rousseau and De Quincey, there is no comparable example of such savagely honest, of such appealing yet unsparingly ruthless self-exposure as appears in Hazlitt's letters which recount the intense struggle of the Romantic temperament with its own violently shifting moods. These letters . . . alone constitute a primary document for the study of the Romantic imagination.[2]

To dwell upon the honesty of the self-exposure is, however, a dubious move. Hazlitt had made a journalistic living variously in the second decade of the century, often with political articles for such liberal papers as the Hunt brothers'. *Examiner* and *Yellow Dwarf*, but his métier was probably theatre criticism, and the line in his writing between theatre and life had long since become indistinct. The 'unsparingly honest' letters to Patmore are written in a highly conscious literary manner, full of dramatic cross-references which Hazlitt sometimes cut before publication. Excised phrases of this sort include 'is it not to write whore, hardened, impudent, heartless whore after her name?'; 'musing over my only subject (Othello's occupation, alas! is gone)'; 'thinking her human and that "below was not all the fiend's"' (pp. 263, 269). From the start he depicts a series of scenes in which he plays, by turns, the parts of Young Werther, Hamlet, Othello, Iago, and Lovelace. The last two roles are significant: Hazlitt's self-image includes the notion of the ingenious contriver who is himself like a stage-manager, or like the author's surrogate within his fiction. It is, then, the most self-conscious, the most continuously literary of love affairs, though some of the sense of

[2] *The Letters of William Hazlitt*, edited by Herschel Moreland Sikes, assisted by Willard Hallard Bonner and Gerald Lahey (New York 1978; London 1979); publisher's advertisement on dustjacket. References to Hazlitt's letters are to this edition. Though floridly written, this description is not otherwise untypical. Compare the extended, 'romantic' accounts in Catherine M. Maclean, *Born Under Saturn: A Biography of Hazlitt* (London, 1943), pp. 415–99; Cyril Connolly, 'Hazlitt's *Liber Amoris*', *London Magazine*, November 1954; Ralph M. Wardle, *Hazlitt* (Lincoln, Nebraska, 1971), pp. 300–65.

contrivance arises because Sarah has scarcely any words of her own, and seems to be waiting, like an actress, for her part to be written. Hazlitt, stage-managing as well as writing and performing, takes all the initiatives and dictates the course of the scenes. He tries Sarah physically by pulling her on to his knee and fondling her; he tests her morally by trusting her with his most prized possession, a little bronze statue of Napoleon. In late May, when he had served his Scottish time but not completed the divorce proceedings, he paid a flying visit to his London lodgings, where he found Sarah chillier than he had hoped for. In his rage he smashed the statue, and thus by a fine symbolic act pronounced the end of the affair.

As if the letters did not reveal an incurable self-dramatizer, they were clearly begun with at least half an eye to publication; by mid-March 1822 Hazlitt was certainly thinking not of a private record but of a book.[3] Henceforth, as he went on wooing Sarah by letter, he did so in the declared knowledge (declared to Patmore but not to Sarah) that he was making copy. The painful feelings were no doubt genuine; the fact that they were stage-managed does not imply that they were under control. Hazlitt at the time was under that compulsion pioneered by the Ancient Mariner, of telling all his friends about his sorrows and, when his friends were not at home, of telling their servants instead.[4] He extended the practice from London to Edinburgh, where he took the professional risk of laying bare his soul to the rather proper and very eminent Francis Jeffrey, editor of the *Edinburgh Review* and one of the leading journalistic patrons of the day.

From its inception as letters to its appearance as a novel, the book is always an inextricable blend of the lover's compulsive self-dramatization and the writer's professional calculation. *The Liber Amoris or the New Pygmalion* was published anonymously early in May 1823. Each of its three sections is based fairly closely on an original document or group of documents, two of which survive. Part I, seven fragments of dialogue between H— and S—, derives from a manuscript notebook (now in the Lockwood Memorial Library of the State University of New York at Buffalo); this must be the notebook Hazlitt told Patmore he had begun at Stamford in February 1822. Part II is based on the letters Hazlitt sent Patmore from Renton, with various cuts, rearrangements, and rewriting: the originals survive in various libraries. Part III is made up of the more polished retrospective letters Hazlitt apparently wrote later in the summer to his new friend, the Scottish dramatist J. S. Knowles, telling of the closing stages of the affair. But two further passages of 'real' material, not used in the novel for, presumably, decency's sake, show Hazlitt at his most Lovelacean, his most knowingly

---

[3] *Letters*, p. 246. A postscript to the letter reads: 'I have begun a book of our conversations (I mean mine and the statue's), which I call *Liber Amoris*'. The text of this letter becomes Letter 1 of Part II of the published *Liber Amoris*.

[4] The amusing account of Hazlitt's communicativeness by B. W. Proctor (the writer Barry Cornwall) is quoted in Richard Le Gallienne's privately printed edition of the *Liber Amoris* (London, 1894), p. xiv. References are to this edition.

literary. One is in a letter of 18 June, in which he describes an overheard kitchen conversation between his 'goddess', her mother, and her brother in such bawdy terms that to his fevered imagination the lodging-house has now taken on the appearance of a brothel. The other is an extraordinary sequence entered in a separate notebook between 4 and 16 March 1823, and thus potentially a fourth episode for the book. The entries record the last and most flamboyantly literary of Hazlitt's contrivances, his procuring of a friend, F—, to test Sarah's virtue by attempting to seduce her. The notebook, which is given as an appendix in the Lahey edition of the *Letters*, consists of Hazlitt's summary of F—'s dealings with Sarah, including a last episode in which they scampered together up the lodging-house stairs, 'he all the way tickling her legs behind' (p. 388). This last document demonstrates not merely that the 'private' material can be more gripping than what was printed in the edition of 1823; it also shows that, if a clear line ever existed in Hazlitt's mind between living his story and making a book of it, this had now broken down. Why was F— procured? To tell Hazlitt something about Sarah that, nine months after their parting, he still emotionally had to know? It was, surely, to discover something about her that readers of the drama needed to know; though in the end Sarah, least manipulable of heroines, proved as incommunicable to F— as she had been to H—.

Ever since the appearance of the *Liber Amoris* in 1823, no clear distinctions between the character H— and the author Hazlitt, the 'novel' and the 'real' manuscripts, have ever proved possible to maintain. When the Tory *John Bull* maliciously printed the unexpurgated letter, it claimed that it did so in the public interest, part of the 'truth' having been improperly withheld. Reviewers and columnists immediately identified Hazlitt, no difficult matter when half London was in his confidence, and their descriptions of the *Liber Amoris* show that they thought they were dealing with the truth and nothing but the truth, even if it was not quite the whole truth. Later in the century the *Dictionary of National Biography* treated the book without demur as an autobiography. Hazlitt, *DNB* supposes, must have been half mad when he wrote it, but 'sane enough to get £100 for rivalling Rousseau's *Confessions*'.

But in fact the crucial question, 'What kind of an autobiography is it?', cannot be settled either by way of the textual evidence (since no text is more private or honest than another) or by biographical speculation. The anecdotes of contemporary literary men tend to support *DNB*'s hypothesis that Hazlitt was deranged, and this is a view which fits well enough a reading of the *Liber Amoris* as 'the intense struggle of the Romantic temperament with its own violently shifting moods'. But writers themselves and their families and friends often give very poor evidence about why a book was written, because its significant context need not be the private firsthand experience they have witnessed so much as the books of other writers, the taste of the public, and the state of the market. Viewed with these considerations in mind, the *Liber Amoris* becomes less unaccountable and considerably less insane.

In early 1822 Hazlitt was in difficulties not only with both his Sarahs, but with his journalistic employers and a number of his creditors; he was to be arrested for debt on 12 February 1823. The political polemic which had been one staple of his writing for the past seven years had become unfashionable, in the quieter and less controversial times that came with the end of the post-war economic crisis and the temporary slackening of reform agitation. Editors wanted something lighter, more personal, and perhaps profitably titillating — such as both Lamb and De Quincey had in their different styles been achieving during 1821 in John Scott's new *London Magazine*, with the first *Essays of Elia* and the serialized *Confessions of an English Opium Eater*. Of these two new journalistic successes, De Quincey's brilliant impressionistic autobiography must have irked Hazlitt more. While Lamb was a friend of Hazlitt's, De Quincey was an ally and political adherent of the Tory Lake poets. A clear hint that Hazlitt was enviously aware of De Quincey as a journalistic rival came later in 1823, when Hazlitt sent a letter to the *London Magazine* claiming that a recent article by De Quincey against Malthus had used an argument in which Hazlitt had anticipated him.[5]

Above all, the *Confessions* made a target because the book could be read as a classic instance of one of those self-flattering idealizing Portraits of the Artist which stimulated emulation and annoyance in the period. De Quincey adapts the exalted conception of the artist and of his imagination that he has found in the work of Wordsworth and Coleridge, cleverly naturalizing the rather grand concepts by telling a story set in the London streets. Instead of glimpsing a tantalizing Muse, as the younger Romantics and their poetic contemporaries had become over-fond of doing, he found and then lost again the haunting young prostitute, Ann, in Oxford Street. The Oriental visions of Beckford, Southey, and Coleridge in 'Kubla Khan' become the no less fantastic and lavishly written, but more psychologically explicable, consequences for De Quincey's dream-life of his ten-year addiction to laudanum. But De Quincey has not lost sight of the theoretical potential of the dream-vision, which in the idealist view of art beginning to emanate from Germany, and being popularized by Coleridge, can stand symbolically for another world created and peopled by the artist's imagination. The *Confessions* works as an *apologia pro vita sua*, because it isolates the artist again from the common world in which he is placed, elevating him to a special magical category on account of his gift of imagination.

De Quincey himself, in the opening passage of his *Confessions*, complains of *his* most obvious model, the *Confessions* of Rousseau, because it is too self-indulgent. That charge was often levelled against Rousseau's sexually-permissive narrative, from an England in the grip of a moralistic religious revival. But when De Quincey is the accuser the effect conveyed, more

---

[5] *London Magazine*, November 1823. De Quincey writes on the subject in October and (replying to Hazlitt) December 1823. See *Letters*, pp. 329–32.

strongly than ever, is of the pot calling the kettle black. De Quincey's own *Confessions*, with their exculpatory approach to addiction, their narcissistic descriptions of dreams, their unrelenting egotism, advertise their author at least as provocatively as Rousseau's book does. So flamboyantly is this the case, indeed, that it comes as no surprise to discern in Hazlitt's Romantic autobiography of the following year what is in effect a counter-example to De Quincey's.

Countering De Quincey meant feeling for the point at which his approach was specially vulnerable. The generalized ground for complaint against Wordsworth, the leading writer of the Lake school, was, as we have seen, his solipsism; a typical counter-move proposed human love, or rather the consummation of the sexual act with one girl, who is explicitly not a mere figment of the fictional poet's fantasy-life and so functions as a challenge to his egotism. Though De Quincey has the London street-girl in his auto-biography, and though he insists that his attitude to her is affectionate and benevolent, he has actually drawn a strangely muted and one-sided relation-ship. It is not, of course, sexual: that, perhaps, makes a rhetorical point against Rousseau, whose early sexual exploits become the burden of the narrative in his *Confessions*. But if De Quincey describes a mere friendship, bestowing material and physical comfort, the sceptical reader cannot help noticing that it is the waif Ann who gives and the adolescent De Quincey who takes. The key relationship in De Quincey's book thus maintains the asexuality and unsociability which had become a matter of complaint in the work of Wordsworth, De Quincey's main literary mentor. Hazlitt ripostes by taking as the subject of his 'memoirs' a common London girl with whom he longs to have sexual intercourse, but whose very nature is hidden by his over-intellectualizing.

Where De Quincey admits to an autobiography (and even, by choosing the title *Confessions*, evokes the most notoriously self-indulgent of auto-biographies), Hazlitt claims, however notionally, to be writing a novel. The formal manœuvre cannot have been adopted in order to hide the author's identity, or he would have changed initials and place-names and other details that made identification certain. Fictionalizing the story is a device for objectifying it, above all for setting up a distance and some measure of control between the author and H—, now formally a character and not Hazlitt himself. Hazlitt was sufficiently conscious of the technical distinction to make a point of it to the painter B. R. Haydon, who passed on to Mary Russell Mitford that the conversations with Sarah and the letters to Patmore were to be published as 'a tale of character'.[6] It is a critical not an apologetic portrait that Hazlitt thinks he is after, and other intellectual novels within

---

[6] *Diary of Benjamin Robert Haydon*, edited by Willard B. Pope, 5 vols (Cambridge, Massachusetts, 1960–63), II, 382, cited by Robert Ready, 'The Logic of Passion: Hazlitt's *Liber Amoris*', *Studies in Romanticism*, 14 (1975), 41–57. This article is one of the few discussions to take seriously the claims of the *Liber Amoris* as a work of art: Ready sees it as a carefully fashioned, if eccentric, novel.

his milieu supply a precedent for this. William Godwin's *Fleetwood* (1805) and *Mandeville* (1817) each make a critical study of an introverted intellectual, through two heroes so neurotically self-absorbed that they are incapable of successfully loving a woman. Godwin's novels fell under the usual curse of books on this topic, of being misread as examples of precisely that complacent misanthropy they were intended to dispel. *Mandeville* becomes one of the satiric targets of Peacock's *Nightmare Abbey*, which borrows its gloomy setting and its misanthropic hero, and lampoons Godwin's novel ('Devilman') as though it is itself uncritical. But *Fleetwood, or the New Man of Feeling* comes nearer to supplying Hazlitt with a useful model, one which its full title, with its revisionist implications, already points to: there is a significant tradition of intellectual novel-writing, as we shall see, which uses the debunking sub-title, 'or the . . .', followed by a pretentious term for an artist. Fleetwood is a Wordsworthian man who has lived solitarily among the Welsh mountains; in middle age, too late, he tries to find happiness in marriage and is instead consumed by egotism and jealousy. The precedents are thus available for a novel which is apparently autobiographical but in spirit critical, itself introverted in pursuit of a critique of introversion. The precedents are also available to have it misread, but of this Hazlitt may have been unaware.

There is documentary corroboration that in the very month in which Hazlitt began to compile the *Liber Amoris*, he was sketching an outline Portrait of the Artist, one which incorporated the very criticisms which De Quincey's book might have been expected to provoke. The sketch in question appears in yet another letter of an essentially open, public type, Hazlitt's Chesterfieldian 'Letter to his Son' which was meant from the beginning for inclusion in *Table Talk*.[7] In advising his son what kind of man to be, Hazlitt bitterly advocates that he should not become a writer, since writers do not prosper in that sphere (the sexual) with which Hazlitt equates, apparently both ironically and seriously, success and happiness in life. The passage was so nakedly autobiographical that much of it was cut when the 'Letter' was first published in 1825, and only appeared in full when Hazlitt's son himself edited his father's *Posthumous Remains* in 1836. Hazlitt has just plainly referred to his ill success with Sarah Walker: 'There is no forcing liking . . . Women care nothing about poets, or philosophers, or politicians. They go by a man's looks and manner.' But in some profound sense, he goes on to argue, authors bring this rejection on themselves:

Authors feel nothing spontaneously. . . . Instead of yielding to the first natural and lively impulses of things, in which they would find sympathy, they screw themselves up to some farfetched view of the subject in order to be unintelligible. Realities are not good enough for them . . . They are intellectual dram-drinkers; and without their necessary stimulus, are torpid, dead, insensible to every thing. . . . Their minds

---

[7] 'I had a letter from my little boy the other day, and I have been writing him a long essay in my book on his conduct in life' (Hazlitt to Sarah Walker (9 March 1822), *Letters*, pp. 243–44).

are a sort of Herculaneum, full of old petrified images; — are set in stereotype, and little fitted to the ordinary occasions of life.

What chance, then, can they have with women?. . . . Do not, in thinking to study yourself into the good graces of the fair, study yourself out of them, millions of miles. Do not place thought as a barrier between you and love; do not abstract yourself into the regions of truth, far from the smile of earthly beauty. . . . Should you let your blood stagnate in some deep metaphysical question, or refine too much in your ideas of the sex, forgetting yourself in a dream of exalted perfection, you will want an eye to cheer you, a hand to guide you, a bosom to lean on, and will stagger into your grave, old before your time, unloved and unlovely . . .

A spider, my dear, the meanest creature that lives or crawls, had its mate or fellow; but a scholar has not mate or fellow. For myself, I had courted thought, I had felt pain; and Love turned away his face from me. I have gazed along the silent air for that smile which had lured me to my doom . . . And as my frail bark sails down the stream of time, the God of Love stands on the shore, and as I stretch out my hands to him in vain, claps his wings, and mocks me as I pass![8]

The significance of this extraordinary passage is that it both reflects Hazlitt's obsession with Sarah Walker and objectifies it, so that it becomes the basis for a satirical view of the modern artist as an impotent and marginal figure. There is a possible allusion to De Quincey in the phrase, 'they are intellectual dram-drinkers'. There is a much clearer anticipation of the entire plot and theme of the *Liber Amoris*, with an emphasis that points up the full implications of the subtitle of that work: *the New Pygmalion*. Aesthete, narcissist, Pygmalion fell in love with the statue he had made, an icon of his own creation. Inserting the word 'new' has the effect of updating the portrait, and of debunking it further. Really, Hazlitt seems to sigh, no matter how up-to-the-minute the cult of the artist, there is nothing new under the sun.[9]

The power and fascination of the *Liber Amoris*, most underrated of Romantic autobiographies, derives precisely from the interplay between what is personal to Hazlitt, genuinely obsessive, and what has a generalized reference to the lives of all artists. H— has two icons, which correspond to Hazlitt's in real life: Sarah herself, sometimes goddess and sometimes whore; and the little bronze statue, or bust, of Napoleon. The presence of these two successive passions in Hazlitt's life is a matter of record, and was already publicly on record by 1823. Hazlitt had even told the public that he saw a continuity between his old veneration for Napoleon, itself an extension of his youthful revolutionary idealism, and the passionate love he now felt for

---

[8] *Letters*, pp. 223–25. Though the 'Letter' was included in *Table Talk* (1825), the entire passage quoted here was omitted.

[9] One precedent for Hazlitt's full title, Godwin's *Fleetwood, or the New Man of Feeling*, has already been noted. But Godwin's daughter, Mary Shelley, also wrote an admonitory fable about the intellectual life: *Frankenstein, or the Modern Prometheus* (1818). The themes of Hazlitt's and Mary Shelley's books have much in common. Frankenstein, too, is a creative figure, purportedly a scientist but allegorically, surely, an artist, who sets out with exaggerated notions of the benefits that he, like the fire-bearer Prometheus, is bringing to mankind. What he actually succeeds in bringing is a murderous Monster, an intensely lonely creature who is the mirror-image of Frankenstein's own egotism. For *Frankenstein*'s link with *Alastor* and with the critique of Wordsworth's *Excursion*, see my *Peacock Displayed* (London, 1979), p. 72.

Sarah Walker. In an essay entitled 'On Great and Little Things', written in January 1821 and printed in the *New Monthly Magazine* (n.s. 4, 1822), he first alludes unmistakably to his unhappy love affair ('to see beauty is not to be beautiful, to pine in love is not to be loved again') and then, in an upsurge of hope, imagines both love and the political hopes of earlier days restored to him: 'The sun of Austerlitz has not set. It still shines here — in my heart; and he, the son of glory, is not dead, nor ever shall, to me'. (Hazlitt admittedly appended the footnote to the paragraph: 'I beg the reader to consider this passage merely as a specimen of the mock-heroic style, and as having nothing to do with any real facts or feelings'.) Within the *Liber Amoris*, Sarah too makes the statue stand for her unrequited sexual desires, since Bonaparte's face reminds her of a man with whom she has been in love. In the stage-direction with which Hazlitt completes the final dialogue of Part I, 'The Reconciliation', H— and Sarah appear precariously at one in their contemplation of the statue:

I got up and gave her the image, and told her it was her's by every right that was sacred . . . I pressed it eagerly, and she took it. She immediately came and sat down, and put her arm round my neck, and kissed me, and I said, 'Is it not plain we are the best friends in the world, since we are always so glad to make it up?' And then I added, 'How odd it was that the God of my idolatry should turn out to be like her Idol, and that it was no wonder that the same face which awed the world should conquer the sweetest creature in it!' How I loved her at that moment! (p. 82)

So long as the bust survives, it can be used, even if ominously, to symbolize their different sexual fantasies. When H— smashes it on his last visit to Southampton Buildings in May 1822, the crash involves not just the icon he has made of Sarah, and thus the current love affair, but the old, thwarted, superseded passions of both, and thus, by implication, the human comedy implicit in the making and breaking of icons.

But if here the *Liber Amoris* generalizes, elsewhere it particularizes. No autobiographical document of the period, and certainly not the novels with which the *Liber Amoris* was compared by an admiring reviewer, Rousseau's *Julie* and Goethe's *Werther*, in fact delved so minutely into the psychopathology of frustrated sexual love.[10] Sarah's behaviour is almost as intriguing to the reader as it was to Hazlitt, for she copes erratically with his long campaign of sexual harassment, sometimes by avoiding her persecutor, most often by a discouraging reserve, but sometimes with passive acquiescence. Hazlitt grows almost delirious with joy when he fancies himself encouraged, as he does when Sarah's young sister says that Sarah prizes his books; he is then plunged into deeper torment as it becomes plain in the course of the next week that Sarah is keeping out of sight (p. 155). He fully recognizes the

---

[10] *Examiner*, No. 798 (11 May 1823): quoted in *Liber Amoris*, p. xxiii. It is interesting that even this sympathetic reviewer remarked on the resemblance neither to Godwin's novels (for which see text) nor to Benjamin Constant's *Adolphe, and the Red Notebook* (1816), which anticipates the *Liber Amoris* in that it purports to be the edited manuscript of a lover now dead.

humiliating spectacle he must make to others, a man of rich inner resources the slave to a girl without conversation, in whom most of his friends do not even see good looks. In the unpublished parts of the letters, still more than in the *Liber Amoris*, he moans over the pleasure, even in memory, of fondling her body, even through clothes, and he moans too at his own abject dependence on her.[11] When *John Bull* alludes to the hero of the muted published version as a 'disappointed dotard' and an 'impotent sensualist', it has the text(s), read unironically, on its side.

Powerful and extraordinary though it is on its own, Hazlitt's Portrait of the Artist seems incomplete until we have contemplated it superimposed upon other portraits. Along with his fellow writers, Hazlitt was caught up in a collective enterprise in which the notion of the stereotypical intellectual was explored, corrected, given Identikit features, one contribution fitting over and losing itself in the last. Hazlitt's sorrowing and ridiculous Pygmalion gains from his dialogic relationship with De Quincey's tormented but vindicated Dreamer. Together, moreover, these two books advance the stereotype and show up how thin, sentimental, and bombastic it was before. De Quincey with his sluttish Muse in Oxford Street, Hazlitt with his in Southampton Buildings, Holborn, are both modern literary men, aeons away from the idealizations of the poets or from the canvasses of historical painters. For its full revisionist impact, the work of De Quincey and Hazlitt should be seen in the context of the craze, at its height across Europe in the first two decades of the nineteenth century, for a mythologized pantheon of artist-heroes: Homer, Tiresias, Dante, Tasso, and Milton recur, victimized but also resplendent, in the poetry of Byron and Shelley, Goethe and Foscolo, and in the paintings of late neo-Classical artists, particularly in France.[12] The figures of Ann and Sarah need comparing, too, with the poets' impressive idealized meetings with their Muses, who for Foscolo are the Graces, for Keats Greek divinities and Queens of the Underworld.

Yet, even though De Quincey and Hazlitt are like one another and unlike the poets in their realistic treatment of detail and setting, they cannot be compared with one another as iconoclasts: it is only Hazlitt who pits literary realism against literary idealism. The *Examiner*'s reviewer hailed the *Liber Amoris* as a very philosophical book, in the tradition of Bishop Berkeley and Sir William Drummond, the sceptical thinker admired by Shelley: these comparisons are not clearly explained, but it is possible to see why a sympathetic fellow-liberal made them.[13]

Since that time the *Liber Amoris* has not received much recognition, and certainly not the *Examiner*'s kind of intellectual recognition. Today copies of

---

[11] Hazlitt to P. G. Patmore (31 May 1822), *Letters*, p. 263.
[12] See Jon Whitely, 'Homer Abandoned: A French Neoclassical Theme', in *The Artist and the Writer in France*, edited by F. Haskell, A. Levi, and R. Shackleton (Oxford, 1974) pp. 40–51. Whitely estimates that no fewer than sixteen French painters before 1830 used mythical themes from Homer's life, further amplified in modern times to suggest that the blind artist was peculiarly neglected and unfortunate.
[13] *Examiner*, No. 798 (11 May 1823); quoted in *Liber Amoris*, p. xxiii.

it are hard to find, and readers even of Hazlitt have often never heard of it. Nevertheless the book represents a crucial breakthrough in Hazlitt's career. He was not only working Sarah, the real girl, out of his system; by interpreting their story symbolically he was defining his position in relation to some extreme contemporary versions of the doctrine of the Imagination, which, in Hazlitt's rendering, kills. The book is of key importance for him because it marks the final transition from his activities in the second decade of the century, when he was a critic and a political journalist, to his final phase as an autobiographical essayist. Oddly, Hazlitt exclaimed with relief to his publisher Colburn as, on 3 March 1822, he finished the second volume of his *Table Talk*: 'I have done with essay writing for ever' (*Letters*, p. 238). What he was really achieving was an extension and enrichment of his life as an essayist, since henceforth these fragments could be seen against a larger project, a critical, intellectual, and generalized portrait of himself. The essayist who wrote 'On Going a Walk', 'Indian Jugglers', 'On Being a Good Hater' remained an autobiographer, as he remained the author of dramatic monologues and the manipulator of real-life experience. The persona and the voice is developed in the *Liber Amoris*; so is the train of critical thinking that contextualizes the portrait, without which Hazlitt's career as a whole would lack an intellectual dimension.

But then the same point might be made about Romantic autobiography, and about most English Romantic writing as we habitually represent it: without its critical element, its corrections, critiques, parodies, and satires, it lacks an intellectual dimension apparent (if uncertainly) to writers and readers of the age. With the passing of time, critics seem to have become less rather than more aware of the satirical and intellectualist strain in Romantic writing. The problem is that all modern professional persons of letters are Romantics, one way or another, and the premises on which most of our procedures rest are biased in favour of aestheticism. Biographers, psychobiographers, editors, textual critics, deconstructionists, critics of the poem or the poet in isolation, take, as a matter of course, the specialized, narrowly restricted view that in the early nineteenth century was still encountering intelligent criticism. The sympathetic portrait of the solitary artist, lifted by his calling above the ordinary obligations of life, initially aroused resistance because it demanded to be read on its own terms, which put aesthetics above ethics. The satirical counter-portrait is hard to read (and was already hard when it first appeared) because it refuses 'Romantic' self-sufficiency. The meaning of a work remains incomplete until it is read alongside another work: *Alastor* alongside *The Excursion*, Book I; the *Liber Amoris* alongside *The Confessions of an English Opium Eater*.

For some tastes, the case for aestheticism was proved philosophically by Kant, Schelling, Hegel, and their adherents (there is a philosopher's equivalent of the Whig Idea of Progress). If this is the case, the gestures of the English younger Romantic generation were a futile rearguard action, soon overtaken by history, or by revelation. From a more sceptical point of view, the sudden prestige of aestheticism around 1800 is itself a historical phenomenon, no more above criticism than any other movement of ideas, and certainly not immune from the observation that the intellectuals and artists who fostered it had an interest. From that angle of vision, it is pleasant to see Romantic aestheticism meeting, at the outset, some pockets of resistance.

Conrad: Satire and Fiction

MARTIN PRICE

Yale University

In the sixth chapter of *The Shape of Utopia* Robert Elliott discussed the conflict between utopian fiction and the novel. 'The novelist's art is to metamorphose ideas into the idiosyncratic experience of complex human beings', but the utopian writer, interested as he is in the ideas for their own sakes, is content to create characters that are stylized, mechanical, flat. 'The expectations we bring to the *Satyricon, Gargantua and Pantagruel, Candide,* Barth's *Giles Goat-Boy* are very different from those we bring to *Emma* or *Sons and Lovers*: it is pointless to require of *Brave New World* that it try to be what they are.'[1]

My concern is with the way that satire and the novel may combine or conflict, and, while I shall start with a few instances from Dickens, my subject is really the uneasy mixture of satire and fiction in Joseph Conrad.[2] In his discussion of the 'great misanthropes', under the rubric 'the satirist satirized', Elliott had occasion to cite Conrad's remarks in *Nostromo* about Charles Gould: 'A man haunted by a fixed idea is insane. He is dangerous even if that idea is an idea of justice: for may he not bring the heavens down pitilessly upon a loved head?'[3] Conrad is, as I have tried to show elsewhere, essentially concerned with the 'idea' and the way in which it possesses men, turning them, as in the case of Gould, into both victims and tyrants.[4] Conrad tries to show how much our lives are governed by ideas or, as he often chooses to call them, illusions. Because the idea always outruns the actual, it is threatened by calm reflection. Such reflection will make us recognize the very unrealizability of ideas. The universe is inhospitable to man's ideas; no human meanings are accommodated in the grand spectacle of nature. Man must choose among roles: he may assert and live by idea in the face of inevitable defeat; he may adapt himself to the world as it is and ignore the

---

[1] *The Shape of Utopia* (Chicago, 1970), pp. 110, 121. Elliott wrote entertainingly here about the literary difficulties presented by the 'new dispensation which eliminates conflict from society' and leaves little place for 'the angularities of character upon which the novel so much depends' (p. 105). He returned to the issue in 'The Costs of Utopia', *Transactions of the Fourth International Congress on the Enlightenment, Studies in Voltaire and the Eighteenth Century*, 152 (1976), 677–92.

[2] I am using the terms 'novel' and 'fiction' loosely; they may be taken to refer to the tradition of mimetic fiction. As Ian Watt has recently shown with thoroughness and acuteness, Conrad's is among the earliest English fiction systematically to displace narrative sequence by thematic; it is also, with Hardy's, among the earliest to make explicit use of metaphysical concerns. Nevertheless, I believe that my rough and exploratory contrast between satire and fiction can be applied to Conrad. Compare Ian Watt, *Conrad in the Nineteenth Century* (Berkeley and Los Angeles, 1980).

[3] *The Power of Satire: Magic, Ritual, Art* (Princeton, New Jersey, 1970), p. 214.

[4] *Forms of Life: Character and Moral Imagination in the Novel* (New Haven, Connecticut, 1983), pp. 235–65.

claims of the idea; he may remain an ironic spectator of others' efforts or obliviousness and enjoy the comic spectacle of quixotic heroism or heroic obtuseness. The first of these roles may create existential tragedy and the second the comic triumph that arises from luck rather than intention. The third comes at times very close to satiric disdain for those who cannot endure the effort of being fully aware.[5]

In Dickens's novels we often move between satire and the novelistic. Some characters exist entirely within a satiric world, and, through that world, create the obstacles, enclosures, and resistances that threaten the hero. Individually these characters may be absurd; collectively, as a world, they become formidable. These characters display, moreover, a great range of triviality, self-absorption, rigid obsession, and darker impulses of cruelty and aggression. The degree to which these characters resemble each other (in devotion to forms, in acquisitiveness, in defensive self-imprisonment) makes them the various aspects of a common identity and of a shared world. But Dickens's characters may, as one critic has put it, serve a double purpose:

They may be simultaneously dramatic (or novelistic) and rhetorical (satiric counters), or they may move from one mode to another. More often the characters are divided into two groups, one dramatic and one rhetorical (with possibly a third group of those who are or can be both), and the difficulty is the incongruity of their appearance together in the same fictional world.[6]

Dickens tends to segregate such characters when they are most fully realizing one mode or the other. When Fanny Dorrit decides to win her revenge upon Mrs Merdle, we see her in dramatic scenes with her sister Amy, who tries to dissuade her from so empty a purpose. But when we see Fanny carry out her resolution, she enters the Merdles' world with all the reductive simplicity of purpose that this world demands. In *Our Mutual Friend* the world of the Veneerings is virtually autonomous; characters who gain their identity there may, however, open out into greater complexity, as Sophronia Lammle does in her warning to Podsnap. Within the Veneering world a major character must be reduced to a virtual triviality that he may want as a refuge from earnestness. 'Eugene Wrayburn, we note, is buried alive in this company: he is dead in the ironic sense that if they are alive the truly living must be dead; and he is dead in the straightforward sense that he is bored to death, but even more in that he has given in to their death by apathetically consenting to join them' (Manning, p. 203). The paradoxes of life and death are raised more explicitly, and in a different mode, by Jenny

[5] Tony Tanner, in an article on *Under Western Eyes*, cites the relevant, if somewhat overweening, speech of the hero of T. S. Eliot's *The Family Reunion*: 'You have gone through life in a sleep, | Never woken to the nightmare. I tell you, life would be unendurable | If you were wide awake.' ('Nightmare and Complacency: Razumov and the Western Eye', *Critical Quaterly*, 4 (1962), 197–214).
[6] Sylvia Bank Manning, *Dickens as Satirist* (New Haven, Connecticut, 1971), p. 9. Further citations are made by parenthetical page numbers in the text.

Wren, whom Mrs Manning likens to the 'type of primitive satirist described by R. C. Elliott': 'The relish of physical punishment, the bitterness, hatred, and abuse, and the sense of outraged justice behind these resemble the state of satire as it passed from magic to art' (p. 223). Jenny Wren can, at different moments, be tender, bitterly angry, parentally severe, radiantly prophetic; and we are somewhat startled by the reduction of her to a partner of Sloppy at the close.

Dickens's freedom in moving between modes has the confidence of an author who is not hobbled by doctrines of realism and who is constantly in touch with the supple conventions of popular art. Conrad learned much from Dickens's verbal wit, but his effects are less exuberant and far more studied. Conrad's idiom and images are saturated, even adrip, with intention. The difficulty is that the intention is sometimes uncontrolled, and what seems to be meant as Dickensian facetiousness may as readily veer into sarcasm:

Mr Verloc went on divesting himself of his clothing with the unnoticing inward concentration of a man undressing in the solitude of a vast and hopeless desert. For thus inhospitably did this fair earth, our common inheritance, present itself to the mental vision of Mr Verloc. All was so still without and within that the lonely ticking of the clock on the landing stole into the room as if for the sake of company.[7]

One could wish away the second of those sentences, which seems more to gloat than to present Mr Verloc's state of mind.

This uncertainty of tone and effect comes from two principal sources: a conflict of attitudes that is insufficiently resolved, and an excess of assertion. There is a counterpart of these difficulties in Conrad's invention of character and situation. I should like to deal with some of these difficulties as they appear in two comparatively early stories, both in *Tales of Unrest* (1898) and as they appear again in *The Secret Agent* (1907) and *Under Western Eyes* (1911).

The first of the two stories from *Tales of Unrest* is one that Conrad himself regarded highly, 'An Outpost of Progress'; the second is a tale that won praise only from Ford Madox Ford, 'The Return'. The first of these stories was, as Conrad put it in his 'Author's Note', the 'lightest part of the loot' he carried off from Central Africa, 'the main portion being of course *The Heart of Darkness*'. The story continues to win high praise; V. S. Naipaul regards it as 'the finest thing that Conrad wrote'.[8] But, while R. A. Gekoski considers it 'the best of the stories in the volume', he is troubled, as I am, by 'the ferocity of Conrad's treatment' of his characters.[9] It is a tale of studied brilliance, and the author detaches himself from his characters from the outset. The two

[7] *The Secret Agent*, Uniform Edition (London, 1923), p. 179. All references to Conrad's fiction will be to this edition, by parenthetical page numbers in the text.
[8] *The Return of Eva Peron* (London, 1980), p. 215.
[9] *Conrad: The Moral World of the Novelist* (London, 1978). This seems to me an important book, and I regret very much that I had not seen it when I wrote on Conrad earlier (see note 4). Lawrence Graver, who draws interesting resemblances to Flaubert and Kipling, speaks of the 'ruthless belligerence' of the work in *Conrad's Short Fiction* (Berkeley and Los Angeles, 1969), p. 11.

Belgians are put in charge of a remote and 'useless' trading station so that the director can dispose of the two 'imbeciles' sent him by the company for six months. Kayerts and his assistant Carlier are 'two perfectly insignificant and incapable individuals, whose existence is rendered possible through the high organization of civilized crowds'. Nor are they exceptional in this: 'Few men realize that their life, the very essence of their character, their capabilities and their audacities, are only the expression of their feeling in the safety of their surroundings.' All our virtues and principles, 'every great and every insignificant thought belongs not to the individual but to the crowd: to the crowd that believes blindly in the irresistible force of its institutions and of its morals, in the power of its police and of its opinion' (p. 89). This is a traditional Conradian theme: it exhibits the superior penetration and disdain of a narrator who sees through all pretensions and presuppositions. A page or two later, this general theme is localized: 'Society, not from any tenderness, but because of its strange needs, had taken care of these two men, forbidding them all independent thought, all initiative, all departure from routine; and forbidding it under pain of death. They could only live on condition of being machines.' Once these men are subjected to 'the negation of the habitual', they are at a loss, 'being both, through want of practice, incapable of independent thought' (p. 91). Although both men look back longingly to their condition as part of a mass mind, they seem at first to get along well enough 'in the fellowship of their stupidity and laziness. Together they did nothing, absolutely nothing, and enjoyed the sense of idleness for which they were paid' (p. 92). They come belatedly to read novels, in which the range of human motives surprises them.

The station is in fact run by a native clerk, who disturbs the two Belgians' serenity by secretly selling the hired station men into slavery in return for a fine lot of ivory. Not only the rather despondent and inefficient station men have been sold, but some members of the friendly local people. The Belgians are horrified. Or are they? 'They believed their words' (p. 105). And then, once more, the narrator opens up their state to suggest a general one: 'Everybody shows a respectful deference to certain sounds that he and his fellows can make.' Meanings give way to sounds; social beliefs to empty rituals. 'But about feelings people really know nothing. We talk with indignation or enthusiasm; we talk about oppression, cruelty, crime, devotion, self-sacrifice, virtue, and we know nothing real beyond the words. Nobody knows what suffering or sacrifice mean — except, perhaps the victims of the mysterious purpose of these illusions' (pp. 105–06).

For all their obtuseness and their wish not to face reality, a measure of fear steals into the two men's minds and brings with it the loss of their sense of safety. They pick quarrels with each other, until finally Kayerts accidentally shoots and kills Carlier. Kayerts now becomes totally demoralized. All he once believed in and lived by appears 'contemptible and childish, false and ridiculous' (p. 114). But, as he hears the whistle of the steamer making its delayed visit to the station, Kayerts hangs himself from the cross that marks the previous agent's grave. As the director finds him, Kayerts's corpse exhibits his late-found wisdom: 'His toes were only a couple of inches above the ground; his arms hung stiffly down; he seemed to be standing rigidly at attention, but with one purple cheek playfully posed on the shoulder. And, irreverently, he was putting out a swollen tongue at his Managing Director' (p. 117). One may feel that the corpse might have been spared this last exhibition of the narrator's intention, even if it might be read as Kayerts's repudiation of all he has unthinkingly lived by. What is troubling about the story is its steady denial of even a shadow of consciousness to its characters; such consciousness as Kayerts attains at the close is the 'wrong-headed lucidity' (p. 115) of a transvaluation of values. Even when Kayerts looks at his daughter's portrait, we are carefully made to see what Kayerts cannot. 'It represented a little girl with long bleached tresses and a rather sour face' (p. 108). The two men are allowed no thoughts but banalities, no conscience but feeble rationalizations, no feelings but clumsy projections. They become a demonstration of the anonymous urban citizen (such as we see in the Geneva of *Under Western Eyes*) becoming demoralized by solitude, unable to sustain the forms of civilization beyond the pale, worked upon by forces they cannot even imagine.

All that is missing from this story can be seen if we compare these men to Marlow and Kurtz in *The Heart of Darkness*. Kurtz is a far more outrageous and guilty figure. The evil he performs is more than tacit complicity, and the good to which he may have originally aspired is altogether beyond the conception of these two men. What we are given, then, is a demonstration performed upon and through them, and we may be led to ask ourselves how adequate the demonstration is. It has, surely, the boldness of satire in its reductive force. These men embody in almost pure form the operations of a collective mind upon the unreflective individual; they seem completely controlled by their society, in a manner which Emile Durkheim called 'mechanical solidarity'. Durkheim speaks of two kinds of consciousness or *conscience*: 'one which we share with our entire group, which, in consequence, is not ourselves, but society living and acting within us; the other which . . . represents only that which is personal and distinctive to each of us, which makes him an individual'. Mechanical solidarity is at its highest pitch 'when the *conscience collective* is exactly co-extensive' with the individual's consciousness 'and coincides at all points with it: but at this moment his individuality is non-existent'. A society created by mechanical solidarity is a system of homogeneous elements, not so much coherent as bounded territorially.[10] Here the mass-men who are homogeneous elements of Western European society are isolated in Africa, which requires powers such men no longer have. Is the story a satire? Is ridicule the primary note? Do these immediate

[10] Cited from *De la Division du travail social* (1893) in his own translation by Steven Lukes, in *Emile Durkheim: His Life and Work* (Harmondsworth, 1975), pp. 149–50. See also *The Division of Labor in Society*, translated by George Simpson (New York and London, 1933), pp. 129 ff.

objects of satire suggest something more general in human behaviour, as we see in some of the narrator's comments? How telling or general is the import of the human deficiencies Conrad presents here? What is left out that we find in the more novelistic treatment of *The Heart of Darkness*? If this is satire, is it as forceful as it might be if it took more of man into account? Is all satiric reduction of equal value?

A second story, much the longest of those in *Tales of Unrest*, caused Conrad enormous pains of effort and seemed to him later 'a left-handed production'. It is not a story that has won much praise, or even much analysis.[11] It seems too long, somewhat as the final dialogue of Verloc and Winnie seems to have been unduly protracted for ironic effect when Conrad revised the serial version of *The Secret Agent*.[12] It is, moreover, a story which draws on the same themes as 'An Outpost', although it is set in London. Alvan Hervey and his wife are examples of the homogeneous elements of mechanical solidarity. They are suddenly isolated by a moral crisis rather than by distance. We first see Hervey coming off the commuters' train with other men: 'Their backs appeared alike — almost as if they had been wearing a uniform; their indifferent faces were varied but somehow suggested kinship, like the faces of a band of brothers who through prudence, drifting, disgust, or foresight would resolutely ignore each other.' Their eyes 'had all the same stare, concentrated and empty, satisfied and unthinking' (pp. 118–19). Hervey has been married for five years to a woman who had been 'intensely bored with her home where, as if packed in a tight box, her individuality — of which she was very conscious — had no play' (p. 120). (It should be said that Mrs Hervey's belief in her individuality is made a tyical manifestation of the middle-class mind.) But they choose to belong to a world 'where nothing is realized and where all joys and sorrows are cautiously toned down into pleasures and annoyances', 'where noble sentiments are cultivated in sufficient profusion to conceal the pitiless materialism of thoughts and aspirations' (p. 121). They are like skilful skaters 'cutting figures on thick ice for the admiration of the beholders, and disdainfully ignoring the hidden stream, the stream restless and dark; the stream of life, profound and unfrozen' (p. 123). All the consciousness is false. Hervey finances a journal because it serves his ambition, because he enjoys 'the special kind of importance he derived from the connection with what he imagined to be literature' (p. 121).

Conrad finds a brilliant image for Hervey's participation in mechanical solidarity. As he stands beside his wife's pier-glass, it multiplies his image

into a crowd of gentlemanly and slavish imitators, who were dressed exactly like himself; . . . who moved when he moved, stood still with him in an obsequious immobility, and had just such appearances of life and feeling as he thought it

---

[11] Graver discusses it briefly (pp. 34–39) and supplies a short list of selected criticism before 1969 (p. 229). For Gekoski, see note 13 below.
[12] On the revisions of *The Secret Agent*, see Walter F. Wright, *Romance and Tragedy in Joseph Conrad* (Lincoln, Nebraska, 1949), pp. 175–97.

dignified and safe for any man to manifest. And like real people who are slaves of common thoughts, that are not even their own, they affected a shadowy independence by the superficial variety of their movements . . . And like the men he respected they could be trusted to do nothing individual, original, or startling — nothing unforeseen and nothing improper. (pp. 124–25)

When Hervey finds a note in which his wife tells him that she has left him for the editor of the journal, Hervey feels 'physically sick'. But he soon works his way into a saving self-righteousness. He is defending 'life', that 'sane and gratifying existence untroubled by too much love or by too much regret' (p. 129). She has defiled it with a show of passion that 'strips the body of life'. It has 'laid its unclean hand upon the spotless draperies of his existence' (p. 130). We have virtually moved into Swift's world of *A Tale of a Tub*, where the soul is our outward clothing.

When his wife returns, unable to carry through her action but also unrepentant, Hervey seems at first to draw back from the intolerable into the safety of moral outrage. But, for all his posturing, he comes to recognize how much he needs the 'certitude of love and faith' (p. 180), and he finds the loss of it intolerable. He tries to blame the loss upon his wife: 'She had no love and no faith for anyone' (p. 183). In the midst of his self-centred grief, his conscience is born: 'It came to him in a flash that morality is not a method of happiness. The revelation was terrible' (p. 183). He wants 'help against himself, against the cruel decree of salvation. The need of tacit complicity, where it had never failed him, the habit of years affirmed itself' (p. 184). But he does not know how to ask for what he now wants, nor does she recognize any change in him. As she wards off what seems a renewed manifestation of his somewhat brutal egoism and suspects him only of 'a fresh fit of jealousy, a dishonest desire of evasion', she defies him. 'Can you stand it?', he asks, thinking of years 'without faith or love'. To what she thinks he means she shouts angrily, 'Yes!'. Thereupon he leaves, never to return (pp. 185–86).

It is a somewhat muddled narrative because it records the events within the mind of a man who is averse to self-analysis, but the story allows Hervey a growth of awareness that seems genuine enough.[13] The result is to make the satirical elements of the story a record of the self from whose constriction he finally breaks — not at once, not altogether clearly, but with sufficient force to become a complex character. 'The Return' is a more diffuse and less efficiently controlled story than 'An Outpost of Progress', but it attempts to treat more complex characters. They create, as such characters will, a narrative richer in dramatic power. Conrad shifts from sardonic exemplification of a theme his characters cannot conceive to the emergence, within the consciousness of a character, of the meaning of his experience.

---

[13] R. A. Gekoski is very interesting on the story. I cannot follow his emphasis on religious conversion and the 'affirmation of the transcendental value of Love'; and I am, as a result, less inclined to think that Hervey's final vision might have been intended to be ironic. See his discussion in *Conrad*, pp. 51 ff. For the possible influence of this story upon *The Waste Land*, see Robert L. Morris, 'Eliot's "Game of Chess" and Conrad's "The Return"', *MLN*, 65 (1950), 422–23.

Some of the puzzles and difficulties that these stories evoke are to be found in the critical response to *The Secret Agent*. Frederick R. Karl feels that the Professor, in 'a somewhat limited sense', reflects 'Conrad's own contempt for the mediocre, for the loss of nerve and vitality, for a world that has become passionless'. Somewhat earlier Karl observed that Conrad's irony appears to 'give the novelist a devastating authority, even an arrogance'.[14] H. M. Daleski seems led by Conrad's ironic levelling to draw some very questionable equivalences. The Assistant Commissioner's 'settling of scores with both the minister and his own subordinate' is a 'civilized — but almost as deadly — variant of the Professor's shovelling of his stuff at street corners'. Or again: 'In his readiness to stick at nothing in protecting himself . . . Heat resembles nobody so much as the Professor.'[15]

F. R. Leavis described the career of Winnie Verloc after the murder of her husband as a 'gruesomely farcical coda in which the gallows-haunted Winnie, whose turn it now is to suppose herself loved for her own sake, clings round the neck of the gallant Comrade Ossipon'.[16] Leavis's use of 'whose turn it is' reduced Winnie's desperation to the same obtuseness we have seen in her husband's complacency. But Daleski sees her 'obsessive self-sacrifice' on her brother's behalf as 'moral nihilism that is similar [to that of Verloc and Heat] in its exclusive concern with an end and its bland indifference to the means employed to achieve it' (pp. 147, 149). Hers, like Stevie's, is a story of the 'disintegration that follows a prolonged state of nullity or vacancy'. Albert J. Guerard suggests that the vividness of Ossipon's 'growing horror and disgust' after finding Verloc's corpse 'effectively destroys much of our sympathy for Winnie. We may come to share his view. But this is not too high a price to pay for such a show of fictional virtuosity'.[17]

Ian Watt corrects Richard Curle's sentimental view of Stevie by insisting that Stevie is regarded with the 'same impartial perspective as everything else' in this 'black comedy of human cross-purposes'. Watt warns against too simple a reading: 'Just as we are denied the pleasure of melodrama — there is no one we particularly want to applaud or hiss — so we are denied the pleasures of parody or satire — the characters are too human for that.' And yet they are all, as Conrad put it in a letter to his French translator, '*imbéciles*'. The characters, as Watt observes, do not 'understand themselves, or really know what they are doing'. Yet if we look to the author's intentions, Watt sees a 'control that approaches serenity', a tale which is 'tonic rather than depressive in its final effect'.[18] It is perhaps in this sense that Daleski (p. 151)

[14] *Joseph Conrad: The Three Lives* (London, 1979), pp. 599, 587.
[15] *Joseph Conrad: The Way of Dispossession* (London, 1977), pp. 167, 170.
[16] *The Great Tradition*, Peregrine Edition (Harmondsworth, 1962), p. 237.
[17] *Conrad the Novelist* (Cambridge, Massachusetts, 1958), pp. 230–31. I should say that these quotations from Guerard and others whose work I greatly admire are meant to be not representative samplings but responses to particular problems.
[18] *Conrad: The Secret Agent. A Casebook*, edited by Ian Watt (London, 1973), pp. 62, 77, 80.

regards *The Secret Agent* as the 'most enjoyable' of Conrad's novels or that Guerard (p. 231) finds it 'an entertaining and easy book'.

What these critics make clear is the way in which the irony seems to effect a moral levelling of all the characters and the way in which the aloofness or comic distance of the novelist makes us associate our feelings more with his virtuosity than with the minds of his characters. There are variations on each of these emphases. The first is extended by J. Hillis Miller to a view of the 'sinister connectedness of all levels of society from bottom to top'. All the 'living deaths of the novel are the same death, and . . . the theme of *The Secret Agent* is the universal death which underlies life'.[19] The second emphasis has been pursued, to a different evaluation from those I have so far cited, by Irving Howe. Conrad's 'ability to make the life of humanity seem a thing of shame reaches an appalling completeness' at times. Howe regards the final scene between Verloc and Winnie as a 'dazzling *tour de force*', but he feels that Conrad's 'insistence upon squeezing the last ounce of sordid absurdity' is in conflict with 'the narrative rhythm of the book'. Conrad's studied irony is constantly 'nagging at our attention'; he 'lacks the talent for self-resistance that is indispensable to a novelist for whom irony has been transformed from a tactic into a total perspective'.[20]

Perhaps the most comprehensive criticism of the novel is that of R. A. Gekoski. He also compares it to 'An Outpost of Progress' and feels that most of the characters in *The Secret Agent*, like those in the story, are 'finally unworthy even of the sustained scorn to which they are subjected' (this might be what Howe means by Conrad's failure of 'self-resistance'; we are troubled by a novelist who sets up easy targets for what must prove excessive scorn). Gekoski (pp. 150–51) finds that Conrad achieves a 'technical masterpiece', but only 'at the cost of complexity of thought and emotion'. Technical masterpiece, *tour de force*, show of fictional virtuosity: the terms all raise the question of how one can relate the satiric brilliance to the fictional adequacy.

Clearly, in this novel as in the stories I have cited, indolence, self-absorption, moral obtuseness — however we wish to name them — are the faults which arouse scorn even as they serve to reduce man to mechanism, to mere matter in motion. Those who live in an habitual world that calls nothing into question are perhaps engaged in a death more than a life. Those, on the other hand, who are obsessed by an extreme view like the Professor's (and perhaps Vladimir's) can shake off the bonds of the familiar and open up to view a radically different kind of reality. Yet these obsessions are such as to make those who hold them victims as much as masters. For while these men may see what others are content to miss, they need not thereby attain to wisdom. Their vision may be the savage distortion of the insane. A perception of the intolerable is not in itself a passport to reality.

---

[19] *Poets of Reality: Six Twentieth-Century Writers* (Cambridge, Massachusetts, 1966), pp. 41, 66.
[20] *Politics and the Novel* (New York, 1957), p. 94.

Conrad, nevertheless, mocks those who are, as he suggests, too timid, too torpid, too shallow to question received truths, or, what may be the same, too lucky to have had to face the intolerable. They are the men in the ranks whom Marlow regards with some disdain (but with some sense of complicity) in *Lord Jim*. They are the counterparts of Heat or Michaelis or Ossipon in *The Secret Agent*. Everything about them is suspect because they have never reached the sense of the 'problematic' that is so critical for Conrad, as it was for Nietzsche. And yet, as we have seen, the effect of Conrad's irony is to impose a moral levelling that makes for perplexity since it includes both those who are without awareness and those who are maddened by what they take to be too much. Or if not for perplexity, perhaps at times for an easy cynicism of the kind Conrad attacks in Martin Decoud. That Conrad attacks it in *Nostromo* does not, of course, acquit him of participation in it elsewhere (or even there). But it does perhaps betray an uneasiness with those ambivalences of satiric disdain that he best surmounts in *Lord Jim*, where Marlow's mixture of sympathy and realism creates a genuinely complex irony and a complex case, if not a complex character, in Jim.

Conrad builds *The Secret Agent* upon an action that is ludicrously pointless and has been ineptly conducted. His first irony is to give the action point. A bold anarchist measure is not undertaken by the anarchists themselves but is forged, so to speak, in their name, by an autocratic power which seeks to bring other nations over to its own repressive policy. The agent of that power (clearly Russia) wishes to cure the English of their 'sentimental regard for individual liberty' (p. 29) by means of a purely destructive act. Traditional targets could not release the 'absurd ferocity' of this attack upon the new 'sacrosanct fetish', science (p. 31). The act must have 'all the shocking senselessness of gratuitous blasphemy', as if one were to 'throw a bomb into pure mathematics' (p. 33).

Vladimir, as we might suspect of so academic a conspiracy, knows little about revolutionaries or secret agents. He is appalled when he finds Adolf Verloc, the 'celebrated agent', to be merely 'vulgar, heavy, and impudently unintelligent' (p. 27). The revolutionaries of *The Secret Agent* are an unattractive, unromantic lot.

All these people [Conrad wrote to his socialist friend, Cunninghame Graham] are not revolutionaries — they are Shams. And as regards the Professor I did not intend to make him despicable. He is incorruptible at any rate. In making him say 'madness and despair — give me that for a lever and I will move the world', I wanted to give him a note of perfect sincerity. At the worst he is a megalomaniac of an extreme type. And every extremist is respectable.[21]

The others share a world that tends to obey regular laws, where contingency preserves a familiar and manageable scale. Or so it seems.

---

[21] *Joseph Conrad's Letters to R. B. Cunninghame Graham*, edited by C. T. Watts (Cambridge, 1969), Letter no. 60 (7 October 1907), p. 170.

More than any other novel of Conrad's, *The Secret Agent* has a constant succession of details that are irrelevant, discordant, inexplicable, incongruous, or suspect. Verloc keeps a shop (it is, of course, in part a blind) where various 'shady wares', from patent medicines to pornography, are sold. The customers who enter are seedy and furtive, and the shop-bell mocks their stealth with its 'impudent virulence' (p. 4: the idea of impudence is the affront to reasonable expectation).

The most striking instance of the grotesque event which observes its own times and seasons is the player piano in the Silenus Café, the keys moving without hands, its jaunty, tinny tunes sounding at unpredictable intervals with a sardonic jocosity. Details carry a strangeness that remains unnoticed by the characters, and we become as a result more aware of the author. Heat finds the Assistant Commissioner in his private office, 'pen in hand, bent over a great table bestrewn with papers, as if worshipping an enormous double inkstand of bronze and crystal. Speaking tubes resembling snakes were tied by the heads to the back of the Assistant Commissioner's wooden armchair, and their gaping mouths seemed ready to bite his elbows' (p. 97). Seemed so to whom? Presumably not to Heat, who is anything but fanciful. We may think of the Assistant Commisioner's dislike of desk work, but Heat knows nothing of that. These details seem gratuitously rather than significantly violent; they awaken expectations that are neither met nor denied. They seem to be created for effect, as coercive as the floating menace of a Gothic novel. As Thomas Mann observed, the 'gaze turned upon the horrible is clear, lively, dry-eyed, almost gratified'.[22]

As an instance of the suspect detail we may take the remarks about Winnie's mother: 'She considered herself to be of French descent, which might have been true.' This suggests a narrator estimating the plausibility of remarks he has heard, but comes in fact from an author who alone can have decided whether his character's remark is truthful. And why should it not be? Pretension? A few sentences later the pretension is affirmed, but not in a way that denies the claim. 'Traces of the French descent which the widow boasted were apparent in Winnie, too. They were apparent in the extremely neat and artistic arrangement of her glossy black hair' (p. 6).

Conrad is creating a world that seems shot through with incongruity and potential violence; yet their sources are not identified and in many cases are not identifiable. Things 'seem' that way: they carry suggestions we can neither ascribe to a clear source nor comfortably ignore. The obliviousness of the characters seems heavy-lidded, lethargic, imperciptient. They lack the power or the will to recognize what should at least cause a measure of disturbance. When Stevie is so moved by the 'pathos and violence' of a horse's fall as to 'shriek piercingly', it is in a crowd 'which disliked to be

22 'Joseph Conrad's *The Secret Agent*' (1926), reprinted in the translation of H. T. Lowe-Porter in *Conrad: The Secret Agent*, edited by Ian Watt (p. 106).

disturbed by sounds of distress in its quiet enjoyment of the national spectacle' (p. 9). The last phrase seems curiously contemptuous. Is their fascination with the fallen horse one of simple enjoyment, with none of the terror or shock we often find in spectators of other accidents? That Stevie's response is appropriately intense seems clear enough on this occasion. Yet shortly we are to learn of the violence he creates in turn by shooting off fireworks when two office-boys, as a practical joke, disturb him with 'tales of injustices and oppression'. The commotion Stevie creates is called an 'altruistic exploit' (p. 10). Does that dry phrase confirm the implication that Stevie is genuinely responsive to 'pathos and violence' or simply that he is more acutely disturbed by the thought of them? Is he, in short, morally superior or simply pathologically sensitive? And shall we say sensitive or irritable?

In the famous scenes of the second chapter, we see Hyde Park through Verloc's 'glances of comparative alertness'. But is it Verloc who sees 'here and there a victoria with the skin of some wild beast inside and a woman's face and hat emerging above the folded hood' (p. 11)? As Byron in *Don Juan* tells us what the court poet 'sung, or would, or could, or should have sung', so, with Conrad, we follow Verloc's eye-beam but observe what he does not. The 'bloodshot' sun turns London into a scene of 'opulence and luxury', at least this part of London, where the 'whole social order favourable to' the 'hygienic idleness' of the rich 'had to be protected against the shallow enviousness of unhygienic labour'. And while that irony evokes our sense of class differences and of the obliviousness of the idle rich, Mr Verloc, alone rusty in this scene of gold, remains an incongruous case, a man 'born of industrious parents for a life of toil' who has embraced indolence as a vocation, 'with a sort of inert fanaticism, or perhaps rather with a fanatical inertness' (p. 12).

The play with terms and witty extravagance recall Dickens, and the method is carried through: 'At the notion of a menaced social order he would perhaps have winked to himself if there had not been an effort to make in that sign of scepticism. His big, prominent eyes were not well adapted to winking. They were rather of the sort that closes solemnly in slumber with majestic effect' (p. 13). The last sentence mockingly converts indolence to solemnity, inertness to majesty. Two paragraphs later the street itself has 'the majesty of inorganic nature, of matter that never dies', the grandeur, as it were, of the lifeless and the mindless (p. 14). Matter keeps slipping out of or away from form. The mind aspires to the condition of matter. It is, once more, a satiric pattern. Verloc's mind is capable of 'moral nihilism' but is hardly energetic enough to become 'diabolic'. Indolence and inertia displace evil as well as good, for inertia is that conservative reluctance to stand outside the system of belief and social order on which one's life has been based. The desire to remain untroubled is far more powerful than the will to create or destroy.

This satiric pattern is clearest in Chief Inspector Heat. Chance and absurdity unnerve him. He can live with crime that has gain as a motive; it is a form of 'work' by which men keep themselves alive. He understands the mind of a burglar as like his own. 'Both recognize the same conventions . . . They understand each other, which is advantageous to both, and establishes a sort of amenity in their relations (p. 92). This is the large area of the normal, the common recognition of traditions and social institutions, however disparate the moral choices of the members. The Professor offends Heat by standing outside, by refusing to participate in the game whose rules most men obey. 'Revolution, legality — counter moves in the same game; forms of idleness at bottom identical . . . . But I don't play; I work fourteen hours a day, and go hungry sometimes' (pp. 69–70). The Professor mocks Ossipon, who has ineptly described the explosion as 'nothing short of criminal'. Ossipon angrily defends his terms: 'One must use the current words', he replies, in effect affirming his participation in the same game as Chief Inspector Heat and the rest of civil society (p. 71). Ossipon's word reveals the toughness of the social structure; it is deeply embedded in the terms by which we think.

The chief enemy of that structure is the Professor, who exhibits an 'ascetic purity' of thought 'combined with an astounding ignorance of wordly conditions'. His conviction of his own merit makes him, like his evangelical father, 'supremely confident in the privileges of his righteousness' (p. 80). But the Professor has replaced radical Protestantism with a 'frenzied puritanism of ambition', which he nurses as something 'secularly holy' (p. 81). Yet he is haunted at moments by the 'unattackable solidity of a great multitude', who are stubbornly resistant, 'numerous like locusts, industrious like ants, thoughtless like a natural force, pushing or blind and orderly and absorbed, impervious to sentiment, to logic, to terror, too, perhaps' (p. 82). With this suspicion of futility to allay, the Professor enjoys thrusting his presence on Chief Inspector Heat; he feels that he is confounding in the Chief Inspector all his enemies at once and 'affirming his superiority over all the multitude of mankind' (p. 84).

Here the satiric pattern becomes troubling, for the standard of energy is itself more repellent and destructive than the torpor it seeks to abolish. Is there a third term? The new Assistant Commissioner has a nature 'not easily accessible to illusions'. He has a healthy mistrust of men's motives, and he does not deceive himself about his own. He wants, if he can, to exculpate Michaelis in deference to an influential lady (one of his wife's valuable 'connections') who is Michaelis's patron. She is a woman of intelligence as well as generosity, 'seldom totally wrong, and almost never wrong-headed' (p. 105). There is much that is imperious about her aristocratic stance: a sympathy with Michaelis's radicalism based on their common dislike of the middle classes, and a reliance upon the status of birth that makes her irresponsibly ready to entertain the idea of the 'economic ruin of the system'. The Assistant Commissioner has an affection for the lady: 'a complex sentiment depending a little on her prestige, her personality, but most of all on the instinct of flattered gratitude. . . . Her influence upon his wife, a woman devoured by all sorts of small selfishnesses, small envies, small jealousies', was 'excellent' (pp. 111–12). He is able to recognize with 'deri-sive self-criticism' (p. 112) his own desire to please her. This self-awareness does not lead him to abandon his attachment to his self-interest, which is happily not in conflict with his duties. In fact, this motive releases in the Assistant Commissioner considerable administrative talent. He is not easily cajoled into believing what his subordinates think it fit he should believe so that they may conduct their affairs as they wish. He has a larger conception of the game to be played than Heat does: 'The existence of these spies amongst the revolutionary groups, which we are reproached for harbouring here, does away with all certitude' (pp. 140–41). The rules must be changed. As he says to Vladimir, 'we don't intend to let ourselves be bothered by shams under any pretext whatever' (p. 227).

Clearly the Assistant Commissioner has the fullest awareness of all these characters. He can act freely and imaginatively. By preventing Heat from victimizing Michaelis in order to conceal his use of Verloc, the Assistant Commissioner undoes Vladimir's scheme. He can abstract Heat from his London setting and see him with detachment:

His memory evoked a certain old fat and wealthy native chief in the distant colony whom it was a tradition for the successive Colonial Governors to trust and make much of as a firm friend and supporter of the order and legality established by white men; whereas, when examined sceptically, he was found out to be principally his own good friend, and nobody else's. Not precisely a traitor, but still a man of many dangerous reservations in his fidelity, caused by a due regard for his own advantage, comfort, and safety. A fellow of some innocence in his naive duplicity, but none the less dangerous. He was physically a big man, too, and (allowing for the difference of colour, of course) Chief Inspector Heat's appearance recalled him to the memory of his superior. (p. 118)

The Assistant Commissioner becomes a satirist himself for the moment. He is, moreover, adroit in handling the cabinet minister as well as his own subordinate. To liken him to the Professor seems to me profoundly mistaken. In a sense, the Assistant Commissioner has the degree of consciousness that might pull *The Secret Agent* from satire to novel, but he has a limited role, largely subservient to the working out of the ironic plot. He participates in the common plight in having a motive of self-interest among others, but he stands outside it in recognizing what must be done.

The other place we might look for a third term, an exception to the contrast of indolence and obsession, is in Winnie Verloc. She is presented ambiguously as a woman of reserve or of indifference; she seems, in fact, a somnambulist in all but her devotion to her retarded brother. She has chosen to marry Verloc in order to insure support for Stevie, and, that ambition realized, she walks through life somewhat as Verloc walks through the Knightsbridge streets. She refuses to take notice of 'the inside of facts' or 'the inwardness of things'. Winnie's mother, in contrast, more sensitive to Verloc's impatience, devises a means of securing Stevie's place with the Verlocs. She inveigles herself into an almshouse in order to halve the number of Winnie's dependents that Verloc must support. But here, too, illusion must play a part. In performing this 'heroic and unscrupulous' act, she assumes (rightly) that Winnie's loyalty to Stevie will endure: 'She excepted that sentiment from the rule of decay affecting all things human and some things divine. She could not help it; not to have done so would have frightened her too much' (p. 162). This movement to the very edge of endurable truth makes her an 'heroic old woman'. Typically enough, Winnie has no real perception of her mother's fears and countermeasures. Yet like her mother she has sacrificed much for the security of Stevie; her marriage to Verloc has been the form of that sacrifice. But, whatever Winnie's motives, she has pleased Verloc as a wife; she has more than lived up to the terms of her secret bargain. Her life has been 'stagnant and deep like a placid pool', only slightly stirred by the flirtation of Comrade Ossipon, 'an existence foreign to all grace and charm, without beauty and almost without decency, but admirable in the continuity of feeling and tenacity of purpose' (pp. 243–44).

Her discovery of Stevie's death is overwhelming, 'altering even the aspect of inanimate things'. All of the bonds which have held her to Verloc, or even to life, have been broken with the loss of her one purpose, her care for Stevie. Awakened at last into an independent life, she does not know 'what use to make of her freedom'. Verloc, on the other hand, has begun to divest himself of responsibility; he blames the label in Stevie's coat for his discovery. 'I don't blame you', he tells his wife, 'but it's your doing all the same' (p. 255). It was she, moreover, who kept thrusting Stevie upon his attention: 'if you will have it that I killed the boy', he concludes, 'then you've killed him as much as I' (p. 258). With that, Winnie's freedom from human ties is complete. When she stabs her husband to death she is 'a woman enjoying her complete irresponsibility and endless leisure, almost in the manner of a corpse' (p. 262).

In what follows, Winnie Verloc, who has achieved intensity and a degree of heroism, shrinks into a pathetic bur sordid hysteria. She is now over-whelmed by the fear of the gallows, desperate to find any way of escape. She turns to Ossipon for help when she comes upon him; he resumes his flirtation and finds her responsive. She tries to be deliberately seductive, perhaps even somewhat persuaded of Ossipon's affection for her. She is like her mother; not to believe in this 'would have frightened her too much'. She tries to hold Ossipon's loyalty, in spite of his horror at the sight of the corpse, by means of the large sum of money Verloc has given her. Ossipon is both foolish and vicious: he 'gazed scientifically at that woman, the sister of a degenerate, a degenerate herself — of a murdering type. He . . . invoked Lombroso, as an Italian peasant recommends himself to his favourite saint' (p. 297). There is farcical misunderstanding; he praises Stevie as 'a perfect type in a way', and Winnie replies tenderly: 'He was that indeed. . . . You took a lot of notice of him, Tom. I loved you for it.' And Ossipon reflects aloud, with new dread:

'Yes, he resembled you.' As Winnie laments, we are told, 'the truth — the very cry of truth — was found in a worn and artificial shape picked up somewhere among the phrases of sham sentiment'. Her last words are one of these phrases: 'I will live all my days for you, Tom!' (p. 298).

Winnie Verloc emerges as a moral being somewhat as Alvan Hervey does in 'The Return' or as Razumov far more powerfully does in *Under Western Eyes*. But her new existence is immediately aborted by her dread of the gallows. This fear seems arbitrary rather than necessary to Winnie's character, and it has the effect of degrading her to desperate wishfulness and a coarse pathos. She can be compared with the Verlocs' charwoman, Mrs Neale:

She followed it with the everlasting plaint of the poor, pathetically mendacious, miserably authenticated by the horrible breath of cheap rum and soap-suds. She scrubbed hard, snuffling all the time, and talking volubly. And she was sincere. And on each side of her thin red nose her bleared, misty eyes swam in tears, because she felt really the want of some sort of stimulant in the morning. (p. 184)

In *Under Western Eyes* Conrad found an adequate 'third term' in Sophia Antonovna. She impresses Razumov by her acuteness and her dedication. He knows little of her history, but he cannot despise her as he has the others he meets in Zurich. There runs through her talk, however, an affectionate maternal impatience with the childishness of men as well as a deeper acceptance of inferiority to them: 'That's where you men have the advantage. You are inspired sometimes both in thought and action. I have always admitted that when you *are* inspired; when you manage to throw off your masculine cowardice and prudishness you are not to be equalled by us' (p. 250). The last words of the novel echo this indispensable faith: 'Peter Ivanovitch is an inspired man.' Her faith, however misdirected, is formidable. As she recalls the oppression of the Russian people, she exclaims: 'One must believe for very pity. This can't go on.' And she is ready to accept the consequences of acting upon that pity: 'You've got to trample down every particle of your own feelings: for stop you cannot. You must not' (p. 345). For Razumov this 'old revolutionary hand, the respected, trusted, and influential Sophia Antonovna', much more 'representative than the great Peter Ivanovitch', is 'the true spirit of destructive revolution' (p. 261). If she is ruthless and obsessed, if she exhibits 'the stupid subtlety of people with one idea' (p. 283), she is at least selfless and sincere. And to call here 'sincere' is not, as in the case of Mrs Neale, a further accusation.

The Secret Agent remains a troubling book. As a satire, it might be seen to assimilate all of its characters to self-absorbed blindness, whether obsessive or indolent. Yet it offers itself as a 'simple tale' and leads us at many points to accept it as a novel. The result, as we have seen from critics' comments, is to direct our attention to the virtuosity of ironic method. Yet it seems questionable to divorce such virtuosity from its thematic and dramatic uses, and it is there that one feels the presence of an author who wavers between the sardonic and the sentimental. We are not allowed the full detachment which might allow us to scorn the shams and bunglers alike. Nor are we allowed to entertain very long or far the sympathy which the more complex characters awaken. The only way we can resolve these conflicts is to move to a level of abstraction that leaves precise motives and actions behind in the search for large covering terms. If we turn instead to the author's motives, we may be troubled by an irony earned at the expense of disabled characters. *The Secret Agent* is an important book for the problems its raises. It makes us ask ourselves what we expect of a novel, at least in its traditional form, what we ask of satire beyond derision and of irony beyond denial.

The New Style of *Sweeney Agonistes*

BARBARA EVERETT

Somerville College, Oxford

When, in the late eighteenth century, the neo-classical system of genres began to break down, formal satire ceased to attract major literary talents. But the satiric impulse itself did not of course disappear. Satire became an incidental element: it no longer prescribed its own form. Much of the best Victorian satirical writing is found in prose fiction (an obvious instance would be the American chapters in *Martin Chuzzlewit*). In the present century only Wyndham Lewis could be called a thoroughgoing satirist; and he too uses the novel as the vehicle for his satiric vision. T. S. Eliot's earliest important poems, 'The Love Song of J. Alfred Prufrock' and 'The Portrait of a Lady', seem also to maintain a relationship with prose fiction, most notably that of Henry James.

But the novel was never Eliot's preferred form. The manuscripts of *The Waste Land* show him attempting to revive the high Augustan modes of satire: attempts rightly dropped from or radically altered in the final version of the poem. The satiric life of *The Waste Land* is in fact strongest where it is most contemporary in reference and most dramatic in presentation. For it was a dramatic medium that the satiric impulse in Eliot seemed most naturally to demand. Conversely, when, a few years later, he made his first strictly dramatic attempt, the result was two fragments of verse dialogue which are best understood in terms of their satiric hinterland. *Sweeney Agonistes* is essentially, and to an almost Jonsonian degree, intended as 'satire-drama'. Indeed, Eliot achieved his breakthrough into drama not by virtue of a painfully-acquired stagecraft, but by the discovery and mastery of a new and essentially modern satiric style.

The dramatic art was clearly attractive to Eliot. And yet it was in other ways alien to a writer as obdurately inward, as introspectively private as Eliot's particular gifts and principles made him. It may be this mixture of attraction and alienation that produces the characteristically dramatic flavour of Eliot's verse *outside* the theatre; exquisitely reserved in its flamboyancy, reticently exact in its expressiveness. But such a 'dramatic' quality has little to do with a working dramaturgy. Symptomatically, all the later part of Eliot's career shows a gradual fissuring of the poetic and the dramaturgical. His later poetry has a tendency to become the more insistently inward: hence, perhaps, his sense of achievement in the amount of the fully 'public' he managed to bring into his last three *Quartets*; and the theatrical verse struggles against the problem of rhetorical thinness.

Much of Eliot's energy in the making of his plays seems to have gone into that dramaturgy which clearly provoked and delighted him by its difficulty. Play-craft was slowly and laboriously acquired, and remained a conscious, even a public matter, with advice and assistance taken from bystanders. It hardly seems surprising that criticism of the plays has followed Eliot in this. Much of the best work has explicated the plays in terms of conscious purpose, often confining itself to what might be called Eliot's 'spiritual dramaturgy'. One of the best studies, Carol H. Smith's *T. S. Eliot's Dramatic Theory and Practice* (Princeton, New Jersey, 1963), stresses that Eliot 'has chosen poetic drama to accomplish his purpose because it can reach a wider public than other poetic means and, more important, because of the possibilities of creating in drama a total dramatic world in which to demonstrate the divine plan' (p. 29). Almost all academic criticism of the plays has been drawn in this way to a faithful mirroring of Eliot's overt purpose: as if it were conscientiously, and sometimes very successfully, building up his working notebooks for the period covered by the play in question. Carol Smith's account of *Sweeney Agonistes* concentrates on Eliot's conscious effort to revive an ancient ritual drama of death and rebirth; another equally able and representative account, Sears Jayne's 'Mr Eliot's Agon', reads more theologically, seeing in Sweeney himself as much of Christ as of Orestes.[1]

Such accounts no doubt reflect Eliot's purposes. But the poet himself has with some force undermined the role of intention in the making of poetry. And it must be added that, if his dramatic work were exactly like what it is often described as being, it would be intellectually fascinating and thoroughly dead in performance. There have always, of course, been good critics and readers who feel that this is precisely the case. In his short discussion of Eliot's work in the theatre, John Bayley found the plays in the end no more than 'a game of moral philosophy in the theatre . . . cut off in technique and theory from the source of everything spontaneous in his art'.[2] But a good deal has happened in the last twenty years to make this seem more questionable. In the period since his death, the writer's extreme authority has ebbed; and as a result the verse is coming to be appreciated more simply on its own merits. Productions of the plays seem to be improving, a matter not to be entirely dissociated from this lapse of reverence, and response to the plays in performance is surely both sharper and warmer. The Round House *Family Reunion* was as successful as it was brilliant, and a recent production of *The Elder Statesman* was throughout both more detached and more profound (though with the same leading actor,

[1] *PQ*, 34 (1955), 395–414.
[2] 'The Collected Plays', *The Review* (Eliot Number), 4 (November 1962), 3–11 (p. 6).

Paul Rogers) than on its first production twenty years ago — and perhaps also more appreciatively received by its rather smaller audiences. Both plays have been seen to 'work' to a remarkable degree; and such success could not be predicted from the usual academic account of these plays.

This is especially true of *Sweeney Agonistes*. The first of Eliot's plays, it is also the most fragmentary; it possesses least of that 'play-craft' which later work may show. And yet it is interesting that a few critics have seen it as peculiarly dramatic in its own way. In the essay already quoted, John Bayley finds it an exception to the general rule of Eliot's practice, possessed of what he calls an almost 'Brechtian' vitality. Katharine J. Worth, too, praises *Sweeney*'s purely theatrical expressiveness, its derivation (as she sees it) from 'music-hall and minstrel show': '*Sweeney* is very much a play of breaking out and acting out rather than talking out'.[3] This remark suggests some of the problems of this more recent essentially 'theatrical' approach to Eliot's plays. Sympathetic as Katharine Worth's appreciativeness is, this strong stress on what she calls 'the music-hall experience' in *Sweeney Agonistes* fails (to my mind) almost as much as does the 'spiritual dramaturgy' approach to respond to the actual linguistic quality of the work. Symptomatically, Katharine Worth protests at the inclusion of *Sweeney Agonistes* among the 'Unfinished Poems' (rather than with the plays) in the 1969 Collected Edition of Eliot. Both 'spiritual dramaturgists' and theatrical experts alike seem to me to have left aside what makes *Sweeney Agonistes* peculiarly interesting, its character as dramatic *poetry*: a medium that brings Eliot's play-writing into being. Not only have critics failed to appreciate this new and rather startling medium; it has been made the object of savage attack:

'Fragment of an Agon' is defective in execution (save the mark) because the farcical music-hall style, without any indication that Sweeney is deliberately talking down, is an improper vehicle for this serious theme. . . . The critic with no interest in Eliot's idea might find the work strained to grotesqueness by its subject matter, and the only audience likely to be gratified is a morose one with a taste for the frivolously macabre. Eliot's failure seems the more abysmal when the theory from which he was working is traced to its apparent model — De Quincey's essay 'On the Knocking on the Gate in *Macbeth*'.[4]

What is getting signally ignored in this account of *Sweeney Agonistes* by Grover Smith — and indeed more than ignored, positively reviled — is that aspect of art that we like to summarize vaguely as its *medium*. Poetry or drama rightly consists (this seems to be the notion) in a 'serious theme', in 'Eliot's idea'. The whole concept of style is here degraded and trivialized into something artistically shallow and superficial. Even Carol Smith, who writes much more appreciatively of *Sweeney Agonistes*, speaks of its 'comic surface', a covering under which the real stuff of interest, the ritual drama of death and

---

[3] *Revolutions in Modern English Drama* (London, 1972), p. 58; see also 'Eliot and the Living Theatre' in *Eliot in Perspective*, edited by Graham Martin (London, 1970), pp. 151–55.
[4] Grover Smith, *T. S. Eliot's Poetry and Plays* (Chicago, 1956), p. 118.

rebirth, lies snugly awaiting discovery. Such language is sometimes enforced by the needs of finer analysis; but it is always dangerous. An uninterest in or cavalier approach to Eliot's literary or linguistic medium leads to errors which may seem slight but which generate an always-increasing departure from the actual work of art. One such trivial error, which, however, bears directly on what *Sweeney Agonistes* is (to my mind) effecting as a work of art, occurs in another of the essays on the play which I have already mentioned, Sears Jayne's study of what he sees as the play's context of Christianized classical learning as reflected in its epigraphs. When its second section, the 'Fragment of an Agon', was first published in *The Criterion* it was glossed as being 'From *Wanna Go Home, Baby?*'. Jayne concludes: 'The title *Wanna Go Home, Baby?* implied that the language of the play was to be that of the London pub in the 1920's' (p. 397). A title so provokingly flamboyant is certainly likely to imply something, but that it could hardly have implied this, the Supplement to the *OED* might have told Sears Jayne, listing as it does three uses only of 'Baby' in the slang sense of 'girl' before 1930, and all of them from *American* texts only. The surprise Jayne's remark must bring to an English (or Londoner's) ear is supported by information from another, quite different, source: an unpretentious but lively and useful scrapbook on the period put together by Alan Jenkins which tells us decisively that 'the word "baby" as an endearment ("Yes, Sir, That's My Baby") never caught on in Britain, so that unsophisticated British listeners, confronted with a song-title like "I Wonder Where My Baby Is Tonight?", tended to imagine a wayward infant in diapers knocking back cocktails'.[5] And, for what it is worth, though my own memories do not reach back with much effectiveness before the 1940s, they do recall enough from that period of G.I.s and transatlantic hit-tunes to preserve *Baby* as a kind of ideograph of pure (or impure) Americanism. Eliot's earlier proposed title, *Wanna Go Home, Baby?*, suggested, in short, an Americanism all the more highlighted by its linguistic formality: cadenced, derisive and self-conscious.

The 'Americanness' of *Sweeney Agonistes* is indissociable from its meaning, and I shall return to this subject. For the moment it is enough to remark the kind of error that arises when a reader, however expert in other areas, is not much interested in *listening* to poetry. His or her interest must necessarily move to what — if not heard to be there — is by contrast presumed to be there. Hence the concern of much academic criticism with the plot of *Sweeney Agonistes*. In the course of his interesting account of the play, Jayne summarizes some of its plot as follows: 'God, then, invites Doris to the divine union mentioned in the epigraph; pleading physical illness, Doris puts him off until Monday, the day after the Sabbath, in order to have the week-end free for "created beings"; in so doing she has chosen spiritual death (this is why she draws the coffin card)' (p. 407). One would not want precisely to contest this

[5] *The Twenties* (London, 1974), p. 151.

as an account of what may be happening in Eliot's play-poem; in outline the plot sounds likely enough. But if this summary is true, God must be Pereira; and if God is Pereira, God is a ponce. If Eliot can compare the Church to a hippopotamus, he can also (presumably) compare God to a ponce. But 1927 was, after all, the very year in which the poet was baptized and confirmed into the Anglican Church. Any account of the play which stresses such peculiar and yet such purposive meanings as these does not seem consistent with such an act of public profession as this.

It is possible to form ideas about Eliot's 'purposes' (ritual or Aristophanic, Christian or classical) which apply very well to some aspects of these dramatic poems; but if pressed home the results are ridiculous or, in the proper sense, improper. Something of this realization may lie behind the warning note which the poet had appended to the fragments when in 1954 they were included in a collection of one-act plays: 'The author wishes to point out that *Sweeney Agonistes* is not a one-act play and was never designed as such. It consists of two fragments. But as the author has abandoned any intention of completing them, these two fragmentary scenes have frequently been produced as a one-act play.'[6] For there is, one suspects, *no* body of learned materials related to the titles and epigraphs that can be used to make good sense of the dialogue without deformation and impropriety of this kind; and, similarly, no proposed plot adds much to the two fragments as we have them. This seems to be true even of Eliot's own plot-draft as it survives in the Hayward Collection at Cambridge. This draft includes a proposed 'Murder of Mrs Porter' by Sweeney. That almost every reader given to such surmises seems in the past to have assumed that Sweeney's victim was Doris does not prove that *Sweeney Agonistes* is incoherent nonsense; but it does or should arouse some scepticism as to the exact relation of the drafts to what in fact got written. These Hayward Collection drafts have against an earlier form of the title and epigraphs a note in Eliot's hand, saying 'Probably precedes the fragments themselves', as though he too were testifying to changes in the materials as they gradually evolved. Such comments underline, that is, the realization that *Sweeney Agonistes* is like every other poem (and to a lesser extent every other play) that Eliot wrote, in its disjunction between what can be formulated (in terms of 'draft', 'plot', formal and rationalizable 'purpose') and the words that found themselves spoken, the lines that got themselves written. The gradual emergence of what Eliot came (after 1932) to call *Sweeney Agonistes* illustrates how vital it is to leave room for discontinuities in its development: how like, that is to say, the work is in this respect to what we now know of the composition of *The Waste Land* and of *Four Quartets*.

This is perhaps the place to recall briefly what we know of the emergence of *Sweeney Agonistes*. We are lucky to have a contemporary reference to its beginnings, though this needs to be treated as cautiously as all the other

6 *Twenty-four One-Act Plays*, edited by John Hampden, revised edition (London, 1954), p. 346.

materials involved. Eliot happened to visit Arnold Bennett and mentioned his plans, and the event was recorded in Bennett's journal (entry for 10 September 1924). The visit is often made to sound purposive, as if Eliot went to Bennett (whom he knew only slightly) specifically to talk about his play; whereas the context makes it plain that the occasion of the visit was merely to solicit an article for *The Criterion*, and what followed was generated partly by the poet's anxious and urbane courtesy, and partly by the novelist's rather vain, though genial, aggressiveness. Bennett bluffly attacked what he called the 'Wastelands'; Eliot hastened to assure him that he had definitely given up that 'form of writing', 'and was now centred on dramatic writing. He wanted to write a drama of modern life (furnished flat sort of people) in a rhythmic prose "perhaps with certain things in it accentuated by drum-beats". And he wanted my advice. We arranged that he should do the scenario and some sample pages of dialogue'.[7] In the next month Eliot sent the scenario and samples, had them criticized, and returned thanks, describing himself as about to reconstruct the play according to Bennett's advice. Nearly three years later, in June 1927, Bennett was writing to ask whatever became of the 'jazz play'. He was apparently unaware that such of it as was ever to exist had been printed in the numbers of *The Criterion* for October 1926 ('Fragment of a Prologue') and January 1927 ('Fragment of an Agon').

It is worth, I think, laying out this train of events in some detail, so as to ponder the interesting gaps and silences that occur within it. Carol Smith is of the opinion that the two *Sweeney* fragments as we have them were those sent to Bennett in October 1924, and this may very well be so. But there are discrepancies which at least ask to be noticed. Bennett may of course be subject to slips, and the journal account somehow suggests a successful and busy man who was not condescending to listen very hard; all the same, the errors (if they are errors) are odd ones for an extremely capable literary man to make. *Sweeney Agonistes* as we know it does not precisely involve 'furnished flat sort of people', which suggests a downgraded Somerset Maugham world, and more importantly it is not in prose, however rhythmical. Interestingly, another fragment does survive (usefully reprinted by Carol Smith in a footnote, as well as in the programme to the Stage Sixty Theatre Club 'Homage to T. S. Eliot'), and this fragment *is* in prose. It is a finale in which Time enters, 'closely resembling Father Christmas', and speaks in a style which Carol Smith calls 'not quite consistent with the rest of *Sweeney Agonistes*' (p. 63). This is a large understatement: the passage is in fact a piece of lightweight, second-rate, and (one would have said) entirely derivative Audenesque prose. Since this fragment was never published with the other two but only included by Eliot in a 1933 letter to Hallie Flanagan on the occasion of her Vassar production of *Sweeney Agonistes* in that year, it is clearly possible that it was written after the other two. I in fact find it difficult to

<hr />

[7] *The Journals of Arnold Bennett*, edited by Newman Flower, 3 vols (London, 1932–33), III, 52.

believe that Eliot did not add this 'Father Christmas' finale some time after December 1928, when Auden sent him for publication his *Paid on Both Sides*, in one of whose prose passages a 'Father Xmas' figures. At all events this Audenesque prose fragment, while it does not offer any clear evidence as to the actual dating of the two verse fragments, does, if it postdates *Paid on Both Sides*, suggest a work that emerged through different stages and versions. It should encourage, that is, a proper hesitancy concerning Eliot's 'intentions'; for the concept of a single purpose, deriving from a single occasion, becomes as untenable as the notion of a single preserved 'draft'.

Introspective verse like Eliot's (and even a rhetorical drama like his, in so far as it approximates to literature) is clearly always so much of a difficult struggle towards daylight that it is vital for a reader *respicere finem*: to read the words as they emerge on the printed page. Whatever its origins or authorial intentions, *Sweeney Agonistes* begins in print in 1932, when it took the form in which we read it now. And as it stands we read first the section which Eliot evidently wrote first, the 'Fragment of a Prologue' that shows Doris and Dusty at home to their gentlemen friends. Those who attempt to tell the story of *Sweeney Agonistes* have most trouble with this first fragment, for such action as the play might be said to have only gets going (or gets staying) when Sweeney himself appears in the 'Fragment of an Agon'. Eliot, too, deprecated the claims of the first fragment, with that impulse in him which always came to prefer his own 'later stages' as the more articulate and rational, as against the perhaps more obscure if fruitful opening moves. On the other hand, if there is no plot, a good deal is at least *going on* in the 'Fragment of a Prologue'. From the very beginning the poem manifests a furious tragi-comic energy. Energy need not be identified with activity, nor activity with action, nor action with plot, for us to use the word 'dramatic' here: for the intensity is integral with anything we can conceive of (in Eliot's work at least) as an event reflecting relation between the characters. To put it in a phrase, *Sweeney Agonistes* starts with something like an electric shock. Drama moves consequentially, and the opening of *Sweeney Agonistes* makes drama out of the mere astonishing linguistic sequence, from the title through the epigraphs to the dialogue that begins. Eliot's final title, *Sweeney Agonistes: Fragments of an Aristophanic Melodrama*, is powerfully yet frigidly intellectualist; the very word *Agonistes*, with its shadow of Milton's austere unworldly drama, 'never intended for the Stage', and the faint suggestion of 'agonies', darkens the opening like a cold cloud passing over: a darkening intensified by the epigraphs, the first a quotation from Aeschylus ('Orestes: *You don't see them, you don't — but* I *see them: they are hunting me down,* I *must move on*') and the second from St John of the Cross ('*Hence the soul cannot be possessed of the divine union, until it has divested itself of the love of created beings*'). Obliquity here complicates negation, as the mind is lost in the structures both of quotation and of argument, in a rhetoric both conditional and abstract. By the time we arrive at the sub-sub-title, 'Fragment of a Prologue', the opening introducing-apparatus has taken the form of an enormously top-heavy structure: which mutates into the Senecan stichomythia of 'DUSTY. DORIS' as the play begins:

DUSTY: How about Pereira?
DORIS: What about Pereira?
         I don't care.
DUSTY: You don't care!
         Who pays the rent?
DORIS: Yes he pays the rent
DUSTY: Well some men don't and some men do
         Some men don't and you know who
DORIS: You can have Pereira.

The extreme formality of this opening can hardly fail to draw to our attention a simple fact: that there is a difference between 'reading' and 'reading in'. The prolegomena reflect (as they attract and justify) the work of scholarship and criticism; in some real sense a Christian ritual drama 'lies behind' *Sweeney Agonistes*, as Eliot's chosen epigraphs from Aeschylus and St John of the Cross 'stand above' his printed fragments, and as the word 'Aristophanic' follows the title he finally settled for. The difficulty occurs when the two kinds of material are brought together (as Grover Smith indignantly recorded): when the superstructure comes in contact with the dialogue. For not to record a hilarious discrepancy is, in some sense that matters extremely in literature, not to read the work at all.

That *Sweeney Agonistes* might be funny (extremely funny — and consequently, and equally, touchingly sad) is a truth not often admitted in orthodox accounts of the poem. This can only be because those who write them do not attend to the actual words: do not notice details like, for instance, the impassive lack of punctuation, which 'answers' the appalling self-contradictory super-literacy of the opening with a subliteracy in the circumstances almost refreshing. A kind of implicit production-note that works equally well on the page or audibly, this absence of pointing makes the girls seem startlingly to be writing *their own dialogue*. Given the extreme intellectualism of the context, this makes Doris and Dusty appear alive and kicking in a world of glossaria: mere commentary, notes and queries. The complex split in sympathies involved here provokes a violent laughter, that specifically 'hysterical' or sad laughter that attends the girls throughout, a tribute to their capacity to collapse empty cultures. This can perhaps be put more technically: the vitality of Eliot's writing in *Sweeney Agonistes* derives from a tension here represented as distance between styles, something anticipated in the satirical styles, burlesque and mock-heroic, of *The Waste Land*. The move into formal drama only accentuates the distance between, and yet the close marriage of, the 'commentary' on the one hand and the agents on the other: the great Christian-classical panoply, and the two girls' squeakily obdurate voices, as basic, as classic in their way as the *Choephoroi* in its way ('I don't care' and 'Who pays the rent?'). It is a part of the construction of this echo-chamber that the given passage from the ancient tragedy ('You don't see them . . . but I see them') just happens to use a form of helplessly self-repeating monosyllabic utterance not unlike the illiterate tautologies of the chattering girls. To marry them truly, to raise the 'low' to the power of the 'high', is the task Eliot has set himself.

Grover Smith has regretted that Eliot made the mistake of utilizing a 'farcical music-hall style' which was improper for the work's 'serious theme'. This is near to the art of sinking in criticism. For throughout *Sweeney Agonistes*, as in these few opening lines, Eliot is moving burlesque towards a brilliant and new dramatic poetry. He is discovering a voice that permits him to do what is most necessary for any dramatist but perhaps for any poet most difficult: to create an idiom that will lastingly give utterance to lives and beings quite unlike his own. He has done so by giving a grave intellectual context to a medium unused in serious English drama, certainly in verse, for centuries: the medium of the comic demotic. And he is enabled to do so because he has learned to call into account a peculiarity of personal situation: his dislocation between two available traditions. The intellectual context is only as alien to the two girls as the character of Sweeney is to that of Doris; or as the ancient European tradition is to the new American, and each equally far away, each equidistant as it were, from the expatriated unacademic Eliot of the Twenties.

For this is (or so I would suggest) the heart of what Eliot is doing in *Sweeney Agonistes*: he is making a dramatic voice for himself by 'calling in the new world to redress the balance of the old', writing, one might say, a European tragi-comedy in American. I have tried elsewhere to suggest that Eliot had originally hoped that *The Waste Land* might bring together a 'poetry of America' (in the rejected opening section) with a 'poetry of Europe'; just as we should perhaps see him in *Four Quartets*, and especially of course in 'The Dry Salvages', 'domesticating' French Symbolism, humanizing and Christianizing it by rooting it in English and American landscape and history.[8] *Sweeney Agonistes* has a place in this exceedingly ambitious programme. It brings together a great if largely 'dead' European culture with a vital if debased modern American speech, marrying (one might say) Seneca to Doris. And like many other large national and racial resettlements, the job is done essentially at the level of language. To appreciate the scale of the enterprise, it will be necessary to pause and consider rather more exactly the language of these two fragments.

I have already referred in passing to Sears Jayne's assumption that *Wanna Go Home, Baby?* calls up 'the London pub of the 1920's': an assumption worth noting, because it summarizes the major critical response to the fragments'

---

[8] 'Eliot's Marianne: *The Waste Land* and its Poetry of Europe', *RES*, 31 (1980), 41–53; and 'Eliot's *Four Quartets* and French Symbolism', *English*, 29 (1980), 1–37.

language, invariably gestured at as 'the common speech of the time'. The exactness of Jayne's slip is fruitful and helpful. For one of Eliot's problems as a dramatist was of course that of localization, of being able to show his characters in terms of a specific habitat: a task made peculiarly difficult by his own cultural displacement, however central that displacement was (in other senses) to a great period of expatriation and exile. All Eliot's poems in fact manage to generate an intense sense of place, without at the same time making it at all easy to say where the place in question actually is.

Sweeney Agonistes is certainly no exception. Jayne's allusion to the 'London pub', though falsely dependent on *The Waste Land* and (I believe) wrong in fact, since the poem does not take place in a pub whether or not in London, at the same time has some point. Many of the speech-intonations of Doris and Dusty certainly seem to be those of smartened-up South London: Balham or Tooting, say, around 1920, and gone up in the world. Sweeney himself equally certainly has relations in or with a distinctively suburban seedy squalor. The murder he is haunted by is of a piece with those great grubby 'mere English' murders, often for love and often by poison, that filled *The News of the World* through the 1920s. This is a milieu of lower-middle-class violence that evidently fascinated Eliot, perhaps by virtue of the way its mixture of the genteel and the seamy offered challenge and resistance to the beglamorizing tastefulness of late Victorian poetry. There are obvious links backward from here to *The Waste Land*, more indeed than are explicit or are usually guessed at by critics. The most notorious murder of the period was the horrifying and pathetic Thompson-Bywaters case of 1922, in which the pitiable romantic Edith Bywaters encouraged her young lover to deal with her brutal older husband by taking a lesson from *Bella Donna*, the Robert Hitchens best-seller of a decade earlier, about a *femme fatale* who attempts to murder her innocent young husband by feeding him digitalis. Eliot was (in my view) perhaps remembering one or two striking moments from this in fact well-written and absorbing novel in his Thames-scapes in 'The Fire Sermon', as well as recalling the title in 'The Burial of the Dead' ('Here is Belladonna, The Lady of the Rocks, | The Lady of Situations'). This interest in a terrain that could be called peculiarly 'English' at that period — an elusive but strong-flavoured, haunting blend of the violent and the seedy, the aspiringly hopeless and the grubbily romantic — is certainly to be found again in *Sweeney Agonistes*, and gives an odd complex substance to its theoretical design.

And yet that Englishness is radically qualified. The speech-style of Doris and Dusty, at the opening, may consciously reproduce the Cockney, but all the same it is wholly unlike the loquacious aggressive drawl of Lil's friend in 'A Game of Chess'. The staccato machine-gun-fire exchanges of the two girls, as it might be a high-kicking chorus-line of two: this is something else again, something nervous and new. Where did Eliot get it from, this jazz-age or machine-gun-fire style that contributes so much to the force of his fragments? Despite its lower-class London sound, it is worth noticing that the girls' phrasing in fact blends perfectly with the diction of their American and Canadian visitors: which, like the predominant style of 'Fragment of an Agon' and indeed of Sweeney himself, is by no means mere English:

> I gotta use words when I talk to you
> But if you understand or if you don't
> That's nothing to me and nothing to you
> We all gotta do what we gotta do
> We're gona sit here and drink this booze
> We're gona sit here and have a tune
> We're gona stay and we're gona go
> And somebody's gotta pay the rent.

The idiom of both fragments is somewhat changeable, just as, in the second, routines from Broadway vaudeville are followed by a pastiche of W. S. Gilbert. All the same, hard listening to Sweeney's idiom added to the Irish connotations of his name hardly leave one in much doubt as to his transatlantic place of origin: a certainty which rapidly grows to positive suspicion that his friend —

> I knew a man once did a girl in.
> Any man might do a girl in

— was surely a Chicago gangster. The American gangsters of the 1920s tended to specialize in the distribution of liquor; and the need to take the drinks to Doris's flat (from which the action never moves, unless Sweeney is to scramble his eggs in that 'London pub') bespeaks the time and place of the speakeasy, the private club and party of the Prohibition period. Alan Jenkins (to stay within the field of sources quoted earlier) actually gives a list of the names of these leading Chicago gangsters: 'Orazio "the Scourge" Tropea, Murray "the Camel" Humphries, Spike O'Donnell, Sam "Golf Bag" Hunt, Dingbat O'Berta, Jake "Greasy Thumb" Guzik, Hymie "Loud Mouth" Levine, and Machine Jack McGurn' (p. 130). Among these, Sweeney 'the Poet' Agonistes would fit with no trouble at all.

It is this predominant Americanness which Eliot was clearly advertising in his first title, *Wanna Go Home, Baby?*; an Americanness which is more than a mere matter of diction — it affects the vision and substance of the whole:

DORIS: I don't care
DUSTY: You don't care!
        Who pays the rent?

This is not like Lil's friend; it is the speech of a different time, a different continent. Seneca may call it stichomythia, but America calls it the wisecrack pure and simple. Moreover, the girls are something new in Eliot's work: Doris and Dusty affront their fate with a blatant insolence that is almost a latterday innocence. The most appropriate critical reaction to the opening of *Sweeney Agonistes* would be the respectful acknowledgement that a learned, obscure, and inward poet had managed to invent the Dumb Blonde in literature: that T. S. Eliot had fathered Marilyn Monroe. For, given the peculiar intellectual and spiritual context that introduces and entraps the two girls, Dumb Blondes are what they contrastingly define themselves as being. From Doris's marvellously dogged dark mindlessness ('I'd like to know about that coffin') to the bright limits of her more cheerfully competent friend Dusty ('Well I never! What did I tell you?'), this farcically blank and yet diamond-hard address to life is, whether Balham or Bronx, the speech of a quite new type, a caricature of the female that lasted for more than a half-century, and is only now going into recession.

Eliot did not, of course, invent the Dumb Blonde. But *Sweeney Agonistes* was put together at a time extremely close to her invention, and I find it difficult to believe that he wrote in complete ignorance of that event. In fact, I would suggest that it may have been that very invention which helped the realization of an impulse towards drama that, for lack of a proper style, was proving little more than abortive; it found him a glittering new set of conventions more seductive than anything his vague sense of 'furnished flat sort of people' could provide. Probably the most significant event in the evolution of the Dumb Blonde occurred in the year before Eliot published his fragments in *The Criterion*. Through the spring and summer of 1925 a young writer brought out, in six monthly episodes in the American *Harper's Bazaar*, a series of little stories which met such enormous success that she was able to publish them in book form in the late autumn of that year (and English publication followed early in 1926). The book proved one of the great best-sellers, not only of the 1920s, but of several succeeding decades: William Empson put bits of it into a poem, and Santayana cited it ('with a grin', so the flattered author says in her autobiography) when asked to name the best philosophical work by an American. The book in question (which is, of course, *Gentlemen Prefer Blondes*, and the writer Anita Loos) is the self-told success story of a cherubic-faced nail-hard amateur whore or 'gold-digger', Lorelei Lee of Little Rock, and her story opens:

A gentleman friend and I were dining at the Ritz last evening and he said that if I took a pencil and a paper and put down all of my thoughts it would make a book . . . I mean I seem to be thinking practically all of the time . . . So this gentleman said a girl with brains ought to do something else with them besides think.

Accompanied by her much nicer, cleverer, but less successful friend Dorothy, Lorelei gets herself educated, her tutors consisting mainly of people like 'Gus Eisman, the Button King', and 'Sam . . . who is a famous playwright who writes very, very famous plays'; although it is always open to the reader to feel that if any educating is done, it is Lorelei who does it: 'When I came out of it, it seems that I had a revolver in my hand and it seems that the revolver had shot Mr Jennings.'[9]

---

[9] Quoted from the English edition, pp. 11, 48.

Gentlemen Prefer Blondes is a splendidly sustained if unrepeatable joke about being a woman in a world usually run by men like Gus and Sam. And most of its peculiar force and flavour come from the brilliant invention of its personal style. This structure of complex crudities, the 'Lorelei style', is a pure urban-pastoral medium of the 1920s, capable of seeming to sum up in its cadences — with a limpidity that hung in the air for decades — the whole difficulty of maintaining innocence at this late point in human history. Thus, sentences like 'Fun is fun but no girl wants to laugh all of the time' (the one which haunted Empson) or the more famous 'Kissing your hand may make you feel very very good but a diamond and safire bracelet lasts forever' manage to absorb into themselves the whole dissolution of Victorian romanticism in the anarchistic unillusioned 1920s (even Lorelei's shoddy-Wagnerian name packs its own specific punch). But this potent and suggestive stylistic device hardly started, strictly speaking, with Anita Loos, whose invention was largely dependent on an acknowledged master, a writer far more serious and accomplished than herself. This was the journalist and humorist, Ring Lardner. Though he himself no doubt learned from predecessors in the American tradition (Mark Twain offers himself as the obvious forebear in the mimetic vernacular line), Lardner was enough of an original genius to have had a real place in the beginnings of *Sweeney Agonistes*. He deserves a moment's consideration on this ground; for he helps, I think, to give quite as sure a sense of what the poem's real background is as does a mere word like 'Aristophanic'.

Beyond the world of the Ph.D. student (if there) Lardner hardly seems to be remembered now, certainly not in England. And yet by 1926, the year of the publication of the first fragment in *The Criterion*, Lardner had become one of the 'ten best-known men' in America. And the year before, writing in *The Saturday Review of Literature*, Virginia Woolf (unlikely as it may seem) spoke of this baseball commentator and comic journalist as writing 'the best prose that has come our way' — a fact which brings Lardner closer to Eliot's world. But Lardner was in fact born within that world. He came from an educated, sophisticated, and highly literate milieu not much unlike Eliot's own, though one that had lost all its money. He was the friend of Scott Fitzgerald, and is said to be portrayed in Abe North of *Tender is the Night*: Abe, 'who was desperate and witty', and 'his achievement, fragmentary, suggestive and surpassed' (Fitzgerald's very description of his work brings him a little closer to *Sweeney*). Grover Smith has postulated, in fact, that *The Great Gatsby* is an important source for *Sweeney Agonistes*, partly on the ground that Eliot is known to have written in admiration to its author when the novel appeared in 1925, partly because the novel contains a list of grotesque names and a comic telephone conversation. But Fitzgerald's romantic novel seems to me extremely unlike Eliot's savagely funny play-poem; Fitzgerald's names and telephone conversations are naturalistically or sociologically used, Eliot's are highly conventionalized and edged towards black farce. But the connexion is interesting on quite other grounds. It was Lardner who read the proofs of *The Great Gatsby* for Fitzgerald, correcting its writer's always shaky grammar and spelling as he went along; and Grover Smith may well be (or so I would suggest) unconsciously remarking the evidences of Lardner's influence on both Fitzgerald and Eliot. For it is Lardner who is the original inventor, both of preposterous American names ('Mr Kloot', 'Rube de Groot', 'Mrs Garrison', 'Mr and Mrs Glucose') far closer to Eliot's own, and also of play and story titles ('Some Like Them Cold', 'What Of It?', 'How to Write Short Stories') that mix the nonsensical and the self-undercuttingly vernacular in a manner very like *Wanna Go Home, Baby?* and *Sweeney Agonistes*. More importantly, it is the now forgotten Lardner who made a whole literary generation suddenly aware of how to use ironic, self-exposing conventions of vernacular speech and habit, such as the telephone monologue: several of his most brilliant stories involve persons who betray their innocently detestable personalities in letter-writing. It is possible, in short, to trace back to Ring Lardner, but certainly not much further, a startling number of the most potent literary inventions of the 1920s and 1930s (Hemingway's intensely idiosyncratic style, for instance, is as much indebted to Lardner as to Gertrude Stein: Hemingway was highly impressed by Lardner when young, though he angrily rejected his influence later). This one man, baseball reporter and short-story writer, seems personally responsible for a surprising number of the conventions of the whole sophisticated, melancholy, nonsensical, and racy humour that develops in America in the 1920s, and of which both the Marx Brothers (or their scriptwriters) and some of the best *New Yorker* writers of the period were products.

Lardner like Eliot worked with success in the theatre, and produced through the 1920s revue-sketches, playlets, and musical numbers against which it makes some sense to see *Sweeney Agonistes*. His 1925 volume, *What Of It?*, for instance, includes three brief (three-page) 'plays', all of them (unlike many other parodies of modernism) marked by real wit, humour, and poetry. After an opening procedure as lengthy as Eliot's introductory apparatus, *I Gaspiri* (or 'The Upholsterers') goes on:

> . . . *Two strangers to each other meet on the bath mat*
> First stranger.
> Where was you born?
> Second stranger.
> Out of wedlock.
> First Stranger.
> That's a mighty pretty country around there.
> Second stranger.
> Are you married?
> First stranger.
> I don't know. There's a woman living with me, but I can't place her.
> (pp. 45–46)

This nonsensicality is not uncharacteristic of Lardner. But all the same, his very best work is a good deal tougher; and it is to be found outside his writing for the theatre. Lardner began life as a baseball reporter, and never entirely lost his connexion with baseball; what he clearly did lose, though, was his early capacity for focusing a kind of personal idealism on the game, for finding in it a quality of inarticulate myth. As Virginia Woolf observed, games are vital to Lardner's art, and 'the game' became in his writing, as disillusionment set in, an image of what we have learned to call the 'rat-race'. Long before Berne, he became expert in 'the games people play', a bitter expertise paralleled if not reflected in what Eliot has learned to do in the card- reading, the dance routines, the lovebird talk, and the story-telling of *Sweeney Agonistes*. In terms of the 'games they play', Lardner moved outward from his baseball players to portray a whole mean and crooked and complacent, small- town-minded, success-obsessed and money-hunting culture: the America of the pre-Slump 1910s and 1920s as he came to see it. There is an immense detailed realism in Lardner's laconically comic writing. His 'reporting' brings alive a whole continent of tiny self-contained worlds, self- defining egos: crooks, baseball players, smalltime business men, haircutters, Hollywood executives, middle-aged housewives, and 'Thurber' husbands (Thurber was influenced by Lardner too). But the talent that achieves this breadth is both specific and peculiar. It was a highly formalized gift for verbal mimesis. Everything in Lardner is ironic monologue (such as the rejected opening of *The Waste Land* tried and failed to be): his characters come alive and address us off the page, unintroduced and uncommented on, in their own purely individual speech or lingo; but they exist only within severe limits of the self-preserving ego, and with a serene self-possession never remotely impaired by the frightful, though usually comic, insights that their sometimes pathetic self-revelations precipitate.

This painfully funny, melancholy and often lethal talent is in no way easy to exemplify. It depends on a flawless art, controlled through a whole story, and on the impressive variety of verbal types Lardner can handle. One characteristic story, 'My Roomy', may be worth mentioning, though; because it is just conceivable that Eliot read this anecdote of a baseball Coriolanus (whose name is, oddly enough, Elliott) when it first appeared in *The Saturday Review of Literature* during the summer of 1914, while the young graduate Eliot was working on his philosophy thesis at Harvard and taking boxing lessons in his spare time. He certainly dated back Sweeney's real-life source to around this time; if he read it (as he might have, given his interest at all periods in the demotic) it left an image in his mind, which at one moment emerged as 'Sweeney Erect' and at another became the grander, more haunted Sweeney 'in conflict', 'in the game'. Elliott, whose story is told by a hard-headed senior player, is a lonely, half-mad, and heroic innocent, winning huge baseball victories simply to earn the money to marry the girl he probably knows all the time is already married anyway and whom in the end he near-murders with a baseball bat, before being taken off to an asylum:

Another o' his habits was the thing that scared 'em, though. He'd brought a razor with him — in his pocket, I guess — and he used to do his shavin' in the middle o' the night. Instead o' doin' it in the bathroom he'd lather his face and then come out and stand in front o' the lookin'-glass on the dresser. Of course he'd have all the lights turned on, and that was bad enough when a feller wanted to sleep; but the worst of it was that he'd stop shavin' every little while and turn round and stare at the guy who was makin' a failure o' tryin' to sleep. Then he'd wave his razor round in the air and laugh, and begin shavin' again. You can imagine how comf'table his roomies felt![10]

It was in this same magazine, *The Saturday Review of Literature*, that just over a decade later, in August 1925, Virginia Woolf published her essay on 'American Fiction' from which I have already quoted. She says there that what most deeply impresses her about Lardner's work is the absolute self-sufficiency which both the writer himself and his characters manifest. 'He is not merely himself intent on his own game, but his characters are equally intent on theirs. . . . Mr Lardner is not merely unaware that we differ; he is unaware that we exist'. Virginia Woolf profoundly admires this (as she takes it) pure Americanism, this calm uninterestedness in the European. It is in this spirit that men like Lardner are, she concludes, creating a new literature:

All the expressive ugly vigorous slang which creeps into use among us first in talk, later in writing, comes from across the Atlantic. Nor does it need much foresight to predict that when words are being made, a literature will be made out of them. Already we hear the first jars and dissonances, the strangled difficult music of the prelude. As we shut our books and look out again upon the English fields a strident note rings in our ears.[11]

It is, it seems to me, this 'note' of the American that we hear in *Sweeney Agonistes*: a specific and new music Eliot is half inventing and half learning for his own purposes. The quality in Lardner that Virginia Woolf sensed unerringly is surely that which attracted Eliot even more strongly: for 'self-sufficiency' is the attribute a would-be dramatist most needs to endow his characters with, and yet one too that is most difficult for an inward poet to learn. It may even be Lardner's supreme possession of it that inclined the poet towards attempting drama in prose, and made him also try to think like the American journalist in terms of a very specific social milieu in *Sweeney Agonistes*. He had already, in the rightly-rejected introductory monologue of *The Waste Land* ('First we had a couple of feelers down at Tom's place'), found out how alluring but how difficult was the colloquial American style perfected by Mark Twain and by Ring Lardner. If in his 'jazz-age' poem Eliot came strikingly nearer to Lardner's subtle and brilliant demotic speech, something that combined the fragmentary sophisticated farce of *I Gaspiri* with the dry pathetic violence of 'My Roomy', then the reason may have been that the task suddenly became easier. Through Lardner's chief pupil, Anita Loos, Lorelei Lee's electric-drilling sweetly-lethal note ('Fun is

---

[10] Reprinted in *How to Write Short Stories* (1926), pp. 181–216 (p. 188).
[11] *Collected Essays*, 4 vols (London, 1966) II, 121.

fun but no girl wants to laugh all of the time') brought the vernacular style straight into the demotic urban present of Prohibition, and gangsters, and Broadway vaudeville; and so offered the poet (always in any case more interested in the metropolitan than the provincial) precisely the medium he needed. Eliot recognized — so we may conjecture — a transcription of Lardner's achievement simple enough to catch the ear and strong enough to be imitated; for a helpless infectiousness is of the essence of this style. Fired, amused, and perhaps even moved, the poet at last 'saw' his prose sketches in 'jazz-age' verse, a highly Eliotic verse but 'after' Lardner and Loos. Some such background is, it seems to me, necessary to explain the peculiar achievement of the style of *Sweeney Agonistes*.

I have dwelt on the medium of *Sweeney Agonistes* and its apparent satirical antecedents because in ignoring this stylistic medium criticism has neglected what is most vital to the work. Drama came to Eliot from the beginning not as a dramaturgy but as an identifying speech, the self-defining language of the isolated. In all his verse the poet is perhaps the greatest literary stylist of the modern period, his inventions and experiments in the verbal medium always cognate with what is deepest in his meaning. This is more than ever so in the first of the dramas, for *Sweeney Agonistes* is a work that *listens*: 'I gotta use words when I talk to you.' Anyone can quote this line from Eliot, a fact that makes us realize that *Sweeney Agonistes* is one of the most commonly quoted, the most rememberable of all the poet's works. Its harsh utterances are somehow conjunct with the ironical and yet normative speech of the mind: it says what we need to say. Its way-out elements, from the *Choephoroi* to Doris, seem to cancel each other out, to reduce each other down to a fantastic metaphor for normalcy. In the process, the limits of an impoverished speech act for Eliot, rather as Lardner's 'games' did for him, as an aesthetic discipline; a narrow vocabulary in constant repetition moves towards an expressive music:

> There's an awful lot in the way you feel
> Sometimes they'll tell you nothing at all
> You've got to know what you want to ask them
> You've got to know what you want to know . . .
>
> I've been born, and once is enough.
> You don't remember, but I remember,
> Once is enough.

Sweeney Agonistes comes to have this effect because the work is the first in Eliot's career which puts into the simplest practice that principle of humility expressed morally in *Four Quartets*. Its universe is a world of sound in which people share a single speech style ('I gotta use words') which scarcely even distinguishes them from the inanimate. The girls 'speak', but so does a telephone: *Ting a ling ling,|Ting a ling ling*; the door says KNOCK KNOCK KNOCK just like Wauchope and co., the cards have a story to tell, as

Sweeney does. In 'A Game of Chess', rich woman and poor were equal in the intensity of their egoism; *Sweeney Agonistes* goes further and envisages the world (almost as in the Elizabethan *Orchestra*) as one uttering and dancing and suffering comic movement, a medium of universal even if degraded speech:

> We're all hearts. You can't be sure . . .
> What comes next? . . . What comes next . . .
> You cut for luck. You cut for luck.
> ~~It might break the spell. You cut for luck.~~

The eloquence of *The Waste Land* lies in the way it turns fragments of broken civilizations into metaphors of feeling. *Sweeney Agonistes* goes in a direction almost opposite, and makes metaphors out of the *uncivilized*. Its author has fallen in love with the expressive power of inarticulacy, with a brute and vulgar lingo of incommunication in which Tooting and Brooklyn meet and mix. Trashy phrases in the poem linger in the mind with a weight that is ironical, but that goes beyond irony into the dramatic; beyond the 'purposive', one might say, into the truly aesthetic: 'We're all hearts. You can't be sure.' The academic critic who demotes or disregards the 'farcical music-hall style', the 'improper vehicle for [a] serious theme', is neglecting plain aesthetic fact. For the two girls' agitated interest in the playing-cards (like the reader, they believe that they exist enough to have a fate) and Sweeney's painfully heavy-breathing and struggling anxiety become equally an expression of an almost vatic utterance freed from pretension or pomposity. Such characters are found a diction, an East Side or East End guttural half invented by the erudite and talented in two continents, that by its taciturn, even Tacitean, omissions achieves wit, even profundity, even a form of necessity. If Eliot did not 'finish' his play it is because he did not need to; it was completed when Sweeney and Doris were found a speech.

For the language of the play itself implies that action sought for in 'plot'. By its omissions and implications, by virtue of what is not quite said, it can imply whole dimensions of human relationship. This is an aspect of Eliot's art more explored by later writers like Beckett or (at a lower level) by Pinter; but in *Sweeney Agonistes* the potentialities are present. Thus, though the two fragments do not have a plot, they gesture towards a dramatic situation by the very nature of their duality, the one against the other. The first is given to Doris's and Dusty's party, the second to Sweeney's apprehension of aloneness. Together they suggest that Sweeney, who has fallen in love with Doris, tries to draw her away from her unindividuated role within the party, her degradedly social existence, to make her a person: to make her help him understand aloneness so they can be together. This implicit dramatic situation, which is perceived simply through 'the way they talk', is reflected in the repetition of two threadbare but enigmatically touching lines, Doris's miserable and silly 'A woman runs a terrible risk' answered by Snow's patient 'Let Mr Sweeney continue his story'. The two lines match, like an unrhymed couplet in bathetic heroic verse; and the situations rhyme too, Doris's second-rate company-seeking fear and dreariness silenced by Sweeney's dogged attempt to understand and hold by such truth as lies to hand. Or this situation will reverse itself: Sweeney's in any case sensational and melodramatic insights take on an essential weakness in the terrible tough absolute presence of Doris ('I'd be bored . . . I'd be bored'). And his failure, under her eyes, like an elephant's before a mouse, comes through the diminuendo of the ironic and pastiche pop-songs of love and death that dissolve into the mechanism of her unvarying negation:

> I don't like eggs; I never liked eggs . . .
> That's not life, that's no life.

There is an important difference between the characters of Sweeney and Doris in this work and those in 'Sweeney Among the Nightingales'. The earlier poem presents its persons with a flat contempt and disgust. But the personages of these fragments, within their curiously universalizing wild rhythms for which the cant term 'swinging' is totally appropriate though not yet invented in that sense — these persons are more like the characters in Eliot's cat poems; they may not be amiable but there is something to be said for them. When Doris here states flatly 'I'd be bored', it is not absolutely clear that there is no virtue in her point of view (as in Dusty's answer to the men's avowal that they 'like London fine': 'Why don't you come and live here then?'). We are, however obscurely, for the moment ready to concede that each has something to say. Eliot has in short achieved the self-sufficient embodiment of drama. Writing much later in life, he glanced back at his own *The Family Reunion* and remarked provocatively that the characters for whom he now felt most sympathy were Amy and the chauffeur. The remark shows how much, when he achieved an actual embodying language, it could leave his persons free to alter despite his purpose, or what at least such things as plot-drafts induce us to call his purpose. The terrible Doris and Dusty are clearly meant to illustrate, morally and satirically, the human inability to be alone, which is 'to be' — and they do; but at the same time the force of what they say puts life into them. Doris's decisive 'I'd be bored' to Sweeney's fierce vision of existence has a kind of authorial amusement inside it: her touching idiocy is sometimes, out of mere self-interest, on the verge of being good sense. Similarly, her sombre 'I'd like to know about that coffin' hovers between the farcical and the troublingly sane, since despite all her self-important superstition she is right in her assumption that coffins are a question demanding sooner or later to be gone into.

Particularly in its relation of Sweeney and the girls the whole of the work has this intense humour that fades into pathos, and a final vision hesitating between farce and pain, with an effect of odd aesthetic beauty deriving from the exactness of their balance. The good-time girls in their rented flat sit waiting for 'gentlemen friends' whose apotheosis is Sweeney: hunted, haunted, brutish and out of touch, intersected by alarming and even nonsensical glimpses of love and death which he can neither wholly possess nor be possessed by, there is not much 'fun' for them here. None the less, the situation is in its poise dramatic. And it is made so by the discovery of a medium that embodies the speaking self by isolating it. The essential quality of the people in *Sweeney Agonistes* is that they are free-standing, unlike the figures of *The Waste Land*, who are always contained within the moral criterion of the presenter, Tiresias. The people in *Sweeney Agonistes* are what they are, despite all the diminution that the purpose of the play seems to impose upon them:

> He didn't know if he was alive
> and the girl was dead
> He didn't know if the girl was alive
> and he was dead
> He didn't know if they were both alive
> or both were dead . . .

It is striking that Sweeney's one action is to try to tell a story. Eliot's plays do maintain a real if ambiguous relation to story: the mind that created them clearly loved stories, but in process what it most seems to love is untelling them, turning them on their head or inside out, as *Four Quartets* does with chronology. Thus, Sweeney defends his own stasis:

> What did he do! What did he do?
> That don't apply.

In *The Cocktail Party*, which opens after the end of a 'story' that may have been well worth hearing but whose point is that 'there *were* no tigers', Julia takes this up with what Eliot may have seen as specifically female perspicuity, not unlike Doris's and Dusty's:

> Then what were you doing, up in a tree,
> You and the Maharajah?

Sweeney and Doris are clearly up in the same gum-tree, illogically planted in an action in which

> Nobody came
> And nobody went

and for which, consequently, there is no plot. But self-evidently something is (as we say) 'going on', something interpretable variously, perhaps a crime or perhaps just a metaphor. But at whatever level we choose to interpret these goings-on, they possess a *style*: the means by which we recognize that what is before us is not *The Cocktail Party* but *Sweeney Agonistes*.

It is for this reason that I have chosen to talk about Eliot's play, not as involving its Christian-classical context, not even as a 'game of moral philosophy' (relevant as these matters certainly are), but in terms of Eliot's capacity to learn from other writers very different in their ends how flexible, how sophisticated, and even at moments how deep a medium the tragicomic vernacular could be. In the hands of its best exponents this demotic medium could do almost anything — anything except reach that poetic absoluteness of utterance that Eliot had to look elsewhere to find (primarily, in my view, in French Symbolist literature). To turn back to Lardner's stories from *Sweeney Agonistes* is to understand why Lardner himself, intelligent and aesthetic as he was, always condemned himself as a total failure. For his narrow, bitter, and accurate reports on experience are a journalist's triumph, but as works of art they are severely limited. Eliot took the style and used it to explore and embody states of mind considerably more inward and (if one wants) metaphysical:

> If he was alive then the milkman wasn't
> and the rent-collector wasn't
> And if they were alive then he was dead.

The effect of this borrowed style is certainly to give to *Sweeney Agonistes* that effect of limitation, even of sterility, which irritates many of its academic critics, who would compare it to its loss with the major poem it follows: the richly eloquent *Waste Land*. But it is precisely this diminishment which is the writer's first decisive step towards dramatic focus and precision. Moreover, the work's final quality is one that is dependent on this very limitation. An inarticulate medium — used as metaphor, and with flaws, dissonances, changes of key within its conventions — generates an odd, dreamy, pathetic, and comic detachment, as of a removed diffused tenderness, which extends and blurs the harshness of the 'story's' outlines. This is a quality summed up in the title Eliot invented for use elsewhere, 'Doris's Dream Songs'; neither Lardner's nor Anita Loos's characters really have the capacity to dream. Through these two fragments of drama by Eliot, injected in them perhaps by the dislocations of their given titles and sub-titles, the assonance between the epigraphs and what follows, there moves an irrational power of reverie: so that the swirling repetitions of the converse seem not merely the resource of empty mindlessness, but the probing hesitancies of uncertain thought; and brute platitude turns into a feeling for the basic such as no mere brute could articulate — rather, the feeling for 'the bottom' that a drowning man might helplessly engage in:

> . . . it might be you
>   Or it might be you
> We're all hearts. You can't be sure.
> It just depends on what comes next . . .
> I've been born, and once is enough . . .
> I tell you again it don't apply
> Death or life or life or death . . .
> KNOCK KNOCK KNOCK

In the French classical theatre the play starts with three knocks. Sweeney's fragment ends with a beginning, an awakening from the dream of the play. Until that moment, a girl runs a terrible risk; but let Mr Sweeney continue his story.

Wyndham Lewis:
The Satirist as Barbarian

HUGH KENNER

The Johns Hopkins University

Satire, unlike song or epos or simple narrative, is a radically *written* genre, impossible — inconceivable — without the textual storage and recall that has been possible for only twenty-eight centuries. It requires that the language by which we recount events be externalized for inspection, the way only writing externalizes: externalized moreover into literature's defined genres with their concomitant apparatus of expectations. By contrast, the talker, performing as he must amid shared acoustic fluidities, can mock, can cruelly mock, but he cannot satirize. Satire's technologies are not at his disposal.

The spoken, as any crowd knows, is experience we share; whereas the written, as English Augustans understood, is an artifact for men of sense to appraise. We share speech by participation; in joining the mocker we turn against his victim, who will be fortunate if he is not hooted out of the tribe before nightfall. But writing is assessed by judgement, cool and external; in detecting the manipulations of the satirist we come to perceive his victim (and likely ourselves) as entrapped in a kind of metaphysical warp. Something has proved to be wrong on a very large scale, and in a way resistant to our analytic habits. These habits may even be part of what is wrong. What were we doing, sagely nodding our heads as the Modest Proposer prattled about the sheer nuisance of being assailed by beggars? Is *that* a way to state the Irish Problem?

Accordingly, satire manipulates whole systems of perception, notably the literary genres and their potential for overlayering. It addresses itself to book-people like ourselves, persuading us that we have picked up a pamphlet about economic distress in Ireland, or a narrative of voyages into several remote nations of the world, or a brief epic to celebrate a lady who kept her virtue at the cost of some hairs.[1] We had expected the apposite satisfaction: social zealotry's lubricious narcissism, the voyage-reader's vicarious escape, connoisseurship's judicious self-congratulation that can appraise a genre-bound performance. But sooner or later, and perhaps

---

[1] Whether *The Rape of the Lock* be satire is not something we'll quibble about, though whoever questions its genre ('mock-epic'?) plays satire's game. So did Pope's contemporaries when, as often, they disputed the authorship of something. For if a wit has written a transparent piece of duncery, then it is satire, but if a dunce, not.

abruptly or perhaps by gradual steps, satire permits us to discover that we are reading, not what we expected but something else entirely. To this we cannot give a name (save 'satire') because what we thought we were reading in the first place cannot quite be exorcized.

So as verbal technologies go, satire is a sophisticated contrivance indeed. 'Technology' seems the term to employ. I am following Eric Havelock, who has taught us to think of alphabetic writing as itself a technology, loosely definable as something no Noble Savage would be likely to think of. 'The ability to document a spoken language is itself a technological feat, one on which the cultures which preceded the Greek placed some reliance, and which has become essential in post-Greek cultures.'[2]

Once people are used to *texts* (etymologically, things *woven*, as by the fingers) they have trouble imagining how words can exist in any way save textually ('freeing ourselves of chirographic and typographic bias in our understanding of language is probably more difficult than any of us can imagine', writes Walter Ong, himself entoiled in texty words like 'bias').[3] For textual man, reader and writer alike, words are external, 'out there' in space. They are pointers to 'things', likewise 'out there' (literate traversers of this page will think of the philosophers of Lagado, who economized breath by rummaging through bags of things). Writers 'arrange' them (in space), and certain distinctive arrangements are identifiable by eye: Sonnets (which look well on quarto pages), Pindarick Odes (elaborately indented), Works of Learning (small-print footnotes), latterly Novels (a hundred or more cubic inches of wood-pulp, with much conversation typographically marked). Other genres are recognized by conventions of titling, hence Swift's care for titles ('A Modest *Proposal* . . .'; 'TRAVELS into several remote Nations . . .'). Moreover the arrangement has been effected 'by' someone; the key-word on a title-page is 'by'. Whereas a book is naturally 'by', spoken words are 'said by', thanks only to the convention of the passive voice; for speech, the natural words are 'Homer said'. But, once book-ridden (on the analogy of bed-ridden), the *Iliad* is something 'by' Homer. *It*, being here in our hands, has precedence over *him*. He is a 'by-line'. (Did he exist? Did Gulliver? Bentley said that 'Phalaris' did not exist, and one prop of antiquity seemed hewn.)

From all that order of technology satire derives, and we should not be surprised to find it emerging in times of technological stress among the genres: in Rome, when the appropriation of Greek genres (the epic, the panegyric) raised questions concerning their applicability to what you might notice around you; in England, when the commercializing of the new commodity we aptly call 'reading matter' could raise doubts concerning the authority of the page itself. What, we are bidden to ask by *A Tale of a Tub*, is

[2] *The Literate Revolution in Greece and its Cultural Consequences* (Princeton, New Jersey, 1982), p. 106.
[3] *Orality and Literacy* (London, 1982), p. 77.

verbal authority worth, if the work of any hack with adequate command of grammar can strike the eye and heft in the hand just like something substantial? That hacks and dunces preoccupied Swift and Pope is something that should not surprise us. By ninety-eight per cent of all empirical tests, the differences between Pope's *Iliad* and anything at all by Ambrose Phillips are imperceptible. Even the inventory of words they 'arrange' is as nearly identical as makes no difference. Words being normally printed, we can now *count* them, and count their component letters, and discern that 'English' has its statistical norms. Those norms make half a writer's decisions for him (try to write a page with no 'e').[4]

A newly-commercialized typographic culture, presided over by 'booksellers' who, as today's undergraduates need informing, did much more than sell books (it was they, for instance, who chose the English Poets before Johnson wrote the Lives), was a milieu both Swift and Pope were acutely aware of. By one stratagem or another, they had had to connive a way into it; otherwise they would not have been allowed to exist as book-men. With some university press or other at his disposal by professional courtesy, the modern academic can have difficulty seeing why hacks and scribbling ninnies preoccupied them so.

Wyndham Lewis (1882–1957) likewise came to the twentieth-century book-world from the outside. By vocation he was a painter, his normal creative impulses flowing down the musculature of shoulder and arm into his strong fingers. It is not irrelevant that there were painters in his lifetime who called themselves *les fauves*, the wild creatures. Though a savage is not aware of being a savage, a painter in London or Paris can be aware how, like the savage and unlike the bourgeois, he spends his most vital time doing something physical. Lewis projected his savage heritage so eloquently that his more articulate contemporaries could not fail to register it. 'The thought of the modern and the energy of the cave man', wrote T. S. Eliot, astonished.

Not surprisingly, writers and readers, the producers of written words and their consumers, were always to the eye of this caveman a trifle strange. What a confidence-game! Someone scribbles, or strikes keys, or even dictates, and after an interval of technological processing gets acclaimed as a magician by thousands who hold in their hands a wood-pulp artifact, distinguished by ink markings.

That was odd, and what was odder was that Lewis all his life could make money at the writing game more readily than by his brush (in later life he lived on advances for books, which the books seldom repaid though he wrote them meticulously). That was because the arrangements for marketing pictures ensure that what gets marketed is a *name*, and require that at any one time no more than a very few names of power shall be acknowledged. The list

---

[4] Almost exactly half, a man who seemed to know once told me, but just what he was counting I did not find out.

is kept by a sanhedrin of middle-men called dealers, and any name's presence on it seems wholly arbitrary. 'Wyndham Lewis' was never in that arcane sense a 'name', so painters less talented routinely fetched bigger fees.

Early in his career, needing money, he accordingly set out to write a potboiler, *Mrs Dukes' Million*. By a characteristic miscalculation it brought him nothing because it went unpublished till after his death (J. B. Pinker himself couldn't market it) but it is readable today and discloses an early preoccupation with provisional worlds.[5] Very simply, the way to affluence and power is to make yourself be thought to be somebody else. The public world, reported in the newspapers, is a web of illusion ('the stunt of an illusionist' was Lewis's brusque later phrase)[6] and to inherit Mrs Dukes's Million you have only to pass yourself off as Mrs Dukes. A master illusionist in command of a company of actors has arranged for this to be effected, also for the real Mrs Dukes to be bundled off to America, by 1908-convention the world's waste-basket.

An actor they are recruiting is told about 'the prime difference between our theatre, which has the world for its stage, and the theatre that you are used to':

We improvise. No pieces are written for us. The actors act the part as they go along. That is what I myself always wanted to do when I was acting.... I wanted to see actors no longer bound by the 'piece' they had to play, but to *act* and *live* at the same time.... [For us] the play goes on sometimes in several places at the same time. One of the present players in my company is playing his part six thousand miles from here, without audience, but none the worse for that.

That 1908 illusionist spoke for Lewis, who sensed, and ever more strongly as he grew older, that the 'real' was always appearance: was contrived. When we have worked our way up the hierarchies of *The Human Age* to God, God, in the only fragment of Part IV that survives, is 'the old magician of the cloudy wastes of heaven'. That God is a *benign* magician goes without saying (though in 1919 Lewis called the Universe 'a gigantic and, from every point of view, dubious concern');[7] but as the levels get lower magicians get more and more corrupt: precisely, Apes of God. At the levels we inhabit, the 'reality' accessible to our casual sight has been contrived in reputation-factories where the staff can seem inextricable from the product: pressmen, politicians, Famous Writers, 'authorities', film stars, gossip stars, yes, art dealers.

Something else to notice about *Mrs Dukes' Million* is the way its 'reality' has been imported from the *fin-de-siècle* novel: from *The Sign of Four*, from *The New Arabian Nights*, from *The Prisoner of Zenda* and *The Man Who Was Thursday*. Apart from some genial detail about boarding-houses and their perky landladies, it

[5] It was published by The Coach House Press, Toronto, in 1977. The typescript had vanished into England's Sargasso Sea of discarded papers, to surface after nearly five decades in a London junkshop. See my essay in *Wyndham Lewis: A Revaluation*, edited by Jeffrey Meyers, (London, 1980), pp. 85–91.

[6] Letter to T. Sturge Moore, 1941, in *The Letters of Wyndham Lewis*, edited by W. K. Rose (London, 1963), p. 293.

[7] *The Caliph's Design* (1919), reprinted in *Wyndham Lewis on Art: Collected Writings 1913–1956*, edited by Walter Michel and C. J. Fox (London, 1969), p. 153.

tells us little about what Lewis had seen and heard, much about what he had been reading. That is unsurprising in an avowed potboiler, but arresting when we consider how *Mrs Dukes' Million* foreshadows what Lewis the committed publicist and satirist would later have us believe about reality's texture. 'The best-seller', he was to write years later, 'is like the camera, it cannot lie'. He was saying that it could not lie about what its readers took for granted; but to the best-sellers of his young manhood, with their mystifications and charades of mistaken identity, Lewis seems to have attributed an insight into what God, 'the old magician', had contrived: a 'reality' that was *always* provisional. Only the artist, 'older than the fish' as he memorably said, can draw on 'the fundamental slime of creation'. 'The creation of a work of art is an act of the same description as the evolution of wings on the sides of a fish, the feathering of its fins; or the invention of a weapon within the body of a hymenopter to enable it to meet the terrible needs of its life' (*The Caliph's Design*, p.152). That attempts, with Darwin's help, to constate the authentic: the authentic is whatever meets needs, 'terrible needs'. Art, so we are being told, does likewise. All else is spurious, commencing perhaps with the Universe (what need did *it* serve?) and including certainly best-sellers, sonnets, grammarians, six-shooters.

It was inventions of this order — the musket, pistol, and breechloader, not to mention the fire-water — which enabled the European to overrun the globe a few centuries ago. And what good has it done to him or anyone else? . . . For in most of the places where the White Man went with his little gun, his polo-ponies and gangster-films, he has destroyed something finer than himself . . .

something Older than the Fish, in fact.[8] How readily we get hypnotized by the spurious! And by the pretence that our alphabetical scratchings on paper can convey anything save the conventions within which they operate.

For here is Bestre, a Breton inn-keeper; and our first thought may be that the barbarian in charge of the pen has not the least idea how to go about a description. Yet the barbaric surface has been carefully contrived ('Bestre' went through two recastings, the first one seismic, between 1909 and 1927) and the words Lewis finally joined say chiefly this, that sentences as they flow from a normal pen can tell us nothing at all about a creature at once so primitive and so agonistic.

His very large eyeballs, the small saffron ocellation at their centre, the tiny spot through which light entered the obese wilderness of his body; his bronzed bovine arms, swollen handles for a variety of indolent little ingenuities; his inflated digestive case, lent their combined expressiveness to say these things; with every tart and biting condiment that eye-fluid, flaunting of fatness the (well-filled), the insult of the comic, implications of indecency, could provide. Every variety of the bottom-tapping resounded from his dumb bulk. His tongue stuck out, his lips eructated with the incredible indecorum that appears to be the monopoly of liquids, his brown arms were for the moment genitals, snakes in one massive twist beneath his mamillary

---

[8] Quotation is from 'Power-Feeling and Machine-Age Art' (1934), in *Wyndham Lewis on Art*.

slabs, gently riding on a pancreatic swell, each hair on his oil-bearing skin contributing its message of porcine affront.[9]

We were all taught to write *sentences*, subject > verb > object. Lewis attacks that assumption at the root. Sentences map actions, but Bestre is a restless stasis, like a picture, Accordingly, amid empty deference to syntactic conventions, this paragraph's unit is not the sentence but the phrase, each one a surreal snapshot: 'the obese wilderness of his body'; 'snakes in one massive twist'; 'gently riding on a pancreatic swell'.

We all believe, too, in sleek organic integrity, when the object of our attention is a Man, someone 'human' like our fine selves. But this man is built up of parts, of oddly-assorted phrases, and the order of the components, from 'his very large eyeballs' to 'each hair on his oil-bearing skin', seems nearly random (are we ourselves more random than we suppose?). A long sentence, a short, a long: their catch-all rhythms govern. When we read 'Bestre', as we must, against something we carry in our heads, the uncodified but substantial tradition of personal description, all that novelists have learned from one another about ways to convey the look of people, then we may suspect a chasm between affrontive reality and literature's suave procedures. Bestre is not so much ushered on to the page, as relentlessly *looked* at, between discharges of metaphoric shells.

In his 1950 *Rude Assignment* Lewis explicitly connected 'Bestre' (1922 or earlier) with his celebrated *The Apes of God* of 1930.[10] He was accurate. Here is *The Apes of God*'s Lady Fredigonde, veteran gossip-star, getting herself upright from a chair:

The unsteady solid rose a few inches, like the levitation of a narwhal. Seconded by alpenstock and body-servant (holding her humble breath), the escaping half began to move out from the deep vent. It abstracted itself slowly. Something imperfectly animate had cast off from a portion of its self. It was departing, with a grim paralytic toddle, elsewhere. The socket of the enormous chair yawned just short of her hindparts.

Next, she sinks into another chair two rooms away:

She lowered her body into its appointed cavity . . . ounce by ounce — back first, grappled to Bridgit, bulldog grit all-out — at last riveted as though by suction within its elastic crater, corseted by its mattresses of silk from waist to bottom, one large feeble arm riding the billows of its substantial fluted brim.

Finally, she speaks:

There was a great bustle all at once. Her head was lived in once again. A strong wheezing sigh, as the new air went in and the foul air went out, and then she realized the tones of a muted fog-horn to exclaim —

'There will come a time Bridget when I shall not be able to move about like that!' (pp. 22–24)[11]

[9] *The Complete Wild Body*, edited by Bernard Lafourcade (Santa Barbara, California, 1982), p. 78. 'Bestre', a rewriting of a 1909 sketch, achieved its present form at some time between the war's end and its publication in *Tyro*, 2 (March 1922, the year of *Ulysses*).
[10] Lafourcade noted this: 'Out of Bestre . . . grew . . . the aged "Gossip Star" at her toilet' (p. 220).
[11] I am using the beautiful 1981 Black Sparrow Press reprint.

Quickly riffled, the pages of *The Apes of God* say 'novel'; do they not display 'conversations'? More closely examined, these conversations prove synthesized. 'There will come a time Bridget when I shall not be able to move about like that': this string of words lacks the two crucial commas that would designate a human utterance. Here we are deep in the technology of writing, to which alone commas pertain (there are no *spoken* commas); deep too in the layered conventions that would have us intuit from the commas, were commas here, a warmth towards Bridget, soul calling unto soul, without our even having to voice the sentence. Reading silently, we do not so much as pretend to be reading aloud; yet having interiorized print, the chief project of our early education, whenever we scan it we adumbrate reading aloud. So lifelong habit makes us want to have Lady Fredigonde's voice solicit a person, Bridget, and the missing punctuation will not let us.

Here, likewise, is a minor heroine the words will not let us warm to:

A lovely tall young lady it was, of a most drooping and dreamy presence — most modest of *Merveilleuses* that ever stepped upon a palpitating planet screwed into position by a cruel polarity of sex — in consequence compelled to advertise a neck of ivory, nipples of coral, a jewelled ankle of heart-breaking beauty-line-extremities, for the rest, superbly plantigrade — a miracle of blunt-heeled — metatarsally-dominant — proportion — under the arch of whose trotter a fairy coach made out of a cobnut could be readily driven. (*The Apes of God*, p. 455)

We do well not to warm; 'she' is Daniel Boleyn in drag. Still, the parodic mechanism repays inspection: all those paratactic dashes, where custom would enjoin subordinate structures; that palpitation, attributed to a planet; the word 'palpitating' in connivance with the word 'screwed'; the lascivious focus on the *feet*, 'a miracle . . .', its ecstasy dashed by the pork-butcher's word, 'trotter'. This sentence goes about its analytic business, the burdens 'cruel polarity' can lay on a girl, all the while recalling, but refusing to endorse or duplicate, much homage to loveliness lying about in books for any literate reader to supply in paraphrase:

> Her azure veins, her alabaster skin,
> Her coral lips, her snow-white dimpled chin.
>
> (*The Rape of Lucrece*, l. 419)

One writer Lewis knew thoroughly was Shakespeare; and ('azure', 'alabaster', 'coral', 'snow'), by convention, Shakespeare's Lucrece is complimented by the seeming assertion that such are her components. We may entertain a momentary suspicion that such a convention is exceedingly odd; does it not protect a Lucrece as synthetic, on the page, as was Bestre? What a baroque agglomeration is Lucrece!

It was by pretending not to understand the literary conventions of English, and the normal ways to construct or punctuate English sentences, that Lewis cast doubt on the normal world they conjure: the world of jolly Jack Falstaff, bluff Sam Johnson, heroines with coral lips, Lloyd George the Welsh Wizard, Lord Peter Wimsey, Lady Chatterley.

That Johnson was a sort of god to his biographer we readily see. But Falstaff as well is a sort of english god, like the rice-bellied gods of laughter of China. They are illusions hugged and lived in; little dead totems. Just as all gods are a repose for humanity, the big religions an immense refuge and rest, so are these little grotesque fetishes.   (*The Complete Wild Body*, p. 151)

So he put that part of his case in 1927, in the course of rephrasing his 1917 'Inferior Religions', an essay T. S. Eliot had called 'the most indubitable evidence of genius, the most powerful piece of imaginative thought, of anything that Mr Lewis has written'.[12] That had been at the outset of the 'modernist' enterprise in England, when they were trying to write English as knowingly as if it were a foreign language, the way Flaubert had written French, and part of Eliot's polemic strategy had been to call (in vain) for someone with a first-hand opinion of Shakespeare. One kind of first-hand opinion would be an intelligent barbarian's. But 'little dead totems': such are the deliverances of canonized literature. Educated minds are furnished with little else.

Great danger lay in the inability of educated minds to distinguish these cherished totems from more sinister abstractions. 'Media creations', we are accustomed now to say of people who woo votes and wield power. Lewis preceded us by two generations in seeing how literature and its totems create the habits whereby anyone who has learned to read apprehends public reality. He distrusted 'romantic' (that is, literary) celebrations of the primitive; he distrusted D. H. Lawrence. But the genuine primitive, in fact the illiterate: that was the 'something finer than himself' that the White Man had destroyed 'with his little gun, his polo-ponies and gangster-films'; in particular, Lewis might have added, with his newspapers.

So he expended his literary energies on letting us watch the strange behaviour of the civilized. A man of the polo-pony set named Sigismund, who keeps a bulldog called Pym and believes in 'breeding', can conduct a courtship not in the gall-wasp's disciplined way or the caveman's but only in so grotesque a fashion as this:

She fell into his arms to signify that she would willingly become his bride. In a precarious crouch he propped her for a moment, then they both subsided on to the floor, she with her eyes closed, rendered doubly heavy by all the emotion with which she was charged. Pym, true to type, 'the bulldog' at once, noticing this contretemps, and imagining that his master was being maltreated by this person whom he had disliked from the first, flew to the rescue. He fixed his teeth in her eighteenth-century bottom. She was removed, bleeding, in a titanic faint.   ('Sigismund', *The Complete Wild Body*, p. 164)

Burlesque? But observe the decorum of the even sentences, their analytic detachment. 'Her eighteenth-century bottom': that is an aspect the prose thinks worth noting, and it is 'eighteenth-century' because she is a woman distinguished, like Pym, by documented 'breeding' (her faints are 'titanic').

[12] Eliot reviewing *Tarr* in *The Egoist* (September 1918); quoted in *The Complete Wild Body*, p. 148.

A caveman's finesse would likely have improved on Sigismund's. Yet Sigismund, should he try to think of a caveman, would no doubt be guided by the literary abstration of a grunting boor. For here is Sigismund's circle, as perceived by his bride:

They smoked bad tobacco, used funny words, their discourse was of their destiny, that none of them could have had any but the slenderest reasons for wishing to examine. They very often appeared angry, and habitually used a chevaleresque jargon: ill-bred, under-bred, well-bred; fellow, cad, boor, churl, gentleman; good form, bad form, were words that came out of them on hot little breaths of disdain, reprobation, or respect.   (p. 164)

That reads like an ethologist's field-notes: *homo domesticus*, as perceived through a lens. 'It is difficult', Lewis observed, 'to see how the objective truth of much that is called "Satire" can be less true than the truth of lyrical declamation, in praise, for instance, of a lovely mistress'.[13] Elsewhere he stated roundly: 'Wherever there is objective truth there is satire.' That is to say, whenever the externalizing inherent in the habits of written language so alienates us from our human interior as to permit us to see what it is that words are saying, then it will prove less creditable than we expect. *All* writing, in short, is satire, except in so far as it has acquired the tricks whereby nothing gets said. These are called, collectively, 'style'. Let us inspect a few sentences lacking in top-hatted style.

An animal in every respect upon the same footing as a rat or an elephant, I imagine you will agree — man, except for what the behaviourist calls his word-habit, is that and no more. . . . So really *the word* — in contrast to the sound or image — is the thing most proper and peculiar to him (the word, and laughter perhaps). That we are merely *talking* monkeys — rats, elephants, bullocks or geese — is obvious. It is a very peculiar situation!   (*Men Without Art*, p. 288)

It is indeed, and especially so since these categories are inseparable from literacy, which insists that we perceive ourselves from 'outside', the outside where the written word exists, and where it situates readers, telling them 'about' what cannot be *us* (for each of us is an interior, an 'I'). Perceived from outside, our activities are value-less, not to say valueless. 'Regarded as great herds of performing animals', the way literature at bottom would regard us were it faithful to the logic whereby it exteriorizes the word (so enabling us to think of 'species' including the human), we can not be deemed to evince any more distinction than might be observed among the whooping cranes.

Yet one of our species wrote,

> Where'er you walk, cool Gales shall fan the Glade,
> Trees, where you sit, shall crowd into a Shade,
> Where'er you tread, the blushing Flow'rs shall rise,
> And all things flourish where you turn your Eyes.

And he also wrote 'Satires', full of 'objective truth'. It is not the 'Atticus' or the 'Sporus', but Pope's 'beautiful' passage, that is most thoroughly

---

[13] *Men Without Art* (London, 1934), p. 122.

contrived, gales, trees, and flowers obeying the fact of her presence; and she, if we search back through preceding lines for the pronoun's antecedent, is a 'Nymph'! 'Come lovely Nymph, and bless the silent Hours.'[14] Why, the intelligent barbarian might ask, must an upholder of western civilization, just when he is evoking its delights, *pretend* so much?

We know that the way to answer is to invoke one of western civilization's arcane strands, the Pastoral Tradition. Lewis knew that as well as any of us. But the way of the satirist is apt to be relentless; one thing he will never let us do is appeal to a history that must be learned. (Is not 'learning' a set of excuses?) Had Gulliver known a little more of history he would have been less discomfited by the Houyhnhnm objections; but Swift accords him no functional knowledge of the past (he is an archetypal barbarian) and Swift's readers are apt to have difficulty recalling the historic customs that, summoned to their aid, might enable them to be diverted instead of vexed.

Lewis likewise contrives to have us spooked by literary history, as we thrash our way through one of his arresting barbaric paragraphs. For we are agreed that our being civilized entails the fineness of imagination that can contrive such a cadence as 'Where'er you walk . . .'. You would never divine, though, Lewis insinuates, the presence of that agreement among us, if you were to watch us simply spending our time. Examine the talking monkeys, and what do you see?

A good dinner, accompanied by as good wine as we can get hold of; a pleasant spin in the fresh air in as satisfactory a petrol-wagon as we can afford; a nice digestive round of golf; a flirtation accompanied by the rhythmical movements prompted by a nigger drum, purging us of the secretions of sex — a nice detective volume, which purges us pleasantly of the secretions proper to us in our capacity as 'killers' and hunting-dogs . . .; all these things are far more *important* than anything that can be described as 'art'. (*Men Without Art*, p. 290)

Those sentences help press Lewis's reckless case home. Yet is not the barbarian observer, by definition, himself just such a creature as he observes? If these field-notes on our animal behaviour describe our days well, then what can be said of the 'arts' on which we vaunt ourselves? Yet if 'art' is nothing for the creatures, it can also be nothing for him, or nearly nothing: he is a 'creature' too. The fine arts become merely 'the very fine manners of the mind', and Lewis performed the satirist's leap when he said in the next breath, calmly, that he took their value for granted. For how could that be?

It could be so in the perspective of a whole unwritten literature, from whose energies value might leap incontestably. Such a literature — vast scintillant tracts — his practice from time to time bids us imagine. It is normal for us to imagine non-existent literature. Now and then, for a few

---

[14] 'Summer: The Second Pastoral, or Alexis', ll. 73–76, 63. Quotation is from *The Poems of Alexander Pope*, in John Butt's one-volume Twickenham edition (London, 1963).

lines at a time, poetry can hint at more than we are used to encountering, and we have all in our heads an intuited spectrum of verbal delight which but a few glints have prompted. Had we the habit likewise of canonizing rare prose-paragraphs, the one I shall next quote could not be excluded; nor could anyone fail to notice how dissimilar it is not only to the prose we chew daily but to prose we are exhorted to admire. It is a barbarian's extravaganza, composed by a newly-recruited professional killer. That is to say that in 1917, newly enlisted as a bombardier, Wyndham Lewis, aged thirty-five, is writing 'Inferior Religions', no doubt by lamplight, in a Dorset army camp, and, far from his studio and from all he feasts on, is drawing for a rare moment on his deepest passions.

But life is invisible, and perfection is not in the waves or houses that the poet sees. To rationalize that appearance is not possible. Beauty is an icy douche of ease and happiness at something *suggesting* perfect conditions for an organism: it remains suggestion. A stormy landscape, and a pigment consisting of a lake of hard, yet florid waves; delight in each brilliant scoop or ragged burst, was John Constable's beauty. Leonardo's consisted in a red rain on the shadowed side of heads, and heads of massive female aesthetes. Uccello accumulated pale parallels, and delighted in cold architecture of distinct colour. Korin found in the symmetrical gushing of water, in waves like huge vegetable insects, traced and worked faintly, on a golden pâte, his business. Cézanne liked cumbrous, democratic slabs of life, slightly leaning, transfixed in vegetable intensity.   (*The Complete Wild Body*, p. 153)

'It remains suggestion': true of painting, that statement is true also of such writing. Even in Lewis, there is very little else like it. It suggests that writing might be in another cosmos: pre-empting, it goes without saying, the flaccid respect we have for our literary heritage. Its authority seems to emanate from beyond that heritage: from a world of *fauves* who do what they wish with paint, and accumulate icons of their satisfactions: not 'subjects', but qualities, timeless, tirelessly reaffirmed. That is the world of the eye: the world to which writing aspires, but from the riches of which it is debarred. Vision, wrote Merleau-Ponty, 'vision dissects'.[15] So it does, and when writing delivered language to the eye it rendered all words dissective: analytical: Aristotelian. They slide: they unravel: they are systems of self-deceit. Dissection, turned against Man, is a terrible thing; and, once they are moved into the domain of scrutiny, written words have an ineluctable proclivity for showing man up as a talking ape. But 'style', a shared system of agreements not to notice the bleak thing written language implies, has for centuries served to conceal so stark an outcome. And 'style' is a set of conventions derived from history.

But the eye denies history: what it sees is *now*. 'A philosophy of the EYE' was how Lewis described his satirist's approach; 'the wisdom of the eye, rather than that of the ear'.[16] The true barbarian is an ear-man, illiterate.

---

[15] Quoted by Ong, *Orality and Literacy*, p. 72.
[16] *Men Without Art*, pp. 118, 128.

Lewis's barbaric pose ('older than the fish') was that of a literate and sophisticated eye-man, seeking homeopathic remedy for distortions introduced by the eye. It distorts, but it need not. History may be an excuse, but it need not be. The root problem is time, in which history is embedded; death-bound, we lack time. If 'wherever there is objective truth there is satire', that is because imperfect man, whenever, pen in hand, he is being objective, cannot long sustain such a vision as phrased 'red rain on the shadowed side of heads' or 'cumbrous, democratic slabs of life'; or, for that matter, such an acoustic delicacy as '. . . all Earth flourish where you turn your Eyes'.

Between Commentary and Comedy:
The Satirical Side of Borges

JOHN STURROCK
London

A writer so personally reserved and literarily aware as Borges could but tend to the satirical. The satire to which he tends is not the slanderous hot-blooded kind which martyrises its victims by name, but the refined Menippean kind which leniently caricatures only defective temperaments or ideas. Borges is closer to Peacock than to *Private Eye*, that is. But it would be reckless to claim him for a satirist or to say that he had written anything so blunt as a satire. The closest he has come to that is in the sardonic short pieces he has produced over the years with his friend and literary playmate, Adolfo Bioy Casares, under the joint name of H. Bustos Domecq. In the Tales and Chronicles which they have attributed to this culturally omnivorous and endlessly credulous pundit, Borges and Bioy guy both the pretentiousness of avant-garde experimentation and the dire adaptibility of the market for it in a metropolis such as Buenos Aires.

But the satire which is present in these slight but cogent *divertissements* is not local to Argentina or limited only to the more preposterous flights of fancy of the modernists. It applies everywhere and it raises what is for Borges the key question: that of artistic creation in general. Bustos Domecq is a joke but his gullibility towards the egregious novelty of so much that confronts him is his undoing. So facile are his expositions and endorsements of the patently worthless that his own folly comes to seem more reprehensible than that of the world he is charged with interpreting. He has read that world awrong, which for Borges is unforgivable. The misunderstandings with which the wide-eyed Bustos Domecq has been saddled matter, and they crop up again and again in the mature fictions which are Borges's glory.

To read these fictions as informed by Borges's discreetly satirical intentions is, I believe, to read them intelligently. Their very dimensions support this view, because within the space of ten or twelve pages at a time Borges invokes ('raises' would be too crude a term) large and intractable questions about the nature of fiction. All his writing life he has made a virtue of brevity, maintaining that he lacked the staying-power or imagination to write a novel or a treatise. Borges's art is founded on disproportion, between the size of the issues he is involved with and the fewness of the words he allows himself. There is in his wonderful reticence an implied rebuke for the portentous and the prolix, who cannot contain themselves or see that literature is an essentially playful, not a vital aspect of life on earth. Borges has no more love for the superhuman than for the supernatural.

He is that precious and edifying anachronism: a literary thinker thoroughly Classical in his beliefs. Borges's Classicism indeed is all the firmer for being reactionary: he is a reformed Romantic whose early writing strained hard after the colourful effects conventionally taken as evidence of literary distinction. But having practised and seen through the meretricious principles on which Romanticism rests, he turned to the writing of sly and fascinating stories which work to undermine them. The satirical component of these stories is of an unusually radical sort, because what Borges is out to do is to purify our understanding of fiction as a whole and of the problematical relation of language to the world. He is not in any orthodox way a moralist, with prescriptions to offer for social betterment, but he does seek to make us share his own scepticism in respect of the mythology of Romanticism. He is the witty adversary of the overblown, of the rhapsodic; and if, as is usually supposed, the parodic originated with the Greeks in counterpoint to the rhapsodic, as its other, less comely face, then Borges can be numbered among our age's most genuine parodists.

Of that complex of indefensible notions which together make up the mythology of Romanticism, the one he concentrates on most tellingly is that of originality. Borges would prefer that we discard this false notion or at least come to redefine the word itself. Originality, as he sees it, is another and a lesser thing from what we are taught. In his campaign to expel the old idea of originality from our minds Borges is the precursor, and a refreshingly succinct one, of the deconstructionists. His whole drift is to expropriate texts from their authors, if by this last term we mean those transcendent beings of whose intimate concerns the text is read as an objective materialization. His own paradoxical modernity lies in this: that he keeps always in front of us the awareness that we ourselves are not the originators of the language in which we write or speak nor even its provisional masters. Language both precedes and exceeds us.

We cannot endow the words of our native language with meaning, they bear meanings already: if it were not so they would not constitute a language. We can only combine them in what we fancy are newly meaningful groups. This is the simple but salutary axiom at the heart of one of Borges's best-known stories, 'The Library of Babel', in which he toys, to our discomfort, with the combinatorial riches of any given language as well as with the knowledge that our human powers of expression are circumscribed by the finite repertoire of signs and intelligible syntagma available to us. Language, in its immense though not truly infinite productivity, is the hero of 'The Library of Babel', and the realization that the specifically authorial task of composition might be taken over by some tirelessly creative machine is, for all its fantasy and obvious irony, corrosive of our self-esteem. Human authorship could come to seem a stop-gap, an antediluvian prelude to the literary mass-production of the future. And who is to say that the electronic dispositions of the word-hoard we get then will not be found as warmly expressive as those of our own and past ages, given the propensity we share to pass beyond what we read to its palpitant 'human' source?

On the other hand, even the prodigious resources of the library of Babel are inadequate inasmuch as they are merely verbal and reality is real. This inadequacy is something else that Borges will not allow us to forget. It is built in to all his finest stories, and it brings with it, inescapably, an element of self-mockery, since all verbal constructs, including his own, the one we are reading, are afflicted by the same unreality. But if language is inadequate to reality it is also relatively stable; indeed, its failure and success in these respects are indivisible. Everything in reality is unique and mutable, it is what it is and it changes through time. But the signs of a language change slowly or not at all, and they are defined by their repeatability. They are, by definition, banal. It is Borges's contention that we would be well advised to accept this necessary banality and work to it rather than, as we so often try to, against it. A pristine language is a contradiction in terms, and the search for one would be strictly anti-social since a pristine language would also need to be a private language. Borges, like any satirist, is on the side of sociability.

These ideas are consummately if secretively dramatized in a story which is full of roundabout hints as to Borges's literary purposes. The story was first collected in *El Aleph* of 1957; its title, in Spanish, is 'La busca de Averroes'. This is the first of many planned and instructive ambiguities: an equivocal title for a tale whose theme is equivocation. 'La busca de Averroes' could be, in English, 'The Search for Averroes' or it could be 'Averroes's search'. Or it could be, and with Borges it must be, both. Averroes is searching, for the true meaning of two terms which he has encountered in Aristotle and which are unfamiliar to him; and the author of the tale (let us call him Borges) is likewise searching, for Averroes, a long-dead Arab philosopher whom he reconstructs from absurdly scant and less than historical evidence. Thus Aristotle is to Averroes as Averroes is to 'Borges' or to the 'I' who comes forward at the end of the narrative to point to the fragility and the symmetry of the whole undertaking. This authorial intervention is made necessary by ignorance: Averroes looks at himself in a mirror and the illusion of his existence is broken because 'Borges' knows nothing of how his hero looked. Borges gives himself the opportunity to play the game of realism, of individuation through physical description, and then refuses the challenge on grounds of scruple: there is no *knowing* what Averroes looked like and to imagine his features would be cheap.

By his sly and graceful capitulation at this late point in his story, Borges is making quiet fun of the illusion of immediacy on which all realism depends. The local colour in 'La busca de Averroes' is of a perfunctory nature: the Cordoban philosopher is surrounded by a few props only, the trite indices of southern Spain, that country 'in which there are few things, but where each one seems to be in a substantive and eternal mode'. This is not Borges's impression of the real Spain that we are being given, as a land unnaturally empty, but a cunning reflection of his own technique of scene-setting. The few things about Averroes are substantive and eternal indeed; they are nouns — a dove, a patio, a fountain: universals which Borges scorns to particularize when it is enough to name them.

'La busca de Averroes' is a comedy of intermediacy. Averroes has no direct access to his distant precursor Aristotle, on whose philosophy he is composing a commentary; Borges has no direct access to Averroes, on whose perplexity he is likewise composing a commentary. Averroes knows no Greek, and must read the works of Aristotle in 'the translation of a translation'; Borges knows no Arabic and must learn about Averroes where he can, in 'snippets' picked up from the French of Renan, from the English of Edward Lane (one of the translators into English of the *1001 Nights*), from the Spanish of Asín Palacios. These three have the merit at least of having existed, but the same is not necessarily true for the various Arabic sources which Borges brings in: Alexander of Aphrodisia, for example, whose pages Averroes has 'wearied' in his quest for elucidation. The historical and the imaginary commingle in Borges, and are accorded the same status, the presence of the first lending spurious weight to the second, the presence of the second casting terrible doubt on the authority of the first. The bogus erudition in which Borges specializes is not just a prank, it is a warning, against what Jacques Derrida calls the 'onto-theological' fallacy, or the presumption that a literary text can be unequivocal and immutable, like the word of God.

Averroes's search for the 'real' Aristotle is worthy but hopeless; the 'real' Aristotle is inaccessible. The Derridan view, which might very well be Borges's own view, is that the 'real' Aristotle always was inaccessible, from the first moment when he consigned his philosophy to writing and thereby alienated it from himself. And yet Averroes is right to have embarked on his search, for important reasons that I shall come to. The lesson that is taught by this story of Borges's is that we should adapt our expectations in such matters to the facts of the case, so that we are clearer in our own minds about what can and cannot be managed in (re)constructing the meaning of what we read.

Averroes's particular difficulty is his failure to understand a pair of terms he has come across many times in reading Aristotle's *Rhetoric* and his *Poetics*: the terms Tragedy and Comedy. Nothing in his own experience, nothing that is in the Islamic culture in which he lives (this, anyway, is what Borges's tale supposes) enables him to construe these terms. Theatrical performances of any sort are unknown to him. On the face of it, therefore, his chances of 'understanding' the *Poetics*, which is almost entirely concerned with the rules and possibilities of Tragedy, are poor. The cultural and linguistic gap between the Greek philosopher and his Arabic would-be commentator has been set very wide, as if Borges were inviting us to laugh at the extravagance of what Averroes is set on. Averroes is adrift in a foreign language without a reliable dictionary to help him. Yet in his way he succeeds, and the laugh ultimately is not on him, it is on us, for failing to acknowledge that he is enacting a parable of the Reader, who understands what he reads as best he can and is not to be derided for a failure to understand it on the author's own presumed terms.

Averroes stands to Aristotle, as all readers stand to what they read, in a dialectical relationship. He is the Harold Bloom of twelfth-century Andalusia, bent though he may not know it on misprision, on a productive misreading. At the start of the story he is in fact at work not on his famous commentary but on something more overtly polemical, his so-called 'Destrucción de la Destrucción', in which he takes issue with the arguments advanced by an Arabic predecessor, Ghazali, in his 'Destruction of Philosophers'. The title of Averroes's refutation is, in Spanish, once more equivocal: he could be writing a 'Destruction of Destruction', though a text answering to that title is barely imaginable, or he could be writing a 'Destruction of *the* Destruction', a title correctly interpretable only by those knowing of the existence of the work by Ghazali.

Whether these are real works of early Arabic thought, or whether Borges has made them up, I do not know. Their existence is, so to speak, immaterial. All that counts is the function they are given within the story and that cannot be affected by their standing ontologically. They are not to be separated from one another. Averroes's work has been called into being by Ghazali's and the memory of Ghazali's is ensured by the continuing existence of Averroes's. Similarly, the unnamed philosophers 'destroyed' by Ghazali (they may include Aristotle) are the *sine qua non* of his work and certain to survive as long as it does. There can be no text which is not in some sense a departure from earlier texts, no text which will not in some degree condition future texts. Such, says Borges, is the history of thought and of literature: text countertext, unendingly. It is thought, and the writing that disseminates it, which irrigate and refresh: they surely are the water whose 'constancy' Averroes takes comfort in and whose 'source' (*manantial*) he takes Aristotle to be, the Greek 'given to mankind to teach them everything which can be known'. The hyperbole is an indication that Aristotle, so conceived, is a convenient fiction, the mythical first cause of articulate thought itself.

At the start of 'La busca de Averroes' Averroes lacks any understanding of the two baffling terms in Aristotle; by the end of his part of the story he has achieved an understanding of them. He has done so apparently without trying, since the story is the record of various distractions which have occurred to take his mind off his problem. It is not clear just how these distractions embody the lesson he has unquestionably learnt. The narrative tells us only that 'something had revealed to him the sense of the two obscure words'. The reader's perplexity, on learning this, is to read the intervening experiences which Averroes has had as the stages of his enlightenment. The understanding he has come to is imperfect but commendable. He writes: 'Aristú gives the name of tragedy to panegyrics and comedy to satires and anathemas. Admirable tragedies and comedies abound in the pages of the Koran and in the *mohalacas* of the sanctuary.'

Aristotle has been naturalized, even down to his name, eroded by its translation through time and space (like Averroes's own name, which the story opens by giving as Abulgulaid Muhammed Ibn-Ahmed ibn-Muhammed ibn-Rushd; this cumbersome appellation has evolved in the space of a century into that of Averroes, but the longer form can be taken as the adumbration of Borges's theme that one text is born of other texts just as one name is born of other names). Averroes's version of Aristotle is well removed from the original yet preserves a filiation with it. It is like a quotation which has passed from mouth to mouth without ever being accurately recorded.

What has survived from Aristotle (or from our own reading of Aristotle) in this Cordoban translation is the essential polarity between tragedy and comedy. As panegyric, tragedy elevates and singularizes; as satire, comedy demeans and collectivizes or renders anonymous. There is no doubting as to which of these alternative modes Borges stands for. The tragic, with its inflation of literary means and ends, is foreign to him, who is unable to see literature as more than a supreme distraction. The comic is the mode he must pursue, if he is to reveal artifice *as* artifice. His is a satire not of society but of art, and his mission is to blow the artificer's cover by making plain the ruses by which he lives.

But Borges has also seen that satire can not be quite free of panegyric: the two modes are not wholly exclusive of one another. This is because the mere act of representation singularizes, it makes an example of whoever or whatever it is representing. The victim of a satire, if it is a person, owes a part or all of his subsequent fame to his satirist; to that extent he has been raised up in the act of being cast down. It might be unusual but it would not be ridiculous to speak of the 'hero' of a satire.

There is a contradiction here between the simple purpose and the mixed effect of any narrative, and it is a contradiction of which Borges has made clever use. The way he chooses to escape the inescapably panegyric effects even of a satire is to reveal those effects for what they are. It is by such extreme self-awareness that Borges absolves himself from connivance in the naïveties of lesser writers. Far from succumbing to the ambivalence of the fictive, he thrives on it. In the story of Averroes, with its Islamic context, he uses the Koran as his shorthand term for Literature in general, and calls on the authority, real or not, of Chahiz of Basra, to declare the Koran 'a substance which can take the form of a man or an animal, an opinion which seems to agree with that of those who attribute to it two faces'. The Koran it is which is eventually held by Averroes to abound in Tragedies and

Comedies, or the two modes in which reality may be represented. Two modes, or two faces: the tragic and the comic, the human and the animal. For Borges it is art which is human and reality which is animal; but because art has to show itself to be art, reality emerges finally as the truer and, regrettably, the victorious principle. Borges's modesty dictates that he offer himself as a magician, not as a saviour. His own performance once over, he must return us to our fallen human state.

But the distraction that the magician provides, and the self-evident play-acting he goes in for, are deeply instructive. We may be absorbed and harrowed by the tragic, we are taught by the satirical. The first distraction which Averroes enjoys once he has put down his pen and turned his mind to the solution of his puzzle is of a satirical kind. To be exact, it is his *second* distraction because his first gesture has been to go to the shelves of his library and turn the pages of the 'many volumes of the *Mokham* of the blind Abensida'. Borges's English readers will do well to hear the word 'mock' or even 'mock'em' in that Arabic title, to prepare them for what is to follow. For from this serious distraction Averroes is further distracted by the parodistic game being played by a few half-naked urchins in the patio beneath his windows: 'One, standing on the shoulders of another, was very obviously playing the part of the muezzin; his eyes tight closed, he was chanting *There is no other god but God*. The one who was supporting him without moving, was the minaret; a third, abject on his knees in the dust, the congregation of the faithful.'

This brief representation is the second, disreputable face, a satirical counterweight to the solemnities of the *Mokham*. The blind Abensida is caustically recalled by the tight-closed eyes of the street-Arab, who is *pretending* not to see. The language in which the children soon fall to disputing is a 'coarse dialect, that is to say the incipient Spanish of the Muslim masses of the peninsula' — the decadent yet at the same time creative process of translation is at work here also: parody may be secondary in respect of its model but it is also additional to it, and the guarantee of its furtherance.

The cause of the disagreement among the three members of the ragged troupe is that they all want to play the role of the muezzin, who stands preternaturally tall on the shoulders of his fellow and has the obedience of the crowd. The muezzin is the hero of this tiny narrative, in its satirical version just as much as in its serious one. For as long as the satire lasts, its star is exalted; unfavoured in life, the boy takes comfort in the pretence of art. This theme is everywhere in Borges. Whoever has a story to tell (or to enact) is temporarily exempt from the degradations of reality and invested with the glory intrinsic to his role.

The predominant story-teller in 'La busca de Averroes' is the traveller Abulcásim Al-Ashari, who is a fellow-guest at dinner with Averroes in the house of the Koranic scholar Farach. Abulcásim is reputed to have travelled in the East, to have reached indeed 'the kingdoms of the empire of Sin'. Sin is a happy inspiration on Borges's part (if I may be forgiven the use of so inaptly Romantic a term as 'inspiration'; a happy discovery is what he would prefer to have it thought). It leads the mind in three different directions, all of them relevant: to China first of all, for which *Sina* was the Latin name; to the English word 'Sin', with its reprobatory implications, hinting that 'travel' of the kind Abulcásim goes in for is morally deplorable (Borges has a comprehensive knowledge of English and often introduces its words to jocular ends like this); and lastly to the Spanish word *sin* meaning 'without', suggesting that wherever the traveller has been it was not to a real country.

The Borgesian traveller is always a maker of fictions, he travels exclusively in the mind. Abulcásim is the locus of a peculiar contradiction: his detractors say that he has never set foot in China *and* that when he was there he blasphemed Allah. This conjunctive where reason should have imposed a disjunctive between incompatible propositions, is, it seems, 'the peculiar logic which comes from hatred'. Abulcásim's detractors will have it both ways: he is a sinner whether or not he has been to China, a liar if he hasn't been there in fact, a blasphemer if he has. This is detraction in its pure state, resourceful yet also dependent, since it can only sustain, never initiate, the dialogue.

The question of the truth of Abulcásim's claims as to where he has been does not arise. The traveller above all is the narrator who must be taken at his word; he cannot be in two places at once: if he is *here*, now, he can only tell us about *there*, he cannot bring *there* with him in order to convince us of his truthfulness. He is the exemplary story-teller, and that is what he is doing in 'La busca de Averroes'. Abulcásim's listeners do not ask for truths from him in any case but 'marvels'; they understand the charms and responsibilities of narration. But this traveller, we suddenly find, is no hero to himself. 'Then as now, the world was a terrible place; the stout-hearted might travel it, but so might the contemptible, those who submitted to everything. Abulcásim's memory was a mirror of intimate cowardices. What could he recount?'

Cowardice is the mark of the anti-hero because it is the negation of the virtue commonly definitive of heroism, which is bravery. The craven anti-hero amuses us by his abjectness and, in so doing, persuades of his own greater realism as compared to his heroic counterpart. Borges uses cowardice (again I would say, satirically) as an inspiration, as representing that intimate lack without which there would be no urge to narration at all. There is something personal to himself in this, to judge by his fondness for comparing his own safe and cautious existence with the daring lives of his ancestors. He likes to belittle literature as the sedentary compensation of an unadventurous man. But if it is personal it is not merely personal: it is a principle with Borges that in narrative there is transfiguration.

The cowardly Abulcásim is all story-tellers, and a necessarily vainglorious man: he would of course be plain-glorious and not vainglorious had Borges not so exposed him at the outset. He is nothing more than a narrative functionary, without personality of his own. When asked whether the city of Canton is far from the wall built by Alexander the Great (like Averroes, a pupil of Aristotle and referred to here as the 'two-horned' as evidence of his potential duplicity) to hold back Gog and Magog (yet another tragi-comic twosome), he answers 'with involuntary haughtiness', involuntary because he could not in his role answer otherwise. He cannot divest himself of the authority of the narrator. Similarly, once he has told what he has to tell, of a stage performance witnessed in a theatre in Canton, he finds himself, in answering a question, 'converted into an apologist for a function he scarcely remembered and which he had found somewhat tedious'. His conversion is the unavoidable effect of the question, which recognizes his independence of the tale he has been recounting and creates an attitude towards it. This is the small act of separation, be it noted, without which we are unable to 'identify' the story-teller with his tale, since identification is not possible unless there are separate entities to be made one.

Abulcásim is thus an actor, on a par with the figures in crimson masks (a rather lurid disguise which it would be hard to confuse with the trappings of realism) he claims to have seen on a stage in Canton. It is pointed out to him by his questioner, the Koranist Farach, that because the twenty actors and actresses on the stage use words in their performance, the same story could as well be told by a single *hablista* or speaker. The audience approve this typically Borgesian economy of means, and so they should, for they have just been attending such a performance themselves, as they listened to the *hablista* Abulcásim telling of his complex experience in Canton. The word *hablista* is an oddity which gives me pause: it seems to have the force in Spanish not really of 'speaker' but of 'scholar' or of someone distinctive for the purity of the language he uses. Borges introduces it, I would say, to make more precise what the role of the story-teller is. It is a role marked before all else by rigour and by unoriginality. The teller serves the tale, not the tale the teller.

The defence of Classicism is, as I began by saying, the cause to which the mature Borges has bent himself. And yet it is a cause which he also weakens by appearing to take it to fanciful lengths. This is his ultimate abdication from seriousness. Following the narration of Abulcásim, the discussion among the guests in 'La busca de Averroes' turns to poetry and to the virtues of metaphor. One disputant argues that metaphors need constant renewal, if they are not to lose their power to amaze. The argument is approved, by men who, as the story mockingly observes, have heard it put forward many times before. That recognition is the cue for Averroes to uphold the opposite point of view, that poets should stick to traditional metaphors, that the aim of poetry is not to instil amazement, that the poet is less inventor than discoverer, that the image which is private to a single individual is anti-social in so far as it will not affect others.

Averroes believes that the poet's highest responsibility is to quote, for 'time, which despoils castles, enriches verses'. This he describes as 'perhaps the essence of my reflections': the essence indeed, for this is Borges's plea for a partly corrective and partly playful essentialism. The premise is that all we can hope to say has already been said, that the quest for novelty in expression is mistaken. Here, once more, we meet with the cruel inequality between a plethoric reality, of unique and transient phenomena, and the parsimony of language, which possesses only general terms in which to allude to it. Language is by its nature Platonic, and in the tract on which he is working at the start of his story Averroes is maintaining against Ghazali that 'the deity only knows the general laws of the universe, that which concerns species, not individuals'. This deity, we might conclude, *is* language. Rather than fight against this necessary limitation of terms, as Romantics in their quest for particularization always will, Averroes asks that we should embrace it and make use of it. In quoting the lines of our literary predecessors when we feel them appropriate to our circumstances, we establish our solidarity with the past. He gives an example:

Thus, tormented years ago in Marrakesh by memories of Córdoba, I took comfort in repeating the apostrophe which Abdurrahman addressed in the gardens of Ruzafa to an African palm-tree:

You also, oh palm tree
Were in this foreign soil . . .

A singular benefit of poetry: words composed by a king pining for the Orient served me, exiled in Africa, in my nostalgia for Spain.

Averroes goes on to condemn the ambition to innovate as 'vain and illiterate'.

His recycling of the earlier poet's couplet is respectful enough. But it needn't have been. Two contradictory attitudes are possible when it comes to using ready-made lines like this, because to the possibility of courteous endorsement of their sentiments must be added the possibility of derision; to the possibility of panegyric that of satire. In other circumstances, Abdurrahman's lines might be cited to comic effect: Averroes has pointed to the simplest form of parody, which is to quote word for word but in circumstances or a context which distort what we take to have been the original bearing and dignity of the words quoted. Parody proves Borges's point, that language enjoys (or suffers from) a terrible autonomy in respect of that world of particulars which gives rise to it. Its sense is unstable the moment it becomes public property. Borges is as radical in his belief in the anonymity of what is written or recorded as Derrida.

But his is a satirical spirit and he knows, as Derrida too knows, though he chooses not to dwell on it, that he is also a cheat and not entirely to be trusted. For innovation is not only possible, it is inevitable; there is more to literary composition than quotation, as Borges's own compositions demonstrate. Innovation is inevitable simply because words break free so anarchically from those who thought to have mastered them in proffering them. Each use of them is a new and unique occasion. The writer who quotes does not vanish without trace into the quotation and become one with the quoted; the act of quotation itself keeps the two apart. This is the point so beautifully made in the most quoted of Borges's own tales, 'Pierre Menard, author of the Quixote'. Menard is an innovator indeed, who has produced something new without departing by so much as a punctuation mark from an existing text. It is perhaps the newest of all twentieth-century texts, for newness is a function of difference and Menard's chapters of Cervantes's work are *pure* difference: the same words arrived at altogether otherwise. The story of Pierre Menard, like that of Averroes, is at once satirical of the thirst for an impossible novelty in literature and a serious plea for modesty and self-effacement among those who write. It is for such modesty that Borges is justly famed.

Index